Lecture Notes of the Institute for Computer Sciences, Social Informatics and Telecommunications Engineering 427

More information about this series at https://link.springer.com/bookseries/8197

Huilong Jin · Chungang Liu ·
Al-Sakib Khan Pathan · Zubair Md. Fadlullah ·
Salimur Choudhury (Eds.)

Cognitive Radio Oriented Wireless Networks and Wireless Internet

16th EAI International Conference, CROWNCOM 2021
Virtual Event, December 11, 2021
and 14th EAI International Conference, WiCON 2021
Virtual Event, November 9, 2021
Proceedings

Springer

Editors
Huilong Jin
Hebei Normal University
Shijiazhuang, China

Al-Sakib Khan Pathan (iD)
United International University
Dhaka, Bangladesh

Salimur Choudhury
Lakehead University
Thunder Bay, ON, Canada

Chungang Liu
Hebei Normal University
Shijiazhuang, China

Zubair Md. Fadlullah (iD)
Lakehead University
Thunder Bay, ON, Canada

ISSN 1867-8211   ISSN 1867-822X (electronic)
Lecture Notes of the Institute for Computer Sciences, Social Informatics
and Telecommunications Engineering
ISBN 978-3-030-98001-6   ISBN 978-3-030-98002-3 (eBook)
https://doi.org/10.1007/978-3-030-98002-3

This Springer imprint is published by the registered company Springer Nature Switzerland AG
The registered company address is: Gewerbestrasse 11, 6330 Cham, Switzerland

Preface

We are delighted to introduce the proceedings of EAI CROWNCOM 2021 - the 16th EAI International Conference on Cognitive Radio Oriented Wireless Networks. This conference brought together researchers, developers, and practitioners around the world who are leveraging and developing cognitive radio systems. The theme of EAI CROWNCOM 2021 was "innovations and applications with cognitive-based solutions in the context of 5G and beyond".

The technical program of EAI CROWNCOM 2021 consisted of 18 full papers, including six invited papers, in oral presentation sessions at the main conference tracks. The 18 full papers were selected from 44 submissions during a rigorous double-blind review process, with a minimum of three reviews per paper, and the invited papers underwent the same process as the regular papers. Aside from the high-quality technical paper presentations, the technical program also featured a keynote speech given by Guo Qing from the Harbin Institute of Technology, China.

Coordination with the steering chair, Imrich Chlamtac, was essential for the success of the conference. We sincerely appreciate his constant support and guidance. It was also a great pleasure to work with such an excellent organizing committee team for their hard work in organizing and supporting the conference. In particular, we are grateful to the Technical Program Committee (TPC), led by TPC Co-chairs Qianbin Chen, Qinyu Zhang, and Guo Qing, who completed the peer-review process for technical papers and put together a high-quality technical program. We are also grateful to Conference Manager Jacqueline Sirotova for her support and all the authors who submitted their papers to the EAI CROWNCOM 2021 conference.

We strongly believe that EAI CROWNCOM provides a good forum for all researchers, developers, and practitioners to discuss all science and technology aspects that are relevant to cognitive radio. We also expect that the future EAI CROWNCOM conferences will be as successful and stimulating as this year's, as indicated by the contributions presented in this volume.

Huilong Jin
Chungang Liu
Shaoru Zhang

Organization

Steering Committee

Imrich Chlamtac   University of Trento, Italy

Organizing Committee

General Chair

Huilong Jin   Hebei Normal University, China

General Co-chairs

Chungang Liu   Hebei Normal University, China
Shaoru Zhang   Hebei Normal University, China

Technical Program Committee Co-chairs

Qianbin Chen	Chongqing University of Posts and Telecommunications, China
Qinyu Zhang	Harbin Institute of Technology, China
Qing Guo	Harbin Institute of Technology, China
Liehuang Zhu	Beijing Institute of Technology, China
Feng Lv	Hebei Normal University, China
Yanwei Pang	Tianjin University, China
Lei Guo	Chongqing University of Posts and Telecommunications, China
Xiaolong Yang	University of Science and Technology Beijing, China

Sponsorship and Exhibit Chairs

Jinjia Wang   Yanshan University, China
Xu Bai   Harbin Institute of Technology, China
Jiayan Zhang   Harbin Institute of Technology, China

Local Chairs

Liyong Qiao   Hebei Normal University, China
Qing Lv   Hebei Normal University, China
Shujing Zhang   Hebei Normal University, China

Workshops Chairs

Zhenyu Na	Dalian Maritime University, China
Yulong Gao	Harbin Institute of Technology, China
Wenbin Zhang	Harbin Institute of Technology, China

Publicity and Social Media Chairs

Cheng Li	Memorial University of Newfoundland, Canada
Shaochuan Wu	Harbin Institute of Technology, China
Hua Zhao	Hebei Normal University, China

Publications Chairs

Shupeng Wang	Institute of Information Engineering, CAS, China
Junying Sun	Hebei Normal University, China
Wenchao Yang	Harbin Institute of Technology, China

Web Chairs

Xinlin Huang	Tongji University, China
Yongkui Ma	Harbin Institute of Technology, China
Bo Li	Harbin Institute of Technology, China

Posters and PhD Track Chairs

Mingliang Li	Hebei GEO University, China
Jingyang Wang	Hebei University of Science and Technology, China

Technical Program Committee

Xinlin Huang	Tongji University, China
Bo Li	Harbin Institute of Technology, China
Hua Zhao	Hebei Normal University, China
Zhenyu Na	Dalian Maritime University, China
Yulong Gao	Harbin Institute of Technology, China
Wenbin Zhang	Harbin Institute of Technology, China
Xu Bai	Harbin Institute of Technology, China
Jiayan Zhang	Harbin Institute of Technology, China
Wenchao Yang	Harbin Institute of Technology, China
Yanrui Du	Hebei Normal University, China
Bing Li	Hebei Normal University, China
Jingmin Wang	Hebei Normal University, China
Jia Zhao	Hebei Normal University, China

Preface

We are delighted to present the proceedings of the 14th edition of the European Alliance for Innovation (EAI) International Wireless Internet Conference (WiCON 2021). This conference brought together the researchers, developers, and practitioners around the world who are developing wireless technologies for Internet Communications.

The technical program of WiCON 2021 had a total of seven full papers, including two invited papers, in oral presentation sessions at the main conference tracks. The papers were selected based on a rigorous double-blind review process, with a minimum of three reviews per paper, and the invited papers underwent the same process as the regular papers. Aside from the high-quality technical paper presentations, the technical program also featured one keynote speech and one tutorial. The keynote speaker was Nguyen H. Tran from the School of Computer Science, University of Sydney, Australia. The tutorial presenter was Leandros Maglaras from the School of Computer Science and Informatics, De Montfort University, UK.

Coordination with the steering committee, comprising, Imrich Chlamtac and Der-Jiunn Deng, was essential for the success of the conference. We sincerely appreciate their constant support and guidance. It was also a great pleasure to work with such an excellent organizing committee team for their hard work in organizing and supporting the conference. We are also grateful to the conference managers, Jacqueline Sirotová and Aleksandra Sledziejowska, for their support and all the authors who submitted their papers to the WiCON 2021 conference.

We strongly believe that this event provides a good forum for all researchers, developers, and practitioners to discuss various science and technology aspects that are relevant to wireless Internet technologies. We expect that the future editions of WiCON will be as successful and stimulating as this year's, as indicated by the contributions presented in this volume.

Al-Sakib Khan Pathan
Zubair Md. Fadlullah
Salimur Choudhury
Mohamed Guerroumi

Organization

Steering Committee

Chair

Imrich Chlamtac — University of Trento, Italy

Member

Der-Jiunn Deng — National Changhua University of Education, Taiwan

Organizing Committee

General Chairs

Al-Sakib Khan Pathan — Independent University, Bangladesh
Zubair Md. Fadlullah — Lakehead University, Canada

Technical Program Committee Chair

Salimur Choudhury — Lakehead University, Canada

Technical Program Committee Co-chair

Qiang Ye — Dalhousie University, Canada

Web Chair

Mohamed Guerroumi — University of Sciences and Technology Houari Boumediene, Algeria

Publicity and Social Media Chairs

Mubashir Husain Rehmani — Cork Institute of Technology, Ireland
Mohiuddin Ahmed — Edith Cowan University, Australia

Workshops Chairs

Md Zakirul Alam Bhuiyan — Fordham University, USA
Mostafa Fouda — Idaho State University, USA

Sponsorship and Exhibits Chair

Homero Toral Cruz   University of Quintana Roo, Mexico

Publications Chairs

Al-Sakib Khan Pathan   Independent University, Bangladesh
Mohamed Guerroumi   University of Sciences and Technology Houari
                                     Boumediene, Algeria

Tutorials Chair

Sharyar Wani   International Islamic University Malaysia,
                                     Malaysia

Posters and PhD Track Chair

Nurilla Avazov   University of Auckland, New Zealand

Local Chair

A. B. M. Bodrul Alam   Lakehead University, Canada

Technical Program Committee

Waleed Ejaz   Lakehead University, Canada
Mohamed Lahby   Hassan II University of Casablanca, Morocco
Hae Young Lee   Cheongju University, South Korea
Rubaiyyaat Aakbar   DocDocAsia, Singapore
Abdulsalam Yassine   Lakehead University, Canada
Khan Muhammad   Sejong University, South Korea
A. B. M. Bodrul Alam   Lakehead University, Canada
Fengxiao Tang   Tohoku University, Japan
Md Motaharul Islam   United International University, Bangladesh
Salama Ikki   Lakehead University, Canada
Wei Zhao   Anhui University of Technology, China
Mahmoud Badr   Tennessee Tech University, USA
Thuan Ngo   Tohoku University, Japan
Saiful Azad   Universiti Malaysia Pahang, Malaysia
Wei Xiang-Lin   National University of Defense Technology,
                                     China
Mohamed Ibrahem   Tennessee Tech University, USA
Dariyush Ebrahimi   Lakehead University, Canada
Bomin Mao   Tohoku University, Japan
Ahmed Shafee   Tennessee Tech University, USA

Contents

Advanced Technology for 5G/6G (CROWNCOM 2021)

Artificial Intelligence (CROWNCOM 2021)

Wireless Communication and Network Technology for Internet of Things (IoT) (CROWNCOM 2021)

Cognitive Radio Systems
(CROWNCOM 2021)

Spectrum Sensing Performance of Cognitive Radio Optimized by Soft Decision Fusion Threshold

Gefan Wang, Xuefei Sun, and Chungang Liu[✉]

Hebei Normal University, Shijiazhuang, China
liuchungang@hebtu.edu.cn

Abstract. The study aims to obtain higher spectrum efficiency of the cognitive radio system, effectively solve the hidden terminal problem caused by single user spectrum sensing, and improve the spectrum sensing performance of cognitive radio. Based on the analysis of the hard decision and soft decision fusion threshold, the linear weighted cooperative sensing algorithm is used. The purpose is to optimize the soft decision fusion cooperative spectrum sensing threshold from the two perspectives of minimizing the error probability and maximizing the average throughput of the cognitive network. The mathematical function model of error probability and throughput sensing threshold is established, the expression of the optimal threshold is derived, and the influence of various spectrum sensing parameters on the optimal decision threshold is analyzed. It is found that: when the appropriate sensing threshold is selected, compared with other algorithm models of radio spectrum sensing, the performance of the optimized soft decision fusion model proposed is better. It can reduce the error probability and improve the detection accuracy. When the throughput capacity of the cognitive network reaches the maximum, the optimal threshold obtained by the soft decision algorithm makes the detection probability higher up to 93.83%, and the overall performance of the cognitive system is better. The results have specific practical significance and practical value for the research of cognitive radio spectrum sensing.

Keywords: Cognitive radio · Soft decision fusion · Spectrum sensing · Threshold optimization · Linear weighting algorithm

1 Introduction

With the rapid development of the economy and society, radio communication technology has developed rapidly, and the number of users of wireless networks has also increased sharply. However, due to technical limitations, radiofrequency spectrum resources have been severely restricted [1]. Therefore, on the one hand, continuously investigating new technologies is necessary to develop new technologically advanced spectrums. On the other hand, it is also necessary to fully improve the utilization rate of the currently limited spectrum [2]. At present, ways to improve the utilization rate of the spectrum are very common. The most commonly used method is using the most advanced modulation encoder to increase the use efficiency of the spectrum and

H. Jin et al. (Eds.): CROWNCOM 2021/WiCON 2021, LNICST 427, pp. 3–23, 2022.
https://doi.org/10.1007/978-3-030-98002-3_1

improve the orthogonal performance of the spectrum through three angles: time, space, and frequency domain [3]. These technologies are adopted by many companies and individuals; however, affected by the quantitative limit of Shannon's capacity, these technologies have limitations in improving the efficiency of spectrum utilization [4]. However, this is far from satisfying users' demands for spectrum. Therefore, intelligent radio frequency spectrum technology has been developed rapidly. The radio technology is not restricted by time and space in propagation. It uses radio waves as the major medium and utilizes frequency to transmit and receive signals [5]. Currently, radio technology has become an inseparable component of life, which has been widely accepted in many fields and has achieved good results [6]. The prerequisite and basis for achieving the cognitive radio function are to quickly and accurately detect the valid signals of authorized users in the target frequency band, learn and reason about the information obtained by spectrum sensing, and make configuration decisions to ensure that cognitive users can access the target frequency band without conflictions [7]. Therefore, studying the cognitive radio frequency spectrum is of great value for promoting social development.

The radio spectrum solves the problem of low spectrum utilization caused by the current static spectrum allocation strategy and greatly improves the utilization rate of existing spectrum resources. Thus, spectrum sensing determines the overall performance of cognitive radio [8]. On the one hand, the performance of spectrum sensing reflects the ability of the cognitive radio to find a free spectrum. The higher the performance of spectrum sensing, the freer spectrum recognized by the cognitive radio. The more opportunities for the cognitive radio to access the free spectrum, the higher the utilization rate of the spectrum [9]. On the other hand, the performance of spectrum sensing reflects the ability of cognitive users to detect authorized users. The higher the perception performance, the weaker the signals of authorized users that can be recognized by the cognitive radio. In this way, interference with authorized users can be avoided [10]. Some unlicensed frequency bands can be used by cognitive users; however, the premise is that they do not cause interference to other users, causing a waste of spectrum resources in the time and space domains. Therefore, the purpose is to obtain higher spectrum utilization efficiency of the cognitive radio system, solve the hidden terminal problem caused by single-user spectrum sensing, and improve the performance of cognitive radio spectrum sensing [11]. As an important foundation and prerequisite for the cognitive radio to access the authorized frequency band, spectrum sensing is the core technology to ensure the normal operation of the cognitive radio, which plays an important role in the cognitive radio system [12]. Therefore, the focus is on the spectrum sensing technology of the cognitive radio, emphasizing the joint spectrum sensing algorithm of the cognitive radio.

Currently, soft decision fusion and hard decision fusion are common methods for collaborative spectrum sensing. However, these two fusion criteria are less used to study and analyze the performance of perception threshold optimization from the aspects of minimum error probability and maximum throughput. Based on the analysis of the hard decision and soft decision fusion thresholds, the linear weighted collaborative sensing algorithm is used to minimize the error probability and maximize the average throughput of the cognitive network. The soft decision fusion collaborative spectrum sensing threshold is optimized, the mathematical function model of error probability and throughput sensing threshold is established, and the optimal threshold expression is deduced. The obtained results can provide research ideas for cognitive radio spectrum sensing.

2   Related work

2.1   Cognitive Radio Model

The access method of cognitive radio technology is opportunistic spectrum access. Cognitive users perceive the dynamic spectrum environment through spectrum sensing technology and get the opportunity to share authorized frequency bands with authorized users, that is, primary users. Therefore, the improvement of spectrum sensing performance is crucial in cognitive radio [13]. In this regard, different scholars have established corresponding cognitive radio models. Wang et al. (2017) adopted a practical nonlinear energy harvesting model to maximize the total throughput of secondary users and optimize parameters such as energy harvesting time, channel allocation, and transmit power [14]. They gave the closed-form expressions of the optimal transmit power and channel allocation. The simulation results showed a trade-off between harvesting energy and the total throughput of secondary users. To improve energy efficiency and spectrum efficiency, Wang et al. (2017) examined a non-orthogonal multiple access cognitive radio network with wireless information and power transmission under the actual nonlinear energy harvesting model. They proposed a multi-target resource and optimized the problem to maximize the harvesting power of each energy harvesting receiver [15]. Li et al. (2018) proposed a new machine learning-based collaborative spectrum sensing model, which appropriately grouped cognitive radio users before using energy data samples and support vector models for collaborative sensing. They used the user grouping method to reduce collaboration overhead and improve detection performance [16]. Based on the Deep Neural Network (DNN) detection framework, Liu et al. (2019) used the sample covariance matrix as the input of the Convolutional Neural Network (CNN) and proposed a spectrum sensing algorithm based on the covariance matrix, which further improved the radio perception performance [17]. Vimal et al. (2020) proposed a modern data communication security scheme that used private key encryption and had sensing results. They introduced the eclat algorithm and used the Advanced Encryption Standard (AES) algorithm to protect data communication security in the Change Request (CR) network. Results found that this model could effectively save resources and improve the security of the system [18].

2.2   Research Status of Spectrum Sensing

In the actual cognitive radio network, the cognitive radio spectrum sensing technology must be able to avoid interference between control systems, adapt to complex and changeable wireless environments, and meet the efficiency requirements of the system itself to improve the speed and accuracy of spectrum sensing and optimize network performance. Spectrum sensing is the core of the cognitive radio network, and the research on spectrum sensing often focuses on local sensing and collaborative sensing

[19]. Single-node energy-sensing is simple to implement. The first proposed local sensing algorithm includes energy detection, matched filtering, and cyclostationary feature detection [20]. Abbadi et al. (2018) proposed a method for sensing unknown signals in the literature, acquiring signals according to Shannon's sampling theorem, giving the probability density distribution with signal energy as a statistic, and deriving the expressions of false alarm probability and detection probability [21]. Due to the limited perception of a single cognitive user, the detection performance is low due to the influence of shadow fading and hidden terminals. To effectively compensate for the impact of the shadow effect, people have studied the spectrum sensing technology of multi-user collaboration [22]. Under the condition that the sum of false alarm probability and missed detection probability was the smallest, Best et al. (2018) found that the optimal K value under K criteria and derived the optimal decision threshold for single node perception under this optimal K value. The optimal number of cooperative users was obtained when the effective throughput of the cognitive network reached the maximum, and the number of cooperative users was optimized [23]. The spectrum sensing performance in the Additive White Gaussian Noise (AWGN) channel and the fading channel was analyzed using relevant criteria. At present, the optimization problem of cooperative detection has also become a research hotspot [24]. Ni et al. (2019) proposed the optimization problem of cooperative detection and studied the optimization problem of the number of user nodes of cooperative spectrum sensing based on hard decisions and criteria [25]. Muhammad et al. (2019) introduced linear weighted fusion criteria based on detection statistics and gave several methods for selecting weighting coefficients under the optimal criteria. The hard decision fusion and soft decision fusion algorithms were simulated and analyzed, and the detection performance of several algorithms was compared. Results suggested that both fusion algorithms could improve the detection performance of a single sensor node. As the number of sensor nodes increased, the detection performance got improved, and the soft decision fusion algorithm had better detection performance than the hard decision fusion algorithm [26].

3   Research Methodology

3.1   Spectrum Sensing Technology and Algorithm

According to the number of cognitive users participating in perception, many researchers have classified spectrum sensing technology, which is divided into single-user spectrum sensing and multi-user collaborative spectrum sensing, as shown in Fig. 1. In single-user spectrum sensing, cognitive users do not need to coordinate and exchange information. The advantage is that it is easier to design, more mature in technology, and easier to implement. Multi-user cooperative sensing performs information fusion of the detection results of multiple users and makes a comprehensive decision, which can improve the detection probability of cognitive users and reduce the probability of false alarms. At the same time, it can reduce the perception time and enhance the flexibility of the communication network itself. In cooperative spectrum sensing, the same channel is monitored by multiple cognitive users; then, the sensing information is sent to the fusion center for decision [27].

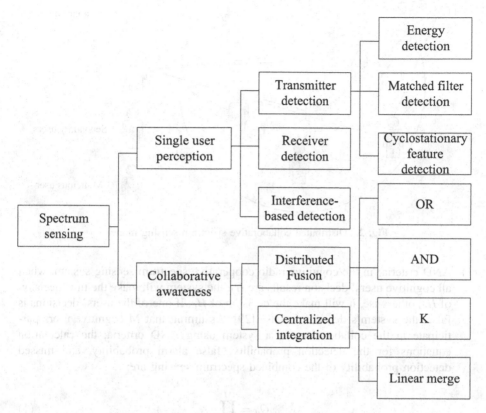

Fig. 1. Classification of spectrum sensing technologies

The focus is on the distributed and integrated spectrum sensing system. Distributed collaborative spectrum sensing is to interact with the messages sensed by each cognitive user independently with other cognitive users. The networking mode of each cognitive user is equal. In this way, each cognitive user makes a fusion decision, and finally, arrives at the decision result. Compared with centralized collaborative spectrum sensing, this sensing method improves the detection performance of the system. Because the detection sensitivity of a single sensing device is reduced, the cost of the device and the difficulty of implementation are also decreased. However, correspondingly, this is all at the cost of increasing network burden and system overhead, and the real-time performance of the system is poor [28]. Figure 2 shows the distributed collaborative spectrum sensing model.

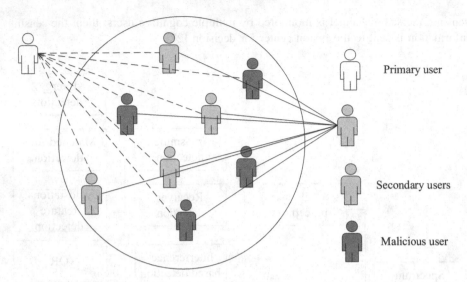

Fig. 2. Distributed collaborative spectrum sensing model

(1) AND criteria: in the cognitive radio cooperative spectrum sensing system, when all cognitive users' decision results are H_1, the system will make the final decision of H_1; otherwise, it will make the decision of H_0. If one of the users' decisions is false, the system's decision is false [29]. Assuming that M cognitive users participate in the collaboration, in a system using AND criteria, the calculation equations for the detection probability, false alarm probability, and missed detection probability of the combined spectrum sensing are:

$$Q_d = \prod_{i=1}^{M} p_{d,i} \tag{1}$$

$$Q_f = \prod_{i=1}^{M} p_{f,i} \tag{2}$$

$$Q_m = 1 - Q_d = 1 - \prod_{i=1}^{M} p_{m,i} \tag{3}$$

In (1)–(3), $p_{d,i}$ refers to the detection probability, $p_{f,i}$ refers to the false alarm probability, and $p_{m,i}$ refers to the missed detection probability. If the detection performance of any cognitive user is very low, the final decision result is very likely to incorrectly determine that there is a spectrum hole, indicating that while increasing the spectrum utilization rate, a greater probability of conflict is needed between the primary user and the cognitive user. Therefore, AND criteria are rarely used as the decision criteria for spectrum sensing in actual radio systems.

(2) OR criteria: if the perception result reported by a cognitive user is H_1, the system will make the final decision of H_1; otherwise, it will make the decision of H_0. When any cognitive user decides the main user signal, the final decision is the main user; otherwise, it decides that the main user does not exist [30]. The OR criteria detection probability, false alarm probability, and missed detection probability are expressed as:

$$Q_d = 1 - \prod_{i=1}^{M} (1 - p_{d,i}) \tag{4}$$

$$Q_f = 1 - \prod_{i=1}^{M} (1 - p_{f,i}) \tag{5}$$

$$Q_m = 1 - Q_d = \prod_{i=1}^{M} (1 - p_{m,i}) \tag{6}$$

(3) K-rank criteria: for a system with M cooperative perception of cognitive users, when the perception result reported by no less than K cognitive users is H_1, the fusion decision center will make the final decision of H_1; otherwise, the decision is H_0. The obtained value is compared with the set threshold. If at least K user decisions are true, the final decision of the fusion center is true [31]. Assuming that the decision result reported by the i-th user is D_i, the decision rule can be expressed as:

$$\begin{cases} \sum_{i=1}^{M} D_i \geq \lambda, H_1 \\ \\ \sum_{i=1}^{M} D_i \leq \lambda, H_0 \end{cases} \tag{7}$$

Assuming that there are independent decisions of M users, using the K rank criteria fusion decision algorithm can get:

$$Q_d = \sum_{j=K}^{M} C_M^i \prod_{i=1}^{M} p_{d,i} \prod_{i=j+1}^{M} (1 - p_{d,i}) \tag{8}$$

$$Q_f = \sum_{j=K}^{M} C_M^i \prod_{i=1}^{M} p_{f,i} \prod_{i=j+1}^{M} (1 - p_{f,i}) \tag{9}$$

$$Q_m = 1 - Q_d = 1 - \sum_{j=K}^{M} C_M^i \prod_{i=1}^{M} p_{d,i} \prod_{i=j+1}^{M} (1 - p_{d,i}) \tag{10}$$

3.2 Soft Decision Fusion Threshold Optimization

In the cognitive network, multiple cognitive users and the fusion center system form a unity. In the system, M cognitive users participate in cooperative spectrum sensing. Each cognitive user i uses an energy detection algorithm to sample the received signal and obtain the energy statistics. After passing through the Gaussian channel and adding channel noise, the energy statistics are sent to the system. The system weights and accumulates the received energy statistics according to the weight distribution criteria, sets a decision threshold in advance, and compares it with the accumulated energy value to make the final decision [32]. The model of the weighted cooperative spectrum sensing system is shown in Fig. 3.

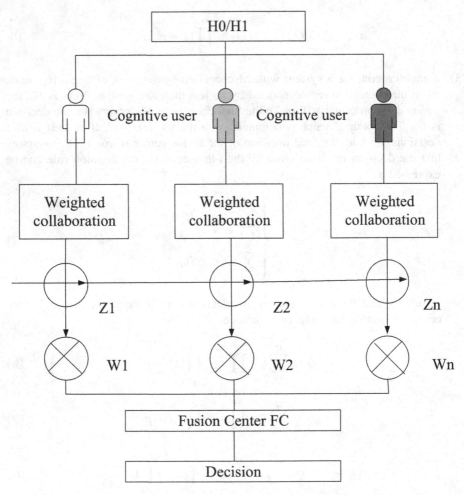

Fig. 3. Weighted collaborative spectrum sensing model

The system collects the energy statistics of M cognitive users, adopts the Signal-to-Noise Ratio (SNR) method of weighted distribution weights, and linearly accumulates these energy statistics to obtain the final decision statistics:

$$Z_c = \sum_{i=1}^{M} \omega_i Z_i = \omega^T z \qquad (11)$$

$$\omega^T = \frac{SNR_i}{\sqrt{\sum_{i=1}^{N} SNR_i}} \qquad (12)$$

In (11) and (12), ω^T represents the weight assigned by the fusion center to user i based on SNR weighting, and Z_i signifies a normal random variable whose linear combination is also a normal random variable; thus, the mean of Z_i is:

$$E(Z_c) = \begin{cases} \mu_0^T \omega, H_0 \\ \mu_1^T \omega, H_1 \end{cases} \qquad (13)$$

In (13), μ_0^T and μ_1^T represent the mean vectors in the case of 0 H and 1 H. There are uncorrelated Gaussian variables in the space, and the mean variance is:

$$Var(Z_c) = \begin{cases} \sum_{i=1}^{N} (\sigma_{0,i}^2 + \delta_i^2)\omega_i^T = \omega^T \sum_0 \omega, H_0 \\ \sum_{j=1}^{N} (\sigma_{0,j}^2 + \delta_j^2)\omega_j^T = \omega^T \sum_1 \omega, H_1 \end{cases} \qquad (14)$$

In (14), $\sum_0 \omega, H_0$ and $\sum_1 \omega, H_1$ are diagonal matrices.

3.3 Model Performance Testing

(1) Minimum error probability: the detection probability, false alarm probability, and missed detection probability based on weighted soft decision cooperative spectrum sensing can be expressed as [33]:

$$Q_d = Q(\frac{\lambda - \mu_1^T \omega}{\sqrt{\omega^T \sum_1 \omega}}) \qquad (15)$$

$$Q_f = Q(\frac{\lambda - \mu_0^T \omega}{\sqrt{\omega^T \sum_0 \omega}}) \qquad (16)$$

$$Q_m = 1 - Q(\frac{\lambda - \mu_1^T \omega}{\sqrt{\omega^T \sum_1 \omega}}) \qquad (17)$$

The overall error probability is:

$$Q_e = P(H_0)Q(\frac{\lambda - \mu_0^T\omega}{\sqrt{\omega^T\sum_0\omega}}) + P(H_1)\left[1 - Q(\frac{\lambda - \mu_1^T\omega}{\sqrt{\omega^T\sum_1\omega}})\right] \qquad (18)$$

The goal of perception threshold optimization aims to minimize Q_e by finding the optimal threshold. The optimized function can be expressed as:

$$\lambda = \arg\min Q_e(\lambda) \qquad (19)$$

The conversion of the mean and variance equations under the two assumptions shows that the optimal detection threshold can be expressed as:

$$\lambda_{out} = \frac{\mu_0}{2} + \mu_0\sqrt{\frac{\sigma_1^2}{4\sigma_0^2} + \frac{\sigma_1^2}{2\mu_0(\mu_1 - \mu_0)}\ln(\frac{P(H_0)}{P(H_0)} \times \frac{\sigma_1}{\sigma_0})} \qquad (20)$$

(2) Average throughput: the optimization goal of the perception threshold aims to find the optimal threshold to maximize the average throughput of the cognitive radio system. After optimization, the objective function [34] can be expressed as:

$$\lambda = \arg\min R(\lambda) \qquad (21)$$

Since the Gaussian function is a monotonically decreasing function, the constraint condition can be converted into a linear constraint condition:

$$\lambda \leq \lambda_{\max} \qquad (22)$$

$$\lambda_{\max} = \mu_1^T\omega + \sqrt{\omega^T\sum_1\omega}Q^{-1}(1 - \varepsilon) \qquad (23)$$

When the false alarm probability and the missed detection probability are both low, it can be converted to a tractable convex optimization problem. The Lagrangian algorithm [35] is used to solve this convex optimization problem, and the Lagrangian function is established:

$$L(\lambda, \mu) = R(\lambda) - \mu[Q_m(\lambda) - \varepsilon] \qquad (24)$$

In (24), μ represents the Lagrangian multiplier factor, and the one-variant quadratic equation can be obtained:

$$\lambda^2 - A\lambda + B = 0 \qquad (25)$$

3.4   Model Parameter Settings

The number of sampling points N is = 512, the SNR of the main user transmitter is = 20 dB, the SNRs of all cognitive users are = 6 dB, the noise variance is both 21, and the number of cognitive users participating in the collaboration is $M = 5$. The probability of H_0 is $P(H_0) = 0.7$, and the probability of H_0 is $P(H_0) = 0.3$, where K in the "K rank" fusion criteria is $= 3$.

4 Results and Analysis

4.1 Spectrum Sensing Performance Analysis

Figure 4A shows the detection performance analysis results of the three fusion criteria. When the false alarm probability is less than 0.1, the detection probability using AND criteria is relatively high. When the false alarm probability is greater than 0.1, the detection probability using OR criteria for the fusion decision is relatively high. Under the same false alarm probability, the detection probability of K criteria among the three fusion criteria is slightly lower. Figure 4B reveals the variation of the error probability with the perception threshold in energy detection. The error probability is a downward convex curve, and there is an optimal λ value. With the increase in SNR, the error probability has a downward trend, which suggests that SNR can reduce the error rate of spectrum sensing, thereby increasing the perception performance. Figure 4C demonstrates how the throughput of a single user changes with the sensing threshold. As the sensing threshold increases, the throughput is also increasing. When the sensing threshold increases to 1.3, the throughput of the system no longer changes, which explains that the threshold cannot be too large; otherwise, the detection probability will be reduced.

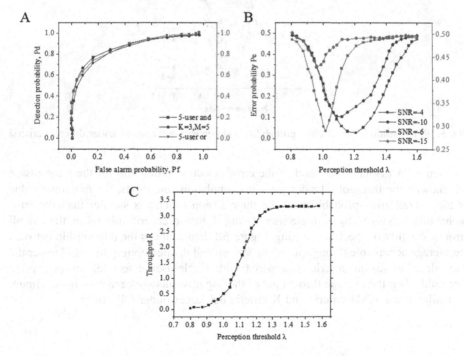

Fig. 4. Spectrum sensing performance analysis

4.2   Model Performance Analysis Under Different Criteria

Figures 5A–5C present the relations among the error probability, the number of users, and the perception threshold under AND, OR, and K criteria, respectively. As the number of perceived users increases, the minimum overall error probability of the three fusion criteria decreases. Therefore, multi-user collaborative sensing can effectively improve the detection performance of spectrum sensing. In K criteria, when $K = M/2$, spectrum sensing performance is the best.

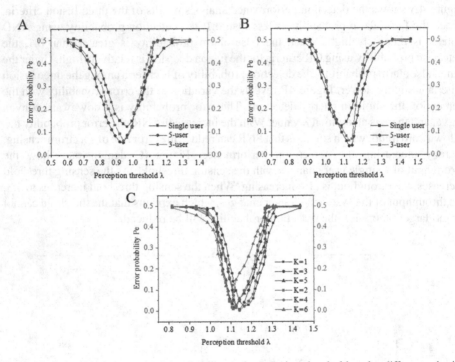

Fig. 5. Relationship between error probability and perception threshold under different criteria

Figure 6A displays the trend of the error detection probability of the three fusion criteria with the threshold. Under the same simulation conditions, the minimum value of the overall error probability of the three fusion criteria is smaller than the error probability perceived by a single user. Using K fusion criteria minimizes the overall error probability of spectrum sensing. Figure 6B demonstrates the relationship between the average achievable throughput of the system and the perception threshold under the three decision fusion criteria. Compared with single-user detection, the perception threshold when the average throughput of the cognitive network reaches the maximum is smaller under AND criteria and K criteria but larger under OR criteria.

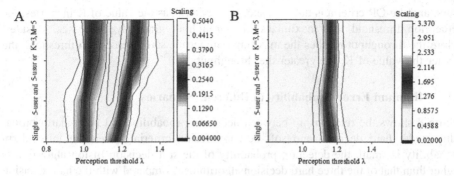

Fig. 6. Error detection probability and throughput results under different OR criteria

Figure 7 shows the relationship between the throughput of the cognitive radio system and the perception threshold under AND, OR, and K criteria. When the average throughput of the cognitive network reaches its maximum value, different fusion criteria have different perception thresholds. In AND criteria, as the number of users participating in collaboration increases, the perception threshold that maximizes throughput decreases, and a smaller perception threshold can increase the detection probability. Moreover, before the throughput reaches the maximum value, when the threshold is perceived, the throughput increases with the increase in the number of

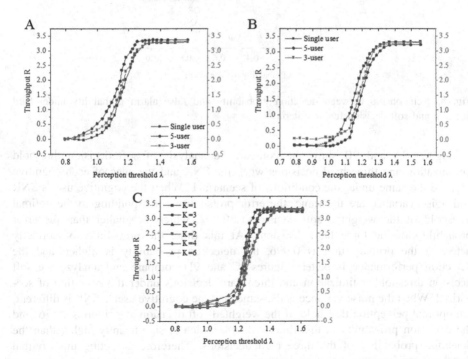

Fig. 7. Relationship between radio system throughput and perception threshold under different criteria

users, and the OR criteria is the opposite. In K criteria, as the value of K increases, the perception threshold that maximizes the throughput gradually decreases. Besides, before the throughput reaches the maximum, under the same perception threshold, the greater the value of K, the greater the throughput.

4.3   Minimum Error Probability in Different Scenarios

Figure 8 shows the relationship between detection probability and false alarm probability under hard decision and soft decision fusion criteria. When the false alarm probability is small, the detection probability of the soft decision fusion algorithm is higher than that of the three hard decision algorithms. Compared with the hard decision algorithm, the soft decision collaborative spectrum sensing collects a large amount of information from authorized users, and the detection performance is relatively high.

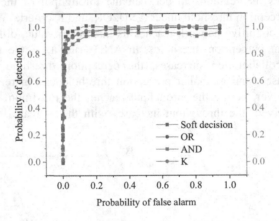

Fig. 8. Relationship between detection probability and false alarm probability under hard decision and soft decision fusion criteria

Figures 9A and 9B show the comparative analysis of soft decision threshold optimization and three hard decisions when the SNR and variance of each cognitive user are the same under the conditions of scenario 1. When the cognitive user's SNR and noise variance are the same, the error probability corresponding to the optimal threshold of the weighted soft decision is 0.002, which is smaller than the error probability of the three hard decisions. At this time, the probability of correctly detecting the primary user is 0.996, the detection probability is higher, and the detection performance is better. Figures 9C and 9D compare and analyze the soft decision threshold optimization and three hard decisions under the condition of scenario 2. When the noise variance is the same, and the cognitive user's SNR is different, the optimal perception threshold of the weighted soft decision algorithm is 2.156, and the detection probability at this time is 0.848, which is significantly higher than the detection probability of the three hard decisions. Therefore, selecting this optimal threshold can improve detection performance.

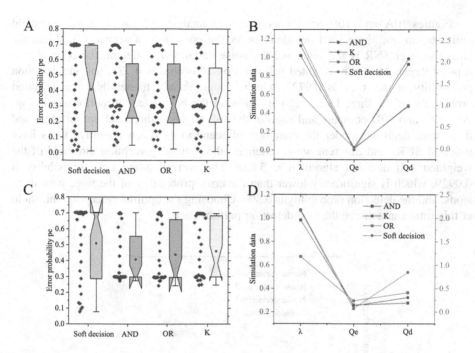

Fig. 9. Comparison and analysis of soft decision threshold optimization and three hard decisions in scenarios 1 and 2

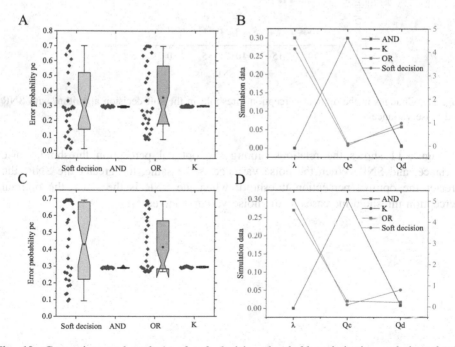

Fig. 10. Comparison and analysis of soft decision threshold optimization and three hard decisions in scenarios 3 and 4

Figures 10A and 10B are the comparative analysis of soft decision threshold optimization and three hard decisions under the condition of scenario 3. When the cognitive user SNR is the same and the noise variance is different, the optimal perception threshold of the weighted soft decision algorithm is 4.138, and the detection probability at this time is 0.9727, which is significantly higher than the detection probability of the three hard decisions, proving the best detection performance. Figures 10C and 10D compare and analyze the soft decision threshold optimization and three hard decisions under the condition of scenario 4. When cognitive users have different SNRs and different noise variances, the optimal perception threshold of the weighted soft decision algorithm is 5.056. The corresponding error probability is 0.0929, which is significantly lower than the error probability of the three hard decisions, and the detection probability is 0.806. Choosing the optimal perception threshold at this time can achieve the best detection performance.

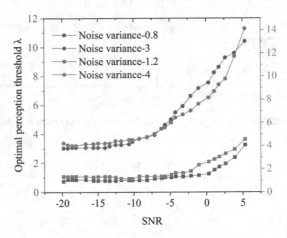

Fig. 11. Changes in the optimal perception threshold in the soft decision algorithm with SNR and noise variance

Figure 11 shows the relations among the optimal perception threshold, noise variance, and SNR. When the noise variance is the same, the greater the SNR, the greater the optimal perception threshold; when the SNR is the same, the optimal perception threshold increases as the noise variance increases.

4.4 Different Spectrum Maximum Throughput

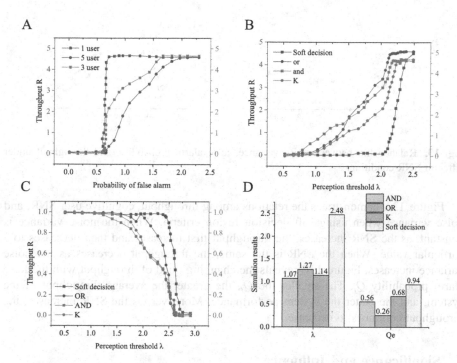

Fig. 12. Relationship between the throughput and the sensing threshold of different cooperative spectrum sensing

Figure 12A demonstrates the relationship between the soft decision fusion algorithm's cooperative spectrum sensing throughput and the sensing threshold. Cooperative spectrum sensing can improve the performance of spectrum sensing. When the throughput of the system reaches the maximum, the perception threshold of different cooperative users is different. Figures 12B–12D illustrate the relations among the cognitive radio system throughput, detection probability, and perception threshold under the four fusion criteria. When the system throughput reaches the maximum, the optimal perception thresholds of the four fusion criteria are different. Among the detection probabilities corresponding to the merit value, the detection probability of soft decision fusion criteria is about 0.938, which is significantly greater than the other three hard decision fusion criteria. Therefore, the optimal perception threshold obtained by soft decision fusion criteria can maximize the throughput and ensure that the detection probability is large enough and the detection accuracy is high. Hence, soft decision fusion criteria is the optimal criteria.

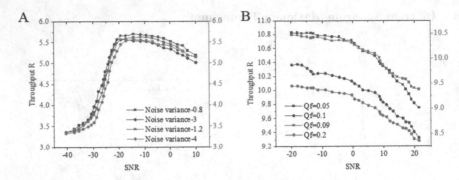

Fig. 13. Relationship between noise variance, false alarm probability, and throughput under different SNR conditions

Figure 13A demonstrates the relations among throughput, cognitive user SNR, and noise variance when using soft decision fusion criteria. When the noise variance is constant, as the SNR increases, the throughput first increases and then decreases to a particular value. When the SNR is the same, the throughput decreases as the noise variance increases. Figure 13B reveals the changing trend of throughput with the false alarm probability Q_f. The smaller the Q_f, the greater the average throughput of the system, and the better the system performance. Moreover, as the SNR increases, the throughput continues to decrease.

5　Significance and Influence

Cognitive radio technology can share spectrum resources with authorized users without interfering and alleviate the contradiction between the scarcity of spectrum resources and the increasing demand for wireless services through cognition and reallocation. To improve the performance of spectrum sensing, people have investigated the spectrum sensing technology of multi-user collaboration from two aspects: error probability and throughput. Moreover, the hard decision fusion and soft decision fusion criteria are used to study the perception threshold optimization, bringing practical significance to the research on cognitive radio spectrum sensing. The contributions are: (1) The spectrum sensing threshold optimization for the three decision fusion algorithms is analyzed in terms of minimum error probability and maximum cognitive network throughput, which not only improves the spectrum sensing performance but also increases the utilization of spectrum resources. (2) Through comparative research with the hard decision algorithm, the accuracy of model detection is improved. When the throughput of the cognitive network reaches the maximum, the optimal threshold obtained by the soft decision algorithm makes the detection probability higher, and the overall performance of the cognitive system is better, which is of great significance to the research on cognitive radio spectrum sensing.

6   Conclusion

The hard decision and soft decision fusion threshold algorithms are studied from the aspects of minimum error probability and maximum cognitive network throughput. By adopting the linear weighted cooperative sensing algorithm, the mathematical function model of the error probability and the throughput sensing threshold is established, the expression of the optimal threshold is deduced, and the influence of various spectrum sensing on the threshold is analyzed. When an appropriate perception threshold is selected, the performance of the soft decision algorithm is better, which can reduce the overall error probability of cognitive radio spectrum sensing and improve the detection accuracy. When the throughput of the cognitive network reaches the maximum, the optimal threshold obtained by the soft decision algorithm makes the detection probability higher; at this time, the overall performance of the cognitive system is better. Although the soft decision fusion threshold algorithm can be optimized, there are several shortcomings. First, the channels of spectrum sensing are ideal Gaussian channels. Whether the algorithm can achieve ideal performance in fading channels, such as the Rayleigh fading channel and the Rice channel, remains to be studied. Second, the involved single user uses energy sensing algorithms and does not include matched filter detection, cyclostationary feature detection, or interference temperature detection. Hence, these two aspects will be researched continuously in the future to improve the optimization algorithm.

References

1. Hu, F., Chen, B., Zhu, K.: Full spectrum sharing in cognitive radio networks toward 5G: a survey. IEEE Access **6**, 15754–15776 (2018)
2. Withey, K.L.: Using apps to develop social skills in children with autism spectrum disorder. Interv. Sch. Clin. **52**(4), 250–255 (2017)
3. Xu, X., Zhao, M., Lin, J.: Detecting weak position fluctuations from encoder signal using singular spectrum analysis. ISA Trans. **71**, 440–447 (2017)
4. Dardikman, G., Turko, N.A., Nativ, N., Mirsky, S.K., Shaked, N.T.: Optimal spatial bandwidth capacity in multiplexed off-axis holography for rapid quantitative phase reconstruction and visualization. Opt. Express **25**(26), 33400–33415 (2017)
5. Sultana, A., Zhao, L., Fernando, X.: Efficient resource allocation in device-to-device communication using cognitive radio technology. IEEE Trans. Veh. Technol. **66**(11), 10024–10034 (2017)
6. Zhang, M., Diao, M., Guo, L.: Convolutional neural networks for automatic cognitive radio waveform recognition. IEEE Access **5**, 11074–11082 (2017)
7. Budati, A.K., Valiveti, H.: Identify the user presence by GLRT and NP detection criteria in cognitive radio spectrum sensing. Int. J. Commun. Syst. **35**(2), 4142–4153 (2019)
8. Arjoune, Y., Kaabouch, N.: A comprehensive survey on spectrum sensing in cognitive radio networks: recent advances, new challenges, and future research directions. Sensors **19**(1), 126–133 (2019)
9. Mu, J., Jing, X., Huang, H., Gao, N.: Subspace-based method for spectrum sensing with multiple users over fading channel. IEEE Commun. Lett. **22**(4), 848–851 (2017)

10. Anandakumar, H., Umamaheswari, K. An efficient optimized handover in cognitive radio networks using cooperative spectrum sensing. Intell. Autom. Soft Comput. 1–8 (2017). https://doi.org/10.1080/10798587.2017.1364931
11. Liu, X., Jia, M., Na, Z., Lu, W., Li, F.: Multi-modal cooperative spectrum sensing based on dempster-shafer fusion in 5G-based cognitive radio. IEEE Access **6**, 199–208 (2017)
12. Wan, R., Ding, L., Xiong, N., Shu, W., Yang, L.: Dynamic dual threshold cooperative spectrum sensing for cognitive radio under noise power uncertainty. HCIS **9**(1), 1–21 (2019). https://doi.org/10.1186/s13673-019-0181-x
13. Khalid, L., Anpalagan, A.: Emerging cognitive radio technology: principles, challenges and opportunities. Comput. Electr. Eng. **36**(2), 358–366 (2010)
14. Wang, Y., Wang, Y., Zhou, F., Wu, Y., Zhou, H.: Resource allocation in wireless powered cognitive radio networks based on a practical non-linear energy harvesting model. IEEE Access **5**, 1–14 (2017)
15. Wang, Y., Wu, Y., Zhou, F., Chu, Z., Wu, Y., Yuan, F.: Multi-objective resource allocation in a NOMA cognitive radio network with a practical non-linear energy harvesting model. IEEE Access **6**, 12973–12982 (2017)
16. Li, Z., Wu, W., Liu, X., Qi, P.: Improved cooperative spectrum sensing model based on machine learning for cognitive radio networks. IET Commun. **12**(19), 2485–2492 (2018)
17. Liu, C., Wang, J., Liu, X., Liang, Y.C.: Deep CM-CNN for spectrum sensing in cognitive radio. IEEE J. Sel. Areas Commun. **37**(10), 2306–2321 (2019)
18. Vimal, S., Kalaivani, L., Kaliappan, M., Suresh, A., Gao, X.-Z., Varatharajan, R.: Development of secured data transmission using machine learning-based discrete-time partially observed Markov model and energy optimization in cognitive radio networks. Neural Comput. Appl. **32**(1), 151–161 (2018). https://doi.org/10.1007/s00521-018-3788-3
19. Abo-Zahhad, M.A., Ahmed, S.M., Farrag, M.A., BaAli, K.A.: Wideband cognitive radio networks based compressed spectrum sensing: a survey. J. Signal Inform. Process. **9**(02), 122–136 (2018)
20. Jia, M., Liu, X., Gu, X., Guo, Q.: Joint cooperative spectrum sensing and channel selection optimization for satellite communication systems based on cognitive radio. Int. J. Satell. Commun. Network. **35**(2), 139–150 (2017)
21. Abbadi, A., Bouhedjeur, H., Bellabas, A., Menni, T., Soltani, F.: Generalized closed-form expressions for CFAR detection in heterogeneous environment. IEEE Geosci. Remote Sens. Lett. **15**(7), 1011–1015 (2018)
22. Liu, S., He, J., Wu, J.: Dynamic cooperative spectrum sensing based on deep multi-user reinforcement learning. Appl. Sci. **11**(4), 1884–1896 (2021)
23. Best, G., Faigl, J., Fitch, R.: Online planning for multi-robot active perception with self-organising maps. Auton. Robot. **42**(4), 715–738 (2017). https://doi.org/10.1007/s10514-017-9691-4
24. Singh, S., Sharma, S. Performance Analysis of Spectrum sensing Techniques over TWDP fading channels for CR based IoTs. AEU – Int. J. Electron. Commun. **80**, 80–92 (2017)
25. Ni, S., Chang, H., Xu, Y.: Adaptive cooperative spectrum sensing based on SNR estimation in cognitive radio networks. J. Inform. Process. Syst. **15**(3), 604–615 (2019)
26. Muhammad, K., Hussain, T., Tanveer, M., Sannino, G., de Albuquerque, V.H.C.: Cost-effective video summarization using deep CNN with hierarchical weighted fusion for IoT surveillance networks. IEEE Internet Things J. **7**(5), 4455–4463 (2019)
27. Rajendran, S., Meert, W., Giustiniano, D., Lenders, V., Pollin, S.: Deep learning models for wireless signal classification with distributed low-cost spectrum sensors. IEEE Trans. Cogn. Commun. Network. **4**(3), 433–445 (2018)

28. Liu, X., Li, F., Na, Z.: Optimal resource allocation in simultaneous cooperative spectrum sensing and energy harvesting for multichannel cognitive radio. IEEE Access **5**, 3801–3812 (2017)
29. Guo, H., Jiang, W., Luo, W.: Linear soft combination for cooperative spectrum sensing in cognitive radio networks. IEEE Commun. Lett. **21**(7), 1573–1576 (2017)
30. Eze, J., Zhang, S., Liu, E., Eze, E.: Cognitive radio-enabled internet of vehicles: a cooperative spectrum sensing and allocation for vehicular communication. IET Netw. **7**(4), 190–199 (2018)
31. Wei, G., Zhang, B., Ding, G., Zhao, B., Guo, K., Guo, D. On the detection of a non-cooperative beam signal based on wireless sensor networks. Secur. Commun. Netw. **2020**, 122–136 (2020)
32. Khan, M.S., Gul, N., Kim, J., Qureshi, I.M., Kim, S.M. A genetic algorithm-based soft decision fusion scheme in cognitive IoT networks with malicious users. Wireless Commun. Mobile Comput. **2020**, 254–263 (2020)
33. El Mahdy, A., Alexan, W.: A threshold-free LLR-based scheme to minimize the Ber for decode-and-forward relaying. Wireless Pers. Commun. **100**(3), 87–801 (2018)
34. Zhang, L., Liang, Y.-C.: Average throughput analysis and optimization in cooperative IoT networks with short packet communication. IEEE Trans. Veh. Technol. **67**(12), 11549–21162 (2018)
35. Birgin, E., Martínez, J.: Complexity and performance of an Augmented Lagrangian algorithm. Optimiz. Meth. Softw. **35**(5), 885–920 (2020)

Methodology for Characterizing Spectrum Data by Combining Quantitative and Qualitative Information

Vaishali Nagpure[1]([⊠]) [iD], Udayan Das[2], and Cynthia Hood[1] [iD]

[1] Illinois Institute of Technology, Chicago, IL 60616, USA
vnagpure@hawk.iit.edu, hood@iit.edu
[2] St. Mary's College of California, Moraga, CA 94575, USA
uddl@stmarys-ca.edu

Abstract. Wideband spectrum data can provide information on how large portions of the spectrum are being used. Spectrograms are typically used to visualize this data. The interpretation of the spectrogram (e.g., identification of bands and patterns) is left to the user, requires significant domain knowledge and is extremely time consuming. In this paper, we present a methodology for combining quantitative and qualitative information to identify channels and changes in spectrum occupancy. Channel identification and change detection algorithms are applied to real spectrum data collected over several years on two different measurement systems in Chicago. These analyses were then used to formulate queries to a knowledge graph implemented on a neo4j graph database. The results of the queries validated the channel identification and provided validation and explanation of the changes detected. This methodology was tested on measurement data from 470–698 MHz.

Keywords: Spectrum measurements · Knowledge graph · Graph database · Change detection

1 Introduction

Wideband spectrum data can provide information on how large portions of the spectrum are being used. Spectrograms are typically used to visualize this data. The interpretation of the spectrogram (e.g., identification of bands and patterns) is left to the user, requires significant domain knowledge and is extremely time consuming. We seek to combine the quantitative analysis of the data with qualitative information to enable continuous, large-scale analysis and to make this type of analysis and interpretation more accessible to those with limited domain knowledge.

Multiband spectrum measurements are spatiotemporal datasets that provide information about spectrum utilization in space, frequency, and time. The characteristics depend on how the frequency band has been allocated (i.e., what type of transmission is legally permitted), how it is used in practice and where the measurements are taken (i.e., what signals can be observed at the given measurement location). In order to effectively characterize true dynamics of spectrum measurements, it is necessary to

H. Jin et al. (Eds.): CROWNCOM 2021/WiCON 2021, LNICST 427, pp. 24–38, 2022.
https://doi.org/10.1007/978-3-030-98002-3_2

explore the underlying structure of the data and automatically provide a descriptive depiction. The goal of characterization is to combine the analysis of the quantitative measurements with qualitative information about how the spectrum is allocated and used in time and space.

Wideband data spans a large number of frequency bands while narrowband usually focuses on small frequency range. For example, one of the Illinois Tech wideband measurement systems captures signals from 30 MHz to 6 GHz, resulting in the sampling of approximately 240K frequencies. Since there are different rules that govern each band, the data must first be separated into bands. Bands can be defined at different levels of abstraction depending on the how the spectrum is allocated. Often bands are subdivided into channels that may or may not have a common use and set of users. Each frequency band has its own unique time-varying characteristics.

Spectrum occupancy measures the percentage of time that a given frequency band or channel is utilized over a given time in each location. The measured utilization of different bands can be found to range from highly utilized, through sporadically used, to not used at all. For example, the TV band includes relatively stable signals coming from transmitters that are stationary and continuously or near-continuously transmitting. Bands that are allocated for Wi-fi and Land Mobile Radio (LMR) introduces mobility plus spatiality. When interpreting the quantitative band occupancy calculation, it is necessary to also consider qualitative or contextual information about the location of potential transmitters and the physics of the signals transmitted. Some signals may be out of range of the measurement system, and some may not be captured due to the measuring system configuration. In this paper, we present a methodology for combining quantitative and qualitative information to identify channels and changes in spectrum occupancy.

2   Background and Related Work

2.1   Spectrum Measurements

Spectrum measurements play a key role in understanding how spectrum is utilized in space, frequency, and time. The design and configuration of the measurement system influences the quality and type of data collected. The Illinois Tech Spectrum Observatory has been using two measurement systems to collect long-term data on spectrum use in Chicago. System 1 measures the spectrum from 30 MHz–6 GHz and System 2 measures the spectrum from 44–900 MHz. Both of the systems use energy detection sensing with specific resolution bandwidths (RBW). The RBW is the bandwidth of a single spectrum measurement obtained during a specific sampling interval. RBW determines frequencies contributing channels based on channel widths. Each system is configured through a band plan which partitions the measurement range into bands where sampling resolution can be specified. The System 1 band plan configures 29 bands where there are 8001 frequencies sampled in each band. There are more than 240,000 frequencies sampled resulting in 93 MB of data per day. The System 2 band plan configures 8 bands with high resolution sampling (1 kHz or 3 kHz) resulting in approximately 200,000 frequencies sampled generating 23 GB of data per day. This work focuses on the analysis of measurements from 470–698 MHz collected from System 1 and System 2. Given the different configurations of these systems as specified above, the resulting data is quite different.

2.2 Analysis with Spectrograms

Analysis of spectrum data usually starts with spectrograms or waterfall charts which are typically used to give a high-level view of spectrum occupancy data. For these charts, time/sweep is represented on the y-axis, frequency is on the x-axis (MHz) and power (dBm) is shown through color. The spectral occupancy is estimated based on noise floor which is a threshold to determine if the measured power exceeds the threshold indicating that a valid signal that was detected. For wideband measurements spanning the 30 MHz to 6 GHz range, the noise floor fluctuates by several dB power levels. Hence, different noise floors must be calculated and used in each sub-band.

Spectrograms allow for the visualization of channels, utilization, and changes/patterns. Spectrograms at different time scales can help identify daily, weekly, and yearly patterns and trends. Figure 1 shows a spectrogram of a band (406–698 MHz) selected from the System 1 spectrum measurements from 2017. From the spectrogram, the channels, and a general sense of occupancy (i.e., whether the channels are occupied throughout the whole year or not) can be determined. This paper describes a methodology to automatically extract this type of information.

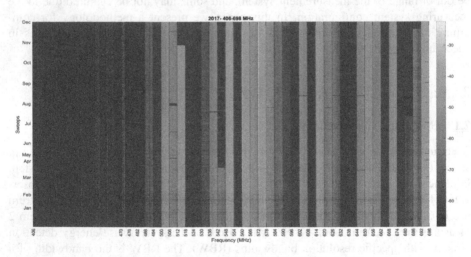

Fig. 1. Spectrogram of 406–698 MHz during 2017.

2.3 Contextual Information

To interpret the visualization of the measurements, contextual information is needed. For example, when looking at the spectrogram in Fig. 1, one is interested in knowing not just that there are channels, but what the channels are used for. To do this one must first find out how the frequencies of interest have been allocated. Since spectrum is a natural resource, each nation decides how the spectrum will be allocated and utilized within its borders. Since this paper involves spectrum measurements collected in Chicago, we focus on the United States spectrum allocation.

In the United States, the National Telecommunications and Information Administration (NTIA) manages the federal spectrum and the Federal Communications Commission (FCC) manages the non-federal spectrum. Figure 2 shows part of the Frequency Allocation Chart. This chart gives a high-level view of how the spectrum is allocated. One or more radio services are indicated in the chart. The narrow, colored band along the bottom of the chart indicates whether the spectrum is federal exclusive (red), non-federal exclusive (green) or federal/non-federal shared (black). Most importantly, this tells us where (i.e., NTIA or FCC) we can find more detailed information about the spectrum usage. In Fig. 2 we can see that the frequencies from 470–512 MHz are reserved for non-federal use and are shared by three different radio services, Broadcast Television, Land Mobile and Fixed.

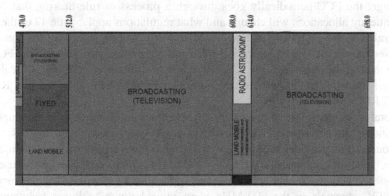

Fig. 2. Snapshot of 470–698 MHz band from the US frequency allocation chart.

A full table of frequency allocations in the US can be found at [1]. Frequency allocations are done per band, where bands are contiguous A band plan defines various characteristics related to the use of spectrum in a specific frequency range. The band plan defines the frequency range to which it applies, parameters related to the use of the spectrum, such as the width of channels, boundaries of sub-blocks within the band, guard bands (if any), etc., and the applications that can use those channels and sub-blocks. The band plans and table of frequency allocations shown in Fig. 3 encode information regarding both what an individual frequency assignment means, as well as the radio service to which it applies.

| 470-608 | 470-512
FIXED
LAND MOBILE
BROADCASTING

NG5 NG14 NG66 NG115 NG149 | Public Mobile (22)
Broadcast Radio (TV)(73)
LPTV, TV Translator/Booster (74G)
Low Power Auxiliary (74H)
Private Land Mobile (90) |
| | 512-608
BROADCASTING

NG5 NG14 NG115 NG149 | Broadcast Radio (TV)(73)
LPTV, TV Translator/Booster (74G)
Low Power Auxiliary (74H) |

Fig. 3. Snapshot of 470–698 MHz band from the US frequency allocation table.

For non-federal spectrum, the FCC maintains data on authorized licenses and publishes regulatory documents defining the proper usage of spectrum in a given geo-temporal context. FCC databases are the primary source of information on current non-federal spectrum allocations. Since the FCC is the regulating authority defining spectrum usage, the FCC periodically goes through a process of rule-making that defines how frequency allocations will change and what regulations apply. Title 47 of the Code of Federal Regulations (CFR) defines rules and regulations regarding telecommunications services in the United States. All rules and regulations pertaining to the FCC are defined there. For example, the CFR contains information on how to calculate parameters such as Height Above Average Terrain (HAAT) and Effective Radiate Power (ERP).

Federal documents are a repository of spectrum information and invaluable in understanding spectrum usage. However, in some cases, secondary sources can be useful sources that provides the spectrum information in a semi-structured manner. For example, spectrum in the 600 MHz to 700 MHz which was previously used for broadcast TV was made available for other applications [2]. Following the incentive auction TV, channels in the 600 MHz were moved down to lower frequencies to channels that were vacated by other applications. Other channels in the sub-600 MHz also changed as part of the band plan changes. This process overall was called the Digital TV repacking.

Table 1. Chicago area broadcast digital TV repacking plan (channel changes).

Old channel number	Old channel frequency (MHz)	New channel number	New channel frequency (MHz)
20	506–512	26	542–548
27	548–554	23	524–530
29	560–566	33	584–590
31	572–578	24	530–536
32	578–584	18	494–500
34	590–595	28	554–560
35	596–602	32	578–584
36	602–608	21	512–518

(continued)

Table 1. (*continued*)

Old channel number	Old channel frequency (MHz)	New channel number	New channel frequency (MHz)
38	614–620	35	596–602
39	620–626	20	506–512
40	626–632	27	548–554
43	644–650	34	590–596
44	650–656	22	518–524
47	668–674	25	536–542
21	512–518	*Did not change*	
45	656–662	*Did not change*	
49	680–686	*Did not change*	
50	686–692	*Did not change*	
51	692–698	*Did not change*	

While details of changes in the band plan due to Digital TV repacking are available through the FCC, the information is fragmented across multiple documents and is often buried in complex, verbose documents. In such a scenario, secondary sources can provide the required information in a semi-structured fashion. The situation is further complicated by there being different repacking plans in different markets. Rabbitears is a website that provides the repacking information in a semi-structured format [3]. When that information is correlated with other secondary sources—Over-the-air-Digital-TV [4] and RadioReference [5]—a complete repacking band plan can be constructed for a market area. Table 1 demonstrates the repacking changes in the Chicago market area [6].

2.4   Related Work

The majority of usable spectrum is allocated in the Unites States [1, 7] and across the world [8, 9] at the same time that the demand for wireless spectrum continues to expand rapidly. A great deal of recent work has been devoted to applying clustering techniques towards spectrum analysis including real-time characterization of spectrum states and spectrum prediction [10–17]. Our previous work [18, 19] has shown the value of semantic information towards spectrum analysis studies. Spectrum occupancy modeling continues to develop as a vibrant field [20, 21].

The TxMiner [22] system has been shown to have the capability to characterize spectrum occupants in an unsupervised fashion using a learning algorithm called Rayleigh-Gaussian Mixture Model (GMM). This gives a very basic but good way of identifying active radio transmitters based on measurements. In [23], Agarwal et al. investigate time series models for occupancy prediction of stationary bands like TV and cellular bands. SpecInsight [24] is an intelligent wideband spectrum sensing and analysis system that learns the characteristics of the signals in each frequency band and adjusts the sensing parameters to maximize detection. A significant innovation is a technique to detect both low and high occupancy signals. Although this system reduces the knowledge necessary for configuration and analysis, a semantic framework could increase the utility of both the data and the analysis results by facilitating linkage with other spectrum measurements and analysis results as well as external data.

In the Dynamic Spectrum Access space there has been some research effort towards modeling spectrum usage, but we do not consider the existing approaches to be aligned with information modeling. While there has been considerable amount of research in the information modeling and knowledge graph space [25–27], since the concept of a knowledge graph was introduced originally by Google [28], to our knowledge, knowledge graphs have not been applied towards getting a deeper understanding of spectrum usage and analysis.

3   Approach

3.1   Quantitative Analysis

Wideband measurements will capture many bands which in turn may contain multiple sub-bands or channels. When there is activity in bands and/or channels, it is quite easy to grasp the organization of the band from a spectrogram as shown in Fig. 1. Along with the structure of the band, we are interested in characterizing the dynamics of the band and in particular identifying changes in the dynamics. Although both the structure and changes can be identified from the visualizations, generating and inspecting spectrograms manually is quite time intensive and is not feasible for continuous and/or wideband measurements. This research seeks to automate the identification of the band structure, characterization of usage, and identification of changes in the identified sub-bands or channels. This paper focuses on identification of the structure and change detection using the measurements from the frequency band 470–698 MHz.

To start with, we use a simple algorithm to determine the structure in the band. Contiguous frequencies with similar measurements are grouped together to form a channel. This is based on the assumption that frequency measurements within a channel will have correlated activity. In this study, we used the mean energy in a frequency over 24 h (one day) as the basis for grouping frequencies. For a given frequency band, the range of mean energy values is divided into buckets based on a threshold which is calculated based on the minimum and maximum value of the range. Correlated frequencies will be grouped together in each bucket. The buckets can be aggregated to give a coarse-grain characterization of the energy level of the correlated frequencies. This roughly corresponds to the colors in the spectrogram. As shown in the Table 2, given the number of correlated frequencies and the resolution bandwidth, the width of the identified channels can be estimated.

Table 2. Snapshot of channels identified on 01-Jan-2017.

Start freq (MHz)	End freq (MHz)	Total freq	RBW (KHz)	Estimated channel width (MHz)
500.06	505.974	163	36.5	5.9495
512.032	517.946	163	36.5	5.9495
536.086	541.962	162	36.5	5.913
614.014	619.963	164	36.5	5.986

Once the channels have been identified and characterized, the focus is on getting a general understanding of the channel dynamics. The first step in this process is to detect when changes have occurred. Change detection techniques detect abrupt changes in time series data by comparing the current measurements to established usual measurements. In this work, an offline change detection mechanism is used [29]. Given the estimates of the channels, we can focus on the center frequencies as a reasonable representation of the channel. Therefore, we focus on the time series of energy measurements of the center frequencies. The type of dynamics identified by the change detection algorithm depends on the time-scale of the features used for change detection. For example, when we use the daily mean energy as input, the minimum changes that can be detected are on a daily basis. More precision can be attained by using finer grain means (e.g., hourly) or by using an online change detection algorithm. There are many possible reasons for changes in the measurements including changes in the spectrum usage (scheduled or unscheduled), changes in allocation and problems with the measurement system. For example, short-term dynamics are possible for TV stations that turn off periodically and long-term dynamics can occur due to allocation changes.

3.2 Modeling of Qualitative Information

In our previous work [30], we proposed an architecture for unifying the different types of spectrum information so that knowledge may be aggregated and reasoned over. This architecture is based on knowledge graphs. A method for modeling various types of information as knowledge graphs was developed. The knowledge graphs are implemented in the Neo4j graph database platform [31]. One of the primary knowledge graphs was implemented with data from the FCC License View API [32]. The FCC License View API provides access to data contained in several FCC licensing databases which collectively represent a majority of publicly available license information for non-federal spectrum. This knowledge graph provides an easy mechanism for making sense of spectrum data in a particular geographic, temporal, and application context. The knowledge graph makes the task of querying and visualizing information much easier than querying the datasets via existing web-based search tools and APIs.

3.3 Combining Quantitative Analysis Results with Qualitative Information

To get an understanding of how the spectrum is being used, a combination of quantitative and qualitative information is needed. The measurements provide information about how the spectrum is actually being used. This includes information about how the measured frequencies are organized into channels as well as characterization of the channel activity and dynamics. To validate and explain the results of the quantitative analysis, qualitative is information is needed to provide the context needed for understanding. The whole process is visualized in Fig. 4, starting with the observations. As seen from Fig. 4, observations include measurements along with configuration parameters of the measurement system such as band plan and RBW. After the data is analyzed to identify the channels, the knowledge graph in the graph database is queried to validate the estimated channel identified. A similar process is used when the analysis of the center frequencies within channels is used to detect changes. The changes detected are then used to formulate queries to try to determine the cause of changes detected. Given that our current knowledge graph is focused on licensing and allocation information, the only changes that can be validated or explained at this time are changes in licensing or allocation. As detailed earlier, this includes the repacking of broadcast TV channels to provide more spectrum for cellular services.

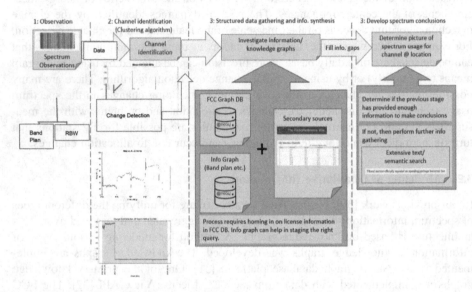

Fig. 4. Process flow diagram of methodology.

4   Results

The research presented in this paper involved the analysis of the 470–698 MHz block from system 1 and 470–700 MHz block from system 2. From Fig. 2, we can see that this block is mostly allocated for broadcast TV. Thus, the channels identified are TV channels. We chose to start in this band because TV transmission is generally continuous thus the channels can be easily detected. Even in this band, we found some challenges and interesting dynamics with the repacking and reallocation. Table 3 shows the channels identified from one day of data from the years 2017–2019 from system1 and from one day of data from 2021 from system 2. Channels with very low signal strength are difficult to identify with our algorithm.

Table 3. Summary number of channels identified.

	2017	2018	2019	2021
Actual-channels	25	21	19	16
Identified channels	22	21	17	13

Table 4 gives an example of some of the channels identified based on the measurements captured using system 1. The number of frequencies grouped is included in the table and using the RBW, the minimum estimated channel width is calculated. Table 5 gives an example of some of the channels identified based on the measurements from system 2. Note that the RBW for system 2 is much smaller than the RBW for system 1 so the sampled frequencies are much closer (only 3 kHz apart). The actual TV channels are 6 MHz so these estimates are close. In Fig. 1, you can observe variations in the channels across the frequencies and at the boundaries between channels. Also, given that these estimates are based on how the systems are configured to sample the frequencies, we do not expect to get an exact value, even in the best case. We are looking for an estimate that we can compare to the response from the knowledge graph.

Table 4. Example of channels identified using system 1 data

Start freq (MHz)	End freq (MHz)	Total freq	RBW (KHz)	Min. estimated channel width (MHz)
488.052	493.928	162	36.5	5.913
500.06	505.974	163	36.5	5.9495
506.12	511.85	158	36.5	5.767
512.032	517.946	163	36.5	5.9495
536.086	541.962	162	36.5	5.913
542.108	547.876	159	36.5	5.8035

Table 5. Example of channels identified using system 2 data

Start freq (MHz)	End freq (MHz)	Total freq	RBW (KHz)	Min. estimated channel width (MHz)
494.208	499.827	1785	3	5.355
500.148	505.875	1910	3	5.73
506.127	511.905	1911	3	5.733
512.115	517.882	1923	3	5.769
518.134	523.834	1874	3	5.622
524.083	529.96	1960	3	5.88

```
ExecutionEngine execEngineTV = new ExecutionEngine(digitalTVbp);

int freqSearch = 491008000;     //491.008 MHz being searched

ExecutionResult execResult = execEngine1.execute("
          MATCH (fa:frequency_assigned) WHERE f.frequency_assigned <= " + freqSearch + "
          MATCH (fu:frequency_upper) WHERE f.frequency_upper >= " + freqSearch + "
          MATCH (fa)<-[*1]-(c:channel)-[*1]->(fu)
          RETURN c, fa, fu;
          "));
```

Fig. 5. Query on TV band for the channel frequency range and channel number.

After identifying the channels, validation is done through the knowledge graph implemented in the graph database. A Java code fragment including the query is shown in Fig. 5. Since the frequency searched in this example is 491.008 MHz, we can look at the spectrum allocations shown in Figs. 2 and 3 and see that the frequency falls within a block that is shared by Broadcast TV, Fixed and Land Mobile Radio services. Since we have implemented the digital TV band plan, we started by querying that knowledge graph and found a match. The highlighted line shows that the channel, lower frequency and upper frequency of the channel are returned when center frequency is searched from the channel. The results confirm that the 491.008 MHz is part of a 6 MHz TV channel from 488–494 MHz.

To determine changes in the identified channels, the change detection algorithm was run on the sampled frequency nearest to the center of each channel. This algorithm was run on 53 months of data from 01-Jan-2017 to 31-May-2021. The spectrogram in Fig. 6 shows a comparison of one day of data from 2017–2019. The data from each day is stacked to visualize the changes. When comparing the visualization from 2017 (on the bottom) to the one from 2019 (on the top), it is evident that there are several channels that are no longer active. There is one channel 524–530 MHz channel where there is new activity in 2019. This stacked visualization gives a general idea of the what changed, but does not provide any information about when the changes occurred. The change detection algorithm identifies the day when the change happened. Figure 7 shows the date when channel 514.989 MHz changed.

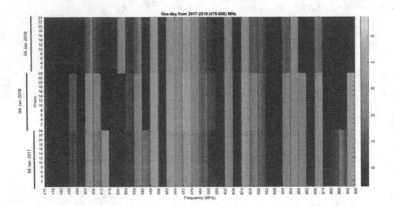

Fig. 6. Spectrogram cascaded three days from 2017–2019

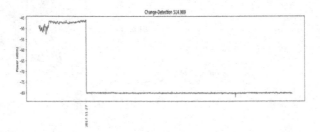

Fig. 7. Change detection for channel 514.989 MHz

The TV band repacking began in 2018 and concluded by July 2020. Figure 8 shows the changes due to repacking. This process was initiated to free up the 600 MHz band for the broadcast incentive auction. As a result of the repacking, the 600–700 MHz band was reallocated to cellular and public safety use. The changes can be seen from spectrogram shown on the right side of Fig. 8 and in Fig. 9. The new and different activity in the 600 MHz band is evident.

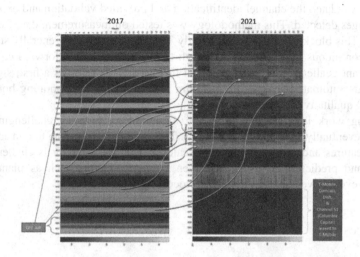

Fig. 8. TV channel changes as a result of Digital TV repacking.

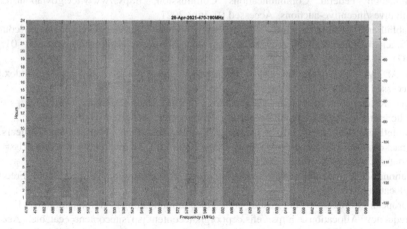

Fig. 9. Spectrogram of 470–700 MHz band in April 2021

5   Conclusion and Future Work

This paper describes a methodology for combining quantitative and qualitative information to characterize spectrum data. Channel identification and change detection algorithms are applied to real spectrum data collected over several years on two different measurement systems in Chicago. These analyses were then used to formulate queries to a knowledge graph implemented on a neo4j graph database. The results of the queries validated the channel identification and provided validation and explanation of the changes detected. This methodology was tested on measurement data from 470–698 MHz. This block is comprised of mostly TV bands which are generally stationary and have continuous transmission. Although this is a very straightforward case, there are significant challenges to automate all of the steps. This result is a first, significant step towards automated analysis of spectrum measurements incorporating both quantitative and qualitative information.

Ongoing work involves extending the methodology to more challenging cases which can eventually span all types of bands. This includes expanding to consider more complex features and also different time scales. Spectrum behavior is challenging to interpret, and prediction of usage is driven by many factors such as planned and unplanned events, weather and human protocols.

References

1. Federal Communications Commission. FCC Online Table of Frequency Allocations (2021)
2. Federal Communications Commission. Broadcast Incentive Auction and Post-Auction Transition Federal Communications Commission. https://www.fcc.gov/about-fcc/fcc-initiatives/incentive-auctions. Accessed 01 July 2021
3. RabbitEars. RabbitEars.Info. https://www.rabbitears.info/repackchannels.php?country=US&city=&state=&mktid=&owner=&sort=oldch&ph=&lss=&status=. Accessed 01 July 2021
4. OTADTV. Television Broadcast Frequencies. https://otadtv.com/frequency/index.html. Accessed 01 July 2021
5. RadioReference. Television Frequencies - The RadioReference Wiki. https://wiki.radioreference.com/index.php/Television_Frequencies. Accessed 01 July 2021
6. RabbitEars. RabbitEars.Info Chicago DTV Repack Plan. https://www.rabbitears.info/repackchannels.php?country=US&city=&state=&mktid=3&owner=&sort=&ph=&lss=&status=. Accessed 01 July 2021
7. National Telecommunications and Information Administration. United States Frequency Allocations. 10.003
8. European Conference of Postal and Telecommunications Administrations. European Frequency Allocations. https://efis.cept.org/sitecontent.jsp?sitecontent=ecatable. Accessed 11 July 2021
9. Ministry of Communications and Information Technology. Egyptian Frequency Allocations. https://www.mcit.gov.eg/en/TeleCommunications/Regulations/Spectrum_Management. Accessed 11 July 2021
10. Wu, J., Li, Y.: A survey of spectrum prediction methods in cognitive radio networks. In: AIP Conference Proceedings, vol. 1834 (2017). https://doi.org/10.1063/1.4981557

11. Gattoua, C., Chakkor, O., Aytouna, F.: An overview of cooperative spectrum sensing based on machine learning techniques. In: 2020 IEEE 2nd International Conference on Electronics, Control, Optimization and Computer Science. ICECOCS 2020 (2020). https://doi.org/10.1109/ICECOCS50124.2020.9314297

12. Rutagemwa, H., Ghasemi, A., Liu, S.: Dynamic spectrum assignment for land mobile radio with deep recurrent neural networks. In: IEEE International Conference on Communications Work. ICC Work. 2018 - Proceedings, pp. 1–6 (2018). https://doi.org/10.1109/ICCW.2018.8403659

13. Agarwal, A., Dubey, S., Khan, M.A., Gangopadhyay, R., Debnath, S.: Learning based primary user activity prediction in cognitive radio networks for efficient dynamic spectrum access. In: 2016 International Conference on Signal processing, Communication. SPCOM 2016 (2016). https://doi.org/10.1109/SPCOM.2016.7746632

14. Kumar, V., Kandpal, D.C., Jain, M., Gangopadhyay, R., Debnath, S.: K-mean clustering based cooperative spectrum sensing in generalized κ-μ Fading channels. In: 2016 22nd National Conference on Communications. NCC 2016 (2016). https://doi.org/10.1109/NCC.2016.7561130

15. Baddour, K.E., Ghasemi, A., Rutagemwa, H.: Spectrum occupancy prediction for land mobile radio bands using a recommender system. In: IEEE Vehicular Technology Conference, vol. 2018-August (2018). https://doi.org/10.1109/VTCFall.2018.8690654

16. Li, Y., Wang, Y., Wan, P., Zhang, S., Zhang, Y., Zhao, T.: A spectrum sensing algorithm based on correlation coefficient and K-means. In: 11th International Conference on Advanced Computational Intelligence. ICACI 2019, pp. 84–89 (2019). https://doi.org/10.1109/ICACI.2019.8778589

17. Ma, J., Zhao, G., Li, Y.: Soft combination and detection for cooperative spectrum sensing in cognitive radio networks. IEEE Trans. Wirel. Commun. 7(11), 4502–4507 (2008). https://doi.org/10.1109/T-WC.2008.070941

18. Nagpure, V., Vaccaro, S., Hood, C.: Spectrum analysis using semantic models for context. In: Kliks, A., et al. (eds.) CrownCom 2019. LNICSSITE, vol. 291, pp. 126–139. Springer, Cham (2019). https://doi.org/10.1007/978-3-030-25748-4_10

19. Nagpure, V., Hood, C., Vaccaro, S.: Semantic models for labeling spectrum data. In: Iliadis, L., Maglogiannis, I., Plagianakos, V. (eds.) AIAI 2018. IAICT, vol. 520, pp. 3–12. Springer, Cham (2018). https://doi.org/10.1007/978-3-319-92016-0_1

20. Chen, Y., Oh, H.S.: A survey of measurement-based spectrum occupancy modeling for cognitive radios. IEEE Commun. Surv. Tutorials 18(1), 848–859 (2016). https://doi.org/10.1109/COMST.2014.2364316

21. Lopatka, J., Malon, K., Kryk, M.: Hybrid model of radio channels occupancy prediction for dynamic spectrum access. URSI 2018 - Baltic URSI Symposium, pp. 238–241 (2018). https://doi.org/10.23919/URSI.2018.8406694

22. Zheleva, M., Chandra, R., Chowdhery, A., Kapoor, A., Garnett, P.: TxMiner: Identifying transmitters in real-world spectrum measurements. In: 2015 IEEE International Symposium on Dynamic Spectrum Access Networks (DySPAN), pp. 94–105 (2015)

23. Agarwal, A., Sengar, A.S., Gangopadhyay, R.: Spectrum occupancy prediction for realistic traffic scenarios: time series versus learning-based models. J. Commun. Inform. Netw. 3(2), 44–51 (2018). https://doi.org/10.1007/s41650-018-0013-6

24. Shi, L., Bahl, P., Katabi, D.: Beyond sensing: multi-ghz realtime spectrum analytics. In: Proceedings of the 12th USENIX Symposium on Networked Systems Design and Implementation (NSDI '15), pp. 159–172 (2015)

25. Auer, S., Kasprzik, A., Kovtun, V., Stocker, M., Prinz, M., Vidal, M.E.: Towards a knowledge graph for science. In: ACM's International Conference Proceedings Series (2018). https://doi.org/10.1145/3227609.3227689

26. Jiang, Z., Chi, C., Zhan, Y.: Research on medical question answering system based on knowledge graph. IEEE Access **9**(Iaeac), 21094–21101 (2021). https://doi.org/10.1109/ACCESS.2021.3055371

27. Ji, S., et al.: A Survey on Knowledge Graphs: Representation, Acquisition and Applications (2021)

28. Google. Introducing the Knowledge Graph: things, not strings.https://blog.google/products/search/introducing-knowledge-graph-things-not/. Accessed on 28 May 2021

29. Aminikhanghahi, S., Cook, D.J.: A survey of methods for time series change point detection. Knowl. Inf. Syst. **51**(2), 339–367 (2016). https://doi.org/10.1007/s10115-016-0987-z

30. Udayan, D., Vaishali, N., Cynthia, H., Ann, M.K.: Simplifying License Information Through the Use of a Knowledge Graph (August 1, 2021). Available at SSRN: https://ssrn.com/abstract=3897187 or https://doi.org/10.2139/ssrn.3897187

31. Neo4j inc. Neo4j Graph Database Platform. https://neo4j.com/product/neo4j-graph-database/. Accessed 18 June 2021

32. Federal Communications Commission. License View API|Federal Communications Commission. https://www.fcc.gov/reports-research/developers/license-view-api. Accessed on 18 June 2021

Computationally Efficient Look-up-Tables for Behavioral Modelling and Digital Pre-distortion of Multi-standard Wireless Systems

Zhaoyang Han[2] , Meabh Loughman[1] , Yiyue Jiang[2] , Rahul Mushini[1],
Miriam Leeser[2(✉)] , and John Dooley[1]

[1] Maynooth University, Maynooth, Ireland
[2] Northeastern University, Boston, MA, USA
mel@coe.neu.edu
https://www.northeastern.edu/rcl/

Abstract. Wireless systems such as cellular networks have begun to
see proposals for increased operational flexibility through reuse of the
same hardware but with different signal standards. This paper presents
an approach to characterise a power amplifier (PA) for multiple signal standards. Following from this, behavioural modeling demonstrates
that the same coefficients trained for a single signal standard can be
effectively applied to multiple signal standards. This result is used to
design and implement a digital predistorter (DPD) capable of lineariz-
ing for different signal standards on a Field Programmable Gate Array
(FPGA). This implementation is experimentally validated on a state-
of-the-art RFSoC FPGA from Xilinx to correct for PA non-linearities
in the transmit chain using an efficient hardware design. Additionally
the behavioural modelling and DPD solutions have been validated using
distinctly different PAs to demonstrate the proposed look up table approach is hardware agnostic and works when the appropriate dimensions
are set for the dynamic nonlinear structure in each case.

Keywords: Behavioural modeling · Pre-distortion · Memory
Polynomial · Software Defined Radio · FPGA

1 Introduction

Software Defined Radio (SDR) has been around for several decades, but the
implementations of such radios, despite including reconfigurable elements such as
Field Programmable Gate Arrays (FPGAs), are surprisingly static. Most SDRs
are configured to support one protocol and a specific design, once deployed, is
seldom changed. In previous work, researchers have addressed the issue by

H. Jin et al. (Eds.): CROWNCOM 2021/WiCON 2021, LNICST 427, pp. 39–55, 2022.
https://doi.org/10.1007/978-3-030-98002-3_3

demonstrating the reception of multiple different protocols with the same front end [11,18]. In this paper, we address the issue of handling multiple different signal standards on the transmit side. The transmitter makes use of a power amplifier (PA) and, to obtain maximum power efficiency, the PA is operated near its saturation point, which leads to nonlinear distortion as well as significant memory effects.

Pre-distortion or linearization of signals to compensate for the non-linearity and memory effects of power amplifiers (PAs) is a broad area of research in telecommunication systems [2,17,24]. The trend for linearization algorithms is to apply increasingly complicated nonlinear structures such as artificial neural networks [12] or vector-switched Volterra series [1] in order to pre-distort the input signal. The nonlinear pre-distorter structures contain weights which must be trained and it is this training operation that introduces the highest computational cost. Look-up tables have been implemented in the past to provide coefficients for the pre-distorter [22], however these solutions have not previously been applied for use with multi-standard radios. A compelling objective for modeling these systems is to identify the most computationally efficient structure which can accurately characterise the PA behaviour and estimate the output signal. A structure that encompasses memory effects, various bandwidths and nonlinearity is the Volterra series, however the number of coefficients used in a Volterra series increases rapidly with increasing nonlinear order or memory depth. More compact memory models can be achieved using the memory polynomial and generalised memory polynomial.

A limitation associated with behavioural modeling of power amplifiers has been that a model trained with one standard of input and output signals is not typically applicable to other signal standards, and thus the resulting behavioural models are traditionally limited to a single protocol. This is in direct contravention to the ethos expected of a software defined radio. Ideally the radio should be capable of transmitting multiple standards; in this research we focus on 3G, 4G and 5G cellular network communications. Wideband Code Division Multiple Access (WCDMA) is widely used in 3G networks [16], while Orthogonal Frequency-Division Multiplexing (OFDM) is utilised in 4G and 5G networks. 5G offers a wider range of configurations for the construction of signals and as a result different signal formats can be generated compared to 4G. In this paper we propose a strategy to model the behaviour of the PA such that the necessary coefficients can be used across these different signal modulation schemes. This structure is then extended to the practical case of providing a digital Pre-Distorter (DPD). The contribution of this paper is describing how the same trained model or DPD coefficients to be used across different signal standards. The result is a look-up-table (LUT) based DPD implementation for multi-standard cognitive radios. The DPD is implemented on a state-of the-art Xilinx RFSoC FPGA which integrates an embedded ARM processor, FPGA fabric, and RF frontend in a single package. In this paper LUT refers to the storage of coefficients for the DPD implementation and not the look up tables that are part of the FPGA fabric.

In Sect. 2 we introduce the background information about power amplifier non-linearity, behavioural modeling, and related work. The two main areas for validation of this work cover behavioural modelling and DPD. In both cases experimentally measured results for power amplifier operation with different input signal standards are collected as described in Sect. 3.1. From these measurements, power level matching between standards can be achieved and the corresponding sets of coefficients applied to different standards, first for behavioural modelling as described in Sect. 3, and next for predistortion as described in Sect. 4. Results of the DPD experiments using signals from different signal standards are presented in Sect. 5. Conclusions from this work are summarised in Sect. 6.

2 Background

2.1 Nonlinear Power Amplifiers with Memory Effects

Power amplifiers perform a critical function in wireless communication systems, which is to transfer the supplied power to a modulated signal at high frequency in order to transmit it over greater distances. Unfortunately, in order to operate the power conversion of the power amplifier efficiently, the resulting PA output signal suffers distortion in the form of dynamic and non-linear behaviours. In particular, Gallium Nitride (GaN) power amplifiers have become the technology of choice for high power applications such as cellular network basestations and satellite communications. This is as a result of GaN devices having a higher breakdown field allowing them to operate at higher output voltages compared to other semiconductor substrates. Additionally electrons on GaN have a higher saturation velocity and large charge capability which allow high current density. GaN devices however demonstrate non-linear behaviour when operated in efficient modes and can experience charge trapping which is more difficult to characterise than for other semiconductor technologies. GaN PAs may be modelled using non-linear digital filters with sufficient order of nonlinearity and number of memory taps.

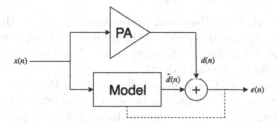

Fig. 1. PA model training

The operation of a digital filter is to take input signal samples x(n), combine the current sample and previous samples, weight all of them and sum the resulting products. A nonlinear filter contains weights H(n), which are multiplied by various combinations of the input samples. The objective is for the output $\hat{d}(n)$ to be comparable to the desired output signal d(n). The operation of training these nonlinear filter or model coefficients, is done in such a way as to minimise the difference between $d(n)$ and $\hat{d}(n)$. Figure 1 depicts this relationship.

2.2   Discrete Dynamic Nonlinear Models and Training Algorithm

For this research, Least Squares (LS) was chosen as the coefficient training technique with the following behavioural models: memory polynomial (MP) and generalised memory polynomial (GMP).

Parameter estimation or training of the behavioural model is as important as the capabilities of the model chosen. Least squares estimation is a direct estimation process where the input and output signals are analysed in vector form and an optimal solution can be derived from direct matrix inversion [15]. The least squares solution can be extracted solely with the input and output sample data. The least squares algorithm chooses weights to minimise the function in Eq. 1.

$$J(N) = \frac{1}{N} \sum_{t=1}^{N} (y(t) - X^T(t)\vec{w})$$ (1)

Where N represents the length of the signal data sets, X and y denote the input and output signal datasets respectively. $\vec{w}$ refers to the calculated weights.

A range of behavioural models were considered for this work. The main difference between them stems from the different number of coefficients used in each to perform behavioural modeling. These models can be classified as subsets of the Volterra model, for which the discrete version is given by Eq. 2. The Volterra model is ideally suited for characterizing nonlinear systems with memory effects such as power amplifiers.

$$y_{VS}(n) = \sum_{i_1=0}^{M-1} \cdots \sum_{i_P=0}^{M-1} h_p(i_1, \cdots, i_p) \prod_{r=1}^{P} x(n - i_r)$$ (2)

Here $x(n)$ and $y(n)$ are the input and output signals to the power amplifier respectively. $h_p(i_1, ..., i_p)$ represents the filter co-efficient expansion utilising P, the highest order for the non-linearity of the Volterra series expansion. M represents the maximum memory depth.

The memory polynomial is a model derived from the Volterra model comprised only of the linear terms and higher order products with the same time-shifts [7]. Combining these higher order products of delayed input signal components into a single array, form the memory polynomial as described by Eq. 3. While the model only considers a fraction of the input signal combinations present in the Volterra series, the addition of delayed input samples allow the characteristic memory effect of the power amplifier to be modelled.

$$y_{MP}(n) = \sum_{p=1}^{P} \sum_{m=0}^{M} a_{pm} x(n-m)|x(n-m)|^{p-1} \qquad (3)$$

where a_{pm} are the estimated model parameters, and P and M represent the highest non linear order and the memory depth of the model, respectively.

The GMP [20] can be considered as taking multiple delayed MP models, given by Eq. 3, to include leading and lagging cross-terms as seen in Eq. 4. In this way a wider range of combinations of delayed input signal samples from the Volterra model are considered compared to the memory polynomial.

$$
\begin{aligned}
y_{GMP}(n) = & \sum_{k \in K_a} \sum_{l \in L_a} a_{kl} x(n-l)|x(n-l)|^k \\
& + \sum_{k \in K_b} \sum_{l \in L_b} \sum_{m \in M_b} b_{klm} x(n-l)|x(n-l-m)|^k \\
& + \sum_{k \in K_c} \sum_{l \in L_c} \sum_{m \in M_c} c_{klm} x(n-l)|x(n-l+m)|^k
\end{aligned}
\qquad (4)
$$

Here K_a and L_a index the arrays for the input signal and its envelope; K_b, L_b and M_b refer to the indexing of the input signal and its lagging envelope; and K_c, L_c and M_c are index arrays for the input signal and its leading envelope. a_{kl}, b_{klm} and c_{klm} are the estimated model parameters.

The Normalised Mean Square Error (NMSE) denotes a common figure of merit used to indicate the accuracy of a model in characterising power amplifiers behaviour [13]. The NMSE is convenient as it only requires a single value to describe the overall deviations between predicted and measured values of the model output $\hat{d}(n)$ and experimentally validated output $d(n)$ over what can be large datasets.

2.3   Related Work

Look-up-table (LUT) solutions for nonlinear power amplifiers have been previously introduced for both behavioural modelling and predistortion. The chronology of these LUT solutions shows new methods have emerged for both applications.

As a means of modeling the behavior of RF power amplifiers, a number of different LUT approaches have been proven to be effective. A data-based nested LUT structure has equivalent performance to the memory polynomial for modeling of power amplifiers exhibiting memory effects as shown in [9]. This LUT approach has been further extended to a 2-D LUT model for transmitters/PAs exhibiting memory effects. With an additional dimension [10], the LUT is expanded to take into account the dependency of the device behavior on the preceding samples. The 2-D LUT models the transfer function of the device under test as a complex gain that is a function of the magnitude of the current and previous samples. More recently, Nunes et al. have demonstrated a LUT solution for high efficiency power amplifier architecture [23]. A newer class of power amplifier behavioral model named hybrid look-up tables (H-LUT) improves the performance of a conventional nested LUT model [6]. Here, a combination of a memoryless LUT and nested LUT are connected in parallel. The accuracy of the proposed model is also better suited for being trained with smaller training datasets compared to the nested LUT model alone.

In [4] a LUT is pre-trained for a power amplifier and used to pre-distort the signal supplied to the PA. At that time, the pretrained LUT demonstrated a solution requiring four orders of magnitude less memory, three orders of magnitude reduction in convergence time and eliminated the reconvergence time needed following a channel switch. FPGA-based LUT solutions have been proposed for switchmode PAs [5]. As a case study a polar configured Class F switch-mode PA is shown to be effectively linearized by the proposed approach. Additional enhancements to the LUT implementation have been proposed [8,21]. Here the aim is to reduce the hardware resources required to implement the solution in an FPGA. Savings of total hardware resources can be made in terms of arithmetic hardware blocks though the structure of the DPD calculations are re-ordered. Molina et al. [19] show how a predistorter with lower complexity than polynomial models translated to a LUT. This is achieved by expressing a DPD function as a system of linear-in-parameter equations. Least squares is used to train the LUT coefficients directly. More recent work on LUT [3] is based on spline-interpolated look-up-tables. While similar to established polynomial-based solutions, a reduction in DPD processing is presented. The use of LUT predistorters has been adopted for optical communications also. Implementations for nonlinear weighted look-up-table predistortion [14] and reduced size LUT [25] show the continued interest in LUT based predistorters. Importantly, this work demonstrates the ability to store sets of coefficients, but determine what set of coefficients to use based on the observed nonlinear performance of the PA, for any given signal. This can avoid the need for the standard LUT approach which has to train a set of coefficients for every possible combination of signal standard and operating power level.

3   Multi-standard Behavioural Modeling

3.1   Data Collection

In order to analyze and study multi-standard behavioural models and implementations, signals were required for each of the standards studied. The signals used were generated in MATLAB using modulation functions from the Communications, LTE & 5G toolboxes. To get the measured results from the PA at different input power levels a testbench was setup, as in Fig. 2 and 3. Here an RFSoC ZCU111 for transmitting and receiving the signals has been used. The signal was generated at the Intermediate Frequency (IF) centred at 1 GHz from the RFSoC DAC with sampling frequency of 737.28 MHz and then with the help of the mixer the signal was upconverted to the required center frequency of 2.6 GHz. After this stage, the signal was passed through the GaN-SiC pallet amplifier (RFHIC RTP26010-N1) and the power of the signal was maintained sufficiently to drive the PA in a nonlinear region of operation. This particular PA has two output ports, one of which was connected to a spectrum analyser and the second coupled output port was connected to the downconverter mixer which uses the same LO frequency as of the upconverter mixer. Here the signal is downconverted back to the IF frequency i.e., 1 GHz and is passed to the RFSoC ADC which also has a sampling rate of 737.28 MSPS. In the case of this PA the model memory depth was chosen to be 3 and the non-linear order of the MP model was chosen to be 3.

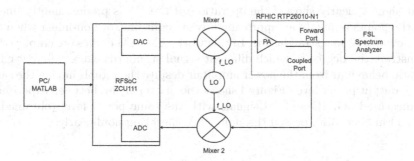

Fig. 2. Test bench block diagram

Fig. 3. Experimental measurement bench RFSoC ZCU111 with RFHIC RTP26010-N1 PA

For measuring at different power levels, the power of the signals generated from the RFSoC was adjusted using the RF Data Converter Interface. The sample length generated in MATLAB for different standard signals was 70,000 samples. To time align the signal and reduce the noise floor to achieve better dynamic range, the length of the signal captured was 10 times the length of the transmitted signal i.e., 700,000 samples. Once the signal has been time aligned, both the transmitted and received signals were normalised with respect to the maximum absolute value of each. The first 30,000 samples of the averaged input and output signals have been used for training the behavioural model and a further 30,000 were used for the validation of the model.

3.2 AM-AM Distortion Characteristics as Guide to Coefficients

A common technique used to illustrate the characteristic behaviour of a nonlinear power amplifier is the AM/AM curve. The data points from the input and output signals clearly show if the operation of the PA is predominantly linear, when the points populate an approximately straight line, or non-linear when the curve deviates from a straight line. In this work, AM/AM curves are employed to demonstrate the degree to which different signal standards cause different characteristic behaviour from the power amplifier despite the signals having the same average output power level. Figure 4 shows the discrepancies between experimentally measured 3G, 4G and 5G signals with the same power level (obtained as described in Sect. 3.1), passed through a PA operating nonlinearly.

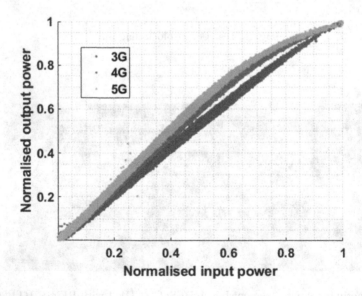

Fig. 4. An experimentally validated illustration of the input-output signal relationship transmitted at 2.6 GHz for 3G, 4G and 5G signals. Signals were transmitted through the same PA at equivalent transmit power.

Further investigations into PA characterisation given different input signals led to the observation that various AM/AM curves of 3G, 4G and 5G-NR, at different power levels, are very similar, as seen in Fig. 5. Therefore by noting the relative difference in the signal power levels for the different signal standards, that all yield the same characteristic AM/AM performance, one can map the power levels for which the same set of model coefficients can work.

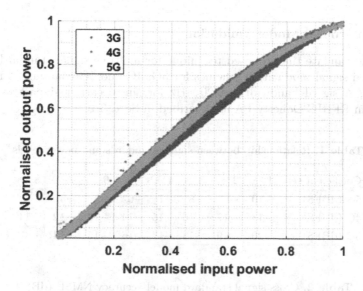

Fig. 5. Experimentally validated AM/AM curve illustrating that 3G, 4G and 5G input signals can produce comparable AM/AM curves given the signals are sent at disparate transmit power levels.

3.3   Multi-standard Behavioural Models

As indicated in Fig. 4, for the same power amplifier excited by different signals with the same average power level and similar bandwidth, there is a noticeable difference in the AM/AM curves. This in turn indicates a difference of behaviour of the hardware as a result of the different signals. It is therefore not sufficient to assume a particular operating behaviour for the power amplifier based on the average output signal power alone; the signal used must also be taken into account.

   This paper presents a means by which a single set of behavioural model coefficients can be extracted and stored in a look-up-table for use with any signal standard so long as the relative power level offsets between different signal types are accounted for. The matching of behavioural model coefficients is implemented across different signal standards. This is performed by extracting coefficients for different power levels for each standard. From the measured output signals the corresponding AM/AM curves are fitted. One set of coefficients are extracted for one signal standard and the AM/AM curve for that standard which best fits the other signal standards is sought.

By exciting the power amplifier using various signals at a range of operating power levels, sets of signals can be compiled and relationships between standards can be learned. Importantly, the signals which match closest in terms of model coefficient performance do not have identical operating power levels.

3.4 Behavioural Model Validation

In order to validate the proposed technique for multiple signal standards, commonly used signal modulation schemes for 3G, 4G and 5G communications are examined. A signal bandwidth of 20 MHz for single carrier signals were sent through an RFHIC Doherty PA as described in Sect. 3.1.

Table 1. Relationship between signal standards and power levels

Coefficient sets	1	2	3	4	5	6	7	8
5G (dBFS)	−10	−9	−8	−7	−6	−5	−4	−3
4G (dBFS)	−18	−17	−16	−15	−14	−13	−12	−11
3G (dBFS)	−20	−19	−18	−17	−16	−15	−14	−13

Table 2. Cross signal standard model accuracy NMSE (dB)

	3G MP/GMP	4G MP/GMP	5G MP/GMP
3G	−38.386/−38.39	−42.008/−41.931	−41.856/−41.804
4G	−42.02/−41.961	−45.874/−45.879	−41.995/−41.918
5G	−42.178/−42.13	−39.623/−30.589	−45.874/−44.067

Pairs of input and output signal datasets are captured for a PA and the AM/AM curves for one signal standard are plotted. A subset of samples from the alternative signal standards at similar power levels are used to check if their AM/AM trace follows a similar trajectory. Comparing these, the relative power levels between standards is determined, and the model coefficients are indexed in the LUT relative to each signal standard power level. The relative power level offsets between standards can be seen in Table 1. In this instance, eight sets of coefficients are matched for the same power amplifier across three different signal standards which each have a relative power level offset.

By knowing the relative power level offsets to use, a behavioral model can be trained for one signal standard and reliably used to model the PA response across the other signal standards. Table 2 illustrates the NMSE comparisons calculated between different signal standards with similar AM/AM curves, which corresponds to one of the columns in Table 1. The columns of Table 2 are populated by training the coefficients using one of the signal standards and validating the model accuracy for all three signal standards. The accuracy for each standard is given in NMSE and placed in its respective row. Independent output signals which were not used to train the models were used for the validation in each case.

4 LUT-Based Multi-standard DPD Transceiver

4.1 DPD Coefficient Estimation

The inverse function of the PA system $f(X)$ can be derived by swapping the input signal x and output signal y in Eq. 3. Applying this inverse function f^{-1} will cancel the effect of the PA system f.

$$x_{MP}(n) = \sum_{p=0}^{P} \sum_{m=0}^{M} d_{pm} \hat{y}(n-m) |\hat{y}(n-m)|^p \qquad (5)$$

Here $\hat{y}$ is the PA output normalized by PA gain G and with a certain offset T introduced by the PA system.

$$\hat{y} = y(n+T)/G \qquad (6)$$

The coefficients d_{pm} of the DPD model can be estimated through different methods. As there are more observations of y and x than the number of coefficients, an over-determined system can be formed. The least squares algorithm is used to estimate the coefficients.

4.2 Hardware Software Co-design

In Sect. 3, different standards' signals at different power levels are shown to have the same AM/AM characteristics. Based on this analysis, a Digital Pre Distortion (DPD) solution for transmitting multi-standard signals is implemented, as shown in Fig. 6. This solution shows a way of pre-distorting different standards' signals with sets of coefficients trained by only one signal standard under different power levels. In this way the resource utilization is minimized and associated power consumption of the entire design optimized.

The proposed design can be divided into two parts: the baseband signal processing and the RF front end. The baseband block handles the predistortion and other necessary signal processing tasks such as filtering and upsampling. The processed signal is then sent through the RF front end.

On the baseband part, the address selection block is used to calculate the addresses of the coefficients based on the signal power level and standard; these are then sent to the look-up table. The coefficients are loaded from the look-up table to the pre-distorter which, for the PA used in this case, required a memory polynomial model with order 5 and memory depth 5. The resulting pre-distorted baseband signals are then forwarded to the RF front end. For the

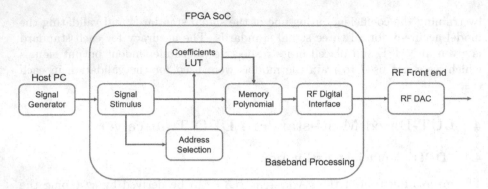

Fig. 6. Proposed system design illustration

FPGA implementation, the original input signal in-phase (I) and quadrature (Q) components are used as the input for the pre-distorter block. This pre-distorter block can be updated through the coefficient I/Q ports where I and Q are the real and imaginary parts of the coefficients. In this work, as the RF front end used has 14-bit DACs and ADCs, the interfaces use 16-bit wide AXI buses where the data are transferred as 16-bit fixed point values.

The data interface of the memory polynomial model is AXI-Stream which has 256 bits of data width. It consists of 8 IQ signal pairs, each with 16-bit width. The memory polynomial core will process 8 input signals per clock cycle. To improve the efficiency of the processing, the core utilizes a CORDIC algorithm to calculate the magnitude term in Eq. 5.

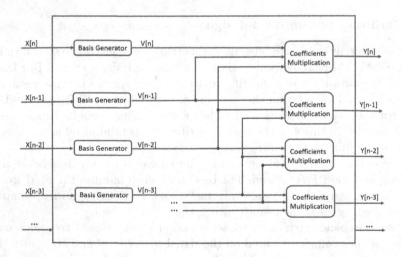

Fig. 7. Parallel processing memory polynomial hardware implementation

Implementation details of the parallel memory polynomial model are shown in Fig. 7. The model processes multiple signal samples per clock cycle. The input data is first disassembled into multiple signal samples. Each sample is connected to a basis generation core. This block along with a CORDIC core, calculates the term $x(n)|x(n)|^{p-1}$ and the results are rerouted to the corresponding coefficient multiplication block. Each coefficient multiplication block requires multiple input bases for the memory taps. For simplicity, the figure here illustrates the design with up to 3 memory taps. In the actual implementation, the memory taps are set to 5. These input bases will be multiplied with the corresponding coefficients. The sum of the results is the output signal.

The addresses selection block requires the transmitted signal as input. The relevant power of the signal is calculated and, along with the chosen signal standard, is used to select the appropriate set of coefficients to use. The update of coefficients is also controlled by this block, where the coefficients are updated constantly.

5 Hardware Implementation and Experimental Validation

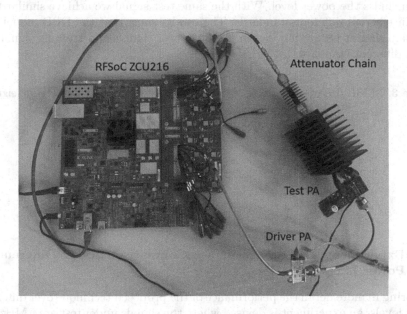

Fig. 8. DPD TestBench RFSoC ZCU216 with NXP's AFSC5G37D37 Doherty PA

The testbench setup is shown in Fig. 8. Xilinx's RFSoC Gen 3 (ZCU216) is used to perform DPD and baseband signal processing. With software and hardware co-design, the address selection block is implemented on the ARM core which utilizes the AXI-Lite bus to update the coefficients based on the input signal. The computationally intensive task of computing the memory polynomial model is performed on FPGA fabric.

The test PA is an AFSC5G37D37 Doherty PA from NXP, which is different from the PA used in the previous validation section. Using a different PA shows the generality of the proposed behaviour modeling and corresponding digital predistortion. Since the output power of the RFSoC is limited, a driver stage PA BGA7210 is used to increase the input power to the test PA. The BGA7210 is a high linearity PA with variable gain which is operating in its linear region. This PA allows us to set the input signal to different power levels.

5.1 Experiment: DPD Performance Comparison with Different Standard's Training Signals

For these experiments, three DPD models are obtained and each model is trained with a particular signal standard. To validate performance of the resulting DPD coefficients, each set of extracted coefficients are tested for three signal standards, namely 3G, 4G and 5G. From these experiments on the PA hardware, Table 3 shows the NMSE performance for different signal standards. In each row, the test signal is the same, independent of the training model it is applied to. This includes the power level. With the same test signal we achieve similar performance across different standards. The results show that the DPD model can maintain similar performance even when the test signals and training signal are under different standards.

Table 3. NMSE (dB) Comparisons with 3G, 4G and 5G training and testing signal

Test \ Training	3G	4G	5G
3G	−26.36	−25.49	−31.13
4G	−26.80	−31.25	−26.33
5G	−24.88	−24.53	−24.97

5.2 Experiment: DPD Performance Comparison Along Different Power Levels

Exploring in more detail the performance of the proposed technique over different power levels, an experiment is devised where the signals under test are 5 MHz 3G signals with different power levels. The different power levels are achieved using the driver PA. The DPD coefficients are trained using 4G signals and to facilitate a direct comparison, the 3G signals. The obtained results are presented in Table 4 and show the NMSE comparison when the input signals are at different power levels. These results show that the proposed DPD has only marginally reduced performance. Additionally, the gap can be narrowed if a greater number of sets of coefficients were trained.

Table 4. NMSE comparison with 3G training signal and 4G training signal for 3G test signal at different power levels

3G test signal power (dBFs)	−9	−9.5	−10	−10.5	−11	−11.5
4G training signal (dB)	−25.22	−27.59	−28.30	−28.64	−28.91	−30.76
3G training signal (dB)	−28.57	−28.73	−29.86	−29.55	−30.84	−31.94
Difference (dB)	−3.35	−1.14	−1.56	−0.91	−1.93	−1.18

6 Conclusions

This paper provides a definitive solution to behavioural modeling and digital pre-distortion for multiple signal standards. By matching the relative AM/AM curves for different signals passed through the same power amplifier, sets of common coefficients that will work across signal standards can be found. While the technique is demonstrated using polynomial models and Least Squares, the relationships between different input signal standards exist irrespective of the model structure used. Experimental validation is performed using input signals of three different signal modulation schemes, and behavioral modelling and DPD are carried out with experimental measurements using two different PAs from two different manufacturers. The LUT approach works well for both cases and the model or predistorter dimensions can be set in the usual way to cover the characteristic behaviour of the chosen PA. The results show that training of a model, the most computationally intensive aspect, can be done for one signal standard and successfully applied to others provided the relative signal power level offsets are known. Thus the same transmitter design can be used for multiple signal standards.

Acknowledgements. This publication has emanated in part from research conducted with the financial support of Science Foundation Ireland (SFI) and is co-funded under the European Regional Development Fund under Grant Number 13/RC/2077 and 18/CRT/6222. This research was also partly supported by MathWorks and by contributions from AMD/Xilinx

References

1. Afsardoost, S., Eriksson, T., Fager, C.: Digital predistortion using a vector-switched model. IEEE Trans. Microw. Theory Tech. **60**(4), 1166–1174 (2012). https://doi.org/10.1109/TMTT.2012.2184295. Conference Name: IEEE Transactions on Microwave Theory and Techniques

2. Cai, J., Yu, C., Sun, L., Chen, S., King, J.B.: Dynamic behavioral modeling of RF power amplifier based on time-delay support vector regression. IEEE Trans. Microw. Theory Tech. **67**(2), 533–543 (2019). https://doi.org/10.1109/TMTT.2018.2884414

3. Campo, P.P., et al.: Gradient-adaptive spline-interpolated LUT methods for low-complexity digital predistortion. IEEE Trans. Circ. Syst. I Regular Papers **68**(1), 336–349 (2021). https://doi.org/10.1109/TCSI.2020.3034825

4. Cavers, J.K.: Amplifier linearization using a digital predistorter with fast adaptation and low memory requirements. IEEE Trans. Veh. Technol. **39**(4), 374–382 (1990). https://doi.org/10.1109/25.61359

5. Cerasani, U., Le Moullec, Y., Tong, T.: A practical FPGA-based LUT-predistortion technology for switch-mode power amplifier linearization. In: 2009 NORCHIP (2009). https://doi.org/10.1109/NORCHP.2009.5397830

6. Dalbah, A.I., Hammi, O., Zerguine, A.: Hybrid look-up-tables based behavioral model for dynamic nonlinear power amplifiers. IEEE Access **8**, 53240–53249 (2020). https://doi.org/10.1109/ACCESS.2020.2973930

7. Ghannouchi, F.M., Hammi, O.: Behavioral modeling and predistortion. IEEE Microwave Mag. **10**(7), 52–64 (2009). https://doi.org/10.1109/MMM.2009.934516

8. Guan, L., Zhu, A.: Low-cost FPGA implementation of Volterra series-based digital predistorter for RF power amplifiers. IEEE Trans. Microw. Theory Tech. **58**(4), 866–872 (2010). https://doi.org/10.1109/TMTT.2010.2041588

9. Hammi, O., Ghannouchi, F.M., Boumaiza, S., Vassilakis, B.: A data-based nested LUT model for RF power amplifiers exhibiting memory effects. IEEE Microwave Wirel. Compon. Lett. **17**(10), 712–714 (2007). https://doi.org/10.1109/LMWC.2007.905627

10. Hammi, O., Ghannouchi, F.M., Vassilakis, B.: 2-D vector quantized behavioral model for wireless transmitters' nonlinearity and memory effects modeling. In: 2008 IEEE Radio and Wireless Symposium, RWS, pp. 763–766 (2008). https://doi.org/10.1109/RWS.2008.4463604

11. Handagala, S., Mohamed, M., Xu, J., Onabajo, M., Leeser, M.: Detection of different wireless protocols on an FPGA with the same analog/RF front end. In: Moerman, I., Marquez-Barja, J., Shahid, A., Liu, W., Giannoulis, S., Jiao, X. (eds.) CROWNCOM 2018. LNICST, vol. 261, pp. 25–35. Springer, Cham (2019). https://doi.org/10.1007/978-3-030-05490-8_3

12. Hongyo, R., Egashira, Y., Hone, T.M., Yamaguchi, K.: Deep neural network-based digital predistorter for Doherty power amplifiers. IEEE Microwave Wirel. Compon. Lett. **29**(2), 146–148 (2019). https://doi.org/10.1109/LMWC.2018.2888955

13. Li, M., Yang, Z., Zhang, Z., Li, R., Dong, Q., Nakatake, S.: Sparsity adaptive estimation of memory polynomial based models for power amplifier behavioral modeling. IEEE Microwave Wirel. Compon. Lett. **26**(5), 370–372 (2016). https://doi.org/10.1109/LMWC.2016.2549024

14. Liang, S., Jiang, Z., Qiao, L., Lu, X., Chi, N.: Faster-than-nyquist precoded CAP modulation visible light communication system based on nonlinear weighted look-up table predistortion. IEEE Photonics J. **10**(1) (2018). https://doi.org/10.1109/JPHOT.2017.2788894

15. Mathews, V.J., Sicuranza, G.L.: Polynomial Signal Processing. Wiley, New York (2000)

16. Milstein, L.: Wideband code division multiple access. IEEE J. Sel. Areas Commun. **18**(8), 1344–1354 (2000). https://doi.org/10.1109/49.864000. http://ieeexplore.ieee.org/document/864000/

17. Mkadem, F., Boumaiza, S.: Physically inspired neural network model for RF power amplifier behavioral modeling and digital predistortion. IEEE Trans. Microw. Theory Tech. **59**(4), 913–923 (2011). https://doi.org/10.1109/TMTT.2010.2098041
18. Mohamed, M., Handagala, S., Xu, J., Leeser, M., Onabajo, M.: Strategies and demonstration to support multiple wireless protocols with a single RF front-end. IEEE Wirel. Commun. **27**(3), 88–95 (2020). https://doi.org/10.1109/MWC.001. 1900224. https://ieeexplore.ieee.org/document/9108998/
19. Molina, A., Rajamani, K., Azadet, K.: Digital predistortion using lookup tables with linear interpolation and extrapolation: direct least squares coefficient adaptation. IEEE Trans. Microw. Theory Tech. **65**(3), 980–987 (2017). https://doi.org/ 10.1109/TMTT.2016.2627562
20. Morgan, D.R., Ma, Z., Kim, J., Zierdt, M.G., Pastalan, J.: A generalized memory polynomial model for digital predistortion of RF power amplifiers. IEEE Trans. Signal Process. **54**(10), 3852–3860 (2006). https://doi.org/10.1109/TSP.2006.879264
21. Mrabet, N., Mohammad, I., Mkadem, F., Rebai, C., Boumaiza, S.: Optimized hardware for polynomial digital predistortion system implementation. In: RWW 2012 - Proceedings: 2012 IEEE Topical Conference on Power Amplifiers for Wireless and Radio Applications, PAWR 2012, pp. 81–84 (2012). https://doi.org/10.1109/ PAWR.2012.6174914
22. Muhonen, K.J., Kavehrad, M., Krishnamoorthy, R.: Look-up table techniques for adaptive digital predistortion: a development and comparison. IEEE Trans. Veh. Technol. **49**(5), 1995–2002 (2000). https://doi.org/10.1109/25.892601. Conference Name: IEEE Transactions on Vehicular Technology
23. Nunes, L.C., Cabral, P.M., Pedro, J.C.: LUT based behavioral model for Doherty power amplifier design. In: Conference on Telecommunications - ConfTele, September 2015
24. Schreurs, D., ODroma, M., Goacher, A.A., Gadringer, M. (eds.): RF Power Amplifier Behavioral Modeling. Cambridge University Press, Cambridge (2008). https://doi.org/10.1017/CBO9780511619960. http://ebooks.cambridge. org/ref/id/CBO9780511619960
25. Zhalehpour, S., Lin, J., Sepehrian, H., Shi, W., Rusch, L.: Experimental demonstration of reduced-size LUT predistortion for 256QAM SiP transmitter. In: 2019 Optical Fiber Communications Conference and Exhibition (OFC), San Diego, CA, USA. IEEE (2019)

Metaheuristic Optimisation for Radio Interface-Constrained Channel Assignment in a Hybrid Wi-Fi–Dynamic Spectrum Access Wireless Mesh Network

Natasha Zlobinsky[1]([✉]) [iD], David Johnson[1] , Amit Kumar Mishra[1] [iD],
and Albert A. Lysko[1,2] [iD]

[1] University of Cape Town, Cape Town, South Africa
natzlob@gmail.com, akmishra@ieee.org
[2] Council for Scientific and Industrial Research, Pretoria, South Africa
alysko@csir.co.za

Abstract. Channel Assignment (CA) in wireless mesh networks (WMNs) has not been well studied in scenarios where the network uses Dynamic Spectrum Access (DSA). This work aims to fill some of this gap. We compare metaheuristic algorithms for optimising the CA in a WMN that has both Wi-Fi and DSA radios (where DSA could be Television White Spaces or 6 GHz). We also present a novel algorithm used alongside these metaheuristic algorithms to ensure that the CA solutions are feasible. Feasible solutions meet the interface constraint, i.e. only as many channels are allocated to a node as it has radios. The algorithm also allows the topology to be preserved by maintaining links. Many previous studies tried to ensure feasibility and/or topology preservation by using two separate steps. The first step optimised without checking feasibility and the second step fixed infeasible solutions. This second step often negated the benefits of the previous step and degraded performance. Other CA algorithms tend to use simple on/off interference models, instead of models that more realistically reflect the physical layer environment, such as the Signal to Interference plus Noise Ratio ($SINR$). We present our more realistic $SINR$-based model and optimisation objective. Simulated Annealing (SA) and Genetic Algorithm (GA) are applied to the problem. Performance is evaluated and verified through simulation. We find that GA outperforms SA, finding higher quality solutions faster, although both metaheuristics are better than random allocations. GA can be used daily to find good CAs in changing conditions.

Keywords: Channel Assignment · Dynamic Spectrum Access · DSA · Wireless Mesh Networks · WMN · CBRS · Wi-Fi 6E · TVWS · Genetic Algorithm · Simulated Annealing

H. Jin et al. (Eds.): CROWNCOM 2021/WiCON 2021, LNICST 427, pp. 56–76, 2022.
https://doi.org/10.1007/978-3-030-98002-3_4

1 Introduction

Recently, Dynamic Spectrum Access (DSA) has been gaining traction again. This is as regulatory bodies around the world have been opening up the spectrum bands that were formerly reserved for licensed users, for opportunistic use by other users. Examples are Citizens Broadband Radio Service (CBRS) Spectrum Access System (SAS) [1] and Automated Frequency Coordination in Wi-Fi 6E [2]. Most of the associated spectrum bands require (or will require) the use of databases to acquire access to channels within the bands. Another technology, Wireless Mesh Networks (WMNs), has proven its usefulness in extending Internet access from a gateway node to a wider area [3–6]. This is especially useful in rural areas or informal settlements where Internet connectivity infrastructure is not reliable. Bringing together DSA and WMN technologies can be very advantageous, especially in bringing connectivity to the unconnected, unreliably connected, or underserved.

This novel type of network comes with new challenges and avenues for research. Channel Assignment in such DSA WMNs is especially challenging. The limited channel availability, the fact that different nodes may have different allowed channels, interference within the network, as well as the possibility of other secondary users causing interference, all add to the complexity of an already NP-complete problem [7].

This work employs two metaheuristic algorithms (Simulated Annealing and Genetic Algorithm) to address the Channel Assignment problem in a WMN that uses DSA. We introduce a novel algorithm that ensures both the radio interface constraint and the connectivity or topology preservation constraint are met. This algorithm is used in conjunction with either Simulated Annealing or Genetic Algorithm. We optimise on Signal to Noise and Interference Ratio ($SINR$), rather than unrealistic binary interference models.

We continue this section with some brief background information on DSA technologies, as well as the metaheuristic optimisation techniques used in this work. An overview of related work is given in Sect. 2. Then, in Sect. 3, we present and formulate models for the problem. The methodology is detailed in Sect. 4. Simulation results are presented and discussed in Sect. 5, before concluding.

1.1 Dynamic Spectrum Access

Dynamic Spectrum Access has emerged as a way for the radio frequency spectrum to be used more efficiently. DSA became more important after it had been found that large parts of the radio spectrum remain unused while being licensed to certain users, creating an artificial spectrum scarcity. DSA refers to any of a number of techniques whereby wireless frequency bands can be shared opportunistically between the primary (licensed) users of the spectrum and secondary (unlicensed) users (SUs). It is enabled by cognitive radio, through spectrum sensing and/or the use of Geolocation Spectrum Databases (GLSDs). While practical spectrum sensing still remains in the research stage, GLSD based approaches have received wide acceptance and practical use. Using DSA methods, radios can adjust their spectrum use according to current environmental conditions while ensuring that Primary Users (PUs) or incumbents are protected from harmful interference.

Television White Spaces (TVWS) is one band in which DSA is used. TVWS refers to the unused portions of the spectrum in the 470–694 MHz range traditionally licensed to TV transmitters. SUs have been allowed to access this spectrum by a number of national regulatory bodies, including the FCC in the United States of America, Ofcom in the United Kingdom, and ICASA in South Africa. Most regulations require the use of a GLSD to ensure compliance and protection of TV broadcast services.

Citizens Broadband Radio Service (CBRS) is a band of spectrum in the 3.5 GHz range that was recently opened for sharing with incumbents for commercial use in the United States [1]. Service providers can deploy networks in this band without requiring spectrum licenses. Access is divided into three tiers: incumbent access, priority access, and general authorised access. CBRS uses a Spectrum Access System (SAS), which grants requests by SUs to access channels in the band, using a database of CBRS radio base stations, similar to the GLSD in TVWS.

To minimise interference with satellite links, Wi-Fi 6E is set to use Automated Frequency Selection (AFC), as the 6 GHz band has been opened up for unlicensed use by either low power indoor Access Points (APs), or standard power outdoor Wi-Fi APs [2]. This will also use a database to coordinate spectrum use among all users. To obtain available channels and request access, APs must consult an AFC provider before starting to transmit.

Our work can be extended to any and all of these DSA technologies and so we expect it to become increasingly useful in time.

1.2   Metaheuristic Algorithms for Optimisation

We give some brief background on the metaheuristic stochastic optimisation algorithms employed in this work. We have selected these algorithms because they are some of the most well-known and readily available algorithms, which are widely applied and verified. This means they would be easier to implement in a real network. It also means that our experiments can be replicated readily using the same algorithms, perhaps in other coding languages or with other simulation frameworks. For these reasons, we have also chosen to implement the most common "vanilla" versions of these algorithms. Variations are left as future work.

Simulated Annealing. Simulated Annealing (SA) is a probabilistic search heuristic used in optimisation problems with complex, often discrete, search spaces. It is based on, and analogous to, the physical process of annealing (of a metal, for example) in statistical mechanics, whereby atoms are cooled in a specific slow way until reaching the state of minimum energy [8]. The aim is always to find the lowest "energy" solution. That is the solution with the lowest cost. The algorithm starts with the system in a certain arbitrary configuration or state, i.e. a solution, and then it computes the "energy", which is the value of the objective function or cost of that solution at that iteration. From there, a new neighbour solution is generated by applying a slight alteration to the system state and its cost value computed and compared to the previous cost. The new solution is either accepted or rejected based on whether it has a lower "energy" value than the first solution and according to the temperature parameter. The new candidate solution is always accepted if the cost value has improved, and accepted probabilistically if the new solution is worse. The probability of acceptance is based on the difference in cost between the new candidate solution and the old solution, as well as on the current temperature value. The accepted solution is then the starting point for the next iteration.

The temperature parameter relates to how likely the algorithm is to choose a worse solution than the current one, which can prevent it from stagnating on a local minimum. The temperature must initially be set to a certain high value and decreased every iteration according to a defined cooling function, the choice of which is up to the implementer. Some examples are exponential multiplicative cooling, logarithmic multiplicative cooling, and linear multiplicative cooling [9]. The process of generating a new neighbour solution and accepting or rejecting the solution continues until the termination conditions are met. These could be a specified number of iterations or when an acceptable running time is reached, or an acceptably low solution has been settled on. Certain tests and rules-of-thumb can be followed to determine whether to stop or continue with the algorithm or estimate the convergence time, e.g., the Geweke test [10].

Genetic Algorithm. The Genetic Algorithm is a well-known metaheuristic algorithm based on the evolution of genes through generations, whereby the fittest individuals are selected as parents, they reproduce, and genes occasionally mutate. The components required are:

- a fitness function (optimisation objective function);
- a population of chromosomes, also called genomes (an encoding for solutions in the solution search space);
- a selection method by which parents for the next generation are selected;
- a crossover or reproduction method to produce the next generation; and
- a mutation method by which random changes are introduced to chromosomes, preventing convergence to local minima.

The algorithm aims to find the solution with the maximum fitness. It continues until a) the fitness value of the chromosome with the best value thus far stays the same for a certain number of iterations, or b) after an acceptable predetermined total number of generations is reached. One of several parent selection methods may be used. A popular method is Roulette Wheel selection, where each chromosome in the current generation is given a probability of being selected that is proportional to its fitness. This method is vulnerable to causing premature convergence. Linear Rank selection tries to prevent a single solution from dominating and causing premature convergence in Roulette Wheel selection by instead ranking individuals according to their inverse fitness and then basing the probability of selection on the rank rather than the actual fitness value. The highest fitness solutions are given the highest value rank. For example, out of ten solutions, the highest fitness will have rank position 10 (not 1).

2 Related Work

While the channel selection and assignment problems may appear to be well studied, there is no other work that presents an algorithm for a WMN using DSA methods, such as a GLSD, along with spectrum sensing. To the best of our knowledge, this paper is also one of the first works to use the $SINR$ perceived by the mesh nodes for CA in a WMN. It is common in the literature to use simplistic binary conflict-based objectives, using unrealistic interference and channel models, and neglecting the requirement to maintain connectivity in the network.

Simulated Annealing is evaluated by Chen and Chen [11] for CA in WMNs, while considering the interface constraint. The interface constraint states that the number of channels assigned to a node cannot exceed the number of interfaces or radios it has. In one method of Chen's work, the interface constraint is modelled with a penalty function for candidate solutions. In the other method, solutions that violate the interface constraint are not allowed, and infeasible solutions are converted to feasible solutions by merge operations. A weakness of this work is that this merge operation once again introduces the interference the first step aimed to minimise. Interference is considered binary, either present or not, and connectivity is ensured by assigning every link a channel.

Sridhar et al. present a CA methodology for multi-radio WMNs that use only Wi-Fi spectrum [12]. The optimisation goal is minimising interference. However, they also introduce a constraint to ensure that each link is assigned a channel for topology preservation. They weight the interference objective by the link traffic, which is predicted from previous averages. Lagrangian relaxation is used to find lower bounds. They also present a GA-based metaheuristic for solving the problem. A distributed algorithm is also presented, but this requires that all radios maintain a channel assignment matrix as well as a radio usage matrix for all nodes in the network, both of which are difficult to realise. Pal and Nasipuri also present a GA, but for joint routing and channel assignment [13]. They optimise on route quality. Balusu et al. combine GAs with learning automata to minimise interference in WMN CA for multicast tree topologies [14]. Multicast tree networks are also investigated by Cheng and Yang, who present GA, SA and Tabu search solutions for joint Quality of Service (QoS) routing and channel assignment in multi-radio multi-channel WMNs [15]. A GA is employed by Ding et al. for minimising total interference and maximum link interference in WMNs with partially overlapping channels [16]. They also model interference simplistically. All these works have differences from ours.

A number of works use Particle Swarm Optimisation (PSO) e.g., [17–19]. Subramanian et al. use Tabu search to minimise binary interference, first ignoring the radio constraint and then merging channel assignments to comply with the interface constraint [20]. This two-step method has the same weakness as [11], where the second step negates the first. Finally, the case of a multi-radio multi-channel network as SUs coexisting with PUs is addressed by Qin et al., using Lyapunov optimisation of throughput and average delay [21].

In view of the existing literature, we bring novelty to this field by tackling CA in WMNs in situations where the networks use the licensed spectrum opportunistically as SUs, in the presence of other SUs. Our approach uses Wi-Fi as an additional option, rather than using only Wi-Fi channels. We also take into account that different nodes may have different allowed channels, since the network is geographically spread out. Furthermore, we bring a realistic $SINR$ model instead of a simple on/off interference model. Ours is the first work to compare metaheuristic optimisation algorithms for such a network and scenario, giving consideration to all these factors. We also present a novel algorithm for ensuring that both the connectivity constraint and the interface constraint are met at once.

3   Problem Formulation

3.1   Network Model

The scenario we consider is a WMN consisting of nodes equipped with both Wi-Fi radios and radios capable of accessing alternative spectrum, such as TVWS or CBRS, as unlicensed or Secondary Users. These mesh nodes also act as APs to clients on another radio interface (this could be 2.4 GHz or 5 GHz Wi-Fi, for example). There are also Primary Users of the alternative spectrum band, which need to be protected from interference. Thus, it is required that devices use a GLSD to get a list of channels that are allowed at a device's location. This is the case for TVWS as well as Wi-Fi 6E 6 GHz AFC. A single node is the gateway to the Internet from the mesh network and also acts as the gateway to the GLSD. Mesh nodes may not all have direct access to the Internet and hence to the GLSD, but all nodes will have a connection path to the gateway node (and thus to the GLSD), which may not be optimal. The gateway node will gather the list of allowed channels and powers for all the nodes in the network.

Ensuring that all the nodes have an initial connection to the GLSD in a way that complies with regulation could be done using the method of Maliwatu [22]. In this method, nodes begin in passive scanning mode, listening for beacons, while one node (the gateway in our case) has Internet access. The node with Internet and GLSD access picks a channel and broadcasts beacon frames on this channel, along with an ordered list of alternative channels. One-hop neighbours receive this beacon frame, tune to that channel, and query the GLSD through the first node. The one-hop neighbour then selects a channel from the list of alternative channels. It can now join the network and start broadcasting beacons for the next-hop neighbour. This then allows second-hop neighbours to repeat the process and join the network, through the one-hop neighbour. This process continues until reaching the outermost set of nodes. We also assume that the gateway node will act as a controller, gathering the average $SINR$ readings from all the nodes and performing any channel assignment optimisation algorithm.

In addition, the network may be in the presence of devices external to the network, which are also making use of the alternate spectrum band and so may cause interference. An example of this scenario is shown in Fig. 1.

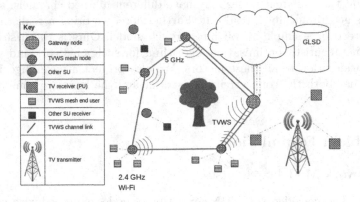

Fig. 1. An infrastructure WMN using both DSA alternative spectrum and Wi-Fi

3.2   Problem Statement and Motivation

Given this scenario, the question arises, "how to allocate channels to the mesh node radio interfaces optimally, according to certain metrics?". The main issues are minimising interference within the network and from external interference sources, while ensuring connectivity is guaranteed. Connectivity must at least be maintained along the most important paths, and between as many nodes as possible. Different channels may be allowed for use by different nodes in the network because they are placed in different geographic locations. In addition, different channels may experience different levels of external interference, loss, fading, and utilisation. Hence, the problem of assigning channels optimally is an important and difficult one in this scenario.

The CA problem is well known to be NP-hard since it is, in essence, a graph-colouring problem [7]. In the context of a WMN, it is even more difficult and goes beyond a basic graph colouring problem. Firstly, this is because the links are not the same, as mentioned, and would require a model of a weighted graph. Secondly, this is because, while interference must be avoided, it is also necessary to maintain connectivity and meet the interface constraint. We have determined that the problem is also not convex, by plotting the objective function for a scaled-down three-node (A, B, C) three-link (A-B, B-C, A-C) version of the problem, shown in Fig. 2. Each of the three axes represents the channels assigned to a link. The sawtooth shape in the one plane, and presence of higher values within the low-value regions (shown by purple, red and orange values inside the black region) make this problem non-convex, even in low dimensions. This justifies our use of metaheuristic optimisation algorithms and not convex optimisation algorithms.

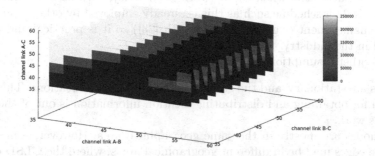

Fig. 2. Map of the objective function value of CA problem in a three-node WMN

3.3 Assumptions

The goal of the CA algorithm is to assign channels to a set of links.

Definition 1. *A link is defined as a pair of radio interfaces between which traffic could potentially flow directly if tuned to the same channel.*

In a network, over the course of a day, the routing algorithm will select and use various paths. Therefore, the set of links used for relaying traffic over the course of a day will vary. The selected paths are dependent on the capacity of the links, which is affected by the channel allocation. On the other hand, channel allocation should consider the links used, especially those with the highest traffic load. So there is a circular dependency between the two problems of routing and CA. While these two issues are very much interlinked, our channel assignment will be quasi-static (or semi-dynamic) and not change according to routing in near real-time.

This is a practical and advantageous decision, rather than a limitation. Suppose the CA attempts to keep up with the rapidly changing routes, and routing is, in turn, trying to keep up with changing channel allocations. This would cause network instability, which leads to a bad user experience, which is not desirable. Channel switching causes loss of network connectivity during the time the Network Interface Card (NIC) switches its channel and tries to re-establish connectivity, and this can be on the order of seconds in reality. Optimisation algorithms, such as those we present here, are time-consuming to run and resource-intensive. This is especially true on commodity mesh radios, which are resource-constrained, even if a dedicated controller node is used with more power. The distribution of the final channel assignment to the nodes in the network also requires time. These factors all point to the fact that we would not want the CA to change, or the optimisation algorithm to run, too often. A reasonable trade-off would thus be to run the optimisation once a day, for example. This could be run at a time when the network is not busy, such as in the middle of the night. A 24-h schedule such as this is already employed by other systems for resource management (e.g., Aruba Airmatch [23]) so it is practical and can be accepted in the industry.

Some other assumptions that apply are:

- Nodes are stationary, and the gateway node knows their locations. The mechanism for obtaining and distributing location information is out of the scope of this work.
- The nodes are mostly in the same geographical area. However, some nodes on the edges may be in different geographical areas, where the GLSD defines the boundaries. If they are not, the WMN can be partitioned into clusters with largely overlapping allowed channel lists. For this reason, we also do not present results for larger WMNs, as a large network would be partitionable into clusters. There are also practical limitations on performance in the case of large WMNs. We consider a network of 50 or more nodes as large.
- If the nodes at the cusp of two clusters do not share a sufficient number of overlapping allowed channels in the DSA band, they can be linked by a Wi-Fi channel.
- Channel widths are fixed to the same value for all channels at all nodes.
- We use average $SINR$ measurements per node in the optimisation. This is because, if the average $SINR$ over the network is large, a high throughput can be expected. $SINR$ is a direct measure of the result of changing channel assignments on the signal reception and interference experienced by nodes. These measurements will be gathered on all the channels by all nodes for different possible channel assignments. An average of all the samples for a particular CA will be used in the optimisation. Either the samples, or the overall averages will be sent to the controller/gateway node to perform the optimisation. The method by which nodes obtain $SINR$ samples could be using acknowledgement (ACK) frames, similarly to Cho et al. [24].
- All links are saturated with traffic, so the total $SINR$ across the network is also a fair objective, and no other fairness criteria is necessary.

3.4   Mathematical Model

In the usual way, we model the network as a graph $G = (V, E)$ where V is the set of nodes (vertices) and edges E are the links between nodes. Edges are potential links and not necessarily carrying traffic at this stage. Each edge $e \in E$ could be tuned to a particular channel at any time, i.e. $E \mapsto C$, where C is the full set of considered allowed channels for the whole network. C is the union of channels allowed in different locations of the WMN according to the GLSD. Each node v has a set $C(v)$ of channels it is allowed to use. For two nodes v_1 and v_2, $C(v_1) \neq C(v_2)$ in general, although they could be equal and should have channels in common $(C(v_1) \cap C(v_2) \neq \emptyset)$, especially if v_1 and v_2 are neighbours. A channel is specified by a channel number, a centre frequency and a channel bandwidth. There might also be other transmitting devices (other SUs) that can influence the reception of nodes in G if they are transmitting with power in the same channel that one of the links E is tuned to. These are added to the conflict graph. Connectivity graph G maps to a conflict graph G_c.

Definition 2. *Conflict graph $G_c = (V_c, E_c)$, where the vertices of the conflict graph are the edges in G i.e. $V_c = E$. An edge $e' \in E_c$ exists between two vertices in V_c if the two links could interfere if tuned to an overlapping channel. This could occur when the interfering signal power is above the receiver sensitivity.*

We add vertices and edges representing outside sources of interference to form $\hat{G}_c$, but note that these are fixed as their channels cannot be switched and their transmit power cannot be controlled.

An edge e' exists if a transmission in link 2 causes power to leak into, or be transmitted in, the channel on which link 1 is operating. This can occur if the two links are tuned to the same channel. This can also happen if the links are tuned to different channels while the spectrum mask of the transmitter node is wide or the receive filtering is poor, so that power leaks into the channel on which link 1 is operating. We can model this as a weighted conflict graph denoted $\langle G_c(V_c, E_c), w \rangle$, where the weight w represents the interference power per link.

Considering this conflict graph, we aim to minimise the conflict but maximise the wanted signal power received by each node and so maintain connectivity in G. We can satisfy both these requirements simply by considering $SINR$. This measure encapsulates the goals of having the highest desired received signal level throughout the network, while also minimising conflict (interference). The optimisation objective is thus to find the channel assignment A, which is a mapping of $E \mapsto C$ that maximises the average $SINR$, i.e.

$$\max_{A=E \mapsto C} \sum_{v \in V} \frac{P_{wanted,v}(A)}{\sum_{i \in I} P_i(A) + N} \implies \min_A \sum_{v \in V} \frac{\sum_{i \in I} P_i(A) + N}{P_{wanted,v}(A)}$$

$$= \min_A \sum_{v \in V} \frac{\sum_{x \in V \setminus u} P_{x,v}(A) + N}{P_{u,v}(A)} \tag{1}$$

$$= \min_A \frac{|V|}{\sum_{v \in V} SINR_v(A)}$$

over all possible channel assignments, subject to the radio interface constraint:

$$|A(v)| \leq R_v \quad \forall\, v \in V \tag{2}$$

where:

$A(v)$ is the channel assignment of node v and $|\cdot|$ indicates the size (number of channels assigned to the node);

R_v is the number of radios at node v;

$P_{u,v}$ is the power received at node v from transmitting node u;

P_i is interfering power received at node v from an interfering transmission i over the whole channel width of channel c to which node v is tuned.

N is the noise power, which in ns3 is modelled as the product of the thermal noise (N_t) and the noise figure (F_N), as shown in Eq. (3).

$$N = N_t \times F_N = kTB \times F_N \tag{3}$$

where k is Boltzmann's constant ($= 1.380649 \times 10^{-23} JK^{-1}$), T is the temperature in Kelvin and B is the channel width.

A transmitting node is considered interfering with v if it is in the set of nodes V minus the node u, the node transmitting the desired signal to v. We only consider there to be one wanted receive signal per time slot.

Each transmitted signal is subject to propagation loss as well as frequency-selective fading. As usual, the received signal power at node v from node u's transmitted power $P_{u,v}$ (in W) before receive filtering is related by the propagation loss L according to the chosen loss model. We apply the basic Friis transmission loss model in Eq. (4). This also implies that we assume an isotropic antenna model, but this can also be changed in the simulation for future work. We note, however, that our method is easily extensible to other propagation loss models and is not limited to work on any particular propagation loss model only. This model is used without loss of generality.

$$P_{u,v} = P_u \frac{G_v G_u \lambda^2}{(4\pi d)^2} = \frac{P_u}{L_{u,v}} \tag{4}$$

where

G_u is the transmission gain of node u's antenna (unitless)

G_v is the receive gain of node v's antenna (unitless)

λ is the wavelength (in m), inversely proportional to the frequency, so is affected by the channel assignment

d is the distance between the nodes (in m)

or, in dB,

$$P_{u,v}(dB) = P_u(dB) - L_{u,v}(dB) \tag{5}$$

where path loss $L(dB)$ is the absolute value of the loss in dB.

Before considering interference, a link only exists if the effective received signal power on that link is above the receive sensitivity s_v of the receiver node v. That is, the link will be pruned unless

$$P_{u,v}(dB) \geq s_v$$
$$SNR_v \times N \geq s_v \tag{6}$$
$$SNR \geq s_v/N$$

SNR can only be measured if it is above the receiver sensitivity/noise. This constraint reduces the number of links that require channel assignment and reduces the edges in the conflict graph that need to be considered. We also have to ensure that in the CA, constraint (6) is met, so that connectivity is maintained. Additionally, interference is only considered if the interference power at the receiver is above the energy detection threshold of the receiver.

In the simulation framework of Network Simulator 3 (ns3), frames are split into constant $SINR$ chunks and overlapping frame chunks are considered as additional contributions to the overall noise. Interfering signals are only considered as interference when the frame chunks actually overlap with those of the wanted frame at each considered receiving node in time. Preamble and payload parts of frames are treated separately because the payload might have a higher modulation and coding rate than the BPSK-encoded preamble.

4   Methodology

The optimisation methods all generate candidate solutions from the CA solution space and obtain $SINR$ measurements from all nodes based on that solution (CA), in order to optimise on that measurement. In a real implementation, over the course of a day, $SINR$ samples for some of these solutions will be taken. For those solutions with insufficient $SINR$ samples, such samples must be gathered during the running of the optimisation algorithm, possibly by generating traffic between nodes for this purpose. The algorithm will start with a randomly generated feasible candidate CA and iteratively improve on that solution. For the results presented here, we have used simulation in ns3 for evaluation purposes, because this provides a controlled environment for ease, efficiency, clarity and cost-effectiveness of experimentation.

4.1   Generating Feasible Candidate Solutions

While we have used the graph analogy for this problem, it is not a simple graph colouring problem. One of the added complexities that distinguishes this problem from normal graph colouring is the interface constraint in Eq. (2). Another is that connectivity must be maintained between links through ensuring Eq. (6) is true and having common channels assigned to link nodes, while collisions should be avoided. In all of the metaheuristic optimisation methods we need to generate a set of possible solutions, that is, the solution space. We can either generate each solution and check for feasibility afterwards, or ensure feasibility within the generation procedure. Our method does the latter. We have developed a simple novel algorithm to generate candidate solutions that are feasible. A feasible solution is one that satisfies the interface constraint while using only allowed channels at each node. In this algorithm, we attempt to allocate channels to all links in the network. However, this might not be possible. Therefore, we allocate DSA channels to as many links as possible out of the full set. To ensure connectivity on the remaining links, Wi-Fi is used. This algorithm is outlined in Algorithm 1.

4.2 Optimisation

The objective is to find a link→channel mapping (A) that maximises the total average $SINR$ in the network. For each considered solution, all nodes scan the environment for a period of time and obtain a large set of sample $SINR$ values for traffic flow through a particular link→channel mapping for a particular interference environment. We then use the average of these values in the cost. In Simulated Annealing, we desire that the objective function (so-called "energy" value E) incorporates these $SINR$ samples in a way that the desired result is the lowest cost. Hence, the selected cost is based on $1/SINR$. For Genetic Algorithm, where we use a fitness value, this is the normalised average of $SINR$. All results are shown as the scaled inverse $SINR$ for direct comparison between optimisation methods.

Simulated Annealing. The cost per iteration j is shown in Eq. (7), where V is the number of nodes, n is the number of $SINR$ samples per node, and $\overline{SINR}$ is the average of the $SINR$ measurements per node.

$$E_j = \frac{1}{V} \sum_{v=1}^{V} \left[\frac{1}{n} \sum_{i=1}^{n} \frac{1}{SINR_j(i)}(v) \right] = \frac{1}{V} \sum_{v=1}^{V} \frac{1}{\overline{SINR_j(v)}} \tag{7}$$

In SA, the change in cost every iteration is used to decide whether to accept or reject the particular CA solution. If the new solution is better than the previous solution, i.e., has a lower cost, the new solution is always accepted. However, if the new CA has a higher cost, this worse solution is accepted with a probability h given by Eq. (8). This is realised by selecting a random value a between 0 and 1 and evaluating if $a < h$.

$$h = \exp(-\frac{\Delta E}{kT}) = \exp(-\frac{E_j - E_{j-1}}{k \cdot T_j}) \tag{8}$$

where
E_j is the "energy" or cost at iteration j, given by Eq. (7)
k is Boltzmann's constant ($1.380649 \times 10^{-23} JK^{-1}$)
T_j is the temperature at iteration j

Algorithm 1: Initial channel allocation

Data: C = allowed channel set, c = single channel in C, n_i = node number i,
$\quad\quad\quad L$ = set of links, l = link in L, A = channels assigned = $\varnothing$, r = number
$\quad\quad\quad$ of interfaces per node=2

Result: complete $A(l) \; \forall \, l \in L$

for $l = (n_i, n_j) \in L$ do
$\quad$ if $A(n_i) < r$ and $A(n_j) < r$ then
$\quad\quad$ c = random channel $\in C(n_i) \cap C(n_j)$;
$\quad\quad$ $A(n_i) = c$;
$\quad\quad$ $A(n_j) = c$;
$\quad$ end
$\quad$ else if $A(n_i) == r$ and $A(n_j) < r$ then
$\quad\quad$ $\{c\} = A(n_i) \bigcup C(n_j)$;
$\quad\quad$ if $\{c\} \neq \varnothing$ then
$\quad\quad\quad$ $c = \{c\}\,[0]$;
$\quad\quad$ end
$\quad\quad$ else
$\quad\quad\quad$ c=choose one of $A(n_i)$;
$\quad\quad\quad$ $A(n_j) = c$;
$\quad\quad$ end
$\quad$ end
$\quad$ else if $A(n_i) < r$ and $A(n_j) == r$ then
$\quad\quad$ $\{c\} = A(n_j) \bigcup C(n_i)$;
$\quad\quad$ if $\{c\} \neq \varnothing$ then
$\quad\quad\quad$ $c = \{c\}\,[0]$;
$\quad\quad$ end
$\quad\quad$ else
$\quad\quad\quad$ c=choose one of $C(n_j)$;
$\quad\quad\quad$ $A(n_i) = c$;
$\quad\quad$ end
$\quad$ end
$\quad$ else
$\quad\quad$ both interfaces already assigned channels;
$\quad\quad$ $\{c\} = A(n_i) \bigcup A(n_j)$;
$\quad\quad$ if $\{c\} \neq \varnothing$ then
$\quad\quad\quad$ $c = \{c\}\,[0]$;
$\quad\quad$ end
$\quad\quad$ else
$\quad\quad\quad$ continue;
$\quad\quad$ end
$\quad$ end
$\quad$ $A(l) = c$;
end
$\forall \, l$ unassigned, assign a 5 GHz Wi-Fi channel

If $a < h$, the solution is accepted. If not, the solution is rejected. If Eq. (8) always evaluates close to 1, higher cost solutions will always be accepted and the SA algorithm will not converge. Conversely, if Eq. (8) always evaluates to a value very close to 0, almost no "worse" solutions will be accepted and the algorithm will converge prematurely on a local minimum that may be much worse than the true optimum.

A careful balance of temperature ranges and ΔE ranges as well as k-value must be formulated to tune the algorithm appropriately. Boltzmann's constant k could be omitted from this relation (or set to 1) in practice if it makes the probability of accepting a point extremely low, leading to converging on a local minimum. Including or leaving this constant out, is part of the parameter tuning required to ensure the algorithm behaves well. We have omitted k but added another constant to scale the $1/SINR$ values appropriately.

The other parameter tuning required is the selection of the starting temperature and the temperature cooling function. A starting temperature that is too high or a cooling function that decreases too slowly will cause much slower convergence. On the other hand, starting with a temperature that is too low or a cooling function that reduces too quickly may result in converging prematurely. Starting temperature and the temperature cooling function must be adjusted in consideration of the number of iterations the algorithm is expected to run for, or that is considered acceptable. We ran experiments with various cooling functions (e.g., logarithmic and exponential functions) in this work before finding a suitable one: the linear temperature cooling function shown in Eq. (9).

$$T_j = T_{start} - \alpha \cdot j \tag{9}$$

where j is iteration count and α is a constant set to 0.02. We selected this value for α by reversing the calculation (9) for appropriate starting temperature (20) and final temperature (0.1) and the desired number of iterations (1000), and confirming by experimentation that it works well. We start with a lower temperature value of 20, selected by observation of the ΔE values for our problem, and scale the $1/SINR$ values appropriately. With these adjustments, the algorithm is able to converge sufficiently within 1000 iterations.

The neighbour generation procedure whereby a new solution is generated is to shuffle the links randomly and perform Algorithm 1.

Genetic Algorithm. For the GA, we encode a genome also as a link→channel mapping, where the links are all node pairs possible in the mesh and where the condition of Eq. (6) is met. To generate a genome, we randomly shuffle the set of links, randomly shuffle the set of allowed channels, and use Algorithm 1 to generate a feasible genome. We then generate a population by generating a number of genomes. We determined from experimentation that a population size of 20 functions well without excessive computational burden. This population is confirmed as a good choice by [25], who find that a population size of 20 presents less structural bias than populations of 5 or 100 individuals in general.

Both Roulette Wheel selection and Linear Rank selection were implemented. For the Roulette Wheel selection, we generated a piecewise constant probability distribution, where the intervals are 1 + the population size and the weights are the fitness values of the chromosomes in the population. For Linear Rank selection, we sort the chromosomes by their inverse fitness value so that the genome with the highest fitness has the lowest rank (highest number). We then create a piecewise constant probability distribution of the ranks and select two parent chromosomes randomly according to that distribution. It was found that Linear Rank selection outperforms Roulette Wheel selection, so only the results for Linear Rank selection are shown. We select as many parents as the current population and each pair of parents generates two children. The previous generation is eliminated once they reproduce, so the size of the population remains stable.

Once two parents have been selected, the next operator is crossover. The crossover operator randomly selects an index in the genome (a link) greater than the first and smaller than the last, as the crossover point. We then split both parents at this crossover point and generate two new children by joining the first section of the first parent with the second section of the second parent, and the first section of the second parent with the second section of the first parent. Mutation is done with a probability of 0.5, by randomly selecting one link and randomly selecting a new channel for that link, and replacing the currently assigned channel with the new one. The 0.5 probability was found to provide a suitable trade-off between exploration and exploitation for the population size and problem. This follows the findings of [26].

5   Results and Discussion

To evaluate the performance of the algorithms, we have simulated the network using ns3. We have built on top of the existing ns3 classes and created a module for the multi-radio multi-channel WMN simulation with interference, which models the spectrum sensing part of the DSA. Additionally, we created new ns3 modules for each of the optimisation techniques. This code can be reused by others wishing to build on this work or replicate these results [27].

Simulations were run on a T2 large Amazon Web Services EC2 instance with 8 GiB of memory and 2 virtual CPUs, both with Ubuntu 16.04 Operating System, and using ns3-dev version [27] forked from the ns3 GitHub [28].

In each iteration of all the optimisation algorithms, the WMN simulation is run for a period of 5 s. This was found to yield sufficient $SINR$ samples for the average to be meaningful. In the mesh simulation, nodes are set up in an equally spaced grid. Each node has two DSA interfaces (representing the DSA band interface). Constant bitrate UDP traffic is generated at the transmit node for every possible link in the network so as to saturate the links. Packets will be received on the other side if there is a common channel between the two nodes and the received signal is above the receive sensitivity. The interference is included in the $SINR$ measurement using ns3's InterferenceHelper class, and interference is counted only if the overlapping packet chunk is above the sensitivity of the receiver. The simulation parameters are given in Table 1.   Table 2 compares the mean and standard deviation of CA final costs for 10 runs of SA and GA, and random CAs. We can see that for all presented WMN sizes, SA is significantly better than random allocations (between 120% and 620% better).

Table 1. Parameters used in simulations

Parameter	Value
Mesh network size	9–49 nodes
Number of interfaces	2
Distance between grid nodes	100 m (vertical and horizontal)
Channel bandwidth	10 MHz
Propagation loss model	Friis
Propagation delay model	ConstantSpeed
Packet interval	0.01 s
Packet size	1024 bytes
Error rate model	NistErrorRateModel
Mesh routing algorithm	OLSR

In comparison, GA is significantly better than both random allocations (between 380% and 1268%) and SA (between 16% and 54% better). While the averages improve significantly, the standard deviation also reduces significantly so that the chances of SA or GA producing a substantially worse solution than those shown here are very low.

The deviations from the average cost values get smaller over time as the algorithms converge. Regardless of the starting point, different runs start to converge on similar values, especially in the GA case. Figure 3 shows the cost of the solutions found by both SA and GA at each iteration averaged over 10 different runs, for different network sizes. For GA the average population costs for the different runs are averaged. We can observe clearly that GA converges much quicker than SA. Different runs of GA also converge on solutions that are closer than SA (as seen by the smaller standard deviations in Table 2. We can obtain a reasonably good solution using GA within 25 iterations (or even less) for a 9-node WMN. Even for the larger 16 and 49-node mesh networks, the solutions within 50 iterations are better than SA after the same number of iterations. We note, however, that for one iteration of GA, we need to perform 20 runs of the WMN simulation (or perform sampling windows for 20 different CAs), since there are 20 individuals per population. This sampling window is the most time-intensive portion of the optimisation. Hence, 1 iteration of GA is roughly equivalent in time to 20 iterations of SA; so 50 iterations of GA are equivalent to 1000 iterations of SA in time. Still, within the same amount of time, we are able to achieve significantly better results with GA than with SA, although both achieve much better results than CAs.

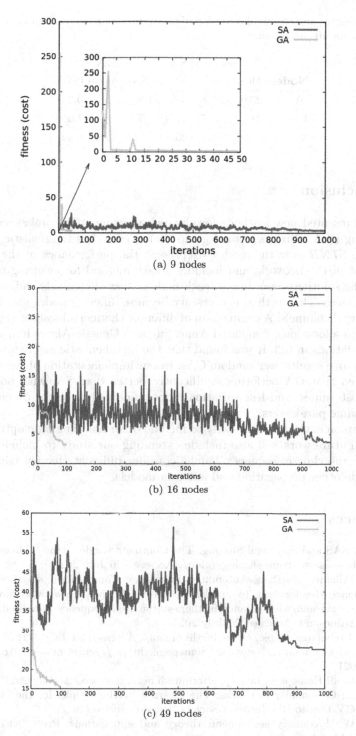

Fig. 3. Average cost of all runs of SA and GA (average cost of population) per iteration compared

Table 2. Average and standard deviation of cost values for random channel allocations, SA and GA for 10 runs of each

	Random	SA	GA
Nodes	Mean (SD)	Mean (SD)	Mean (SD)
9	26.0 (±35.8)	3.6 (±1.6)	1.9 (±0.25)
16	28.1 (±35.7)	4.3 (±2.7)	3.6 (±1.0)
49	56.0 (±51.7)	25.4 (±4.9)	11.6 (±5.2)

6   Conclusion

We have presented new methods for channel assignment in wireless mesh networks using DSA. Our work is unique in that it considers the realistic measure of average $SINR$ over the mesh to represent the performance of the channel assignment in the network, and includes a new method for ensuring the feasibility of the solutions according to each node's allowed channels and number of radio interfaces. This method is necessary because different nodes may have different allowed channels. A comparison of different channel allocation algorithms, i.e., random allocations, Simulated Annealing and Genetic Algorithm, was done using simulations in ns3. It was found that the metaheuristic algorithms significantly improve results over random CAs. In our implementation of the problem, we observed that GA performs significantly better than SA, with both lower average cost values, and less variation among final solutions for different runs with the same parameters.

We plan on extending this study to include other metaheuristic optimisation methods. Future work will also include extending our study to include aspects specific to the chosen frequency bands, consider different channel bandwidths and include other propagation and antenna models.

References

1. CBRS, SAS and Spectrum Sharing: The Complete Guide. https://blinqnetworks. com/cbrs-sas-spectrum-sharing-guide/. Accessed 26 July 2021
2. Wi-Fi Alliance®furthers Automated Frequency Coordination specification and compliance development to accelerate Wi-Fi 6E. https://www.wi-fi.org/news-events/newsroom/wi-fi-alliance-furthers-automated-frequency-coordination-specification-and. Accessed 26 July 2021
3. iNethi Homepage. https://www.inethi.org.za/. Accessed 24 July 2021
4. Zenzeleni Community Networks Homepage. https://zenzeleni.net/. Accessed 24 July 2021
5. AlterMundi Homepage. https://altermundi.net/. Accessed 24 July 2021
6. Belli, L.: Community Networks: The Internet by the People, for the People, 1st edn. FGV Direito Rio, Internet Society, Rio de Janeiro (2017)
7. Hale, W.: Frequency assignment: theory and applications. Proc. IEEE **68**(12), 1497–1514 (1980)

8. Kirkpatrick, S.: Optimisation by simulated annealing. Science **220**(4598), 671–680 (1983)
9. Nourani, Y., Andresen, B.: A comparison of simulated annealing cooling strategies. J. Phys. A Math. Gen. **31**(41), 8373–8385 (1998)
10. Geweke, J., Tanizaki, H.: Bayesian estimation of state-space models using the Metropolis-Hastings algorithm within Gibbs sampling. Comput. Stat. Data Anal. **37**(2001), 151–170 (2001)
11. Chen, Y., Chen, C.: Simulated annealing for interface-constrained channel assignment in wireless mesh networks. Ad Hoc Netw. **29**(2015), 32–44 (2015)
12. Sridhar, S., Guo, J., Jha, S.: Channel assignment in multi-radio wireless mesh networks: a graph-theoretic approach, In: First International Communication Systems and Networks and Workshops, Bangalore, India, vol. 2009, pp. 1–10 (2009)
13. Pal, A., Nasipuri, A: JRCA: a joint routing and channel assignment scheme for wireless mesh networks. In: Conference Proceedings of the 30th IEEE International Performance, Computing, and Communications Conference, pp. 1–8 (2011)
14. Balusu, N., Pabboju, S., Narsimha, G.: An intelligent channel assignment approach for minimum interference in wireless mesh networks using learning automata and genetic algorithms. Wireless Pers. Commun. **106**(3), 1293–1307 (2019). https://doi.org/10.1007/s11277-019-06214-3
15. Cheng, H., Yang, S.: Joint QoS multicast routing and channel assignment in multiradio multichannel wireless mesh networks using intelligent computational methods. Appl. Soft Comput. J. **11**(2011), 1953–1964 (2011)
16. Ding, Y., Huang, Y., et al.: Channel assignment with partially overlapping channels in wireless mesh networks. In: Proceedings of the 4th Annual International Conference on Wireless Internet, pp. 1–9. ICST, Maui (2008)
17. Zhuang, X., Cheng, H., Xiong, N.: Channel assignment in multi-radio wireless networks based on PSO algorithm. In: 2010 5th International Conference on Future Information Technology, FutureTech 2010 - Proceedings, pp. 1–6 (2010)
18. Shawkat, A., et al.: On the use of particle swarm optimisation techniques for channel assignments in cognitive radio networks. In: Multidisciplinary Computational Intelligence Techniques: Applications in Business, Engineering, and Medicine, pp. 202–214, Information Science Reference, United States of America (2012)
19. Chakraborty, M., Chowdhury, R., Basu, J., Janarthanan, R. Konar, A.: A particle swarm optimisation-based approach towards the solution of the dynamic channel assignment problem in mobile cellular networks. In: IEEE Region 10 Annual International Conference, Proceedings/TENCON, pp. 1–6 (2008)
20. Subramanian, A.P., Gupta, H., Das, S.R.: Minimum interference channel assignment in multi-radio wireless mesh networks. In: 2007 4th Annual IEEE Communications Society Conference on Sensor, Mesh and Ad Hoc Communications and Networks, pp. 481–490 (2007)
21. Qin, A., et al.: Opportunistic scheduling and channel allocation in MC-MR cognitive radio networks. IEEE Trans. Veh. Technol. **63**(7), 3351–3368 (2014)
22. Maliwatu, R.: A new connectivity strategy for wireless mesh networks using dynamic spectrum access. Ph.D. thesis, Cape Town (2020)
23. AirMatch. https://www.arubanetworks.com/techdocs/ArubaOS_81_Web_Help/Content/ArubaFrameStyles/ARM/mCell.htm. Accessed 31 July 2021
24. Cho, S.: $SINR$-based MCS level adaptation in CSMA/CA wireless networks to embrace IoT devices. Symmetry **9**(10), 236–253 (2017)
25. Kononova, A.V., et al.: Structural bias in population-based algorithms. Inf. Sci. **298**(2015), 468–490 (2015)

26. Deb, K., Agrawal, S., et al.: Understanding interactions among genetic algorithm parameters. Found. Genet. Algorithms **5**(5), 265–286 (1999)
27. ns-3-dev-git. https://github.com/natzlob/ns-3-dev-git/tree/mrmc-fresh. Accessed 31 July 2021
28. ns-3-dev-git. https://github.com/nsnam/ns-3-dev-git. Accessed 31 July 2021

Performance of Cooperative Spectrum Sensing Based on Random Transition of the Primary User in Laplacian Noise

Khushboo Sinha$^{(\boxtimes)}$ (iD) and Y. N. Trivedi (iD)

Nirma University, Ahmedabad 382470, Gujarat, India
{18ftphde24,yogesh.trivedi}@nirmauni.ac.in

Abstract. In this paper, cooperative spectrum sensing (CSS) of dynamic primary user (PU) is considered in Laplacian noise environment. The dynamic PU is characterized by its transitions from ON (present) state to OFF (absent) state and vice-versa. It means, during the entire sensing duration, the PU appears or disappears intermittently. We assume that each cognitive radio (CR) uses conventional test-statistics such as energy detection (ED), absolute value cumulation detection (AVCD) and improved AVCD (i-AVCD). The hard decision from each CR fuses at the fusion center (FC) according to CSS based on OR rule (CSS-OR), CSS-AND rule and CSS-majority rule to make a final decision on the appearance or disappearance of the PU. We further consider dynamic nature of the PU in terms of its arrival rate (θ_A) and departure rate (θ_D). We present performance of the CSS of dynamic PU using receiver operating characteristic (ROC) and detection probability (P_D) versus average signal-to-noise ratio (SNR), denoted by γ, using Monte Carlo simulations. We conclude that the CSS-OR rule based spectrum sensing outperforms CSS-majority rule and CSS-AND rule based spectrum sensing over a wide range of average SNR, i.e., $-10 < \gamma < 10$ dB. We further conclude that CSS-AND rule is unsuitable for enhancing the detection probability of conventional sensing schemes. Furthermore, CSS-majority rule outperforms conventional sensing schemes ED, AVCD and i-AVCD beyond $\gamma = -1, -5$ and -6 dB, respectively.

Keywords: Energy detection · Cooperative spectrum sensing · Fusion center · Dynamic primary user · Laplacian noise · Detection probability

1 Introduction

In the current era of 5G communication, the world has evolved with the massive use of Internet of Things (IoT) devices. Progressive and sound technologies such as cloud computing, big data analytic and wireless communication have led to the widespread use of bandwidth consuming IoT devices [1]. These IoT devices exploit huge bandwidth in the existing limited microwave spectrum and

© ICST Institute for Computer Sciences, Social Informatics and Telecommunications Engineering 2022
Published by Springer Nature Switzerland AG 2022. All Rights Reserved
H. Jin et al. (Eds.): CROWNCOM 2021/WiCON 2021, LNICST 427, pp. 77–93, 2022.
https://doi.org/10.1007/978-3-030-98002-3_5

are extensively used in sectors such as smart manufacturing, smart cities and cyber-physical systems [2]. In the real time scenario, the prevailing microwave spectrum is limited. Although, millimeter wave can relieve spectrum scarcity problem by providing sufficient spectrum, drastic changes in the wireless network are required [3]. Besides the spectrum scarcity problem, the insufficient or under utilization of existing spectrum is a major concern i.e., large segment of the spectrum remains unutilized [4]. The unutilized segment of spectrum is commonly known as spectrum hole [5]. Cognitive radio (CR) is an advanced futuristic and sophisticated technology which uses three major spectrum utilization model, i.e. interweave model, underlay model and overlay model [6]. Amongst which interweave model is the most popular model and sometimes it is also known as opportunistic model [7]. In this model, spectrum holes are periodically or continuously monitored by the unlicensed spectrum user, also known as secondary user (SU), in a way such that licensed user or primary user (PU) suffers minimum interference [6,7]. The process through which these spectrum holes are sensed to identify the presence of PU is known as spectrum sensing [8].

In CR, there always exists a trade off between the detection probability of PU and the throughput, i.e. with increase in sensing samples, detection probability increases but as a result of no data transmission during sensing period, throughput decreases [9]. The PU traffic which remains steady or varies slowly with time is an ideal assumption for the case of static PU. The assumption of static PU can be well observed in television broadcast and radar systems [10]. On the other hand, dynamic nature of PU is suitable for PU traffic which varies quickly with time as in case of wireless medical networks (medical body area network) and wireless local area network (WLAN) [11]. During the sensing period, the static behaviour of PU is well documented in [12,13] and dynamic behaviour in [14,16].

Additive white Gaussian noise (AWGN) has been considered in many spectrum sensing schemes as the noise is assumed to model the thermal noise or Johnson noise in the receiver [17–19]. However, in the current scenario of multi user communications, multiple access interference (MAI) serves as a dominant noise source [20]. In such case, AWGN fails to accurately model the MAI. The MAI is modelled by various noise models such as Laplacian noise model, Gaussian mixture model (GMM) and Middleton Class A model (MCA) [21]. It has been proved that the Laplacian noise model precisely models the MAI in time-hopped ultra-wideband (TH-UWB) wireless communication system under static PU scenario [20,21]. The CSS, based on majority rule (k_m out of L rule, where $k_m \leq L$), has been considered in Laplacian noise environment under the static PU scenario [22]. In [23], it has been shown that the detection performance of CSS based on Rao detector (CSS-Rao) is superior to the performance based on classical ED (CSS-ED) in non-Gaussian noise, which is modelled by Generalized Gaussian distribution (GGD). In fact, the Laplacian noise and Gaussian distributions are special cases of GGD.

The CSS based on dynamic double threshold energy detection (DDTHED) was proposed in [24] with circularly symmetric Gaussian noise and in the environment of mobile cognitive radio network. It was shown that CSS-DDTHED outperformed CSS-ED.

In this paper, we consider the CSS based on dynamic PU in additive Laplacian noise environment. We assume that there are total L number of CRs and out of which k_m are active CRs. These k_m CRs independently sense the presence of PU by applying test-statistics such as ED [25], absolute value cumulation detection (AVCD) [26] and improved AVCD (i-AVCD) [27]. Then, All CRs send their hard decisions via reporting channel to a central controlling center known as Fusion center (FC). The FC fuses these decisions via different rules such as 'AND rule', 'OR rule' or 'majority rule (k_m out of L rule). The detection probability and false alarm probability at each active CR are denoted by P_d and P_f, respectively. The detection probability and false alarm probability at the FC are denoted as P_D and P_F, respectively. Further, we assume that the random transitions of the PU, i.e. PU's random arrival and departure, are modelled by Poisson distribution. Moreover, the random transition time of the PU is modelled by exponential distribution [15].

The rest of the paper is organised as follows. Section 2 presents the system model. Section 3 presents performance analysis of the dynamic PU in detail. Section 4 presents simulation results followed by brief conclusion in Sect. 5.

2   System Model

In the considered dynamic scenario, H_o denotes the hypothesis when PU is present up to a specified sample ψ_o and thereafter PU is absent. In a similar way, H_1 denotes the alternate hypothesis when PU is absent up to a specified sample ψ_1 and thereafter PU is present. Thus, the received signals at each of the L cognitive terminals are expressed as

$$
\begin{aligned}
H_o : y_k &= \begin{cases} s_k + w_k, & k = 1, \ldots, \psi_o \\ w_k, & k = \psi_o + 1, \psi_o + 2, \psi_o + 3 \ldots, N \end{cases} \\
H_1 : y_k &= \begin{cases} w_k, & k = 1, \ldots, \psi_1 \\ s_k + w_k, & k = \psi_1 + 1, \psi_1 + 2, \psi_1 + 3 \ldots, N \end{cases}
\end{aligned}
\tag{1}
$$

where $k = 1, 2, 3 \ldots, N$. The N is the aggregate samples present during the sensing period. The s_k is the unknown PU signal and w_k is the Laplacian noise having mean as 0 and variance as $2b_o^2$. The b_o is known as the scale parameter of the Laplacian noise. Average signal-to-noise ratio (SNR) is well expressed as

$$
\gamma = \frac{1}{N} \sum_{k=1}^{N} \frac{s_k^2}{2b_o^2},
$$

where ψ_o and ψ_1 indicate the first level transition points of the PU under hypotheses H_o and H_1 respectively. The random transition (departure) of the PU occurs between the samples ψ_o and $\psi_o + 1$ while the random transition (arrival) of the PU occurs between the samples ψ_1 and $\psi_1 + 1$. The probability density function (PDF) of the Laplacian noise is expressed as [22]

$$
f_{w_k}(i) = \frac{1}{2b_o} \exp\left(-\frac{|i|}{b_o}\right).
\tag{2}
$$

Each of the L cognitive terminals then uses ED, AVCD and i-AVCD as test-statistics to decide the presence or absence of PU. Hard decisions from each CR are then sent to FC, where they are fused according to specified CSS fusion rule, i.e., CSS-AND rule, CSS-OR rule and CSS-majority rule. P_F and P_D at the FC can be derived as

$$P_F = Prob\{H_1|H_o\} = \sum_{i=k_m}^{L} \binom{L}{i} P_f^i (1 - P_f)^{L-i},$$

$$P_D = Prob\{H_1|H_1\} = \sum_{i=k_m}^{L} \binom{L}{i} P_d^i (1 - P_d)^{L-i}, \tag{3}$$

where P_f and P_d are false alarm probability and detection probability at each L cognitive terminal. k_m denotes the number of active CRs present. $k_m = 1$ represents OR rule, $k_m = L$ represents AND rule and $k_m < L$ represents majority rule.

3   Performance Analysis

In this section, we present two subsections. In the first subsection, we present three different cases of CSS-ED. The first case presents the case static PU as a special case of dynamic PU while the second and third case being the dynamic PU random arrival case and random departure case, respectively. In the second subsection, we presents all the three cases of PU in CSS-i-AVCD. We also discuss AVCD as a special case of i-AVCD. Further, we derive P_D and P_F in each of the considered cases in CSS-ED and CSS-i-AVCD.

3.1   CSS Based on Energy Detection (CSS-ED)

ED is one of the simplest spectrum sensing techniques in the field of cognitive radio. Considering ED as the test-statistic, the likelihood functions under hypothesis H_o and H_1 are expressed as [15]

$$f(\mathbf{y}|\mathbf{s}_{co}, H_o) = \frac{1}{(2b_o)^N} \exp\left\{ -\sum_{k=1}^{\psi_o} \frac{|y_k - s_k|^2}{b_o} - \sum_{k=\psi_o+1}^{N} \frac{|y_k|^2}{b_o} \right\},$$

$$f(\mathbf{y}|\mathbf{s}_{c1}, H_1) = \frac{1}{(2b_o)^N} \exp\left\{ -\sum_{k=1}^{\psi_1} \frac{|y_k|^2}{b_o} - \sum_{k=\psi_1+1}^{N} \frac{|y_k - s_k|^2}{b_o} \right\}, \tag{4}$$

where $\mathbf{y} = [y_1, y_2, y_3 \ldots, y_N]$, $\mathbf{s}_{co} = [s_1, s_2, s_3 \ldots, s_{\psi_o}]$ and $\mathbf{s}_{c1} = [s_{\psi_1+1}, s_{\psi_1+2}, s_{\psi_1+3} \ldots, s_N]$. As s_k is unknown PU signal, it is necessary to omit it from the likelihood function. Maximum likelihood (ML) estimation of s_k is used for this purpose. It results in

$$\frac{f(\mathbf{y}|\hat{\mathbf{s}}_{c1}, H_1)}{f(\mathbf{y}|\hat{\mathbf{s}}_{co}, H_o)} = \frac{\frac{1}{(2b_o)^N} \exp\left\{\sum_{k=1}^{\psi_1} -\frac{|y_k|^2}{b_o}\right\}}{\frac{1}{(2b_o)^N} \exp\left\{\sum_{k=\psi_o+1}^{N} -\frac{|y_k|^2}{b_o}\right\}} \underset{H_o}{\overset{H_1}{\gtrless}} \lambda_o, \tag{5}$$

where $\hat{\mathbf{s}}_{co} = [\hat{s}_1, \hat{s}, \hat{s}_3, \ldots, \hat{s}_{\psi_o}]$ and $\hat{\mathbf{s}}_{c1} = [\hat{s}_{\psi_1+1}, \hat{s}_{\psi_1+2}, \ldots, \hat{s}_N]$. $\hat{s}_k$ is the ML estimate of s_k which is calculated manually and found to be y_k, i.e., $\hat{s}_k = y_k$. At this point, ψ_o and ψ_1 are also unknown and random. Simplifying (5), the likelihood ratio test can be expressed as

$$Z_{ED} = \sum_{k=\psi_o+1}^{N} |y_k|^2 - \sum_{k=1}^{\psi_1} |y_k|^2 \underset{H_o}{\overset{H_1}{\gtrless}} \lambda'_o, \tag{6}$$

where $\lambda'_o = b_o \cdot ln(\lambda_o)$ is the threshold and decision statistic is Z_{ED}. It is obtained using Neyman-Pearson (NP) test. The values of ψ_o and ψ_1 are averaged out in (6) over their distributions. The detection probability (P_d) and false alarm probability (P_f) at each CR are expressed as

$$P_d = Pr\left\{Z_{ED} > \lambda'_o | H_1\right\},$$

$$P_f = Pr\left\{Z_{ED} > \lambda'_o | H_o\right\}. \tag{7}$$

At the FC, hard decisions from each CR using (7) are then forwarded to the FC. The P_D and P_F at the FC are derived from (3). If X denotes random variable signifying PU non-arrival, then its probability mass function (pmf) is expressed as

$$f(r; \theta_A T) = Prob(X = r)$$
$$= \frac{\exp\{-\theta_A T\} \cdot \{\theta_A T\}^r}{r!}, \tag{8}$$

where θ_A denote the PU arrival rate. T is the time interval at which the PU signal is sampled. r denotes the number of occurrence of events (arrivals) within time interval T. Here, we assume $r = 0$. The same case applies when PU randomly departs with θ_D represents the PU departure rate. Hence, the probability with which the PU arrives or departs during sample interval T is given by $1 - \exp\{-\theta_A T\}$ and $1 - \exp\{-\theta_D T\}$, respectively. The probability of the random transition of the PU in the ψ_o^{th} and ψ_1^{th} sample are expressed as [15]

$$Prob\{\psi_o\} = \left\{1 - \exp\{-\theta_D T\}\right\} \cdot \left\{\exp\{-\theta_D T\}\right\}^{\psi_o},$$

$$Prob\{\psi_1\} = \left\{1 - \exp\{-\theta_A T\}\right\} \cdot \left\{\exp\{-\theta_A T\}\right\}^{\psi_1}, \tag{9}$$

where $Prob\{\psi_o\}$ and $Prob\{\psi_1\}$ are the probability of random departure and random arrival of the PU, respectively. The three cases of PU are discussed in the following sections.

(1) **Static PU:** Static PU signify a low traffic scenario case when $\psi_o = 0$ and $\psi_1 = 0$. Decision statistic at each L CR which use ED as test-statistic in static scenario is expressed as

$$Z_{ED_{(s)}} = \sum_{k=1}^{N} |y_k|^2 \underset{H_o}{\overset{H_1}{\gtrless}} \lambda_{ED_{(s)}}, \tag{10}$$

where $\lambda_{ED_{(s)}}$ is the detection threshold of ED based test statistic $Z_{ED_{(s)}}$ obtained by applying NP test. For large values of N, Central limit theorem (CLT) is used to approximate the probability density function (PDF) of $Z_{ED_{(s)}}$ as Gaussian with mean m_s and variance σ_s^2, i.e.,

$$Z_{ED_{(s)}} \sim N(m_s, \sigma_s^2), \tag{11}$$

where $m_s = 2Nb_o^2$ and $\sigma_s = 2\sqrt{5N}b_o^2$. Using (11), $\lambda_{ED_{(s)}}$ is expressed as

$$\lambda_{ED_{(s)}} = Q^{-1}(P_f)\sigma_s + m_s, \tag{12}$$

where $Q(.)$ represents the Q-function given by $Q(l) = \frac{1}{\sqrt{2\pi}} \int_l^{+\infty} \exp\left(-\frac{t^2}{2}\right) dt$. At the FC, P_F can be obtained using (3).

(2) **Random Transition in Dynamic PU (Arrival Case):** The case of $\psi_o = 0$ signifies the absence of PU during the complete duration of sensing period. However, it also marks the beginning of transmission of the PU. Here, if we assume ψ_1 follows exponential distribution, then using (6) and (9), decision statistic under this scenario can be obtained as [15,28]

$$Z_{ED_{(a)}} = \sum_{\psi_1=0}^{N-1} \{1 - \exp\{-\theta_A T\}\}\{\exp\{-\theta_A T\}\}^{\psi_1} \left[\sum_{k=1}^{N} |y_k|^2 - \sum_{k=1}^{\psi_1} |y_k|^2\right] \underset{H_o}{\overset{H_1}{\gtrless}} \lambda_{ED_{(a)}}$$

$$= \sum_{k=1}^{N} \{1 - \exp\{-\theta_A Tk\}\} |y_k|^2 \underset{H_o}{\overset{H_1}{\gtrless}} \lambda_{ED_{(a)}}, \tag{13}$$

where $\lambda_{ED_{(a)}}$ is the detection threshold of ED based decision statistic $Z_{ED_{(a)}}$ during PU random arrival. In this case, it can be seen that the arrival time of the PU follows exponential distribution within sensing period. For large values of N, CLT can be applied so that $Z_{ED_{(a)}}$ tends to be Gaussian with mean μ_{A_o} and variance $\sigma_{A_o}^2$. Thus, $\lambda_{ED_{(a)}}$ is expressed as

$$\lambda_{ED_{(a)}} = Q^{-1}(P_f)\sigma_{A_o} + \mu_{A_o}, \tag{14}$$

where μ_{A_o} denotes the mean and $\sigma^2_{A_o}$ denotes the variance of the decision statistic $Z_{ED_{(a)}}$ obtained in (13) under hypothesis H_o. The expression of μ_{A_o} and $\sigma^2_{A_o}$ can be derived and expressed as [28]

$$\mu_{A_o} = \mu_s \left\{ N - \left(\frac{\exp\left(-\theta_A T\right) \left\{1 - \exp\left(-\theta_A TN\right)\right\}}{1 - \exp\left(-\theta_A T\right)} \right) \right\},$$

$$\sigma^2_{A_o} = \sigma^2_s \left\{ N - \left(\frac{\exp\left(-2(\theta_A T + 1)\right) \left\{1 - \exp\left(1 - N\right)\right\}}{1 - \exp\left(-1\right)} + \exp\left(-2\theta_A T\right) \right) \right\},$$

$$(15)$$

where μ_s and σ^2_s denotes the mean and variance of the decision statistic $Z_{ED_{(s)}}$ which can be obtained from (11). At the FC, P_F is obtained using (3).

(3) Random Transition in Dynamic PU (Departure Case): The case of $\psi_1 = 0$ signifies the presence of PU during the whole sensing period. However, it also marks the beginning of the last phase of the PU active transmission. Here, if we assume ψ_o follows exponential distribution, then using (6) and (9), decision statistic under this scenario is expressed as

$$Z_{ED_{(d)}} = \sum_{\psi_o=0}^{N-1} \left\{1 - \exp\{-\theta_D T\}\right\} \left\{ \exp\{-\theta_D T\}\right\}^{\psi_o} \left[\sum_{k=1}^{N} |y_k|^2 - \sum_{k=1}^{\psi_o} |y_k|^2 \right] \underset{H_o}{\overset{H_1}{\gtrless}} \lambda_{ED_{(d)}}$$

$$= \sum_{k=1}^{N} \left\{1 - \exp\{-\theta_D Tk\}\right\} |y_k|^2 \underset{H_o}{\overset{H_1}{\gtrless}} \lambda_{ED_{(d)}}, \qquad (16)$$

where $\lambda_{ED_{(d)}}$ is the detection threshold of decision statistic $Z_{ED_{(d)}}$ when PU randomly departs. In this case, it can be seen that the departure time of the PU follows exponential distribution within sensing period For large values of N, by applying CLT, $Z_{ED_{(d)}}$ tends to be Gaussian with mean μ_{D_o} and variance $\sigma^2_{D_o}$. Thus, $\lambda_{ED_{(d)}}$ is expressed as

$$\lambda_{ED_{(d)}} = Q^{-1}(P_f)\sigma_{D_o} + \mu_{D_o}, \qquad (17)$$

where μ_{D_o} denote the mean and $\sigma^2_{D_o}$ denote the variance of the decision statistic $Z_{ED_{(d)}}$ obtained in (16) under hypothesis H_o. The expression of μ_{D_o} and $\sigma^2_{D_o}$ can be derived and expressed as [28]

$$\mu_{D_o} = \mu_s \left\{ N - \left(\frac{\exp\left(-\theta_D T\right) \left\{1 - \exp\left(-\theta_D TN\right)\right\}}{1 - \exp\left(-\theta_D T\right)} \right) \right\},$$

$$\sigma^2_{D_o} = \sigma^2_s \left\{ N - \left(\frac{\exp\left(-2(\theta_D T + 1)\right) \left\{1 - \exp\left(1 - N\right)\right\}}{1 - \exp\left(-1\right)} + \exp\left(-2\theta_D T\right) \right) \right\},$$

$$(18)$$

where μ_s and σ^2_s are the mean and variance of the decision statistic $Z_{ED_{(s)}}$ which is from (11). At the FC, P_F is obtained using (3).

3.2 CSS Based on i-AVCD (CSS-i-AVCD)

In the scenario of Laplacian noise, AVCD and i-AVCD are the two actively used test-statistics. In i-AVCD, received samples at the cognitive terminal are raised to a positive exponent P in the range $0 < P \leq 2$. Being a special case of i-AVCD at $P = 1$, AVCD test-statistic's corresponding parameters can be obtained by substituting the value of $P = 1$ in the expressions obtained for i-AVCD. Considering i-AVCD as the test-statistic, the likelihood functions under hypothesis H_o and H_1 are expressed as

$$f(\mathbf{y}|\mathbf{s}_{co}, H_o) = \frac{1}{(2b_o)^N} \exp\left\{ -\sum_{k=1}^{\psi_o} \frac{|y_k - s_k|^P}{b_o} - \sum_{k=\psi_o+1}^{N} \frac{|y_k|^P}{b_o} \right\},$$

$$f(\mathbf{y}|\mathbf{s}_{c1}, H_1) = \frac{1}{(2b_o)^N} \exp\left\{ -\sum_{k=1}^{\psi_1} \frac{|y_k|^P}{b_o} - \sum_{k=\psi_1+1}^{N} \frac{|y_k - s_k|^P}{b_o} \right\}, \quad (19)$$

As s_k is unknown PU signal, it is necessary to omit it from the likelihood function. Maximum likelihood (ML) estimation of s_k is used for this purpose. It results in

$$\frac{f(\mathbf{y}|\hat{\mathbf{s}}_{c1}, H_1)}{f(\mathbf{y}|\hat{\mathbf{s}}_{co}, H_o)} = \frac{\frac{1}{(2b_o)^N} \exp\left\{ \sum_{k=1}^{\psi_1} -\frac{|y_k|^P}{b_o} \right\}}{\frac{1}{(2b_o)^N} \exp\left\{ \sum_{k=\psi_o+1}^{N} -\frac{|y_k|^P}{b_o} \right\}} \underset{H_o}{\overset{H_1}{\gtrless}} \lambda_m, \quad (20)$$

where $\hat{\mathbf{s}}_{co} = [\hat{s}_1, \hat{s}, \hat{s}_3, \ldots, \hat{s}_{\psi_o}]$ and $\hat{\mathbf{s}}_{c1} = [\hat{s}_{\psi_1+1}, \hat{s}_{\psi_1+2}, \ldots, \hat{s}_N]$. $\hat{s}_k$ is the ML estimate of s_k which is calculated manually and found to be y_k, i.e., $\hat{s}_k = y_k$. Simplifying (20), the expression becomes

$$Z_{i-AVCD} = \sum_{k=\psi_o+1}^{N} |y_k|^P - \sum_{k=1}^{\psi_1} |y_k|^P \underset{H_o}{\overset{H_1}{\gtrless}} \lambda'_m, \quad (21)$$

where λ'_m is the detection threshold of decision statistic Z_{i-AVCD} which is equal to $b_o \cdot ln(\lambda_m)$. It is obtained using Neyman-Pearson (NP) test. Detection Probability (P_d) and false alarm probability (P_f) at each CR are expressed as

$$P_d = Pr\left\{ Z_{i-AVCD} > \lambda'_m | H_1 \right\},$$

$$P_f = Pr\left\{ Z_{i-AVCD} > \lambda'_m | H_o \right\}. \quad (22)$$

At the FC, hard decisions from each CR using (22) are then forwarded to the FC. The P_D and P_F at the FC are derived from (3). The probability of the random transition of the PU in the ψ_o^{th} and ψ_1^{th} sample can be derived from (9).

(1) **Static PU:** Static PU signify a low traffic scenario case when $\psi_o = 0$ and $\psi_1 = 0$. Decision statistic at each L CR which use i-AVCD as test-statistic in static scenario is expressed as

$$Z_{i-AVCD_{(s)}} = \sum_{k=1}^{N} |y_k|^P \underset{H_o}{\overset{H_1}{\gtrless}} \lambda_{i-AVCD_{(s)}}, \tag{23}$$

where $\lambda_{i-AVCD_{(s)}}$ is the detection threshold of i-AVCD based test statistic $Z_{i-AVCD_{(s)}}$ obtained by applying NP test. For large values of N, Central limit theorem (CLT) is used to approximate the probability density function (PDF) of $Z_{i-AVCD_{(s)}}$ as Gaussian with mean m_s and variance σ_s^2, i.e.,

$$Z_{i-AVCD_{(s)}} \sim N(\mu_o, \sigma_o^2), \tag{24}$$

where μ_o and σ_o^2 can be expressed as

$$\mu_o = b_o^P \Gamma(P+1)$$
$$\sigma_o^2 = b_o^{2P} \left(\Gamma(2P+1) - \Gamma^2(P+1) \right), \tag{25}$$

where $\Gamma(v) = \int_0^{+\infty} e^{-t} t^{v-1} dt$ [29]. Using (24), $\lambda_{i-AVCD_{(s)}}$ is expressed as

$$\lambda_{i-AVCD_{(s)}} = Q^{-1}(P_f)\sigma_o + \mu_o, \tag{26}$$

where $Q(.)$ represents the Q-function given by $Q(l) = \frac{1}{\sqrt{2\pi}} \int_l^{+\infty} \exp\left(-\frac{t^2}{2}\right) dt$. At the FC, P_F can be obtained using (3).

(2) **Random Transition in Dynamic PU (Arrival Case):** The case of $\psi_o = 0$ signifies the absence of PU during the complete duration of sensing period. However, it also marks the beginning of transmission of the PU. Using (9) and (21), decision statistic under this scenario can be obtained as

$$Z_{i-AVCD_{(a)}} = \sum_{\psi_1=0}^{N-1} \{1 - \exp\{-\theta_A T\}\}\{ \exp\{-\theta_A T\}\}^{\psi_1} \left[\sum_{k=1}^{N} |y_k|^P - \sum_{k=1}^{\psi_1} |y_k|^P \right]$$
$$= \sum_{k=1}^{N} \{1 - \exp\{-\theta_A Tk\}\} |y_k|^P \underset{H_o}{\overset{H_1}{\gtrless}} \lambda_{i-AVCD_{(a)}}, \tag{27}$$

where $\lambda_{i-AVCD_{(a)}}$ is the detection threshold of i-AVCD based decision statistic $Z_{i-AVCD_{(a)}}$ during PU random arrival. For large values of N, CLT can be applied so that $Z_{i-AVCD_{(a)}}$ tends to be Gaussian with mean μ_{A_o} and variance $\sigma_{A_o}^2$. Thus, $\lambda_{i-AVCD_{(a)}}$ is expressed as

$$\lambda_{i-AVCD_{(a)}} = Q^{-1}(P_f)\sigma_{A_o} + \mu_{A_o}, \tag{28}$$

where μ_{A_o} denotes the mean and $\sigma_{A_o}^2$ denotes the variance of the decision statistic $Z_{i-AVCD_{(a)}}$ obtained in (27) under hypothesis H_o. The expression of μ_{A_o} and $\sigma_{A_o}^2$ can be derived and expressed as

$$
\mu_{A_o} = \mu_o \left\{ N - \left(\frac{\exp\left(-\theta_A T\right)\left\{1 - \exp\left(-\theta_A TN\right)\right\}}{1 - \exp\left(-\theta_A T\right)} \right) \right\},
$$

$$
\sigma_{A_o}^2 = \sigma_o^2 \left\{ N - \left(\frac{\exp\left(-2(\theta_A T + 1)\right)\left\{1 - \exp\left(1 - N\right)\right\}}{1 - \exp\left(-1\right)} + \exp\left(-2\theta_A T\right) \right) \right\},
$$

$$(29)$$

where μ_o and σ_o^2 denotes the mean and variance of the decision statistic $Z_{i-AVCD_{(s)}}$ which can be obtained from (24). At the FC, P_F is obtained using (3).

(3) Random Transition in Dynamic PU (Departure Case): The case of $\psi_1 = 0$ signifies the presence of PU during the whole sensing period. However, it also marks the beginning of the last phase of the PU active transmission. Using (9) and (21), decision statistic under this scenario is expressed as

$$
Z_{i-AVCD_{(d)}} = \sum_{\psi_o=0}^{N-1} \left\{1 - \exp\{-\theta_D T\}\right\}\left\{\exp\{-\theta_D T\}\right\}^{\psi_o} \left[\sum_{k=1}^{N} |y_k|^P - \sum_{k=1}^{\psi_o} |y_k|^P \right]
$$

$$
= \sum_{k=1}^{N} \left\{1 - \exp\{-\theta_D Tk\}\right\} |y_k|^P \underset{H_o}{\overset{H_1}{\gtrless}} \lambda_{i-AVCD_{(d)}}, \tag{30}
$$

where $\lambda_{i-AVCD_{(d)}}$ is the detection threshold of decision statistic $Z_{i-AVCD_{(d)}}$ when PU randomly departs. For large values of N, by applying CLT, $Z_{i-AVCD_{(d)}}$ tends to be Gaussian with mean μ_{D_o} and variance $\sigma_{D_o}^2$. Thus, $\lambda_{i-AVCD_{(d)}}$ is expressed as

$$
\lambda_{i-AVCD_{(d)}} = Q^{-1}\left(P_f\right)\sigma_{D_o} + \mu_{D_o}, \tag{31}
$$

where μ_{D_o} denote the mean and $\sigma_{D_o}^2$ denote the variance of the decision statistic $Z_{i-AVCD_{(d)}}$ obtained in (30) under hypothesis H_o. The expression of μ_{D_o} and $\sigma_{D_o}^2$ can be derived and expressed as

$$
\mu_{D_o} = \mu_o \left\{ N - \left(\frac{\exp\left(-\theta_D T\right)\left\{1 - \exp\left(-\theta_D TN\right)\right\}}{1 - \exp\left(-\theta_D T\right)} \right) \right\},
$$

$$
\sigma_{D_o}^2 = \sigma_o^2 \left\{ N - \left(\frac{\exp\left(-2(\theta_D T + 1)\right)\left\{1 - \exp\left(1 - N\right)\right\}}{1 - \exp\left(-1\right)} + \exp\left(-2\theta_D T\right) \right) \right\},
$$

$$(32)$$

where μ_o and σ_o^2 are the mean and variance of the decision statistic $Z_{i-AVCD_{(s)}}$ which is obtained from (24). At the FC, P_F is obtained using (3).

4   Results

In this section, performance of the CSS in dynamic PU environment with additive Laplacian noise is presented in terms of receiver operating characteristic (ROC) and P_D vs. γ using Monte Carlo simulations. The values of ψ_o and ψ_1 are taken to be 10 and 15 respectively. For static PU environment, $\psi_o = 0$ and $\psi_1 = 0$. Similarly, for random transitions of the PU, i.e., in dynamic environment, both are less than N. We have used constant value of $P = 0.8$ throughout our simulation results as it is known that the detection performance of i-AVCD improves with decrease in the value of P and vice-versa in the presence of Laplacian noise. Further, the value of N is also assumed to be constant at $N = 50$ as detection performance improves with increase in the value of N and vice-versa. The value of b_o is assumed to be 1 throughout our simulation result.

Figure 1 shows the ROC comparison of conventional i-AVCD with CSS-OR in case when there is random transition of the PU. The values of $\theta_A T$, $\theta_D T$ are assumed to be 10 and 0.1. N is assumed to be 50 and $\gamma = -2$ dB. It is observed that the performance in the dynamic scenario outperforms the performance in the static scenario for $\theta_A T = 10$ while the same is not true for $\theta_A T = 0.1$. We have further observed that the performance of CSS-OR based on test-statistic i-AVCD is better than the performance achieved with conventional i-AVCD.

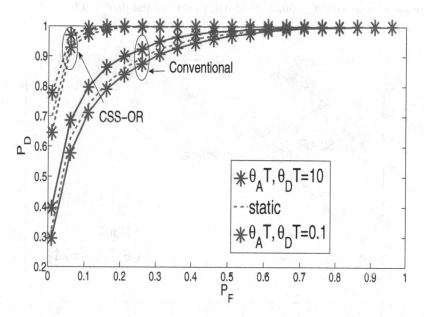

Fig. 1. Comparison of ROC plots for i-AVCD based on conventional scheme and CSS-OR fusion scheme with $N = 50$, $\gamma = -2$ dB, $\theta_A T = 10$ and $\theta_D T = 0.1$.

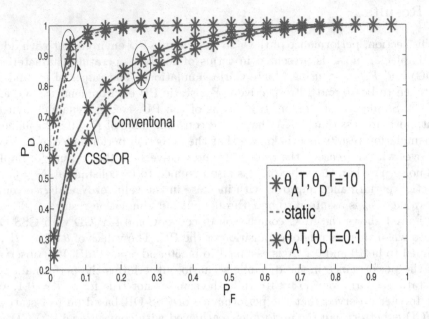

Fig. 2. Comparison of ROC plots for AVCD based on conventional scheme and CSS-OR fusion scheme with $N = 50$, $\gamma = -2$ dB, $\theta_A T = 10$ and $\theta_D T = 0.1$

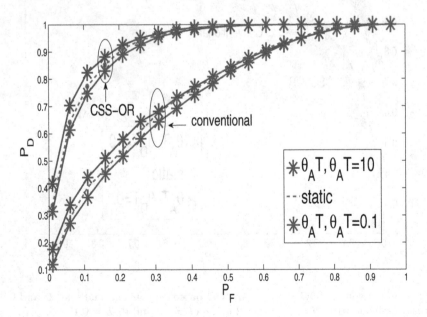

Fig. 3. Comparison of ROC plots for ED based on conventional scheme and CSS-OR scheme with $N = 50$, $\gamma = -2$ dB, $\theta_A T = 10$ and $\theta_D T = 0.1$

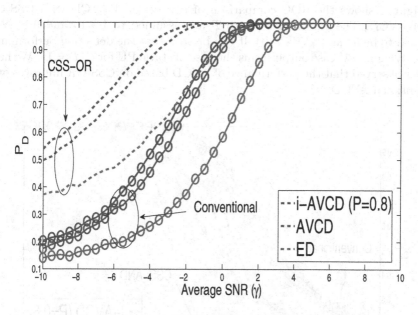

Fig. 4. P_D vs γ comparison of conventional and CSS-OR based test-statistic at $N = 50$, $P = 0.8$ and $P_F = 0.1$ when PU randomly arrives or departs.

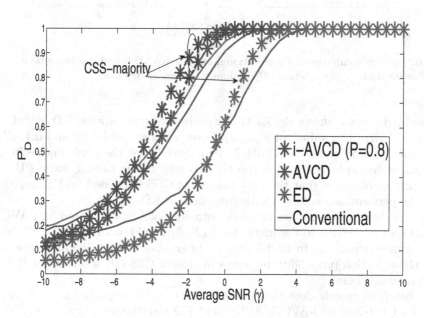

Fig. 5. P_D vs γ comparison of conventional and CSS-majority based test-statistic at $N = 50$, $P = 0.8$, $k_m = 2$, $L = 3$ and $P_F = 0.1$ when PU randomly arrives or departs.

Figure 2 shows the ROC comparison of conventional AVCD with CSS-OR based AVCD. The values of $\theta_A T$, $\theta_D T$ are assumed to be 10 and 0.1. N is assumed to be 50 and $\gamma = -2$ dB. It can be seen that the detection performance in the dynamic PU case outperforms the case of static PU for $\theta_A T = 10$. We have further observed that the performance of AVCD based on CSS-OR improves over conventional AVCD.

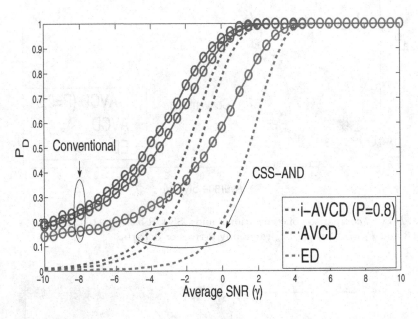

Fig. 6. P_D vs γ comparison of conventional and CSS-AND based test-statistic at $N = 50$, $P = 0.8$ and $P_F = 0.1$ when PU randomly arrives or departs.

Similarly, Fig. 3 shows the ROC comparison of conventional ED with CSS-OR based ED. The values of $\theta_A T$, $\theta_D T$ are assumed to be 10 and 0.1. N is assumed to be 50 and $\gamma = -2$ dB. It is observed that the performance in the dynamic scenario is better than the performance in the case of static PU. We have further observed that the performance of CSS-OR based on ED improves over the performance achieved with conventional ED.

In Fig. 4, we represent detection performance of CSS-OR based on i-AVCD, AVCD and ED based test-statistic for $\theta_A T$, $\theta_D T = 1$ with $P = 0.8$, $N = 50$ and γ ranges from -10 to 10 dB with an interval of 0.5 dB. We have observed that the detection probability improves in case of CSS-OR scheme over that of conventional scheme.

Figure 5 represents detection performance of CSS-majority ($k_m = 2$ out of $L = 3$ CRs) based on i-AVCD, AVCD and ED test-statistic for $\theta_A T$, $\theta_D T = 1$ with $P = 0.8$, $N = 50$ and γ ranges from -10 to 10 dB with an interval of 0.5 dB. Here, we have observed that for a specified low range of SNR, conventional scheme perform better while for a specified high range of SNR, CSS-majority based test-statistic perform better. CSS-majority scheme outperform conventional ED, AVCD and i-AVCD beyond $-1, -5, -6$ dB, respectively.

In Fig. 6, we represent detection performance of CSS-AND based on i-AVCD, AVCD and ED based test-statistic for $\theta_A T$, $\theta_D T = 1$ with $P = 0.8$, $N = 50$ and γ ranges from -10 to 10 dB with an interval of 0.5 dB. Here, we have observed that for the considered wide range of SNR, conventional scheme performs better than CSS-AND scheme.

5 Conclusion

In this paper, we considered the CSS scheme over the conventional sensing schemes such as ED, AVCD and i-AVCD in the additive Laplacian noise environment. Further, we considered the dynamic nature of primary user in terms of $\theta_A T$ and/or $\theta_D T$ assuming its random transition within the sensing interval. We presented the detection performance of the considered spectrum sensing schemes using simulations in terms of receiver operating characteristics and detection probability versus average SNR. We conclude that CSS-OR scheme outperforms conventional sensing schemes over a wide SNR range of $-10 < \gamma < 10$ dB. It is because, in CSS-OR rule, there exists at least one CR which have local decision based on hypothesis H_1. Hence, CSS-OR rule is much reserved to let CRs access the licensed band. Also, interference caused to the PU is minimized drastically. Conventional scheme outperforms CSS-AND scheme over the considered SNR range. Hence, we conclude that CSS-AND scheme is unsuitable for enhancing the detection probability of conventional schemes unlike that in the case of Gaussian noise. Further, we also conclude that CSS-majority scheme outperforms the conventional schemes beyond specified values of SNR which is $-1, -5, -6$ dB, respectively, for ED, AVCD and i-AVCD.

References

1. Li, F., Lam, K., Li, X., Sheng, Z., Hua, J., Wang, L.: Advances and emerging challenges in cognitive internet-of-things. IEEE Trans. Indus. Inform. **16**(8), 5489–5496 (2020). https://doi.org/10.1109/TII.2019.2953246
2. Lin, H., Hu, J., Ma, J., Xu, L., Yu, Z.: A secure collaborative spectrum sensing strategy in cyber-physical systems. IEEE Access **5**, 27679–27690 (2017). https://doi.org/10.1109/ACCESS.2017.2767701
3. Rappaport, T.S., et al.: Wireless communications and applications above 100 GHZ: opportunities and challenges for 6G and beyond. IEEE Access **7**, 78729–78757 (2019). https://doi.org/10.1109/ACCESS.2019.2921522
4. Karimzadeh, M., Rabiei, A.M., Olfat, A.: Soft-limited polarity-coincidence-array spectrum sensing in the presence of non-gaussian noise. IEEE Trans. Veh. Technol. **66**(2), 1418–1427 (2017). https://doi.org/10.1109/TVT.2016.2570139
5. Choi, K.W., Hossain, E.: Opportunistic access to spectrum holes between packet bursts: a learning-based approach. IEEE Trans. Wirel. Commun. **10**(8), 2497–2509 (2011). https://doi.org/10.1109/TWC.2011.060711.100154

6. Liang, Y., Chen, K., Li, G.Y., Mahonen, P.: Cognitive radio networking and communications: an overview. IEEE Trans. Veh. Technol. **60**(7), 3386–3407 (2011). https://doi.org/10.1109/TVT.2011.2158673
7. Wang, W., Zhang, H.: Slotted secondary transmission with adaptive modulation and coding under interweave cognitive radio. IEEE Trans. Veh. Technol. **68**(5), 4800–4809 (2019). https://doi.org/10.1109/TVT.2019.2904285
8. Ali, A., Hamouda, W.: Advances on spectrum sensing for cognitive radio networks: theory and applications. IEEE Commun. Surv. Tutor. **19**(2), 1277–1304 (2017). https://doi.org/10.1109/COMST.2016.2631080
9. Liang, Y., Zeng, Y., Peh, E.C.Y., Hoang, A.T.: Sensing-throughput tradeoff for cognitive radio networks. IEEE Trans. Wirel. Commun. **7**(4), 1326–1337 (2008). https://doi.org/10.1109/TWC.2008.060869
10. Tang, L., Chen, Y., Hines, E.L., Alouini, M.: Performance analysis of spectrum sensing with multiple status changes in primary user. Traffic **16**(6), 874–877 (2012). https://doi.org/10.1109/LCOMM.2012.041112.120507
11. Zandi, M., Dong, M., Grami, A.: Distributed stochastic learning and adaptation to primary traffic for dynamic spectrum access. IEEE Trans. Wirel. Commun. **15**(3), 1675–1688 (2016). https://doi.org/10.1109/TWC.2015.2495154
12. Liu, M., Zhao, N., Li, J., Leung, V.C.M.: Spectrum sensing based on maximum generalized correntropy under symmetric alpha stable noise. IEEE Trans. Veh. Technol. **68**(10), 10262–10266 (2019). https://doi.org/10.1109/TVT.2019.2931949
13. Zou, Y., Yao, Y., Zheng, B.: Outage probability analysis of cognitive transmissions: Impact of spectrum sensing overhead. IEEE Trans. Wirel. Commun. **9**(8), 2676–2688 (2010). https://doi.org/10.1109/TWC.2010.061710.100108
14. Pradhan, H., Kalamkar, S.S., Banerjee, A.: Sensing-throughput tradeoff in cognitive radio with random arrivals and departures of multiple primary users. IEEE Commun. Lett. **19**(3), 415–418 (2015). https://doi.org/10.1109/LCOMM.2015.2393305
15. Beaulieu, N.C., Chen, Y.: Improved energy detectors for cognitive radios with randomly arriving or departing primary users. IEEE Signal Process. Lett. **17**(10), 867–870 (2010). https://doi.org/10.1109/LSP.2010.2064768
16. Chang, K., Senadji, B.: Spectrum sensing optimisation for dynamic primary user signal. IEEE Trans. Commun. **60**(12), 3632–3640 (2012). https://doi.org/10.1109/TCOMM.2012.091712.110856
17. Unnikrishnan, J., Veeravalli, V.V.: Algorithms for dynamic spectrum access with learning for cognitive radio. IEEE Trans. Signal Process. **58**(2), 750–760 (2010). https://doi.org/10.1109/TSP.2009.202
18. MacDonald, S., Popescu, D.C., Popescu, O.: Analyzing the performance of spectrum sensing in cognitive radio systems with dynamic PU activity. IEEE Commun. Lett. **21**(9), 2037–2040 (2017). https://doi.org/10.1109/LCOMM.2017.2705126
19. Yilmaz, Y., Guo, Z., Wang, X.: Sequential joint spectrum sensing and channel estimation for dynamic spectrum access. IEEE J. Sel. Areas Commun. **32**(11), 2000–2012 (2014). https://doi.org/10.1109/JSAC.2014.141105
20. Win, M.Z., Scholtz, R.A.: Ultra-wide bandwidth time-hopping spread-spectrum impulse radio for wireless multiple-access communications. IEEE Trans. Commun. **48**(4), 679–689 (2000). https://doi.org/10.1109/26.843135
21. Hu, B., Beaulieu, N. C.: On characterizing multiple access interference in TH-UWB systems with impulsive noise models. In: 2008 IEEE Radio and Wireless Symposium, pp. 879–882, January 2008. https://doi.org/10.1109/RWS.2008.4463633

22. Tan, F., Song, X., Leung, C., Cheng, J.: Collaborative spectrum sensing in a cognitive radio system with laplacian noise. IEEE Commun. Lett. **16**(10), 1691–1694 (2012). https://doi.org/10.1109/LCOMM.2012.080312.120517
23. Xiaomei Z., Champagne, B., Wei-Ping Z.: Cooperative spectrum sensing based on the RAO test in non-Gaussian noise environments. In: 2013 International Conference on Wireless Communications and Signal Processing, pp. 1–6 (2013). https://doi.org/10.1109/WCSP.2013.6677074
24. Wu, J., Wang, C., Yu, Y., Song, T., Hu, J.: Performance optimisation of cooperative spectrum sensing in mobile cognitive radio networks. IET Commun. **14**, 1028–1036 (2020). https://doi.org/10.1049/iet-com.2019.1083
25. Düzenli, T., Akay, O.: A new spectrum sensing strategy for dynamic primary users in cognitive radio. IEEE Commun. Lett. **20**(4), 752–755 (2016). https://doi.org/10.1109/LCOMM.2016.2527640
26. Ye, Y., Li, Y., Lu, G., Zhou, F., Zhang, H.: Performance of spectrum sensing based on absolute value cumulation in Laplacian noise. In: 2017 IEEE 86th Vehicular Technology Conference (VTC-Fall), 1–5 September 2017. https://doi.org/10.1109/VTCFall.2017.8287978
27. Ye, Y., Li, Y., Lu, G., Zhou, F.: Improved energy detection with Laplacian noise in cognitive radio. IEEE Syst. J. **13**(1), 18–29 (2019). https://doi.org/10.1109/JSYST.2017.2759222
28. Sinha, K., Trivedi, Y.N.: Spectrum sensing based on dynamic primary user with additive Laplacian noise in cognitive radio. In: Caso, G., De Nardis, L., Gavrilovska, L. (eds.) CrownCom 2020. LNICSSITE, vol. 374, pp. 16–28. Springer, Cham (2021). https://doi.org/10.1007/978-3-030-73423-7_2
29. Geddes, K.O., Glasser, M.L., Moore, R.A., et al.: Evaluation of classes of definite integrals involving elementary functions via differentiation of special functions. Alegbra Eng. Commun. Comput. **1**(2), 149–165 (1990)

Assessment of Spectrum Management Approaches in Offshore Private Industrial 5G Networks

Pekka Ojanen[1(✉)], Seppo Yrjölä[2,3], and Marja Matinmikko-Blue[3]

[1] Co-Worker Technology Finland Oy, Turku, Finland
pekka.ojanen@co-workertech.com
[2] Nokia, Oulu, Finland
[3] Centre for Wireless Communications, University of Oulu, Oulu, Finland

Abstract. Wireless communication research has recently expanded to address the use of 5G in enterprise application, which has led to the introduction of local private industrial networks. At the same time, the use of wireless communication services offshore has increased both in improving the productivity of the incumbent oil and gas segment, and particularly in enabling sustainable windmill park implementations. These developments call for novel, flexible and scalable spectrum management models to meet the operational requirements of these critical infrastructure verticals. This paper investigates spectrum management approaches and regulatory decisions for private mobile industrial communication networks for the offshore applications. The findings indicate that in offshore areas where significant natural resources, such as oil have been utilized, the regulators have defined mechanisms to make spectrum available while the regulation varies between countries. Traditionally, the regulators have been oriented towards public mobile networks and their service areas have been land oriented. The basis for the jurisdiction for offshore deployments is very different, and also the radio environment at sea differs significantly from that on land which calls for new authorization mechanisms and coordination approaches, and different technical requirements.

Keywords: Cognitive radio · Private networks · Offshore · Radio access · Radio spectrum administration · Radio spectrum management · Spectrum sharing · 5G mobile communication

1 Introduction

Wireless solutions are increasingly targeting to digitalize different sectors of society, especially through the use of 5G. To help the different verticals in serving of their end users, the concept of local micro-operators was introduced to 4G discussions way before the 5G spectrum awarding decisions were made [1]. As a result, private industrial networks have emerged, and local spectrum licenses have been made available for them. Ever-expanding variety of frequencies allocated to wireless communication from sub-giga Hertz to mm-wave spectrum bands with novel local requirements of verticals industrial use cases have fragmented spectrum regulation [2].

© ICST Institute for Computer Sciences, Social Informatics and Telecommunications Engineering 2022
Published by Springer Nature Switzerland AG 2022. All Rights Reserved
H. Jin et al. (Eds.): CROWNCOM 2021/WiCON 2021, LNICST 427, pp. 94–107, 2022.
https://doi.org/10.1007/978-3-030-98002-3_6

Traditional long-term spectrum assignments with nationwide coverage obligation are being complemented with local licensing [3], shared spectrum access [4–6] and license-exempt access [7], which signifies a transformation in spectrum administration and management for mobile communication networks. The 3.5 GHz citizens broadband radio service (CBRS) system in the US [5] and licensed shared access (LSA) [6] managed spectrum sharing concept in Europe were found to extend business models towards locality [8] and openness [9]. Furthermore, studies on the valuation of spectrum [2] and spectrum pricing models [3] in the context of private local networks found the spectrum sharing concepts as essential enablers in the spectrum regulation. Assessment of spectrum management requirements [7], approaches to private industrial networks was addressed in [10], and the feasibility of the CBRS concept in [11]. Vuojala et al. [12] reviewed different spectrum access options to meet the 5G vertical sectors' requirements and urged regulators to make versatile spectrum access options available to boost vertical network service provider businesses. A recent study [13] describes a coordinated space, terrestrial and ocean network architecture and discusses related spectrum management challenges.

To the authors' knowledge, this is the first paper assessing the applicability of recent spectrum management approaches in the context of private offshore industrial 5G mobile networks. The focus is on private networks deployed at sea for installations such as oil platforms or wind farms. The rest of this paper is organized as follows. Section 2 presents an overview of spectrum management approaches, and Sect. 3 presents the use cases for offshore communications, an overview of offshore spectrum requirements and the regulation for offshore private wireless networks. Section 4 introduces the state of the art of offshore spectrum management approaches globally, and Sect. 5 discusses their applicability for offshore applications. Finally, suggestions for future research and conclusions are provided in Sect. 6.

2 Overview of Spectrum Management Approaches

Spectrum management generally aims at maximizing the value of spectrum by allocating spectrum bands among different radio communication services and assigning related spectrum access rights. Here, we consider three types of spectrum management approaches: administrative allocation, market-based mechanisms, and the unlicensed commons approach, especially from the viewpoint of offshore private industrial networks [2].

Administrative allocation is a method for regulators to decide themselves through their own criteria who gets spectrum access rights. Examples include beauty contests or direct awards. Typically, rules are created to minimize harmful interference between different users. Several countries have introduced local licenses that allow different stakeholders to establish local private networks and award them through administrative allocation, for example on first come first serve basis. In *market-based mechanisms* the regulator relies on market forces to define who gets the spectrum access rights. Typically, auctions are used by the regulators to assign spectrum access rights to deploy cellular mobile communication networks in many countries. Additionally, the right to sell or lease the rights of use is a form of market-based mechanisms where the licensee can allow another stakeholder to use the band or part of the band, depending on the licensing agreement terms. For example, in Europe, licenses awarded through auctions for mobile communication networks come with this right, which would allow different stakeholders to gain access to spectrum locally on a mobile network operator (MNO) band if they reach a commercial agreement. The *unlicensed commons* approach is based on spectrum sharing and allows several systems to access the same spectrum band under pre-defined rules and conditions, typically on maximum transmission power and duty cycle. Often the transmission power limits set the operational area to be local. Thus, local networks could also be established in these bands, but without guarantees for the service quality as the band is often shared with an unlimited number of systems.

3 Offshore Private Industrial Networks

This chapter introduces offshore applications and discusses their implication to spectrum requirements and regulation.

3.1 Applications and Use Cases

Trustworthy communication is essential for the critical offshore infrastructure applications and services characterized by remoteness, harsh sea conditions, strong and unpredictable winds, extreme temperatures, and distance from the shore. Traditional oil and gas industry is exploring ways to improve productivity and reduce costs through digital automation leveraging technologies such as Internet of things (IoT), machine learning (ML), robotics and 5G. 5G connectivity platforms add value by providing reliable and secure ultra-high speed low latency connectivity between drilling sites, service vessels, and offshore platforms. Compared to "voice only" dedicated satellite link technology widely utilized today, 5G can provide substantial cost savings [14]. While the global offshore oil and gas market has flattened out, the offshore windmill market is set to expand significantly over the next decades matching investments in gas- and coal-fired capacity over the same period [15]. Reinforced by the sustainability development goals and the lower cost technology innovations, the capacity of offshore windmill farms is projected to increase fifteen-fold to 2040, becoming a $1 trillion industry. Trustworthy and reliable high speed broadband connectivity is essential to enable digital automation beyond current supervisory control and data acquisition (SCADA) capabilities [16] and further to trigger growth as expected. Key offshore applications and use cases utilizing 5G-ACIA categorization [17] consist of employee voice and video group communications, as well as broadband data for safety, productivity and general corporate services; campus area connectivity for fixed-position or mobile devices such as drives, robots, machines, sensors, actuators, screen terminals, and other interacting systems; remote monitoring, surveillance and awareness analytics for process automation via IoT sensors, high definition video, thermal and radar; remote control-to-control communication for autonomous devices that normally interact with their local controller and only need remote communication occasionally or for maintenance; remote control and management of mobile robots and automated guided vehicles (AGVs) such as drones, cranes and robot arms; closed-loop control of interacting components within a control loop, such as sensors, actuators and control units for process automation, and service operation vessel (SOV) services on-site, roaming to land mobile network. These applications set distinct technical requirements for reliability and availability, security, end-to-end (e2e) latency, quality diagnostics, and network privacy and isolation.

3.2   Spectrum Requirements

Building on the above-mentioned applications and use cases, we will next define high level spectrum requirements for private offshore networks. The use of harmonized bands, e.g. 3GPP defined bands, provides economies of scale through existing device ecosystem. Therefore, their use is also desirable for the considered offshore operations. The spectrum assignments should include wide enough bandwidths for parallel wideband applications. As many of the applications are related to safety and critical reliability services, guaranteed spectrum availability and protection from harmful interference are required. Both indoor and outdoor coverage is typically required, as well as mobility around the facility. Transmit power levels allowing for outdoor coverage are needed, as well as flexibility of the uplink/downlink (UL/DL) ratio that enables capacity flexibility for various applications. Individual authorizations, i.e. licensing, are the preferred authorization method, and license application submission should be possible any time. The authorization duration should facilitate regulatory certainty and flexibility within the expected facility lifetime. The license fees should be known in advance and affordable industry grade pricing is preferred. Table 1 summarizes the identified high level spectrum requirements for offshore private networks.

Table 1.   Spectrum requirements for offshore private networks

	Private offshore network preference
Band type	Harmonized for the scale and device ecosystem, low to medium frequencies for wide area coverage
Bandwidth	Support for multiple wideband applications
Availability	Guaranteed full time availability
Interference protection	Exclusive, protected band preferred
Sharing conditions	Static, pre-defined conditions, locally exclusive coverage
Mobility	Support for employee, machine and SOV mobility
Location and coverage area	Local outdoor (farm/rig wide) and indoor (service platform) coverage. One or multiple areas. Coverage for SOV service
Transmit power	High output power outdoors
UL/DL ratio	Flexible, uplink orientated
Authorization method	Individually authorized, application possible any time, time-to-deployment critical
Authorization duration	Flexible and renewable. In line with typically long facility life cycle and varying service contracts
Cost/pricing	Known, stable and affordable industrial license fee
Regulatory certainty	High, beyond authorization duration

3.3   Offshore Spectrum Regulation

Traditionally, offshore radiocommunication has comprised of UHF and VHF radio services focused on safety issues, such as on monitoring radio frequencies for distress messages and broadcasting of weather warnings. The emergence of cellular communications created new opportunities at sea, especially close to the shore. The United Nations Convention on the Law of Sea (UNCLOS) defines the maritime zones from the shore towards the sea and the rights of the states within those zones [18] as illustrated in Fig. 1. Individual states have sovereign rights to regulate spectrum use within their territories, including the territorial waters. Terrestrial mobile networks are typically authorized to provide coverage over the land area, but also, depending on the country and the band, in many cases, towards the sea. The Radio Regulations (RR) of the ITU-R define the global framework for utilization of specific frequencies for specific purposes globally, regionally or per country [19]. Border coordination is dealt by bilateral agreements between the countries including border coordination towards the sea. There is a need to ensure the offshore usage of spectrum for the required services, while the creation of harmful interference by offshore applications towards the land-based spectrum usage must be avoided.

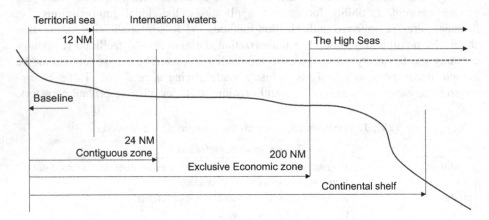

Fig. 1. Maritime zones (1 NM = 1852 m).

As an overall rule, based on UNCLOS, spectrum use within the territorial waters, reaching 12 nautical miles (NM) from the baseline, i.e., the low water line of the coast, falls into the jurisdiction of the state by the sea and is therefore regulated by the national authorities. Spectrum use outside the terrestrial waters is generally outside of the national jurisdiction. This has an impact on private mobile networks on board vessels. On-board networks operating on 3GPP bands are authorized by the flag state, and the networks can be used in international waters, in the "high seas", as long as they operate in accordance with the applicable provisions of the RR. When the vessel enters the territorial waters, unless the system use is specifically authorized by the local authorities, the on-board mobile system must be switched off to avoid harmful interference to local terrestrial mobile networks, as shown in Fig. 2. The crew and the passengers should get then connected to the local terrestrial mobile networks. Similar operational restrictions do not apply to on-board Radio LAN or other networks operating on license exempt bands.

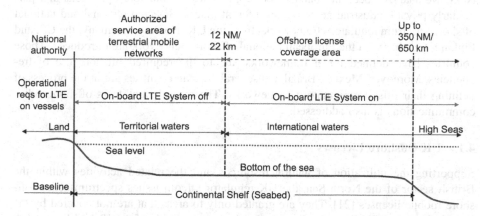

Fig. 2. Authorizations and operational rules depend on distance from baseline.

There are specific cases, where the deployment and operation of networks beyond the territorial waters is to be authorized by the national authorities. The countries have sovereign rights to utilize the water column and the continental shelf within their Exclusive Economic Zone (EEZ) extending up to 200 NM from the baseline. These rights include, e.g. fishing and utilization of wind and oil. Furthermore, beyond the EEZ the countries have the sovereign rights to utilize the continental shelf. Due to these rights, several countries are regulating the spectrum use of installations and devices related to petroleum activities or to utilization of renewable energy resources within their EEZ or ever further on the continental shelf, as illustrated in Fig. 2. This is the case for example on the North Sea, where the surrounding states authorize mobile spectrum use within their "sectors", i.e. portions of the North Sea dedicated as their EEZs. Due to oil drilling at the North Sea, there is a need for wireless and mobile communications on oil platforms and vessels. Depending on which sector this takes place, the corresponding country can authorize spectrum use within the sector, ensuring that there is no harmful interference to the mobile networks using the same bands at shore or in the neighboring sectors. For example, the regulators of Norway, Germany, Denmark, and the Netherlands have agreed on the coordination measures, which include maximum field strength limits and coordinated use of preferential Physical Cell-layer Identifiers (for LTE, 5G) and Scrambling Codes (for 3G) [20].

4   Spectrum Management Approaches for Offshore Private Industrial Networks

Next, we analyze spectrum management approaches for offshore operations and particularly private industrial networks in different places. Selected regional and national offshore spectrum regulatory frameworks from the UK, Norway, Germany, the US, and Finland, together with the European regional offshore framework are introduced. Those countries have defined novel frameworks due to the required offshore use of frequencies. Moreover, Mexico, Brazil and several African countries are in the process of defining their offshore regulatory frameworks. The role of satellite in offshore radio-communications is also addressed.

4.1   UK Offshore Licenses

Supporting the utilization of natural resources and the related activities within the British sector of the North Sea, the UK regulator Ofcom issues spectrum access offshore mobile licenses [21]. They are granted only to areas that are not covered by the rights of existing mobile network operators, i.e. areas outside of the 12 NM limit. Such licenses can cover the most common mobile bands of 800 MHz, 900 MHz, 1800 MHz, 2100 MHz, 2.3 GHz, and 3.4 GHz. There is no restriction on the number of licenses, and none of the licenses will be technically coordinated by Ofcom. However, the licenses for the 2.3 GHz and 3.4 GHz bands need to be coordinated with the Ministry of Defense. There is an administrative fee of 5000 £/every 5 years for the license. The offshore license authorizes use of spectrum on a non-protection/non-interference basis. The licensees need to coordinate between themselves to resolve any emerging interference problems. The emissions must meet at the UK coast the transmission levels defined by Ofcom, and in the borders of the UK EEZ the coordination agreements with the neighboring states when the systems are deployed.

4.2   Norwegian Offshore Licenses

In 2019, the Norwegian regulator Nkom announced that it makes available spectrum for offshore use in the 900 MHz and 700 MHz bands with updated regulation. The bandwidths were 2×5 MHz and 2×10 MHz. As the demand exceeded the supply, the spectrum was auctioned. There were 4 participants, and spectrum was awarded to three companies. The prices paid by each licensee ranged from 92 k€ to 120 k€. The auctioned spectrum can be traded or leased, which can be an opportunity for deployment on new offshore networks. 70 km was used as a coordination distance between the land-based networks and the offshore spectrum use, but the rules allow other arrangements, if so agreed between the land based and offshore license holders. In late 2020, the Nkom offered further 2×5 MHz from both bands based on applications to be used at facilities in connection with petroleum activities on the continental shelf, on Norwegian ships, and at facilities for utilization of renewable energy resources at sea [22]. Coordination with neighboring countries is carried out by Nkom and based on international coordination values for field strength. The licenses will be valid until end of 2033. The annual license fee for 2020 is approximately 13500 € per 5 MHz duplex block. If the demand will exceed the supply, auctions will be arranged.

4.3 Local Licensing in Germany

The German regulator BNetzA issues licenses for local use of the 3.7–3.8 GHz band within Germany [23], and the same regulation applies to offshore areas within the German Exclusive Economic Zone EEZ. The frequencies 3.7–3.8 GHz are available for local broadband networks at sea and can be applied for via the standard application process. The deployment areas can be defined by the applicants and the regulator performs the compatibility calculations for protection of incumbents. The neighboring operators are requested to coordinate between the networks. For border coordination, the maximum allowed field strength at the border is 32 dBµV/m/5 MHz at a height of 3 m. In the Baltic Sea, the border is the dividing line between the exclusive economic zones of the countries. The bandwidth can be a multiple of 10 MHz. The license period is 10 years and there is an annual fee, depending on the used bandwidth, requested license duration and the deployment area. The eligibility to apply for frequencies in the 3.7–3.8 GHz range is connected to the ownership of a piece of land or any other right to use the land, therefore the Federal Maritime and Hydrographic Agency (BSH) may have to approve the use of the frequency at sea.

   The 26 GHz band is also available for locally deployed, licensed broadband networks, both for mobile network operators (MNOs) and other entities including industry. The licensing conditions are rather similar to those of the 3.7 GHz band. Assuming that the band can be used also offshore, it can provide sufficient bandwidth for future industrial offshore applications.

4.4 US Offshore Regulation

The US regulator FCC authorizes spectrum use within the territory of the United States, usually not covering the sea. In general, the FCC rulings do not address offshore spectrum use and there are no mechanisms for offshore authorizations. However, the FCC regulates spectrum use within their side of the Gulf of Mexico (GoM): there are specific service areas covering the gulf area, reaching outside of the 12 NM from the baseline down to the southern edge of the continental shelf. This applies to spectrum bands for several services, for example to use of the AWS bands [24]. Usage for any application is allowed and not only for those related to the utilization of natural resources of the continental shelf. The 1.7/2.1 GHz AWS band can offer room only for 2 × 5 or 2 × 10 MHz bandwidths. Spectrum for private networks in the GoM area has to be acquired from the secondary market, and the cost may be high, as the licensee had to buy the spectrum from an auction. On the other hand, the access will be dedicated. In the US, the CBRS band, 3550–3700 MHz is available for private LTE and 5G networks, but it cannot be used airborne or at sea, due to the requirement for naval incumbent protection [5].

4.5   Mobile Network Coverage on the Gulf of Finland

Mutual agreements between coastal states can override the generic geographical limitations of frequency use and the mobile network coverage. The coverage of the Finnish 700 MHz band is allowed to reach near the Estonian coast, and the Estonian coverage is allowed to reach near the Finnish coast, spanning both ways over the narrow international area between the two countries [25]. Similar agreements exist between Finland and Sweden over the Gulf of Bothnia, as well as between Finland and Russia in the eastern part of the Gulf of Finland for the use of the 700 MHz band. The coordination agreement facilitates a continuous mobile network connection on board boats and ferries traveling at sea between Finland and the neighboring countries. Such network coverage would be usable by SOVs, but for the actual private network, a separate and preferably a dedicated band would need to be made available. In Finland, 20 MHz from the 2.3 GHz band is available for local private deployments, and spectrum from all auctioned bands can be leased to 3rd parties. The license conditions for the 3.5 GHz band require that unused spectrum resources are made available for third parties, which could be owners of private networks. Spectrum from the 26 GHz band was auctioned recently for public mobile use, and the sub-band 24.25–25.1 GHz is reserved for local/private 5G networks. Availability of the band for offshore use will depend on the final regulation.

4.6   EU Regulation for Visiting Vessels

The mobile communication systems on board vessels (MCV) must usually be switched off within the territorial waters, i.e. closer than 12 NM from shore, to avoid causing harmful interference to land based networks as depicted in Fig. 2. In Europe, the EU/CEPT regulation allows the visiting vessels to use certain 3G and 4G frequencies down to distance of 2 or 4 NM from the shore under specific technical and operational restrictions [26–28]. Conditions for 5G are being considered. For LTE systems using the 1800 MHz or 2.6 GHz bands the rules are: between 0 and 4 NM (0–7.4 km) from the baseline the on board LTE system shall be off, between 4 and 12 NM (7.4–22 km) from the baseline the LTE system outdoor antennas shall be off and the maximum UE transmission power is limited to 0 dBm, and for distances between 12 and 41 NM (22–76 km) from the baseline the EU recommends that the UE transmit power would be restricted to a defined, distance-depending value [29]. There are also other technical and operational requirements that apply. This regulation provides an opportunity for SOVs to communicate in the area of offshore facilities and towards the shore down to a distance of 2 or 4 nm, from where there is a possibility to roam to land based public networks. MCV's operating under this regulation may cause interference to offshore operations within territorial waters if they use the same frequencies. Similar regulation is adopted also outside of Europe, e.g. by the UAE [30].

4.7   Role of Satellite

Fixed and mobile satellite services have an important role in offshore communications. Backhaul connections for vessels and offshore platforms which are not within the coverage of terrestrial fixed links, mobile systems or underwater cables must be implemented through satellites. Several companies and international organizations such as Inmarsat, Intelsat and Eutelsat provide such services. Furthermore, there are mobile satellite systems (MSS) such as Globalstar and Echostar that offer connectivity. The MSS systems can have a terrestrial network as a component of the overall system: a Complementary Ground Component (CGC) or Ancillary Terrestrial Component (ATC). The use of a MSS system, and especially the use of the associated ground component requires an individual authorization from the national regulatory authority. Both MSS systems have been authorized by a number of countries, Globalstar by the US, Canada [31], two other American countries and six African countries, Echostar satellite component by the EU [32] and its CGC by a few European countries. The MSS systems can provide connectivity over the whole country, not only over the land-based area, but also over the territorial sea and beyond. A private LTE network could be used as part of the CGC or ATC. The capacity of the MSS systems is limited as the available bandwidth is typically not more than 10 MHz. The pricing is determined by the MSS provider.

5 Discussion on Spectrum Options

The regulation for offshore spectrum use is highly fragmented between countries as analyzed in Sect. 4. The consideration of spectrum options for the specific vertical use cases is of utmost importance in making the wide-spread use of mobile communication technology a reality for vertical usage. The 4G and 5G networks are typically authorized and deployed to provide coverage over the land areas, but in some countries the authorizations can extend over the territorial waters or even further. In areas where significant natural resources, such as oil are exploited, some regulators have defined regulatory mechanisms to make spectrum available for offshore use.

The level of regulatory radio environment coordination varies between no coordination, and coordination towards the incumbents. Typically, resolving harmful interference between the offshore licensees is left to the licensees; that is the case in the UK and Germany. In the UK, the license is issued on non-protection/non-interference basis.

In the previous examples the available bands are all harmonized 3GPP bands. The available bandwidth can be wide, several tens of MHz's, in the UK and Germany, while the Norwegian 700 MHz and 900 MHz bands offer bandwidths that can only support voice and basic data. The same applies to the US, where the cellular bands can be utilized through a secondary market. For example, the AWS band, 3GPP band 4, available in the Gulf of Mexico can offer only limited bandwidths, i.e. 2×5 MHz, or 2×10 MHz. In Finland, the band 40 can allow access to the full 20 MHz sub-band, but even this will not allow for several parallel wideband services. The release of the 26 GHz band can provide wide bandwidths, as the total amount of spectrum in the band is 850 MHz. The EU regulation for MCV has been based on usage of voice-oriented services and simple data, which can be supported by the designated bands. The analyzed available carrier frequencies and bandwidths and related interference coordination mechanisms vary a great deal between countries, making it a highly case-specific decision to for connectivity in offshore operations.

None of the presented local licensing examples can offer guaranteed spectrum availability, although in Norway, Germany, US, and Finland the bands are dedicated to the licensees and in Germany available only in a defined, authorized local area. In Europe, the visiting ships can use any regionally allocated mobile band in the international waters but within the territorial waters only specific bands defined under the EU/CEPT regulation. The sharing conditions for offshore use are defined by the regulator, and thus known beforehand.

Mobility within and around the offshore network deployment is not restricted in the example cases, though a possible field strength limit at the edge of the coverage area must be considered. This can have a significant impact on the possible transmit power, especially if the transmitter is several meters above the sea level, e.g. on oil platform. The UL/DL ratio can be changed in the TDD bands, which are available in the UK, Finland, and Germany. In case there are networks operating in the same band in adjacent locations, synchronization between TDD networks could be beneficial as the regulation allows in some cases, like within the North Sea, higher maximum field strengths at the borderline if the networks are synchronized. The decision on actual synchronization is left to the licensees.

A wide range of authorization methods is used: the UK has no restriction on the number of authorizations (all-come-all-served), Norway has used auctions in case the demand exceeds the supply, Germany uses administrative authorization, in the US and Finland the access is based on secondary markets. The authorization duration is relatively long in all cases. The duration in the US and Finland depends on the duration of the license of the lessor. The EU regulation is valid on a permanent basis, like the UK Offshore licenses. The pricing is based on a fee in the UK, Germany, and Norway. But in case of high demand Norway uses an auction for awarding the licenses. The pricing for spectrum leasing depends on negotiations with the licensee, that is the case with examples from the US and Finland.

Satellite connections can have a significant role in providing the backhaul connection between the offshore network and the shore. In addition, 4G or 5G based ground component network of an MSS system could act as an offshore private network. The band for the ground component would be a 3GPP band, spectrum assignment would be dedicated, and its availability guaranteed, but the bandwidth in the MSS bands would be limited.

6 Conclusions

The use of 5G to serve vertical sectors' specific needs has gained increasing attention while the actual deployment of private industrial networks involves a number of spectrum regulation challenges. These challenges further depend on the vertical sector in question. Regarding offshore private networks, globally only a few countries have so far introduced offshore regulatory frameworks. Mainly countries, where offshore oil drilling takes place, have defined their regulatory frameworks and the related authorization mechanisms. Additional demand for such regulation is emerging when offshore wind farms are being deployed worldwide in new countries. One challenge for the regulators is the fact that traditionally the mobile communications has been very much oriented towards public mobile networks and their service areas have been land oriented. This challenge appears more widely in the use of mobile communication technology for vertical specific service delivery and needs to be thoroughly addressed. In the specific case of offshore deployments, the basis for the jurisdiction is very different, and also the radio environment at sea differs significantly from that on land which calls for new authorization mechanisms, coordination approaches and different technical requirements. Many of the spectrum preferences for offshore use are still partly or fully similar to the requirements of locally deployed terrestrial industrial networks, e.g. requirement for harmonized bands, guaranteed spectrum availability, protection from harmful interference, wide bandwidths, application based assignment, fee based costs, etc. Therefore, it would be very beneficial, if the ITU-R or the regional organizations such as the CEPT in Europe could define a common basis for offshore spectrum requirements, taking into account the specific radio environment and if the regional organizations would provide guidance on suitable authorization mechanisms and frameworks in support of individual regulators facilitating offshore radio communication. The common basis and guidance should take into account the ongoing regulatory trend to reserve spectrum for land based industrial local use. Expanding local licensing and spectrum sharing to sea could be a viable basis, especially when realizing the specific nature of offshore operations – the physical locations of these connectivity solutions are often away from other spectrum usage, which makes interference coordination more viable.

Acknowledgment. The research has been supported by the Business Finland 5G Vertical Integrated Industry for Massive Automation (5G-VIIMA) program.

References

1. Matinmikko, M., Latva-aho, M., Ahokangas, P., Yrjölä, S., Koivumäki, T.: Micro operators to boost local service delivery in 5G. Wireless Pers. Commun. **95**(1), 69–82 (2017)
2. Matinmikko-Blue, M., Yrjölä, S., Seppänen, V., Ahokangas, P., Hämmäinen, H., Latva-aho, M.: Analysis of spectrum valuation elements for local 5G networks: case study of 3.5 GHz band. IEEE Trans. Cogn. Commun. Netw. **5**(3), 741–753 (2019)
3. Kokkinen, H., Yrjölä, S., Engelberg, J., Kokkinen, T.: Pricing private LTE and 5G radio licenses on 3.5 GHz. In: Moerman, I., Marquez-Barja, J., Shahid, A., Liu, W., Giannoulis, S., Jiao, X. (eds.) Cognitive Radio Oriented Wireless Networks. CROWNCOM 2018. LNICSSITE, vol. 261, pp. 133–142. Springer, Cham (2019). https://doi.org/10.1007/978-3-030-05490-8_13
4. FCC: Second Memorandum Opinion and Order in ET Docket Nos. 02-380 and 04-186. 25 FCC Rcd 18661, vol. 23 (2010)
5. FCC: CFR Title 47, Part 96 - Citizens Broadband Radio Service (2021)
6. ECC: Report 205 Licensed Shared Access (LSA) (2014)
7. Ojanen, P., Yrjölä, S., Matinmikko-Blue, M.: Assessing the feasibility of the spectrum sharing concepts for private industrial networks operating above 5 GHz. In: EuCAP 2020, Copenhagen, Denmark (2020)

8. Ahokangas, P., et al.: Business models for local 5G micro operators. IEEE TCCN **5**(3), 730–740 (2019)
9. Yrjölä, S., Ahokangas, P., Matinmikko, M.: Evaluation of recent spectrum sharing concepts from business model scalability point of view. In: 2015 IEEE International Symposium on Dynamic Spectrum Access Networks (DySPAN), Stockholm, Sweden, pp. 241–250 (2015)
10. Ojanen, P., Yrjölä, S.: Assessment of spectrum management approaches to private industrial networks. In: Kliks, A., et al. (eds.) CrownCom. LNICSSITE, vol. 291, pp. 277–290. Springer, Cham (2019). https://doi.org/10.1007/978-3-030-25748-4_21
11. Yrjölä, S., Jette, A.: Assessing the feasibility of the citizens broadband radio service concept for the private industrial internet of things networks. In: Kliks, A., et al. (eds.) CrownCom. LNICSSITE, vol. 291, pp. 344–357. Springer, Cham (2019). https://doi.org/10.1007/978-3-030-25748-4_26
12. Vuojala, H., et al.: Spectrum access options for vertical network service providers in 5G. Telecomm. Policy **44**, 101903 (2020)
13. Yin, L., Jiang, C., Jiang, C., Qian, Y.: Collaborative spectrum managements and sharing in coordinated space, terrestrial and ocean networks. IEEE Netw. **34**(1), 182–187 (2020)
14. Verma, S., Kasem, A.: 5G a Critical Enabler for Digitalization in Oil and Gas: Emerging Use Cases and Opportunities. Frost & Sullivan (2019). https://ww2.frost.com/frost-perspectives/5g-a-critical-enabler-for-digitalization-in-oil-and-gas-emerging-use-cases-and-opportunities/. Accessed 21 Apr 2021
15. IEA: Offshore Wind Outlook 2019. International Energy Agency, Paris (2019). https://www.iea.org/reports/offshore-wind-outlook-2019. Accessed 21 Apr 2021
16. Khan, Z.H., Thiriet, J.M., Genon-Catalot, D.: Wireless network architecture for diagnosis and monitoring applications. In: 2009 6th IEEE Consumer Communications and Networking Conference, Las Vegas, NV, pp. 1–2 (2009)
17. 5G-ACIA: White Paper: Key 5G Use Cases and Requirements from the Viewpoint of Operational Technology Providers. ZVEI – German Electrical and Electronic Manufacturers' Association, 5G Alliance for Connected Industries and Automation (5G-ACIA), Frankfurt am Main, Germany (2020)
18. United Nations Convention on the Law of Sea
19. ITU-R: Radio Regulations, Volume 1: Articles (2020)
20. Nkom: Agreement between the Communications Authorities of Denmark, Germany, Norway and the Netherlands, concerning the offshore use of the following frequency bands: 700 MHz, 800 MHz, 900 MHz, 1400 MHz, 1800 MHz, 2100 MHz, 2600 MHz, 3600 MHz for wideband systems capable of providing terrestrial electronic communications services in the border areas of exclusive economic zones of the respective countries (2019). https://www.nkom.no/frekvenser-og-elektronisk-utstyr/tillatelse-til-a-bruke-frekvenser/mobil-radiokommunikasjon. Accessed 21 Apr 2021
21. Ofcom: Radiocommunication licenses; Offshore mobile (2020). https://www.ofcom.org.uk/manage-your-licence/radiocommunication-licences. Accessed 21 Apr 2021
22. Nkom: Utlysning av ledige frekvensressurser til offshore (2020). https://www.nkom.no/aktuelt/utlysning-av-ledige-frekvensressurser-til-offshore. Accessed 21 Apr 2021
23. BNetzA: Regionale und lokale Netze (2020). https://www.bundesnetzagentur.de/DE/Sachgebiete/Telekommunikation/Unternehmen_Institutionen/Frequenzen/OeffentlicheNetze/LokaleNetze/lokalenetze-node.html. Accessed 21 Apr 2021
24. FCC: CFR Title 47, Part 27 – Miscellaneous Wireless Communications Services (2021)
25. Traficom: Agreement between the Finnish Communications Regulatory Authority and the Technical Regulatory Authority of Estonia concerning the use of the 700 MHz frequency band (694 – 791 MHz) for Terrestrial Services in the border areas (2016)

26. ECC: Report 237: Compatibility study between wideband Mobile Communication services on board Vessels (MCV) and land based MFCN networks (2015)
27. EC: Decision 2010/166/EU on harmonised conditions of use of radio spectrum for mobile communication services on board vessels (MCV services) in the European Union (2010)
28. EC: Commission Implementing Decision 2017/191/EU, amending Decision 2010/166/EU, in order to introduce new technologies and frequency bands for mobile communication services on board vessels (MCV services) in the European Union (2017)
29. ECC: Decision (08)08 The harmonised use of GSM systems in the 900 MHz and 1800 MHz bands, UMTS systems in the 2 GHz band and LTE systems in the 1800 MHz and 2.6 GHz bands on board vessels (2017)
30. UAE Telecommunications Regulatory Authority: Regulations, Mobile Communications On-Board Vessels, version 2.0 (2018)
31. ISED: SMSE-009-20, Decision on Globalstar Canada's Application for Ancillary Terrestrial Component (ATC) Authority in the 2.4 GHz Band (2483.5-2500 MHz) (2020)
32. EC: Decision 2009/449/EC on the selection of operators of pan-European systems providing mobile satellite services (MSS) (2009)

An Eigenvalue Based Cooperative Spectrum Sensing for Multiuser MIMO Cognitive Radio Networks Under Correlated Fading Scenario

Abhishek Kumar[1]($\boxtimes$), Rajarshi Bhattacharya[2], Seemanti Saha[2], and Naveen Gupta[3]

[1] G S Sanyal School of Telecommunications, Indian Institute of Technology Kharagpur, Kharagpur 721302, India
abhishek.ece14@nitp.ac.in
[2] Department of Electronics and Communication Engineering, NIT Patna, Patna 800005, India
{rajarshi,seemanti}@nitp.ac.in
[3] Department of Electrical and Electronics Engineering, BITS-Pilani KK Birla Goa Campus, Sancoale 403726, India
naveeng@goa.bits-pilani.ac.in

Abstract. In this work, the performance of an eigenvalue-based cooperative spectrum sensing for multiuser multiple-input multiple-output (MIMO) cognitive radio networks is investigated under a correlated fading scenario. The secondary user (SU) is modeled as a MIMO system to detect the presence of primary user signal under incomplete channel state information (CSI) and Rayleigh faded channel model. At each SU, an energy detector is used to obtain the local decision statistic. Next, SU's local decision is sent to the fusion center (FC) via numerous transmit antennas in order to get the transmitting diversity gain to combat the hidden node problem. Further, FC received the local decision statistic with multiple antennas under Racine faded correlated channel with perfect CSI. Finally, a global decision is made at FC based on an eigenvalue-based detection algorithm. The closed-form expression for the detection probabilities is derived at both SUs and FC. A simulation study shows that the target detection probability $P_d \geq 0.95$ is achieved even at a very low signal to noise ratio value of -5 dB.

Keywords: Cognitive radio · Cooperative spectrum sensing · Multiple input multiple output · Eigenvalue based detection

1 Introduction

The continuous development of new technologies and wireless communication systems applications increases the demand for high data rates and bandwidth for individual users. Consequently, the frequency spectrum band is getting crowded

© ICST Institute for Computer Sciences, Social Informatics and Telecommunications Engineering 2022
Published by Springer Nature Switzerland AG 2022. All Rights Reserved
H. Jin et al. (Eds.): CROWNCOM 2021/WiCON 2021, LNICST 427, pp. 108–119, 2022.
https://doi.org/10.1007/978-3-030-98002-3_7

day by day [1]. According to an FCC analysis, the current fixed spectrum allocation strategy results in inefficient use of the licensed spectrum band [2]. Cognitive radio (CR) is a promising technology that enables the secondary users (SUs) to utilize the available spectrum resources of the licensed/primary users (PUs) opportunistically [3]. SU must ensure the minimum interference to PUs by dynamically changing the value of transmit power, carrier frequency, modulation, and other parameters while accessing the PU band opportunistically [1]. To access PU band opportunistically, spectrum sensing techniques are employed to exploits the wireless spectrum and find the spectrum white spaces band [4]. Thus, it is important to perform the spectrum white space detection accurately for the efficient operation of CR systems. Ambient noise and channel defects, on the other hand, have a significant impact on white space recognition, resulting in detection mistakes and PU interference [1,4,5].

Recently, cooperative spectrum sensing (CSS) and multiple input multiple output (MIMO) antenna systems is attracted researcher attention to exploit spatial diversity the spectrum white spaces by combating wireless channel defects to find spectrum [1,6]. In CSS, each cooperating CR network (CRN) user performs local sensing to determine the availability of spectrum white spaces and then sends the local sensed decision value to the fusion center (FC) to make a global decision on white space availability. Specifically, the FC receives the locally sensed energy information in soft combining (SC) and local hard decisions information in hard combining (HC) schemes from SUs [3,6]. Finally, FC aggregates the data from the SUs to arrive at a global sensing decision [6]. Due to numerous advantages such as energy efficiency, better reliability, fault tolerance, low cost, scalability, and restricted bandwidth requirements, it is preferable to communicate the local hard decision to FC rather than sending real sensed data [7].

In [8], author proposed a CSS scheme which incorporate multiple antennas at the FC and single antennas at each SUs to sense the PU signal, this configuration minimize the sensing error by exploiting the spatial diversity in reporting channel. However, MIMO configuration at individual SUs is not examined, which is critical for combating the fading imperfection effect in local sensing channels. A multiuser MIMO CR network in which SUs sends local hard decisions to the FC via multiple transmit antennas and the FC receives them via multiple receive antennas is presented in [9]. The installation of numerous reception antennas at FC aids in the reduction of fading and noise in the reporting channel [9–11]. It's worth noting that multi-antenna sensing at SUs could improve performance even more by combating the imperfect channel conditions of the sensing channel as well. In [9–11], the energy detection based spectrum sensing technique is performed at both SUs and FC for ease of implementation. Recent study shows that the eigenvalue based spectrum sensing in MIMO scenario outperforms the energy detection with the cost of slightly higher computation complexity [12,13]. To the best of authors' knowledge eigenvalue based multiuser MIMO CSS with SUs equipped with multiple antenna for the PU signal sensing is not reported so far.

Further, multiuser MIMO CSS is practically feasible as most of the SUs/end user equipment for sixth generation (6G) cellular technology will have multi antenna system [14,15].

Motivated by the above, in this paper, we propose a novel eigenvalue based multiuser MIMO CSS for CRNs in fading scenario. Here, at each SU, an energy detector is used to obtain the local decision statistic under uncertain channel state information (CSI). Next, SU send the obtained local hard decision to the FC via numerous transmit antennas in order to get the transmitting diversity gain to combat the hidden node problem. Further, FC received the local decision statistic with multiple antennas under Racine faded correlated channel with perfect CSI. Finally, a global decision is made at FC based on an eigenvalue-based detection algorithm. The main contributions of this paper are listed below:

- An energy detection is adopted at the SUs for local sensing decision and eigenvalue based detection at FC for global sensing decision, as SUs are assumed to have a low computation capability and FC is assumed to have higher computation complexity.
- A more realistic scenario is assumed, where the sensing channel is modelled as a Rayleigh faded channel and reporting channel is modelled as a correlated MIMO channel with Rician fading as the CRNs users are placed in a close proximity area.
- The closed form expressions are derived at both SU for local sensing performance and at FC global sensing performance.
- The receiver operating characteristic (ROC) plot is obtained, which shows that the proposed spectrum sensing technique achieve the target detection probability (P_d) $P_d \geq 0.95$ is achieved even at a very low signal to noise (SNR) value of -5 dB with the proposed scheme.

2   System Description

A multiuser MIMO CSS architecture for the detection performance analysis of SUs and FC is shown in Fig. 1. The spectrum sensing technique is modeled as the binary hypothesis detection problem at both SUs and FC [6,9]. Let, assume that the mth SU senses the PU signal with the N_r antenna, then the corresponding received signal vector, $\mathbf{y}_m(k) \in \mathbb{C}^{N_r \times 1}$ at k^{th} observation is given by;

$$\mathbf{y}_m(k) = \mathbf{h}_m x(k) + \mathbf{w}_m(k), \tag{1}$$

here, $x(k) \in \mathbb{C}^{1 \times 1}$ is the PU signal at k^{th} interval, $\mathbf{h}_m \in \mathbb{C}^{N_r \times 1}$ is the sensing channel vector, and $\mathbf{w}_m(k) \in \mathbb{C}^{N_r \times 1}$ is additive white Gaussian noise (AWGN) $\mathcal{N}(0, \sigma^2)$. $\hat{\mathbf{h}}_m$ is imperfect minimum mean square estimation (MMSE) of $\mathbf{h}_m$, which is known to SU. Thus, $\mathbf{h}_m$ is given by [16],

$$\mathbf{h}_m = \hat{\mathbf{h}}_m + \mathbf{e} \tag{2}$$

where, $\mathbf{e}$ is an error vector, and $\sigma^2_{\mathbf{h}_m} = \sigma^2_{\hat{\mathbf{h}}_m} + \sigma^2_e$, here $\sigma^2_{\mathbf{h}_m}$ denotes the variance of $\mathbf{h}_m$, $\sigma^2_{\hat{\mathbf{h}}_m}$ denotes the variance of . The distribution of $\hat{\mathbf{h}}_m$ and $\mathbf{e}$ are $\hat{\mathbf{h}}_m \approx$

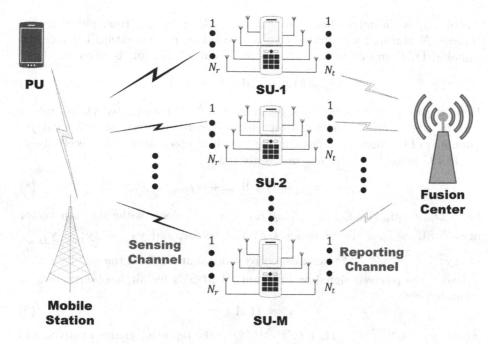

Fig. 1. A multiuser MIMO cooperative CRN architecture

$\mathcal{CN}(0,1)$ and $\mathbf{e} \approx \mathcal{CN}(0, \sigma_e^2)$ respectively [17]. Now, the received signal at m^{th} SU is rewritten as:

$$\mathbf{y}_m(k) = (\hat{\mathbf{h}}_m + \mathbf{e})x(k) + \mathbf{w}_m(k). \tag{3}$$

In the absence of PU signal the (3) is given by;

$$\mathbf{y}_m(k) = (\hat{\mathbf{h}}_m + \mathbf{e})x(k) + \mathbf{w}_m(k). \tag{4}$$

The hypotheses H_1 and H_0 is correspond to the presence and absence of the PU signal which is the case (3) and (4). The likelihood ratio test (LRT) $\Lambda_m = p(\mathbf{y}_m(k)|H_1)/p(\mathbf{y}_m(k)|H_0)$ for the energy detection is performed at each SU to obtained the local decision. The obtained local decision at m^{th} SU gives the local decision $d_m(k)$, which is given by,

$$d_m(k) = \begin{cases} 0 & \Lambda_m < \eta_m \ H_0 \\ 1 & \Lambda_m \geq \eta_m \ H_1 \end{cases}. \tag{5}$$

Here, η_m is the given LRT threshold value, and $d_m(k) \in D = [0,1]$ is the obtained local decision.

η_m is determined using Neyman Pearson criteria where,

$$P_{fa} = \int_{\eta_m}^{\infty} p(\mathbf{y}_m(k)|H_0)dy \leq \alpha_m \tag{6}$$

where, α_m is the upper bound of $P_{m,fa}$. $d_m(k)$ is further transmitted to FC through N_t transmit antennas to combat the hidden node problem. The received signal at FC from m^{th} SU for k^{th} observation at j^{th} antenna is given as:

$$y_{j,m}(k) = \mathbf{h}_{j,m}^h \mathbf{d}_m(k) + w(k). \tag{7}$$

Here, $\mathbf{d}_m(k) \in \mathbb{C}^{N_t \times 1}$ is the local decision of mth SU transmitted via N_t antennas, $\mathbf{h}_{j,m} \in \mathbb{C}^{N_t \times 1}$ is the reporting channel vector between m^{th} SU and j^{th} antenna of FC. Next, by concatenating the all K observations, the received signal at FC from j^{th} receive antenna is given as:

$$\mathbf{y}_{j,m} = \mathbf{D}_m \, \mathbf{h}_{j,m} + \mathbf{w}_{j,m}, \tag{8}$$

here, $\mathbf{D}_m = [\mathbf{d}_m(1), \mathbf{d}_m(2), \cdots, \mathbf{d}_m(K)] \in \mathbb{C}^{N_t \times 1}$ denotes the decision vector of mth SU, $\mathbf{w}_{j,m} \in \mathbb{C}^{K \times 1}$ denotes AWGN vector, and $\mathbf{y}_{f_m} = \left[\mathbf{y}_{f_{1,m}}^T, \mathbf{y}_{f_{2,m}}^T, \cdots, \mathbf{y}_{f_{N_{rf},m}}^T\right] \in \mathbb{C}^{N_{rf}K \times 1}$ denotes received signal at FC from the mth SU.

Now, the received signal at FC from all M SUs for all K observations, is given by;

$$\mathbf{y}_f = \mathbf{H}_r \mathbf{d} + \mathbf{w}, \tag{9}$$

where, $\mathbf{y}_f \in \mathbb{C}^{MKN_{rf} \times 1}$, $\mathbf{H}_r \in \mathbb{C}^{MKN_{rf} \times N_t}$ is the reporting channel matrix, and $\mathbf{w} \in \mathbb{C}^{MKN_{rf} \times 1}$ is AWGN vector.

2.1 A Correlated Reporting Channel Model

An antenna correlation at SU's transmit antennas as well as at FC's receive antennas are considered for the sensing performance evaluation at FC. $\mathbf{H}_r$ is the correlated channel matrix between SUs and FC, and given by [18]:

$$\mathbf{H}_r = \frac{1}{\sqrt{tr\left(\mathbf{R}_{Rx}\right)}} \mathbf{R}_{Rx}^{\frac{1}{2}} \mathbf{H}_u \mathbf{R}_{Tx}^{\frac{1}{2}}. \tag{10}$$

Here, the transmit antenna covariance matrix is $\mathbf{R}_{Tx} = \frac{1}{N_t}\mathbb{E}\left[\mathbf{H}^H\mathbf{H}\right] \in \mathbb{C}^{N_t \times N_t}$, the receive antenna covariance matrix is $\mathbf{R}_{Rx} = \frac{1}{N_{rf}}\mathbb{E}\left[\mathbf{H}\mathbf{H}^H\right] \in \mathbb{C}^{N_{rf} \times N_{rf}}$, and $\mathbf{H}_u$ denotes the uncorrelated channel matrix, which contains independent identically distributed (i.i.d) complex fading channel coefficients [19]. $\mathbf{R}(i,j) = \rho_0^{\left|\frac{(d_i - d_j)}{\lambda/2}\right|}$ denotes the correlation between i^{th} and j^{th} antennas, where ρ_0 signifies the correlation between two co-located antennas and λ is the wavelength. Due to pattern/polarization diversity, the correlation coefficient value is $\|\rho_0\| \leq 1$.

3 Analytical Study of the CSS for Multiuser MIMO CRNs

A novel multiuser MIMO CSS for CRNs is proposed in this section. First, multiple sensing antennas are used to perform LRT-based PU link detection at each

SU in order to get a local hard decision over a Rayleigh faded channel with imperfect CSI situation. Then, through multiple transmit antenna, each SU sends its obtained local decision to FC to achieve transmit diversity and address the hidden node problem at FC. In addition, eigenvalue detection is used at FC to obtain the global decision. The assumptions to employ energy detection technique at SUs and eigenvalue detection at FC are more suitable to implement the CRN practically as the SUs are user equipment, which is less computational efficient and FC have high computation capacity [9,18]. The closed form expression for P_{fa} and P_d have been derived in both cases.

3.1 MIMO Energy Detection Based Local Spectrum Sensing at SU over Rayleigh Faded Scenario

In this subsection, each SU used the maximal ratio combining (MRC) and LRT detection to find the availability of spectrum white spaces with multiple sensing antennas to resist the fading/shadowing impact in sensing channels with imperfect CSI. The LRT test of the PU's signal for k^{th} observation at m^{th} SU is given by;

$$T(\mathbf{y}_m(k)) = \Lambda_m = \frac{p(\mathbf{y}_m(k), H_1)}{p(\mathbf{y}_m(k), H_0)}. \tag{11}$$

The PDF of the received signal at m^{th} SU under H_1 and H_0 are $p(\mathbf{y}_m(k), H_1)$ and $p(\mathbf{y}_m(k), H_0)$, respectively. The test statistic could be further obtained by approximating these PDFs with Gaussian distribution and is given by;

$$T(\mathbf{y}_m(k)) = \frac{\left(\frac{1}{2\pi\sigma^2}\right)^{\frac{1}{2}} \exp\left[\frac{-1}{2\sigma^2}\left(\mathbf{y}_m(k) - \mathbf{h}_m x(k)\right)^2\right]}{\left(\frac{1}{2\pi\sigma^2}\right)^{\frac{1}{2}} \exp\left[\frac{-1}{2\sigma^2}\left(\mathbf{y}_m(k)\right)^2\right]}. \tag{12}$$

$$= \exp\left[\frac{-1}{2\sigma^2}\mathbf{h}_{s,m}^2 x^2(k) - 2\mathbf{h}_{s,m}x(k)\mathbf{y}_{s,m}(k)\right]. \tag{13}$$

The test statistic is further reduced to by calculating logarithm on both sides and excluding the data independent factors,

$$T'(\mathbf{y}_m(k)) = ln(T(\mathbf{y}_m(k))) = \mathbf{h}_m x(k)\mathbf{y}_m(k). \tag{14}$$

By incorporating all the sensing antennas (N_r) in the above equation, the $T'(\mathbf{y}_m(k))$ is given by;

$$T'(\mathbf{y}_m(k)) = \sum_{n=1}^{N_r} \mathbf{h}_m x(k)\mathbf{y}_m(k). \tag{15}$$

In case of imperfect CSI of the sensing channel, (15) is given by;

$$T'(\mathbf{y}_m(k)) = \sum_{n=1}^{N_r} \hat{\mathbf{h}}_m x(k)\mathbf{y}_m(k). \tag{16}$$

The mean and variance of $T'(\mathbf{y}_m(k))$ under H_1 is obtained as $\mu_{T'(\mathbf{y}_m(k))|H_1} = N_r|\hat{\mathbf{h}}_m|^2 x^2(k)$ and $\sigma^2_{T'(\mathbf{y}_m(k))|H_1} = N_r|\hat{\mathbf{h}}_m|^2 x^2(k)\left[\sigma_e^2 x^2(k) + \sigma^2\right]$ respectively. Further, the local hard decision $d_m(k)$ for the kth observation of the PU signal is then given by m^{th} SU as:

$$d_m(k) = \begin{cases} 1 & T'(\mathbf{y}_m(k)) \geq \lambda_m \\ 0 & T'(\mathbf{y}_m(k)) \leq \lambda_m. \end{cases} \tag{17}$$

$d_m(k) \in [0,1]$ depending upon the value of $T'(\mathbf{y}_m(k))$ and λ_m. The probability of detection $(P_{d,m})$ and probability of false alarm $(P_{fa,m})$ at m^{th} SU is given by [9]:

$$P_{d,m} = Q\left(\frac{\lambda - \mu_{T'(\mathbf{y}_m(k))|H_1}}{\sigma^2_{T'(\mathbf{y}_m(k))|H_1}}\right), \tag{18}$$

and

$$P_{fa,m} = Q\left(\frac{\lambda - \mu_{T'(\mathbf{y}_m(k))|H_0}}{\sigma^2_{T'(\mathbf{y}_m(k))|H_0}}\right). \tag{19}$$

Here, $\mu_{T'(\mathbf{y}_m(k))|H_1}$ is the mean and $\sigma^2_{T'(\mathbf{y}_m(k))|H_1}$ is the variance of $\mathbf{y}_m(k)$ under H_1, and similarly $\mu_{T'(\mathbf{y}_m(k))|H_0}$ is the mean and $\sigma^2_{T'(\mathbf{y}_m(k))|H_0}$ is the variance of $\mathbf{y}_m(k)$ under H_0.

3.2 Eigenvalue Based Spectrum Sensing at FC Under Correlated Rician Faded MIMO Reporting Channel

The analysis of the global decision at FC is presented in this subsection, where correlated MIMO reporting channel is considered between SUs and FC with perfect CSI. Perfect CSI and Rician fading channel is considered by assuming that there is at least one line of sight (LOS) link is present between each SU and FC in case of cooperative CRNs. The received signal at FC from M SUs for K observations is concatenated and given by, $\mathbf{y}_{fc} = [\mathbf{y}_{fc,1}^T, \mathbf{y}_{fc,2}^T, \cdots \mathbf{y}_{fc,M}^T]^T \in \mathbb{C}^{MKN_{rf} \times N_t}$. Here, $\mathbf{y}_{fc,m}^T \in \mathbb{C}^{KN_{rf} \times N_t}$ is the received K decision vector at FC by m^{th} SU. The ratio of maximum eigenvalue to the average eigenvalue is considered as the decision test statistic owing to its advantage presented in [13] and the corresponding detection performance metric at FC is derived. The block implementation of eigenvalue based spectrum sensing at FC is presented in Fig. 2. The L consecutive sub samples of the received signal $(\hat{\mathbf{y}}_{fc}(n))$ is given by,

$$\hat{\mathbf{y}}_{fc}(n) = \mathbf{H}_r \hat{\mathbf{D}}(n) + \hat{\mathbf{w}}(n), \tag{20}$$

here, $\mathbf{H}_r \in \mathbb{C}^{L \times (N+L)}$ is the correlated reporting channel matrix, and is given as:

$$\mathbf{H}_r = \begin{bmatrix} h_r(0) & \cdots & h_r(N) & \cdots & h_r(0) \\ & \ddots & & \ddots & \\ h_r(N) & \cdots & h_r(0) & \cdots & h_r(N) \end{bmatrix}. \tag{21}$$

Fig. 2. A schematic model of eigenvalue based detection at FC

Thus, the covariance matrix ($\mathbf{R}_{y_{fc}}$) of $\hat{\mathbf{y}}_{fc}(n)$ is:

$$\mathbf{R}_{y_{fc}} = \mathbb{E}\left[\mathbf{y}_{fc}[n]\mathbf{y}_{fc}^H[n]\right],$$

$$\mathbf{R}_{y_{fc}} = \frac{1}{N} \sum_{n=L}^{L-1+N} \mathbf{y}_{fc}[n]\, \mathbf{y}_{fc}^H[n]. \tag{22}$$

Next, the covariance matrix of SUs decision is given as:

$$\mathbf{R}_d = \mathbb{E}\left[\mathbf{d}[n]\mathbf{d}^H[n]\right],$$

$$\mathbf{R}_d = \frac{1}{N} \sum_n \mathbf{d}[n]\mathbf{d}^H[n], \tag{23}$$

and the noise covariance matrix is given by;

$$\mathbf{R}_w = \mathbf{E}\left[\mathbf{w}[n]\mathbf{w}^H[n]\right],$$

$$\mathbf{R}_w = \frac{1}{N} \sum_{n=L}^{L-1+N} \mathbf{w}[n]\mathbf{w}^H[n] = \sigma_w^2 \mathbf{I}_L. \tag{24}$$

Here, $\mathbf{I}_L \in \mathbb{C}^{L \times L}$ is the identity matrix, σ_w^2 is the noise variance. Next, for large N, the relationship among covariance matrices is given by;

$$\mathbf{R}_{y_{fc}} = \mathbf{H}\mathbf{R}_d\mathbf{H}^H + \sigma_w^2 \mathbf{I}_L. \tag{25}$$

It is inferred that, if there is absence of primary signal corresponding to H_0 then $\mathbf{R}_d = 0$, which means that the off-diagonal elements of the received signal covariance matrix $\mathbf{R}_y$ are zero. Further, the maximum eigenvalue (λ_{max}) and average eigenvalue (λ_{avg}) of the covariance matrix $R_{y_{fc}}$ are obtained, and the global decision test statistic at FC is given by;

$$T(y_{fc}) = \frac{\lambda_{max}}{\lambda_{avg}} \underset{H_0}{\overset{H_1}{\gtrless}} \delta. \tag{26}$$

The approximated value of the λ_{max} and λ_{min} is given by [20],

$$\lambda_{max} = \frac{\sigma_w^2}{K}\left(\sqrt{K} + \sqrt{P}\right)^2, \tag{27}$$

and

$$\lambda_{min} = \frac{\sigma_w^2}{K}\left(\sqrt{K} - \sqrt{P}\right)^2, \tag{28}$$

where, $K = N - 1$ and $P = N_{rf}L$, where N_{rf} is total number of receiving antennas at FC. Thus, λ_{avg} is given by;

$$\lambda_{avg} = \frac{\lambda_{max} + \lambda_{min}}{2},$$

$$= \frac{\frac{\sigma_w^2}{K}\left(\sqrt{K} + \sqrt{P}\right)^2 + \frac{\sigma_w^2}{K}\left(\sqrt{K} - \sqrt{P}\right)^2}{2},$$

$$= \frac{\sigma_w^2}{K}(K + P). \tag{29}$$

In case of random matrices the distribution of the λ_{max} is the Tracy-Widom distribution of the second order and given by [21]:

$$\mathbf{Q} = \frac{N}{\sigma_w^2}\mathbf{R}_w, \tag{30}$$

$$\mu = \left(\sqrt{K} + \sqrt{P}\right)^2,$$

and

$$\nu = \left(\sqrt{K} + \sqrt{P}\right)\left(\frac{1}{\sqrt{K}} + \frac{1}{\sqrt{P}}\right)^{\frac{1}{3}}. \tag{31}$$

Here, μ and ν are the mean and variance of distribution of λ_{max} respectively. The probability of false alarm P_{fa} for the global decision is give as [20]:

$$P_{fa} = P\left(\lambda_{max} \geq \delta\lambda_{avg}\right) \quad : H_0,$$

$$\approx 1 - F_2\left(\frac{\delta(K + P) - \mu}{\nu}\right). \tag{32}$$

Thus, the threshold value is given by;

$$\delta = \frac{\nu F_2^{-1}(1 - P_{fa}) + \mu}{(K + P)}, \tag{33}$$

by putting the value of μ and ν in (33) the threshold value is given by;

$$\delta = \frac{1}{(K + P)}\left(\left(\sqrt{K} + \sqrt{P}\right)\left(\frac{1}{\sqrt{K}} + \frac{1}{\sqrt{P}}\right)^{\frac{1}{3}}\right.$$
$$\left. F_2^{-1}(1 - P_{fa}) + \left(\sqrt{K} + \sqrt{P}\right)^2\right). \tag{34}$$

Similar to the derivation presented in [22,23], the probability of detection (P_d) of the global sensing is given by;

$$P_d = 1 - F_1\left(\frac{\delta K + \frac{K(\delta\lambda_{avg} - \lambda_{max})}{\sigma_w^2} - \left(\sqrt{K} + \sqrt{P}\right)^2}{\left(\sqrt{K} + \sqrt{P}\right)^2\left(\frac{1}{\sqrt{K}} + \frac{1}{\sqrt{P}}\right)^{\frac{1}{3}}}\right). \tag{35}$$

4   Performance Evaluation

In this section, detection performance of the proposed eigenvalue based multiuser MIMO CSS for CRNs is evaluated in fading scenario. In the proposed system architecture presented in Fig. 1, is considered where the sensing antenna at each SU is $(2 \leq N_r \leq 6)$, and transmitting antenna at each SU is $(N_t = 2)$, is taken to evaluate the sensing performance. Next, receiving antenna at FC is $(2 \leq N_{fc} \leq 4)$ and $\rho_0 = 0.15$ is considered for correlated reporting channel, 10000 Monte-Carlo simulation is performed to obtained the ROC plot at both SU and FC. Thus, the sensing scenario at each SU is modeled as MIMO system and the decision reporting scenario at the FC is modeled as SIMO system as presented in Fig. 1. The detection performance at SU for local decision is presented in Fig. 3. Next, the detection performance for global decision at FC is depicted in Fig. 4.

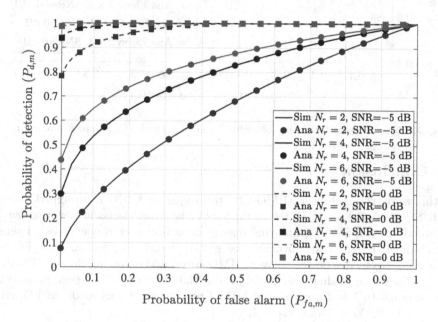

Fig. 3. A $P_{d,m}$ vs. $P_{fa,m}$ plot at m^{th} SU. (Color figure online)

The ROC plot for local sensing performance at each SU is presented in Fig. 3. It has been observed that as the number of sensing antennas grows, so does the sensing diversity, resulting in improved sensing performance.

The ROC plot for global decision at FC is depicted in Fig. 4. In Fig. 4, it is shown that the global decision at FC imposes a better performance compared to the individual performance of each SU, because of the cooperative gain at FC, which enhances the overall detection performance. It has also been observed that the detection performance is almost equal to 1 under correlated MIMO reporting channel model at FC with $SNR = 0\ dB$, $N_t = 2$ and $N_{rf} = 4$.

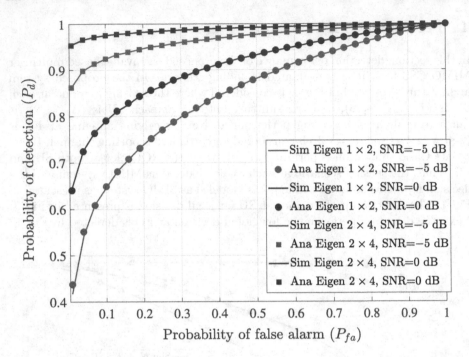

Fig. 4. P_d vs. P_f plot for both eigenvalue based detect at FC. (Color figure online)

5   Conclusion

In this work, the multiuser MIMO CSS technique for CRNs is presented, where each SU is model as MIMO system. First, the local decision performance is obtained at each SU by employing energy detection over Rayleigh faded sensing channel. Further, we obtained the global decision performance at FC by employing eigenvalue detection over MIMO correlated reporting channel. Finally, the performance evaluations at FC show that the detection performance is almost equal to 1 under correlated MIMO reporting channel model at FC with $SNR = 0\ dB$, $N_t = 2$ and $N_{rf} = 4$.

References

1. Akyildiz, I.F., Lo, B.F., Balakrishnan, R.: Cooperative spectrum sensing in cognitive radio networks: a survey. Phys. Commun. **4**(1), 40–62 (2011)
2. Commission, F.C., et al.: Notice of proposed rule making and order. ET Docket no. 03–222 (2003)
3. Kumar, A., Saha, S., Tiwari, K.: A double threshold based cooperative spectrum sensing with novel hard-soft combining over fading channels. IEEE Wirel. Commun. Lett. **8**, 1154–1158 (2019)
4. Atapattu, S., Tellambura, C., Jiang, H.: Energy Detection for Spectrum Sensing in Cognitive Radio. Springer, Cham (2014). https://doi.org/10.1007/978-1-4939-0494-5

5. Kumar, A., Saha, S., Bhattacharya, R.: Wavelet transform based novel edge detection algorithms for wideband spectrum sensing in CRNs. AEU-Int. J. Electron. Commun. **84**, 100–110 (2018)
6. Yucek, T., Arslan, H.: A survey of spectrum sensing algorithms for cognitive radio applications. IEEE Commun. Surv. Tutor. **11**(1), 116–130 (2009)
7. Saha, S., et al.: An LLR based cooperative spectrum sensing with hard-soft combining for cognitive radio networks. In: XXXIInd General Assembly and Scientific Symposium of the International Union of Radio Science (URSI GASS), pp. 1–4. IEEE (2017)
8. Rossi, P.S., Ciuonzo, D., Romano, G.: Orthogonality and cooperation in collaborative spectrum sensing through MIMO decision fusion. IEEE Trans. Wirel. Commun. **12**(11), 5826–5836 (2013)
9. Patel, A., Ram, H., Jagannatham, A.K., Varshney, P.K.: Robust cooperative spectrum sensing for MIMO cognitive radio networks under CSI uncertainty. IEEE Trans. Signal Proc. **66**(1), 18–33 (2018)
10. Song, Z., Zhang, Z., Liu, X., Liu, Y., Fan, L.: Simultaneous cooperative spectrum sensing and wireless power transfer in multi-antenna cognitive radio. Phys. Commun. **29**, 78–85 (2018)
11. Lei, A., Schober, R.: Coherent max-log decision fusion in wireless sensor networks. IEEE Trans. Commun. **58**(5), 1327–1332 (2010)
12. Zhao, W., Ali, S.S., Jin, M., Cui, G., Zhao, N., Yoo, S.J.: Extreme eigenvalues based detectors for spectrum sensing in cognitive radio networks. IEEE Trans. Commun. **70**, 538–541 (2021)
13. Kumar, A., Khan, A.S., Modanwal, N., Saha, S.: Experimental studies on energy and eigenvalue based spectrum sensing algorithms using USRP devices in OFDM systems. Radio Sci. **55**(8), 1–11 (2020)
14. Viswanathan, H., Mogensen, P.E.: Communications in the 6G era. IEEE Access **8**, 57063–57074 (2020)
15. Pinchera, D., Migliore, M.D., Schettino, F.: Optimizing antenna arrays for spatial multiplexing: towards 6G systems. IEEE Access **9**, 53276–53291 (2021)
16. Yoo, T., Goldsmith, A.: Capacity and power allocation for fading MIMO channels with channel estimation error. IEEE Trans. Inf. Theory **52**(5), 2203–2214 (2006)
17. Potter, C., Kosbar, K., Panagos, A.: On achievable rates for MIMO systems with imperfect channel state information in the finite length regime. IEEE Trans. Commun. **61**(7), 2772–2781 (2013)
18. Kumar, A., Saha, S., et al.: A decision confidence based multiuser MIMO cooperative spectrum sensing in CRNs. Phys. Commun. **39**, 100995 (2020)
19. Bouida, Z., et al.: Reconfigurable antenna-based space-shift keying (SSK) for MIMO Rician channels. IEEE Trans. Wirel. Commun. **15**(1), 446–457 (2016)
20. Zeng, Y., Liang, Y.-C.: Eigenvalue-based spectrum sensing algorithms for cognitive radio. IEEE Trans. Commun. **57**(6), 1784–1793 (2009)
21. Bai, Z.D.: Methodologies in spectral analysis of large dimensional random matrices, a review. In: Advances in Statistics. World Scientific, pp. 174–240 (2008)
22. Zeng, Y., Liang, Y.-C.: Maximum-minimum eigenvalue detection for cognitive radio. In: 18th International Symposium on Personal, Indoor and Mobile Radio Communications, pp. 1–5. IEEE (2007)
23. Awin, F., Abdel-Raheem, E., Tepe, K.: Blind spectrum sensing approaches for interweaved cognitive radio system: a tutorial and short course. IEEE Commun. Surv. Tutor. **21**(1), 238–259 (2018)

Low-Profile Frequency Reconfigurable Patch Antennas for Cognitive Radio Applications

Yasser M. Madany[1], Hassan M. Elkamchouchi[1],
and Sara I. Abd-Elmonieum[2](✉)

[1] IEEE, Communications and Electronics Department,
Alexandria University, Alexandria, Egypt
helkamchouchi@ieee.org
[2] Electronics and Communications Department, College of Engineering
and Technology, Arab Academy for Science, Technology and Maritime
Transport, Alexandria, Egypt

Abstract. In this paper, low-profile frequency reconfigurable patch antennas for cognitive radio applications are proposed on the ultra-wideband (UWB) frequency range. The methodology of the proposed antennas is described in this paper, and is achievable by controlling the electrical length of the antenna. additionally, miniaturized patch antennas are achieved by using shorting post technique and partial ground plane. The substrate used in the proposed antennas is the Rogers duroid 6010 with a dielectric constant of 10.2 and thickness of 0.635 mm. The presented antennas are designed and simulated using High-Frequency Structure Simulator (HFSS). The advantage of the proposed antenna designs is the compact size 8 mm × 8 mm (and smaller). The proposed antennas are designed, analyzed, and compared to a conventional microstrip patch antenna, and the total area size reduction is about 89% to meet the size requirements of wireless miniaturized systems and cognitive radio applications.

Keywords: Frequency reconfigurable · Cognitive radio applications ·
Miniaturized patch antenna · Shorting post technique

1 Introduction

Cognitive radio is an intelligent radio system that can sense and learn from the surrounding environment to adjust its mode of operation to provide a high quality of service [1]. There are a lot of parameters that cognitive radio depends on such as: modulation, transmit power, carrier frequency, polarisation, and radiation pattern as it learns and understands more about its surroundings. The operating frequency is the most critical parameter to change for a cognitive radio system [1]. Thus, a reconfigurable antenna is crucial to meet this need. The compact size of antenna is also needed in modern portable wireless communication systems, a miniaturized antenna size is also required for many applications, like the internet of things (IoT) sensors and actuators, and fifth-generation evolution (5G) portable systems [2–9]. Microstrip patch antennas are a popular choice for that type of integrated technology due to their characteristics. There are many methods for miniaturizing patch antenna size namely,

H. Jin et al. (Eds.): CROWNCOM 2021/WiCON 2021, LNICST 427, pp. 120–127, 2022.
https://doi.org/10.1007/978-3-030-98002-3_8

making slots, using a defected ground structure, loading material, and folded and shorting post [10–14]. The resonance frequency of the patch antenna loading with shorting post (connecting the patch with a ground plane) depends on the size and position of the post. In this paper, a low-profile frequency reconfigurable patch antenna for cognitive radio applications is presented. The proposed approach depends on varying the operating frequency of patch antenna configurations into a tunable frequency by changing the partial ground length in addition to the miniaturized patch dimensions using shorting post technique. The proposed antennas are much smaller in size compared to the corresponding antennas proposed in the literature, which gives them the advantage of being more suitable for modern applications.

This paper is organized as follows. Section 2 presents the proposed antenna design. Then, Sect. 3 introduces the results and discussion. Finally, the conclusion is provided in Sect. 4.

2   Proposed Patch Antenna Design

The proposed loaded square patch antenna design is introduced and analyzed at operating frequencies around 3 GHz, 4 GHz, and 5 GHz. The proposed loaded frequency reconfigurable patch antenna is printed on a 0.635 mm thicker, using dielectric

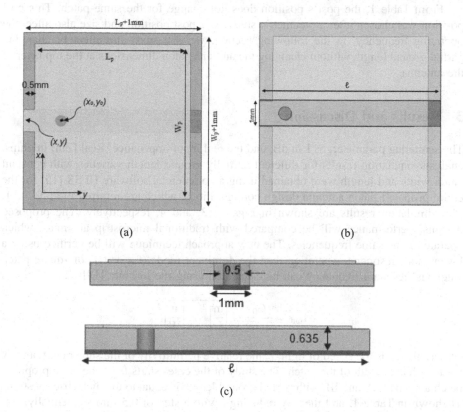

(a)   (b)

(c)

Fig. 1. The geometry of the proposed antennas: (a) top view, (b) bottom view, and (c) side view.

substrate Rogers duroid 6010 (ε_r = 10.2, and tan(δ) = 0.0023). The suggested patch antenna dimensions in mm were chosen to form part of the $\lambda/4$ ($\lambda/4q$), where q is a rational number proportional to the dielectric constant of the substrate $\left(q \approx \sqrt{\varepsilon_r}\right)$. The bottom layer is a partial ground plane in the form of a microstrip transmission line (TL), where the partial ground width is 1 mm and length is the same as the dielectric length, at the first, and then different length, ℓ, depending on the desired patch antenna configuration. Figures 1(a), (b), and (c) show the proposed frequency reconfigurable patch antenna's configuration top view, bottom view, and side view, respectively.

The main proposed antenna geometry has been shown in Fig. 1, and the entire proposed patch antennas (I to III) have been designed using the new design approach introduced in this paper, and simulation results are tabulated in Table 1.

Table 1. The specification of designed antennas

Antennas #	Wp	Lp	ℓ	Shorting post (x_o, y_o)	f (GHz)	S11 (dB)
I	8 mm	8 mm	9 mm	(0, 1.4)	3.6	−8
II	7 mm	7 mm	8 mm	(0, 1.7)	4.26	−17.7
III	6 mm	6 mm	7 mm	(0, 1.6)	5.13	−17.7

From Table 1, the post's position does not change for the same patch. This post position was chosen after a parametric study. The post position and size also affect the operating frequency. In the following section, we will study the effect of changing partial ground length without changing the antenna patch dimensions at the top layer of the antenna.

3   Results and Discussion

The scattering parameter, $S11$ in dB, and the real input impedance, Real [Zin] in ohms, analysis simulation results for different partially ground length varieties with constant patch width and length were obtained using a commercial software HFSS [15] for the entire proposed patch antenna design configurations, which are referred to in Table 1. The simulation results are shown in Figs. 2, 3, and 4, respectively. The proposed designs' performance will be compared with traditional microstrip antennas, which operate on the same frequencies. The new approach technique will be verified using a lower mode resonance operation than the dominant mode (f_{10} or f_{01}) of square patch antennas' resonant frequency can be calculated using the formula [13]:

$$f_{mn} = \frac{C_0}{2\sqrt{\varepsilon_r}} \sqrt{\left[\frac{m}{L}\right]^2 + \left[\frac{n}{W}\right]^2}$$

Where the C_0 is the speed of light, ε_r the relative permittivity of the substrate, L and W the length and width of the patch. The study of the cases starts from the main proposed patch antenna I, II, and III, with partial ground length is equal to the dielectric substrate, as shown in Table 1, and then by reducing l with a step of 0.5 mm sequentially.

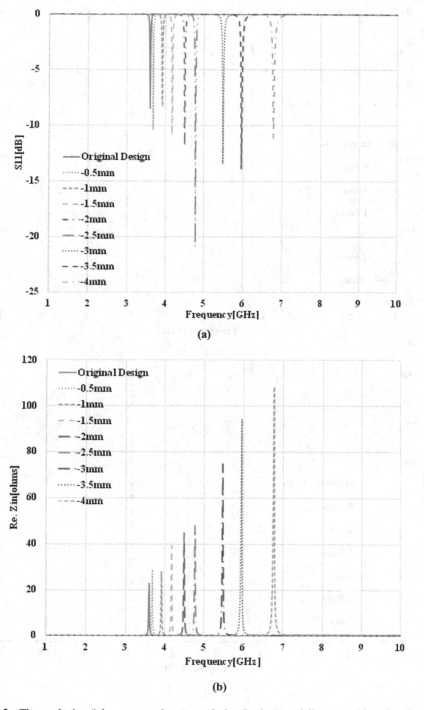

Fig. 2. The analysis of the suggested antenna design I when partially ground length reduces.

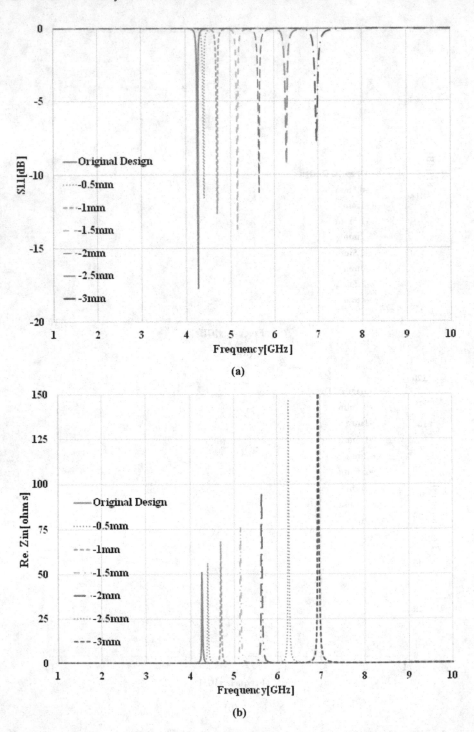

Fig. 3. The analysis of the suggested antenna design II when partially ground length reduces.

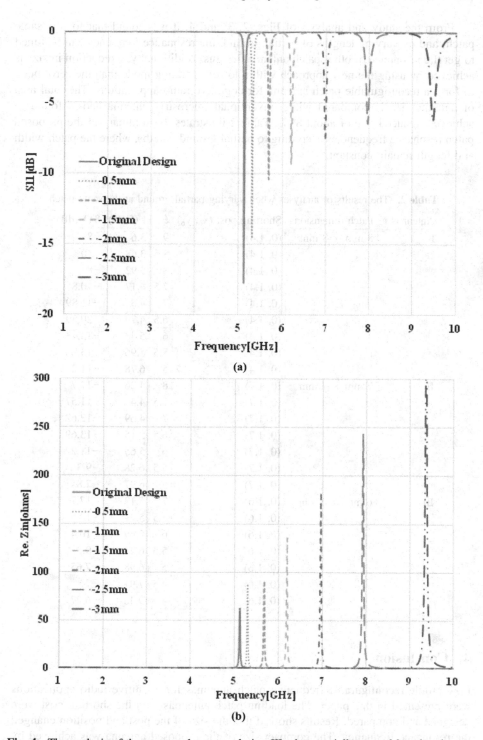

Fig. 4. The analysis of the suggested antenna design III when partially ground length reduces.

From the study and analysis of Figs. 2, 3, and 4, it was found that for the same patch, and by varying lengths of partial ground, the resonance frequency can be tuned to get the resonance of other patch antenna designs. Additionally, a reduction in size is achieved by using the new approach with a lower operating mode than the zero-mode to form a reconfigurable patch antenna for cognitive radio applications. The total area of antenna size is compared with conventional microstrip antenna and is found to achieve a reduced size of about 89%. Table 2 illustrates the summary of the proposed patch resonance frequencies according to partial ground lengths, where the patch width and length remain constant.

Table 2. The results of analyses when varying partial ground at the same patch

Antennas #	Patch dimensions	Shorting post (x_o, y_o)	ℓ	f (GHz)	S11 (dB)
I	8 mm × 8 mm	(0, 1.4)	9	3.6	−8
		(0, 1.4)	8.5	3.68	−10
		(0, 1.4)	8	3.92	−8
		(0, 1.4)	7.5	4.17	−10.8
		(0, 1.4)	7	4.5	−11.89
		(0, 1.4)	6.5	4.79	−20.89
		(0, 1.4)	6	5.48	−13.43
		(0, 1.4)	5.5	5.96	−13.88
		(0, 1.4)	5	6.78	−11.2
II	7 mm × 7 mm	(0, 1.7)	8	4.26	−17.7
		(0, 1.7)	7.5	4.4	−11.57
		(0, 1.7)	7	4.69	−12.62
		(0, 1.7)	6.5	5.15	−13.69
		(0, 1.7)	6	5.65	−11.2
		(0, 1.7)	5.5	6.28	−9.3
		(0, 1.7)	5	6.97	−7.8
III	6 mm × 6 mm	(0, 1.6)	7	5.13	−17.7
		(0, 1.6)	6.5	5.31	−14.5
		(0, 1.6)	6	5.69	−10.4
		(0, 1.6)	5.5	6.2	−9.3
		(0, 1.6)	5	6.98	−7.65
		(0, 1.6)	4.5	7.97	−7
		(0, 1.6)	4	9.48	−6.27

4 Conclusion

Low-profile reconfigurable frequency patch antennas for cognitive radio applications were presented in this paper. The loading patch antennas with the shorting post were designed and compared. Results showed that the size of the post and position changed the resonance frequency. The compact size of the proposed antenna was achieved by using shorting post and a partial ground plane. The total area of the proposed antenna resulted in reduction in the size of 89% compared to conventional microstrip antenna. The length of the partial ground plane affected the operating frequencies, which in turn can be tuned to meet the cognitive radio applications requirements.

References

1. Ilesanmi, O.A., Ndujiuba, Ch.U., Idowu-Bismark, O., Wikiman, O.O., Thomas, S., Muhammad, I.: State of the art techniques for cognitive radio antenna design. Int. J. Electromagnet. Appl. **9**(1), 7–13 (2019)
2. Daud, N., Osman, M.N., Kamarudin, M.R., Kram, A.R., Mokhzaini, A.: A compact antenna design for fifth generation wireless communication system. In: MATEC Web of Conferences (2017)
3. Shuhrawardy, M., Chowdhury, M.H.M., Das, D.: Design of a compact wideband antenna for 5G applications. In: 2018 4th International Conference on Electrical Engineering and Information and Communication Technology (iCEEiCT), pp. 174–177 (2018)
4. Praveena, A., Aqeel, S., Ponnapalli, V.A.S., Sireesha, P.: A study on compact microstrip antenna design for advanced wireless applications. In: 2021 International Conference on Computer Communication and Informatics (ICCCI), pp. 1–6 (2021)
5. Kaeib, A.F., Shebani, N.M., Zarek, A.R.: Design and analysis of a slotted microstrip antenna for 5G communication networks at 28 GHz. In: 2019 19th International Conference on Sciences and Techniques of Automatic Control and Computer Engineering (STA), pp. 648–653 (2019)
6. Ayomikun, A., Mokayef, M.: Miniature microstrip antenna for IoT application. Mater. Today Proc. **29**(1), 43–47 (2020)
7. Arum, T., Caiado, J., Matos, J.N.: Compact ultra-wideband series-feed microstrip antenna arrays for IoT communications. Appl. Sci. **11**(14), 62–67 (2021)
8. Satheesh, A., Chandrababu, R., Rao, I.S.: A compact antenna for IoT applications. In: 2017 International Conference on Innovations in Information, Embedded and Communication Systems (ICIIECS), pp. 1–4 (2017)
9. Garg, R., Bhartia, P., Bahl, I., Ittipiboon, A.: Microstrip Antenna Design Handbook. Artech House, Norwood (2001)
10. Balanis, C.A.: Antenna Theory: Analysis and Design, 4th edn. John Wiley & Sons. Inc., New York (2016)
11. Khan, M.U., Sharawi, M.S., Mittra, R.: Microstrip patch antenna miniaturization techniques: a review. IET Microwaves Antennas Propag. **9**, 913–922 (2015)
12. Pozar, D.M.: Microwave Engineering, 4th edn. John Wiley & Sons, New York (2012)
13. Kumar, P., Singh, G.: Microstrip antennas loaded with shorting post. Engineering **01**, 41–45 (2009)
14. Madany, M., Elkamchouchi, H.M., Abd-Elmonieum, I.S.: Design and analysis of loaded square microstrip patch antenna with shorting post for miniaturized wireless communication applications. In: 26th Telecommunications Forum (TELFOR), pp. 420–425 (2018)
15. ANSYS electronics desktop package: ANSYS v18, Ansoft Corporation

A Full-Duplex Multicarrier Cooperative Device-to-Device Communications System with MMSE Based RSI Cancellation

Rahul Bajpai[1(✉)], Ronak Soni[1], Naveen Gupta[1], and Abhishek Kumar[2]

[1] Department of Electrical and Electronics Engineering, BITS-Pilani KK Birla Goa Campus, Sancoale 403726, India
{p20190003,f20180450,naveeng}@goa.bits-pilani.ac.in
[2] Department of Electronics and Communication Engineering, BIET Hyderabad, Hyderabad 501510, Telangana, India
abhishek.ece14@nitp.ac.in

Abstract. Integration of full-duplex (FD) technology with cooperative device-to-device (CD2D) communications system has recently emerged as a potential candidate for the fifth-generation (5G) and beyond technologies to improve the spectral efficiency of a cellular system. This paper investigates the outage performance of a multicarrier FD CD2D communications system wherein, the D2D link source node (S) serves as an FD relay for uplink cellular transmission. The self-interference (SI) occurring at S is suppressed using analog cancellation schemes, and the residual SI (RSI) is further suppressed using digital domain (DD) RSI cancellation techniques. A probabilistic mathematical model is established for the performance evaluation of the proposed system. The closed-form expressions for D2D and cellular outage probability are derived. Simulation results show that the proposed FD CD2D communications system, along with minimum mean square error-based DD RSI cancellation, gives the optimum performance compared to the least square-based RSI cancellation scheme.

Keywords: Cooperative D2D communications system · Full-duplex · OFDMA · Outage probability

1 Introduction

With the emergent growth in wireless devices and multimedia applications, there is an urgent need to upgrade the current wireless infrastructure to achieve ultra-high data rates requirements within the limited spectrum resource. Adopting multiple prominent technologies, namely device-to-device (D2D) communications, cooperative relaying, and full-duplex (FD) radio, enables the fifth-generation (5G) cellular networks to match the growing capacity requirement

© ICST Institute for Computer Sciences, Social Informatics and Telecommunications Engineering 2022
Published by Springer Nature Switzerland AG 2022. All Rights Reserved
H. Jin et al. (Eds.): CROWNCOM 2021/WiCON 2021, LNICST 427, pp. 128–140, 2022.
https://doi.org/10.1007/978-3-030-98002-3_9

for immensely dense indoor surroundings. D2D communication has evolved as one of the vital technologies for 5G and beyond cellular networks [1,2] to enhance data rates, spectral efficiency and reduce latency for short-range communication. D2D communications allow direct data transfer between two or more users in proximity without traversing the data through the base station (BS).

D2D communication adopts either one of the three predefined frameworks in a wireless system: overlay, underlay, or cooperative D2D (CD2D). As seen in [3], the CD2D framework achieves less outage probability (OP) in comparison to the other two frameworks. In the CD2D framework, single or multiple user equipment (UE) operates as a cooperative relay for cellular uplink/downlink (UL/DL) transmissions [4]. An FD node transceives the signals concurrently at the same time-frequency resource block (TFRB) [5]. However, simultaneous transmission and reception (STAR) generate self-interference (SI), which restricts the performance of the FD systems. Hence, a major challenge in the operation of FD systems is suppressing the SI, which makes the STAR feasible.

SI cancellation (SIC) is usually carried out in the analog domain (AD) and digital domain (DD). The active and passive AD cancellation is performed in the space and radio frequency (RF) circuit domain. The remaining SI, called residual SI (RSI), is further suppressed by applying reliable and efficient DD SIC algorithms [6]. The performance of the SIC technique depends significantly on the accuracy of the SI channel estimation [7]. In [6], the least square (LS) based SI channel estimation is used for RSI cancellation, where noise is ignored for the channel estimation computation, resulting in a high estimation error. To reduce the channel estimation error, the minimum mean square error (MMSE) estimator is proposed in [8] for the FD communications system. However, the analysis is limited to the two legitimate nodes operating in FD mode, and the prospective advantages of the LS and MMSE estimator are not explored for CD2D systems. Moreover, the analysis in [6,8] is limited to a single carrier transmission, and hence, there is a need to explore the LS and MMSE estimator for a multicarrier transmission-based CD2D communications system. The MMSE outperforms the LS-based SI canceler at the cost of implementation complexity.

Recently, the merits of the orthogonal frequency division multiple access (OFDMA) and CD2D communication framework have been combined by many researchers for efficient spectrum utilization in a short distance communications system [9,10]. In [9], OFDMA based CD2D system is proposed, and the OP expressions for UL transmission from the cellular user (CU) and D2D links are derived. However, the analysis is confined to half-duplex (HD) mode exclusively. In [10], an outage analysis of the FD relay (FDR) assisted CD2D framework has been proposed with an optimal power allocation framework for maximizing the achievable transmission rate of cellular and D2D links. However, the proposed scheme uses a single carrier system and incurs overhead by deploying an extra relay node. Additionally, [9,10] have not explored the advantages of DD SIC techniques to reduce RSI.

To the best of our knowledge, no existing literature has investigated the RSI cancellation for an OFDMA based FD CD2D communications system. Hence, motivated by the existing literature on the CD2D communications system, in this paper, we propose an OFDMA based FD CD2D communications system wherein, a single D2D user is mapped with a CU on a specific TFRB. Using OFDMA, the available cellular bandwidth is divided into N independent and orthogonal subcarriers, where each subcarrier carries equal sub-channel bandwidth. The system works as an in-band D2D mode, wherein the D2D pair shares the cellular spectrum for D2D transmission. According to the proposed scheme, BS broadcasts N subcarriers to CU and D2D pair. Out of N received subcarriers, D (where $D < N$) subcarriers are allocated to FD node (S) for relaying the DL cellular transmission signal, and the remaining $N - D$ subcarriers are allocated to the D2D user for its own transmission. SI occurred at the FD node is suppressed using active and passive cancellation schemes in the AD. Further, this paper adopts LS and MMSE-based RSI channel estimation to suppress the RSI in the DD. The main contributions of the proposed work are summarised below:

- An OFDMA based FD CD2D communications system is proposed, wherein the D2D node operates as an FDR for cellular UL transmission.
- The closed-form expressions of achievable rate and OP for cellular UL transmission utilizing FD relaying and D2D transmission have been derived.
- MMSE-based DD RSI cancellation scheme is adopted at D2D node to reduce the RSI. Further, the performance is compared with the LS-based RSI cancellation scheme.
- An OP analysis of D2D and cellular transmission is shown with respect to the number of allocated subcarriers for different RSI parameters.
- A comparison of MMSE and LS-based RSI cancellation schemes is shown for the proposed FD CD2D communications system in terms of mean square error (MSE).

2   System Model

Figure 1 shows the proposed FD CD2D system consisting of a BS denoted as B, one UE acting as CU, denoted as C, and two UEs acting as the D2D transmitter and receiver denoted as S and T, respectively. Node S works as an FD relay utilizing the decode and forward (DF) protocol. Please note that due to physical obstacles or heavy shadowing, there is no direct communications link between the C and B [11]. Using OFDMA, the available bandwidth at C is divided into N orthogonal subcarriers, and these subcarriers are distributed among C and S by the B in accordance with the traditional in-band D2D communications system [12]. The communication channels between the nodes are modelled as Rayleigh block fading with channel coefficient denoted by $g_{xy,k} \sim \mathcal{CN}(0, d_{ij}^{-\mu})$; where $x, y \in \{C, S, R, B\}$ and d is the distance between the transmitting and receiving nodes, and μ is the path loss exponent [9]. The parameter k represents the index of subcarrier ($1 \leq k \leq N$). Hence, the channel coefficient for C-S link is $g_{CS,k}$ over k^{th} subcarrier. Similarly, the channel coefficient for S-B link and S-T link are $g_{SB,k}$ and $g_{ST,k}$, respectively. For each subcarrier, the instantaneous channel gain is defined as $h_{xy,k} = |g_{xy,k}|^2$. The communication between each pair of nodes is affected by additive white Gaussian noise (AWGN), represented as $n_x \sim \mathcal{CN}(0, \sigma_{max}^2)$, where σ_{max}^2 is the maximum AWGN variance observed at each pair of nodes. AWGN variance at node y is denoted by σ_y^2. The subcarrier power transmitted by C and S is denoted by $p_{C,k}$, and $p_{S,k}$, respectively. It is worth mentioning that $x_{C,k}$ and $x_{S,k}$ are presumed to have mean zero, and $\mathbb{E}[x_{C,k}^* x_{C,k}] = \mathbb{E}[x_{S,k}^* x_{S,k}] = 1$, here $\mathbb{E}[\cdot]$ is the mean estimation operator.

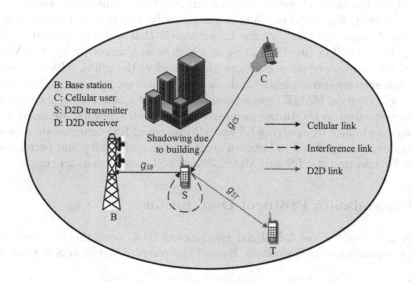

Fig. 1. System model

2.1   Residual Self-interference Model

The occurrence of SI due to STAR at the FD node S deteriorates the system performance. In [13], it has been shown that if the SI is adequately managed, then STAR is possible. However, SI can not be fully canceled due to some pragmatic constraints, which results in RSI. From [14,15] we model the RSI as an additive Gaussian random variable:

$$v_{S,k} \sim \mathcal{CN}\left(0, \beta p_{S,k}^\lambda\right),\tag{1}$$

where, $p_{S,k} \in (0, P_S)$ denotes the power of the signal transmitted from the source S, and P_S is the maximum power available at the source. Here, $\beta, \lambda \in [0, \infty)$ are based on the parameters of the best fit line [7].

The transmit-power-to-RSI-ratio (TRR) without RSI cancellation is defined as:

$$TRR = \frac{p_{S,k}}{\beta p_{S,k}^\lambda}.\tag{2}$$

2.2   Residual Self-interference (RSI) Cancellation Schemes

RSI is reduced further to improve the performance of an FD CD2D system. A good DD RSI channel estimate is required for RSI cancellation. In this paper, two such techniques (LS and MMSE) are used at S for RSI cancellation. In LS-based RSI channel estimation, we multiply the frequency response of the received self transmitted signal with the inverse of the transmitted signal in the absence of the C signal. LS exhibits less complexity, and it is easy to implement. However, a major drawback of the LS scheme is that noise is ignored for estimating the DD RSI channel, resulting in a high estimation error [8]. The MMSE channel uses autocorrelation matrices and considers the noise, which results in high implementation complexity and computational cost as compared to the LS technique. However, MMSE channel estimation gives a much lesser mean-square error as compared to LS. In the proposed FD CD2D framework, we analyze the system performance by applying LS and MMSE-based RSI cancellation schemes. There is always a trade-off in between computation complexity and performance output for selecting the LS and MMSE-based RSI cancellation scheme.

3   Transmission Protocol Description

Let, $x_{C,k}(t)$ denotes the UL signal transmitted by C over the kth subcarrier, which is represented as hypothesis H_1 and the received signal at S is given by,

$$H_1: \quad y_{S,k}(t) = \sqrt{p_{C,k}}g_{CS,k}x_{C,k}(t) + v_{S,k}(t) + n_{S,k}(t); \quad 1 \le k \le N, \quad (3)$$

where, $v_{S,k}(t) = h_{si} * x_{S,k}(t)$ represents the RSI, and $n_{s,k}(t)$ represents the zero mean AWGN for k^{th} subcarrier. Here, h_{si} is assumed to be a single tap Rayleigh fading RSI channel coefficient, and $*$ denotes the convolution operator.

Next, we have adopted LS and MMSE-based DD RSI cancellation schemes to mitigate the SI further. Here, first, S estimates the DD RSI channel in the absence of a C signal. The estimated RSI channel is used for the RSI cancellation. In the absence of C signal, the received signal at S is represented as hypothesis H_0 and is given by,

$$H_0: y_{S,k}(t) = h_{si}(t) * x_{S,k}(t) + n_{S,k}(t) \quad 1 \le k \le N. \quad (4)$$

The frequency-domain representation of received signal at S is given by,

$$Y_{S,k}(f) = X_{S,k}(f)H_{si}(f) + W_{s,k}(f), \quad (5)$$

where, $Y_{S,k}(f) \xleftarrow{\mathscr{F}} y_{S,k}(t)$, $X_{S,k}(f) \xleftarrow{\mathscr{F}} x_{S,k}(t)$, and $W_{s,k}(f) \xleftarrow{\mathscr{F}} n_{S,k}(t)$. $\xleftarrow{\mathscr{F}}$ represents the Fourier transform operator. Next, the LS-based RSI channel estimate is obtained by,

$$\hat{H}_{si}(f) = \frac{Y_{S,k}(f)}{X_{S,k}(f)} = H_{si}(f) + W'_{s,k}(f), \quad (6)$$

where, $W'_{s,k}(f)$ denotes a noise component present at the estimated SI channel coefficient. Further, the time-domain SI channel estimate is acquired by getting inverse fast Fourier transform (IFFT) of (6) and is given by,

$$\hat{h}_{si}(t) = \text{IFFT}(\hat{H}_{si}(f)). \tag{7}$$

As mentioned before, LS-based estimation is not accurate due to the absence of noise. A more statistical channel estimation MMSE can be employed for a better RSI channel estimate. As MMSE depends on the statistical parameter, the statistical mean of the received signal (4) under H_0 is given by,

$$\mathbb{E}[y_{S,k}(t)] = \mathbb{E}[h_{si} * x_{S,k}(t)] + \mathbb{E}[n_{S,k}(t)]; \quad 1 \leq k \leq N, \tag{8}$$

$$\mathbb{E}[y_{S,k}(t)] = x_{S,k}(t) * \mathbb{E}[h_{si}] + \mathbb{E}[n_{S,k}(t)]; \quad 1 \leq k \leq N. \tag{9}$$

Since, $n_{S,k}(t)$ is the zero mean independent identically distributed (i.i.d) random variable, $\mathbb{E}[n_{S,k}(t)] = 0$, and the approximate mean estimate of the received signal is given by,

$$\mathbb{E}[y_{S,k}(t)] = x_{S,k}(t) * \mathbb{E}[h_{si}]; \quad 1 \leq k \leq N. \tag{10}$$

Hence, the MMSE channel estimate $\hat{h}_{si}(t)$ using the statistical algorithm is given as,

$$\hat{h}_{si}(t) = R_{hy}(t)R_{yy}(t)(y_{S,k}(t) - \mathbb{E}[y_{S,k}(t)]), \tag{11}$$

where, R_{hy} is the cross co-variance of h_{si}; $y_{S,k}$ and R_{yy} is the co-variance matrix of $y_{S,k}$.

Now, using the estimate of RSI channel coefficient based on the LS and MMSE schemes as per (7) and (11), we may further reduce the effect of RSI in H_1, and is given by,

$$y_{S,k}(t) = \sqrt{p_{C,k}}g_{CS,k}x_{C,k}(t) + v_{S,k}(t) + n_{S,k}(t)$$
$$- \hat{h}_{si}(t)x_{S,k}(t); \quad 1 \leq k \leq N \cdots H_1. \tag{12}$$

The TRR followed by LS/MMSE based DD RSI cancellation scheme is given by,

$$\text{TRR} = \frac{p_{S,k}}{\beta p_{S,k}^\lambda - var(\hat{h}_{si}(t)x_{S,k}(t))},$$
$$= \frac{p_{S,k}}{\beta p_{S,k}^\lambda - \hat{\beta} p_{S,k}^\lambda} = \frac{p_{S,k}}{\Delta \beta p_{S,k}^\lambda}. \tag{13}$$

Here, $\Delta \beta p_{S,k}^\lambda$ is the RSI power after DD cancellation scheme. Further, S decodes $x_{C,k}$ from (12), and the decoded signal is represented as $\hat{x}_{C,k}(t)$. This is forwarded to the B over D subcarriers. The signal received at the B is given by,

$$y_{B,k}(t) = \sqrt{p_{S,k}}g_{SB,k}\hat{x}_{C,k}(t - t_0) + n_{B,k}(t); \quad 1 \leq k \leq D, \tag{14}$$

where, t_0 is the processing delay. Here, the remaining $N - D$ subcarriers are used to send the D2D data to node T.

The D2D signal is denoted by $x_{S,k}(t)$ and the signal received at T is given by,

$$y_{T,k}(t) = \sqrt{p_{S,k}}g_{SD,k}x_{S,k}(t) + n_{D,k}(t); \quad 1 \leq k \leq N - D. \tag{15}$$

4   Performance Analysis

4.1   Cellular Uplink Outage Probability

The instantaneous rate at the C-S link,

$$R_{CS} = \sum_{k=1}^{N} \log_2 \left(1 + \frac{p_{C,k} h_{CS,k}}{\sigma_S^2 + \Delta\beta p_{S,k}^{\lambda}} \right). \tag{16}$$

If R_S represents the target transmission rate, the probability that FD node S cannot decode the cellular UL signal is obtained as,

$$P_1 = Pr\left(R_{CS} < R_S \right). \tag{17}$$

From [3],

$$p_{S,k} = p_S, \forall k;\ p_{C,k} = p_C, \forall k;\ h_{CS,k} = h_{CS}, \forall k. \tag{18}$$

Since, $h_{CS} \sim \exp(d_{CS}^{\mu})$, using (16), (17) and (18), we get the OP P_1 of the exponential distribution as,

$$\begin{aligned}
P_1 &= Pr\left(N \log_2 \left(1 + \frac{p_C h_{CS}}{\sigma_S^2 + \Delta\beta p_S^{\lambda}} \right) < R_S \right) \\
&= Pr\left(h_{CS} < \frac{\left(2^{\frac{R_S}{N}} - 1 \right) \left(\sigma_S^2 + \Delta\beta p_S^{\lambda} \right)}{p_C} \right), \\
&= 1 - e^{\frac{-d_{CS}^{\mu} \left(2^{\frac{R_S}{N}} - 1 \right) \left(\sigma_S^2 + \Delta\beta p_S^{\lambda} \right)}{p_C}}. \tag{19}
\end{aligned}$$

Now, the instantaneous rate for the S-B link (R_{SB}) is,

$$R_{SB} = \sum_{k=1}^{D} \log_2 \left(1 + \frac{p_{S,k} h_{SB,k}}{\sigma_B^2} \right). \tag{20}$$

Let P_2 be the probability that S to B link does not satisfy the target rate (R_B). Hence,

$$\begin{aligned}
P_2 &= Pr\left(R_{SB} < R_B \right) \\
&= Pr\left(D \log_2 \left(1 + \frac{p_s h_{SB}}{\sigma_B^2} \right) < R_B \right) \\
&= Pr\left(h_{SB} < \frac{\left(2^{\frac{R_B}{D}} - 1 \right) \sigma_B^2}{p_s} \right). \tag{21}
\end{aligned}$$

On solving further using the cumulative distribution function (CDF) of an exponential distribution, the result obtained for P_2 is,

$$P_2 = 1 - e^{\frac{-d_{SB}^\mu \left(2^{\frac{R_B}{D}} - 1\right)\left(\sigma_B^2\right)}{p_S}}. \tag{22}$$

To find the OP of the C-S-B link (UL), we consider the cases where an outage occurs:

1. S cannot decode the data sent by C.
2. S decodes the data from C successfully and S-B link cannot achieve the required target rate.

Hence, using (13) and (18), the OP of the C-S-B link can be written as,

$$P_{out,UL} = P_1 + (1 - P_1)P_2. \tag{23}$$

4.2   D2D Link Outage Probability

This section comprises achievable D2D rate and OP expressions. Here, an FD node S forwards cellular UL data with D subcarriers, and the remaining $N - D$ subcarriers are used for D2D communications. The instantaneous rate received by the node T is written as,

$$R_{ST} = \sum_{k=1}^{N-D} \log_2 \left(1 + \frac{p_{S,k}h_{ST,k}}{\sigma_D^2}\right). \tag{24}$$

If R_T is the target rate of transmission, then probability that node T cannot decode the signal from node S is given as,

$$P_3 = Pr\left(R_{ST} < R_T\right),$$

$$= 1 - e^{\frac{-d_{ST}^\mu \left(2^{\frac{R_T}{N-D}} - 1\right)\left(\sigma_T^2\right)}{p_S}}. \tag{25}$$

Let P_4 be the probability, when S is not able to decode the signal received from C. Hence,

$$P_4 = 1 - e^{\frac{-d_{ST}^\mu \left(2^{\frac{R_T}{N}} - 1\right)\left(\sigma_D^2\right)}{p_S}}. \tag{26}$$

To find the OP of the D2D link, we consider the following two cases:

1. S cannot decode the data sent by the CU. Then, S uses all N subcarriers for D2D transmission.
2. S decodes the data from CU successfully and forwards D out of N subcarriers to B, and remaining $N - D$ subcarriers are used for D2D transmission.

Hence, using (13), (22) and (23), the OP of the D2D link can be written as,

$$P_{out,D2D} = P_1 P_4 + (1 - P_1)P_3. \tag{27}$$

Table 1. Simulation parameters

d_{CS}	d_{SB}	d_{SD}	p_S, p_C	N
200 m	300 m	50 m	100 mW	32

5   Theoretical and Simulation Results

This section presents the theoretical and simulation results for the outage probabilities of the D2D and cellular links. The simulation parameters are listed in Table 1. Figure 2 shows the theoretical and simulation results of cellular OP vs. D, with varying RSI parameter β. The RSI parameter λ is set to 5, as most of the SI power is suppressed in analog and propagation domain and remaining RSI is canceled in DD [6]. As shown in Fig. 2, cellular OP decreases with an increase in the number of subcarriers D forwarded by node S to B. This is due to the fact that as the value of D increases, UL transmission is more reliable and tends to have a lower probability of outage. The value of β is varied in decreasing powers of 10. It is observed that cellular OP decreases with a decrease in value of β. This is due to the fact that as β decreases, the magnitude of the RSI term decreases consequently lesser SI at the FD node, resulting in low OP. After $\beta = 10^{-9}$, the cellular OP reaches a minimum saturated value.

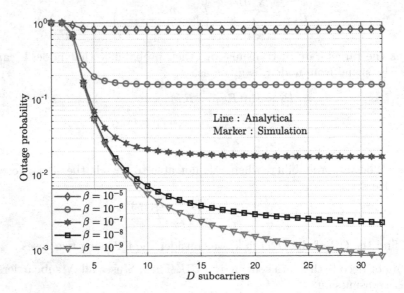

Fig. 2. Cellular OP vs D subcarriers (varying β)

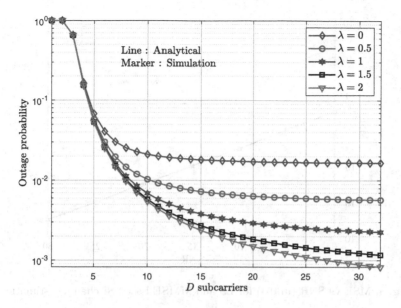

Fig. 3. Cellular OP vs D subcarriers (varying λ)

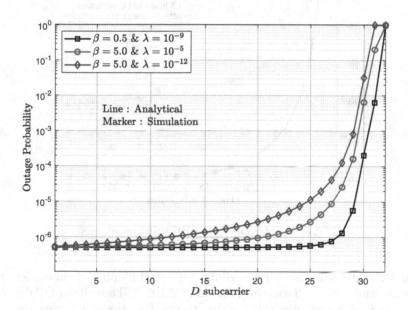

Fig. 4. D2D OP vs D subcarriers (varying λ and β)

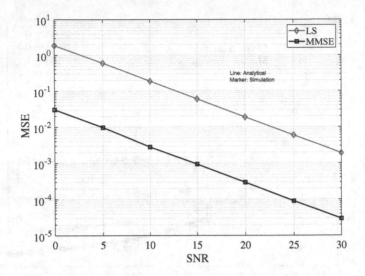

Fig. 5. MSE vs SNR (in dB) for LS and MMSE based SI channel estimation

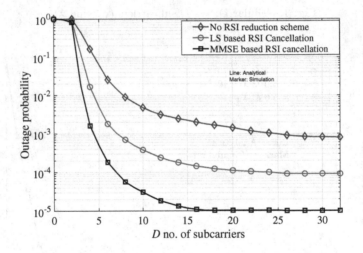

Fig. 6. Cellular OP vs D with RSI cancellation

Similarly in Fig. 3, we observe cellular OP vs D number of subcarriers with varying λ, while setting β to a constant value of 10^{-12}. The cellular OP decreases as the value of λ increases. This is due to the fact that increasing the value of λ decreases the value of the RSI term, since $p_S \leq 1W$. Hence, with lesser interference, the OP of the C-S communication link decreases. Beyond $\lambda = 5$, the value of P_{out} appears to be saturated and does not decrease much with further increase in λ.

Similarly, Fig. 4 shows D2D OP for different values of the parameters β and λ varying with D number of subcarriers. An increase in OP is observed with an increase in D. This increment in D2D OP is due to the fact that as D increases, $N - D$ decreases, and hence, the number of subcarriers allocated to the S-T link decreases. We obtain a probability of the order 10^{-6} when the parameters are set to $\beta = 10^{-12}$ and $\lambda = 5$, which appear to be optimal values for both the D2D and cellular links. The chosen optimum values of β and λ are justified by the analysis done in [10].

Figure 5 shows the comparison between LS and MMSE channel estimation techniques in terms of the MSE with respect to signal to noise ratio (SNR) (in dB) received at S under H_0. It could be clearly observed that MMSE completely outperforms LS-based DD SI channel estimation for a wide range of SNR 0 to 30 dB. Figure 6, shows the cellular OP vs. D number of subcarriers with and without RSI cancellation scheme. Here, we consider $\beta = 10^{-12}$ and $\lambda = 0.5$, it is found that by employing LS based RSI cancellation, the obtained estimate of β is $\hat{\beta} = 10^{-13}$ and by employing MMSE RSI $\hat{\beta} = 10^{-14}$. It is clearly observed from Fig. 6 that the proposed FD enables CD2D along with MMSE-based RSI cancellation gives the optimum performance compared to the proposed system with LS based RSI cancellation.

6 Conclusion

This paper proposes an OFDMA-based FD CD2D communications system, wherein the D2D source node acts as an FDR that DF the cellular UL data with D out of N orthogonal subcarriers received by CU. In exchange for relaying the cellular data, FD node S uses the remaining $N - D$ subcarriers for its own transmission. An LS and MMSE-based RSI cancellation scheme is used at the D2D source for RSI mitigation. The closed-form expressions of D2D and cellular outage probabilities were derived using a probabilistic mathematical model in the presence of LS and MMSE-based RSI cancellation. Results demonstrate the variation in the OP for the D2D and cellular links with the RSI parameters β and λ and the impact of the RSI cancellation scheme on outage analysis of the C-D link.

References

1. Ansari, R.I., et al.: 5G D2D networks: techniques, challenges, and future prospects. IEEE Syst. J. **12**(4), 3970–3984 (2018)
2. Tehrani, M.N., Uysal, M., Yanikomeroglu, H.: Device-to-device communication in 5G cellular networks: challenges, solutions, and future directions. IEEE Commun. Mag. **52**(5), 86–92 (2014)
3. Gupta, N., Bohara, V.A.: Rate and outage trade-offs for OFDMA based device to device communication frameworks. IEEE Access **5**, 14095–14106 (2017)
4. Bajpai, R., Kulkarni, A., Malhotra, G., Gupta, N.: Outage analysis of OFDMA based NOMA aided full-duplex cooperative D2D system. In: 2020 27th International Conference on Telecommunications (ICT), pp. 1–5 (2020)

5. Zhang, Z., Chai, X., Long, K., Vasilakos, A.V., Hanzo, L.: Full duplex techniques for 5G networks: self-interference cancellation, protocol design, and relay selection. IEEE Commun. Mag. **53**(5), 128–137 (2015)
6. Masmoudi, A., Le-Ngoc, T.: Self-interference cancellation for full-duplex MIMO transceiver. In: IEEE Wireless Communications and Networking Conference (WCNC), New Orleans, LA, USA, pp. 141–146, March 2015
7. Duarte, M., Dick, C., Sabharwal, A.: Experiment-driven characterization of full-duplex wireless systems. IEEE Trans. Wirel. Commun. **11**(12), 4296–4307 (2012)
8. Din, F.U., Labeau, F.: In-band full-duplex discriminatory channel estimation using MMSE. IEEE Trans. Inf. Forensics Secur. **15**, 3283–3292 (2020)
9. Gupta, N., Kumar, D., Bohara, V.A.: A novel user selection and resource allocation framework for cooperative D2D communication. In: 2018 IEEE Global Communications Conference (GLOBECOM), pp. 1–7, December 2018
10. Liu, G., Feng, W., Han, Z., Jiang, W.: Performance analysis and optimization of cooperative full-duplex D2D communication underlaying cellular networks. IEEE Trans. Wirel. Commun. **18**(11), 5113–5127 (2019)
11. Bajpai, R., Gupta, N., Bohara, V.A.: An adaptive full-duplex/half-duplex multiuser cooperative D2D communications system with best user selection. IEEE Open J. Commun. Soc. **2**, 1445–1457 (2021)
12. Bajpai, R., Gupta, N.: Outage trade-offs between full/half-duplex relaying for NOMA aided multicarrier cooperative D2D communications system. IETE Tech. Rev. 1–13 (2021)
13. Soriano-Irigaray, F.J., Fernandez-Prat, J.S., Lopez-Martinez, F.J., Martos-Naya, E., Cobos-Morales, O., Entrambasaguas, J.T.: Adaptive self-interference cancellation for full duplex radio: analytical model and experimental validation. IEEE Access **6**, 65018–65026 (2018)
14. Rodríguez, L.J., Tran, N.H., Le-Ngoc, T.: Performance of full-duplex AF relaying in the presence of residual self-interference. IEEE J. Sel. Areas Commun. **32**(9), 1752–1764 (2014)
15. Rodriguez, L.J., Tran, N.H., Le-Ngoc, T.: Optimal power allocation and capacity of full-duplex AF relaying under residual self-interference. IEEE Wirel. Commun. Lett. **3**(2), 233–236 (2014)

Realization and Simulation of Watermarking Algorithm Based on Spread Spectrum and DFT

Tian Wen, Wanming Liu[✉], Ruiyan Du, and Jiangfan Xie

Hebei Normal University, Shijiazhuang 050024, China
Liuwm@hebtu.edu.cn

Abstract. In order to protect image copyright and anti-counterfeit authentication, digital watermarking technology arises at the historic moment. The contradiction between robustness and invisibility affects the development of watermarking technology. To solve this problem, a watermarking algorithm based on spread spectrum and DFT is proposed. The main work of this paper is as follows: firstly, image embedding watermarking: the original image is segmented into two-dimensional discrete Fourier transform, then the watermark information through sequence even spread spectrum is superimposed, and finally the image with watermark is obtained by the inverse discrete Fourier transform. Secondly, extracting watermark information: the discrete Fourier transform is applied to the blocks of the original image and the image with watermark, the spread spectrum watermark information is extracted by comparing the amplitude and the original watermark is obtained by the final solution and expansion. Finally, the simulation results show that the proposed algorithm has good performance in robustness and invisibility.

Keywords: DFT · Spread spectrum · Sequence pairs · Digital image watermarking

1 Introduction

1.1 Introduction to Digital Image Watermarking

Digital watermarking was formally proposed by Trikel et al. in the paper of "Electronic Watermark" in 1990s [1]. In this paper, a digital watermarking method based on least significant bit is proposed, but its anti-attack ability is weak and its robustness is not satisfactory. Since then, digital watermarking technology began to develop rapidly.

Digital image watermarking technology is usually divided into two categories: embedding watermarking into carrier space domain [2] and embedding watermarking into image transform domain. The spatial domain algorithm includes least significant bit algorithm (LSB) [3] and Patchwork algorithm [4]. The advantages of spatial domain algorithm are direct and simple, but its anti-attack performance is poor.

The frequency-domain transforms commonly used in change domain algorithms include DFT (discrete Fourier transform), DCT (discrete cosine transform) and DWT (discrete wavelet transform). Cox et al. proposed a digital watermarking scheme based

H. Jin et al. (Eds.): CROWNCOM 2021/WiCON 2021, LNICST 427, pp. 141–148, 2022.
https://doi.org/10.1007/978-3-030-98002-3_10

on spread spectrum communication technology, embedding the watermark into the DCT region of the image [5], after which DCT domain algorithm developed rapidly. Uraniid et al. proposed a digital watermarking algorithm based on discrete Fourier transform. However, its computational complexity is high and its application value is not high [6]. Saini L K et al. proposed a combination algorithm based on DWT-DCT and verified the algorithm through common attacks [7]. At present, deep learning networks are also used to study image watermarking. For example, Zhou et al. proposed a robust watermarking scheme based on geometric correction codes, which improved the robustness of watermarking against common geometric transformation attacks [8].

1.2 Introduction to Spread Spectrum Communication

Spread spectrum communication is characterized by the bandwidth used for transmitting information is much larger than the bandwidth of the information itself. The basic idea and theoretical basis is to use the bandwidth transmission technology in exchange for the benefits of SNR.

In communication system, there will be various interference, which can be reduced or eliminated by using spread spectrum sequence. Sequence studies have been going on, but the results have not been significant. The concept of sequence pairs is derived from sequence analogy. In the spread spectrum communication system, the spread spectrum sequence of the transmitting end and the unspread sequence of the receiving end are not necessarily the same sequence, as long as the two sequences (called sequence couple) meet certain conditions can meet the engineering requirements for the best signal, which is the difference between sequence couple spread spectrum system and other systems. Thus, the concept of sequence pairs is introduced: suppose X and Y are two one-dimensional sequences of length N, then X and Y are said to form a sequence pair of N length, denoted as (X,Y); If the values of the elements of sequence X and Y are plus or minus 1, the sequence pairs (X,Y) are called binary sequence pairs.

When sequence pairs, Gold sequence [9] and m sequence [10] are used as spread spectrum sequences, the former has worse bit error rate performance than the latter two, but it can exist in any length, which makes up for the limitation that Gold and m sequences can only exist in some fixed length. It is found in the experiment that the bit error rate performance of the system may be better than that of Gold sequence and m sequence when there is a large sinusoidal interference in the system if the proper sequence pair is selected. Based on the above analysis, this paper adopts sequence pairs to spread spectrum processing of watermark information.

2 Realization and Simulation of Watermarking Algorithm Based on Spread Spectrum and DFT

2.1 Watermark Embedding Algorithm

Firstly, the original carrier image is divided into 8*8 data blocks, and then two-dimensional discrete Fourier transform is performed on each data block. Next, sequence pairs are generated and the original watermark information is repeated 61 times bit-by-bit, that is, the length of sequence pairs used in this paper. Then spread spectrum processing is carried out to generate a new spread spectrum sequence code. After all the above work is completed, the generated spread spectrum sequence code is superimposed with the amplitude spectrum of the carrier image after sub-block segmentation and DFT transformation, which is equivalent to successfully loading the watermark information after expansion into the original carrier image. After successful embedding, the image with watermark information can be obtained by inverse discrete Fourier transform. The block diagram of watermark embedding principle is shown in Fig. 1.

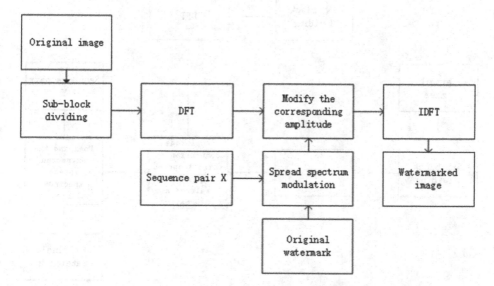

Fig. 1. Watermark embedding algorithm flow

2.2   Watermarking Extraction Algorithm

This algorithm uses the steps similar to the embedding algorithm mentioned above. It divides the carrier image that already contains watermark information into sub-blocks, and then makes DFT changes to each sub-block. After that, it compares the amplitude with the original carrier image that has also undergone segmentation and DFT transformation, so as to extract the spread spectrum watermark information effectively. After the steps are completed, sequence pair Y is used to de-expand the extracted spread spectrum information, that is, the spread spectrum watermarking information is multiplied bit by bit with sequence even Y within the length of a sequence even code element, then the sequence is added in the code cycle and compared with the decision threshold. Due to the sequence pairs have negative correlation, so if the comparison result is greater than 0, judgment is 0; If the comparison result is less than 0, judgment is 1. Finally, the original watermark information is obtained. The block diagram of watermark extraction principle is shown in Fig. 2.

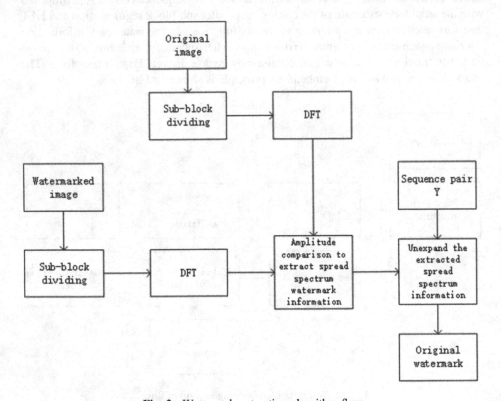

Fig. 2. Watermark extraction algorithm flow

3   Simulation Results and Analysis

In this paper, WIN10 and MATLAB R2016a are used as the experimental simulation environment, and the image size is 512 * 512 pixels. Figure 3 is the original image. Figure 4 shows watermark images. Figure 5 shows the watermark information obtained after sequential even spread spectrum.

Fig. 3. Original image

(a)   (b)

Fig. 4. (a) Original image 128 *1 28 pixels watermark image, (b) 64 * 64 pixels watermark image

watermark information obtained after sequence even spread spectrum

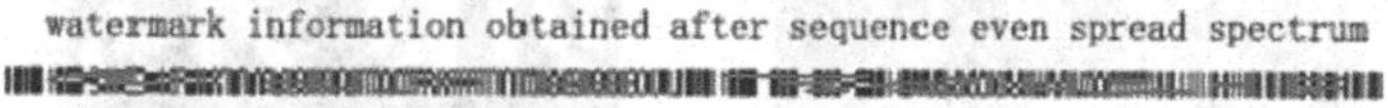

Fig. 5. 64 * 64 pixels watermark image watermark information after sequence even spread spectrum

In this paper, the Normalized Coefficient (NC) and Peak Signal to Noise Ratio (PSNR) are selected to evaluate the algorithm performance. NC is used to evaluate the similarity between the original watermark image and the extracted watermark image, and its value ranges from 0 to 1 [11]. The larger the NC is, the stronger the robustness of the algorithm is. PSNR is used to evaluate the distortion degree between the watermark carrier image and the original image, and its value ranges from 0 to 100 [12]. The larger the PSNR is, the better the visibility of the algorithm is.

Change the embedding strength K to 0.015, 0.02, 0.025 and 0.03 respectively, run the program, calculate the value of PSNR and NC. The experimental comparison results are as follows (Figs. 6, 7, 8, and 9).

1. When k = 0.015, the result is shown as follows, and get the PSNR = 93.522, NC = 0.98013.

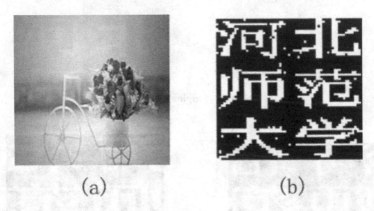

(a)   (b)

Fig. 6. (a) Carrier image with watermark, (b) Extract the watermark image

2. When k = 0.02, the result is shown as follows, and get the PSNR = 87.671, NC = 0.98279.

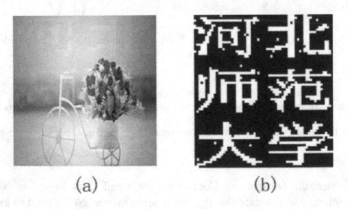

(a)   (b)

Fig. 7. (a) Carrier image with watermark, (b) Extract the watermark image

3. When k = 0.025, the result is shown as follows, and get the PSNR = 83.119, NC = 0.98281.

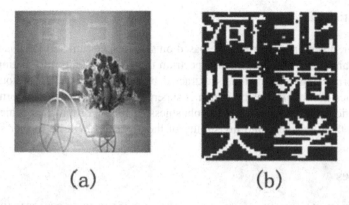

(a)   (b)

Fig. 8. (a) Carrier image with watermark, (b) Extract the watermark image

4. When k = 0.03, the result is shown as follows, and get the PSNR = 79.385, NC = 0.98409.

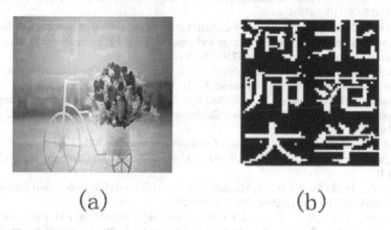

(a)   (b)

Fig. 9. (a) Carrier image with watermark, (b) Extract the watermark image

According to the above experimental results, with the increase of K, PSNR gradually decreases and NC gradually increases, which proves that there is a contradiction between watermark visibility and robustness. The values of NC are all above 0.98 and have good robustness.

4 Conclusion

In this paper, a watermarking scheme based on spread spectrum and DFT is proposed. Sequence pairs are selected to spread spectrum the watermarking information, and the useful watermarking information is extracted by using the excellent autocorrelation characteristics of sequence pairs, which is superposed in the image transform domain. The simulation results show that the robustness of the algorithm has achieved good results, and the robustness and invisibility of the algorithm will be further studied.

References

1. Tirkel, A., Rankin, G.: Electronic watermark. ResearchGate **40**(4), 222–223 (1993)
2. Milad, A., Jasper, R.S., Bryan, T.B., Mark, A.F.: High-speed all-optical Haar wavelet transform for real-time image compression. Opt. Express **25**(9), 9802–9811 (2017)
3. Somwanshi, D., Chhipa, I., Singhal, T., Yadav, A.: Modified Least significant bit algorithm of digital watermarking for information security. In: Pant, M., Ray, K., Sharma, T., Rawat, S., Bandyopadhyay, A. (eds) Soft Computing: Theories and Applications, Advances in Intelligent Systems and Computing, vol. 584. Springer, Singapore (2018). https://doi.org/10.1007/978-981-10-5699-4_44
4. Narawade, N.S.: Robust reversible watermarking using integration of histogram shifting and patchwork algorithm to improve quality and capacity. In: IEEE International Conference on Information Processing, 2016, pp.625–630 (2016)
5. Cox, I.J., Kilian, J., Leighton, F.T., Shamoon, T.: Secure spread spectrum watermarking for multimedia. IEEE Trans. Image process. **6**(12), 1673–1687 (1997)
6. Ruanaidh J.J.K.O., Dowling W.J., Boland F.M.: Phase watermarking of digital images. In: Proceedings of 3rd IEEE International Conference on Image Processing, 1996, pp.239–242 (2016)
7. Saini, L.K., Shrivastava, V.: Analysis of attacks on hybrid DWT-DCT algorithm for digital image watermarking with MATLAB. Int. J. Comput. Sci. Trends Technol. **2**(3), 123–125 (2014)
8. Zhou, Z., Zhu, J., Su, Y., Wang, M., Sun, X.: Geometric correction code-based robust image watermarking. IET Image Proc. **2021**, 1–10 (2021)
9. Veni, M., Meyyappan, T.: Digital image watermark embedding and extraction using oppositional fruit fly algorithm. Multimedia Tools Appl. **78**(19), 27491–27510 (2019). https://doi.org/10.1007/s11042-019-7650-0
10. Dong, Z., Hu, N.: A method for the detection of long pseudo-random code DSSS signals based on the processing of delay-multiply (II) - the estimation of the information symbol period and the pseudo-random code sequence. In: 2008 11th IEEE International Conference on Communication Technology, 2008, pp. 233–236 (2008)
11. Moosazadeh, M., Ekbatanifard, G.: A new DCT-based robust image watermarking method using teaching-learning-Based optimization. J. Inf. Security Appl. **47**, 28–38 (2019)
12. Roy, S., Pal, A.K.: A blind DCT based color watermarking algorithm for embedding multiple watermarks. AEU Int. J. Electr. Commun. **72**, 149–161 (2017)

The Performance Research of LTE-A Cellular Network Based on Relay and Pass-Through D2D Technology

Liyan Zhang[1], Wenbin Zhang[1,2]([⊠]) [iD], Wenke Li[1], and Jiaqi Su[1]

[1] Harbin Institute of Technology, Harbin 150001, People's Republic of China
zwbgxy1973@hit.edu.cn
[2] Science and Technology on Communication Networks Laboratory,
Shijiazhuang 050050, Hebei, People's Republic of China

Abstract. With the development of 5G technology, the demand for communication quality has shown exponential growth. Regarding the problem of low communication quality at the edge of the LTE-Advanced cellular network, we can expand the coverage and share base station traffic by introducing relay technology and D2D technology, thereby increasing the throughput of the communication system. The research background of this paper is to combine pass-through (direct) D2D mode with LTE-A relay cellular network in LTE-A cells, and then construct the MINLP optimization problem with maximizing system throughput as the objective function. The convex optimization method is used to realize the optimal allocation of power resources. The final simulation results show the growth of system throughput and user fairness.

Keywords: LTE-Advanced cellular network · Relay technology · D2D technology · Convex optimization · Throughput

1 Introduction

The addition of relay nodes in the LTE-A system can cover a wider area and achieve higher-quality communication, while it also greatly increases the complexity of the communication system, so it has become the research focus of scholars at home and abroad. To improve system throughput, we should first consider to control the channel interference, the solutions mainly adopt the partial frequency reuse. [1] proposes a method for selecting relay nodes in a mobile Ad hoc network. Based on the messages received from one or other nodes, the list of adjacent relay nodes is updated, and the adjacent relay nodes in the first hop is updated. In the relay nodes and the updated relay list, the relay with the highest value of the selection counter is selected as the MPR node. The method

Supported by National Nature Science Foundation of China (NSFC) under Grant 62071148.

H. Jin et al. (Eds.): CROWNCOM 2021/WiCON 2021, LNICST 427, pp. 149–165, 2022.
https://doi.org/10.1007/978-3-030-98002-3_11

can prevent unnecessary channel competition and conflict between nodes, so it can improve network performance. A new round-robin scheduling algorithm using location information is proposed in [2], so that some frequencies can be reused by base stations or relays after selection. It has been proved that this algorithm can effectively control channel interference and improve the system throughput. [3] proposes an optimization algorithm based on energy efficiency in a large-scale LTE network in a dense urban area. The optimization variables include the relevant parameters of the base station and the relay antenna, such as the azimuth, transmission power, and antenna height. Through overall optimization, the energy consumption of users is reduced, and the communication performance of users is improved. [4] studies the power allocation scheme of subcarriers aiming at maximizing energy efficiency in a cooperative relay network, it mainly studies the situation that the destination nodes receive signals from the source nodes and relay nodes at the same time. [5] in the context of OFDMA downlink, resource allocation is performed by maximizing the minimum weighted rate under the constraint of the transmission power of each base station. This allocation method ensures that the information rate of each cell is roughly the same at the expense of the total data rate of the system, so as to make the system have better fairness. [6] is similar to [5], it also sacrifices the overall throughput of the system to ensure the QoS of each user. Under the condition of a certain total power, the allocation strategies of subcarrier, power and relay are combined at the same time to establish a complex optimization problem, which is solved combined with the optimization theory.

Due to the advantages of D2D technology in sharing data traffic in cellular networks, it has recently become a hot research topic. [7] studies the resource allocation algorithm for single-cell users and multiple D2D users using game theory methods in high-density D2D user scenarios. [8] discusses the link sharing mechanism and user resource allocation strategy of the multi-user D2D communication system. With the purpose of improving the energy efficiency of users, a distributed resource allocation scheme is proposed by using game and noncooperative game methods. [9] studies the interference coordination problem of D2D communication under homogeneous network. Under the condition of satisfying QoS, a channel allocation and power control method based on partial location information is proposed.

The main research content of this paper is to establish the resource sharing model between direct D2D users and cellular users in LTE-A cellular network by combining relay technology and direct D2D technology, establish the objective function of maximizing system throughput, and use convex optimization method to solve this problem. Finally, the throughput and user fairness are analyzed.

Notation: a^* represent the conjugate.

2   System Model for the Coexistence of Direct D2D Users and Cellular Users

The system model is shown in Fig. 1, which contains both direct D2D users and cellular users. The cellular network adopts Time Division Duplex (TDD) mode.

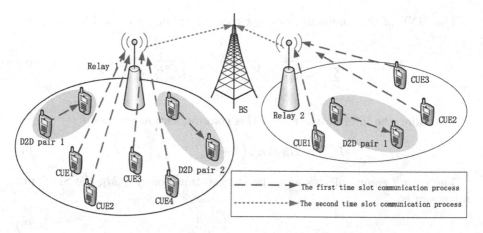

Fig. 1. System model of coexistence of direct D2D users and cellular users.

The entire communication process is divided into two time slots, and all relays communicate synchronously in these two time slots. All cellular users (not using D2D mode) are represented by set M, and all direct D2D users is represented by set D^p, the system bandwidth is divided into N resource blocks (RBs), the set of resource blocks is $N = \{1, 2, \cdots, |N|\}$, the set of resource blocks that can be used in each relay is N, and the bandwidth of each resource block is represented by B_{RB}. The relay set is denoted by $L = \{1, 2, \cdots |L|\}$, $U_l, \forall l \in L$ represents the set of all users who communicate through relay l, the set of cellular users under the relay l coverage is $M_l = M \cap U_l$, the set of direct D2D users under the relay l coverage is $D_l^p = D^p \cap U_l$. Therefore, the following formulas are established: $U_l \subseteq \{D_l^p \cup M_l\}, \forall l \in L$, $\cup_l U_l = \{D^p \cup M\}$, $\cap_l U_l = \varphi, \forall l \in L$. The Signal to Interference plus Noise Ratio (SINR) of the direct D2D pair is:

$$\gamma_{u_l,u_l,1}^{(n)} = \frac{h_{u_l,u_l}^{(n)}}{\sum\limits_{\substack{u_j \in D_j^p \\ j \neq l, j \in L}} Q_{u_j,u_j}^{(n)} \cdot g_{u_j,u_l}^{(n)} + \sum\limits_{\substack{u_j \in M_j \\ j \neq l, j \in L}} Q_{u_j,j}^{(n)} \cdot g_{u_j,u_l}^{(n)} + \sigma^2} \tag{1}$$

Where, $Q_{a,b}^{(n)}$, $h_{a,b}^{(n)}$, $g_{a,b}^{(n)}$ respectively represent the transmit power, the channel coefficient of the communication link, and the gain of the interference link on the resource block n in the communication process from the transmitter a to the receiver b. $\sigma^2 = N_0 B_{RB}$, N_0 is the power spectral density of thermal noise. Therefore, the information rate of this communication process is:

$$R_{u_l,u_l}^{(n)} = B_{RB} \log_2 \left(1 + Q_{u_l,u_l}^{(n)} \gamma_{u_l,u_l,1}^{(n)}\right) \tag{2}$$

The SINR of the communication between the cellular user and the relay is:

$$\gamma_{u_l,l,1}^{(n)} = \frac{h_{u_l,l}^{(n)}}{\sum\limits_{\substack{u_j \in D_j^P \\ j \neq l, j \in L}} Q_{u_j,u_j}^{(n)} \cdot g_{u_j,l}^{(n)} + \sum\limits_{\substack{u_j \in M_j \\ j \neq l, j \in L}} Q_{u_j,j}^{(n)} \cdot g_{u_j,l}^{(n)} + \sigma^2} \tag{3}$$

Therefore, the information rate of this communication process is:

$$R_{u_l,l}^{(n)} = B_{RB} \log_2 \left(1 + Q_{u_l,l}^{(n)} \gamma_{u_l,l,1}^{(n)}\right) \tag{4}$$

The relay l communicates with the base station, for $u_l \in M_l$, the SINR per unit power is:

$$\gamma_{l,eNB,2}^{(n)} = \frac{h_{l,eNB}^{(n)}}{\sigma^2} \tag{5}$$

Therefore, the information rate of this communication process is:

$$R_{l,eNB}^{(n)} = B_{RB} \log_2 \left(1 + Q_{l,eNB}^{(n)} \gamma_{l,eNB,2}^{(n)}\right) \tag{6}$$

In summary, for user u_l under relay l coverage, the total information rate consists of two parts:

(1) direct D2D mode: the user u_l communicates in direct D2D mode, and the information rate is:

$$R_D^{(n)} = R_{u_l,u_l}^{(n)} \tag{7}$$

(2) Cellular mode: The user u_l communicates in the cellular mode, and the information rate of this communication process is:

$$R_M^{(n)} = \frac{1}{2} \min \left\{ R_{u_l,l}^{(n)}, R_{l,eNB}^{(n)} \right\} \tag{8}$$

The above formula is multiplied by $1/2$ because the cellular users within the relay range need two time slots to realize two-way communication through relay forwarding, while the direct D2D communication process only uses one time slot, so there is no need to multiply it.

Set the maximum value of user transmission power as $Q_{u_l}^{max}$ and the maximum value of relay transmission power as Q_l^{max}. Introduce resource block allocation factor $x_{u_l}^{(n)}$, $x_{u_l}^{(n)} \in \{0,1\}$, they are binary integer variables: When $x_{u_l}^{(n)} = 1$, it means that the resource block n is allocated to user u_l, otherwise $x_{u_l}^{(n)} = 0$, $\bar{x}_{u_l}^{(n)} = 1 - x_{u_l}^{(n)}$. The users' QoS requirement is expressed by R_{QoS}. This optimization problem can be described as:

$$\max_{x_{u_l}^{(n)}, Q_{u_l,u_l}^{(n)}, Q_{u_l,l}^{(n)}, Q_{l,eNB}^{(n)}} \sum_{l \in L} \sum_{u_l \in U_l} \sum_{n=1}^{N} x_{u_l}^{(n)} R_D^{(n)} + \bar{x}_{u_l}^{(n)} R_M^{(n)} \tag{9}$$

$$0 \leq \sum_{u_l \in U_l} x_{u_l}^{(n)} \leq 1, \quad \forall n \in N \tag{10}$$

$$\sum_{n=1}^{N} x_{u_l}^{(n)} Q_{u_l,u_l}^{(n)} \leq Q_{u_l}^{\max} , \forall u_l \in D_l^p, \sum_{n=1}^{N} \bar{x}_{u_l}^{(n)} Q_{u_l,l}^{(n)} \leq Q_{u_l}^{\max} , \forall u_l \in M_l \quad (11)$$

$$\sum_{u_l \in M_l} \sum_{n=1}^{N} \bar{x}_{u_l}^{(n)} Q_{l,eNB}^{(n)} \leq Q_l^{\max} \quad (12)$$

$$\sum_{\substack{u_l \in D_l^p}} x_{u_l}^{(n)} Q_{u_l,u_l}^{(n)} g_{u_l,u_l^*,1}^{(n)} \leq I_{th}^{(n)}, \quad \sum_{u_l \in M_l} \bar{x}_{u_l}^{(n)} Q_{u_l,l}^{(n)} g_{u_l,l^*,1}^{(n)} \leq I_{th}^{(n)},$$
$$\forall n \in N, \forall l \in L, l \neq l^*, \forall l^* \in L \quad (13)$$

$$R_{u_l} \geq R_{\mathrm{QoS}}, \qquad \forall u_l \in U_l \quad (14)$$

$$Q_{u_l,u_l}^{(n)} \geq 0, Q_{u_l,l}^{(n)} \geq 0, Q_{l,eNB}^{(n)} \geq 0, \forall n \in N, u_l \in U_l \quad (15)$$

Where, (10) is the condition that each indicator coefficient needs to meet, each resource block can only be allocated to one user under each relay, (11) and (12) limit the transmission power not to exceed the maximum power, (13) indicates that the interference from D2D users under other relays and the interference from cellular users under other relays must meet the interference threshold, (14) ensures that the system meets the minimum QoS requirements, (15) indicates that the transmission power is non-negative.

The unit power SINR of direct D2D users is:

$$\gamma_{u_l,u_l,1}^{(n)} = \frac{h_{u_l,u_l}^{(n)}}{I_{u_l,u_l,1}^{(n)} + \sigma^2} \quad (16)$$

Where, $I_{u_l,u_l,1}^{(n)}$ is the interference of direct D2D user u_l on the resource block n.

$$I_{u_l,u_l,1}^{(n)} = \sum_{\substack{u_j \in D_j^p \\ j \neq l, j \in L}} x_{u_j}^{(n)} Q_{u_j,u_j}^{(n)} \cdot g_{u_j,u_l}^{(n)} + \sum_{\substack{u_j \in M_j \\ j \neq l, j \in L}} \bar{x}_{u_j}^{(n)} Q_{u_j,j}^{(n)} \cdot g_{u_j,u_l}^{(n)} \quad (17)$$

For cellular users, the unit power SINR during the first time slot communication process is:

$$\gamma_{u_l,l,1}^{(n)} = \frac{h_{u_l,l}^{(n)}}{I_{u_l,l,1}^{(n)} + \sigma^2} \quad (18)$$

Where, $I_{u_l,l,1}^{(n)}$ is the interference of the cellular user u_l on the resource block n in the first time slot.

$$I_{u_l,l,1}^{(n)} = \sum_{\substack{u_j \in D_j^p \\ j \neq l, j \in L}} x_{u_j}^{(n)} Q_{u_j,u_j}^{(n)} \cdot g_{u_j,l}^{(n)} + \sum_{\substack{u_j \in M_j \\ j \neq l, j \in L}} \bar{x}_{u_j}^{(n)} Q_{u_j,j}^{(n)} \cdot g_{u_j,l}^{(n)} \quad (19)$$

The total information rate of all cellular users on the resource block n is $R_M^{(n)}$:

$$R_{\mathrm{M}}^{(n)} = \frac{1}{2} \min \left\{ R_{u_l,l}^{(n)}, R_{l,eNB}^{(n)} \right\}$$
$$= \frac{1}{2} \min \left\{ B_{\mathrm{RB}} \log_2 \left(1 + Q_{u_l,l}^{(n)} \gamma_{u_l,l,1}^{(n)} \right), B_{\mathrm{RB}} \log_2 \left(1 + Q_{l,eNB}^{(n)} \gamma_{l,eNB,2}^{(n)} \right) \right\} \quad (20)$$

When $Q_{u_l,l}^{(n)}\gamma_{u_l,l,1}^{(n)} = Q_{l,eNB}^{(n)}\gamma_{l,eNB,2}^{(n)}$ is established, $R_M^{(n)}$ can reach the maximum value. At this time, $Q_{l,eNB}^{(n)}$ in the second time slot can be expressed by the power in the first time slot, that is $Q_{l,eNB}^{(n)} = \frac{\gamma_{u_l,l,1}^{(n)}}{\gamma_{l,eNB,2}^{(n)}}Q_{u_l,l}^{(n)}$. Therefore, the total information rate of cellular users on the resource block n can be rewritten as

$$R_{\mathrm{M}}^{(n)} = \frac{1}{2}B_{\mathrm{RB}}\log_2\left(1 + Q_{u_l,l}^{(n)}\gamma_{u_l,l,1}^{(n)}\right), \qquad u_l \in M_l \tag{21}$$

3   Power Distribution Method Based on Lagrangian Multiplier Method

Optimization problem (9) is difficult to solve because it contains both continuous variables and binary integer variables, and the objective function is nonlinear. Such problems can be called mixed-integer nonlinear programming (MINLP). In order to simplify the problem, we first relax the resource block allocation factor $x_{u_l}^{(n)}$ into a continuous variable, that is $x_{u_l}^{(n)} \in [0,1]$, which represents the proportion of time that the resource block n is allocated to user u_l, and it still meets the aforementioned restriction conditions $0 \le \sum_{u_l \in U_l} x_{u_l}^{(n)} \le 1, \forall n \in N$, $0 < \sum_{u_l \in U_l} x_{u_l}^{(n)} \le 1, \forall n \in N$. In addition, two new variables $S_{u_l,u_l}^{(n)} = x_{u_l}^{(n)}Q_{u_l,u_l}^{(n)}$, $T_{u_l,l}^{(n)} = \bar{x}_{u_l}^{(n)}Q_{u_l,l}^{(n)}$ are introduced, which are respectively used as power allocation variables for direct D2D users and cellular users to represent the actual transmit power of the user u_l on the resource block n. The optimization problem after relaxation and adjustment can be expressed as

$$\max_{x_{u_l}^{(n)},S_{u_l,u_l}^{(n)},T_{u_l,l}^{(n)}} \sum_{l \in L}\sum_{u_l \in U_l}\sum_{n=1}^{N}\left[x_{u_l}^{(n)}B_{\mathrm{RB}}\log_2\left(1 + \frac{S_{u_l,u_l}^{(n)}h_{u_l,u_l}^{(n)}}{x_{u_l}^{(n)}\omega_{u_l}^{(n)}}\right)\right. \tag{22}$$

$$\left. + \bar{x}_{u_l}^{(n)}\frac{1}{2}B_{\mathrm{RB}}\log_2\left(1 + \frac{T_{u_l,l}^{(n)}h_{u_l,l}^{(n)}}{\bar{x}_{u_l}^{(n)}\mu_{u_l}^{(n)}}\right)\right]$$

$$\text{s.t. } 0 < \sum_{u_l \in U_l} x_{u_l}^{(n)} \le 1, \qquad \forall n \in N \tag{23}$$

$$\sum_{n=1}^{N} S_{u_l,u_l}^{(n)} \le Q_{u_l}^{\max}, \forall u_l \in D_l^p, \sum_{n=1}^{N} T_{u_l,l}^{(n)} \le Q_{u_l}^{\max}, \forall u_l \in M_l \tag{24}$$

$$\sum_{u_l \in M_l}\sum_{n=1}^{N} \frac{\gamma_{u_l,l,1}^{(n)}}{\gamma_{l,eNB,2}^{(n)}}T_{u_l,l}^{(n)} \le Q_l^{\max} \tag{25}$$

$$\sum_{u_l \in D_l^p} S_{u_l,u_l}^{(n)}g_{u_l,u_l^*,1}^{(n)} \le I_{th}^{(n)}, \sum_{u_l \in M_l} T_{u_l,l}^{(n)}g_{u_l,l^*,1}^{(n)} \le I_{th}^{(n)}, \forall n \in N \tag{26}$$

$$\sum_{n=1}^{N} \left[x_{u_l}^{(n)} B_{RB} \log_2 \left(1 + \frac{S_{u_l,u_l}^{(n)} h_{u_l,u_l}^{(n)}}{x_{u_l}^{(n)} \omega_{u_l}^{(n)}} \right) \right.$$
$$\left. + \bar{x}_{u_l}^{(n)} \frac{1}{2} B_{RB} \log_2 \left(1 + \frac{T_{u_l,u_l}^{(n)} h_{u_l,u_l}^{(n)}}{\bar{x}_{u_l}^{(n)} \mu_{u_l}^{(n)}} \right) \right] \geq R_{QoS}, \forall u_l \in U_l \tag{27}$$

$$S_{u_l,u_l}^{(n)} \geq 0, u_l \in D_l^p, T_{u_l,l}^{(n)} \geq 0, u_l \in M_l, \forall n \in N \tag{28}$$

$$I_{u_l,u_l,1}^{(n)} + \sigma^2 \leq \omega_{u_l}^{(n)}, u_l \in D_l^p, I_{u_l,l,1}^{(n)} + \sigma^2 \leq \mu_{u_l}^{(n)}, u_l \in M_l, \forall n \in N \tag{29}$$

Where, $\omega_{u_l}^{(n)}, \mu_{u_l}^{(n)}$ are auxiliary variables, when the number of RBs is extremely large, the dual spacing of the optimization problem that satisfies the time allocation condition can be ignored. The optimization problem studied in this paper satisfies the time allocation condition, so the relaxed optimization problem has an asymptotic optimal solution. From the above formulas, the constraint condition (27) is convex, and other constraints are linear. If the objective function is a concave function, then the optimization problem (22) is a convex problem, and there is an optimal solution. Next, we must first prove that the objective function is a concave function.

Define the function $\Re\left(S_{u_1,u_l}^{(n)}, T_{u_l,l}^{(n)} \right)$ as

$$\Re\left(S_{u_1,u_l}^{(n)}, T_{u_l,l}^{(n)} \right) = - \left[x_{u_l}^{(n)} B_{RB} \log_2 \left(1 + \frac{S_{u_l,u_l}^{(n)} h_{u_l,u_l}^{(n)}}{x_{u_l}^{(n)} \omega_{u_l}^{(n)}} \right) \right.$$
$$\left. + \bar{x}_{u_l}^{(n)} \frac{1}{2} B_{RB} \log_2 \left(1 + \frac{T_{u_l,l}^{(n)} h_{u_l,l}^{(n)}}{\bar{x}_{u_l}^{(n)} \mu_{u_l}^{(n)}} \right) \right] \tag{30}$$

Find the Hessian matrix H about $\left(S_{u_l,u_l}^{(n)}, T_{u_l,l}^{(n)} \right)$ for function $\Re\left(S_{u_l,u_l}^{(n)}, T_{u_l,l}^{(n)} \right)$, and find the first derivative about $S_{u_l,u_l}^{(n)}, T_{u_l,l}^{(n)}$ for function $\Re\left(S_{u_l,u_l}^{(n)}, T_{u_l,l}^{(n)} \right)$ respectively, and get formula (31) and formula (32)

$$\frac{\partial \Re}{\partial S_{u_l,u_l}^{(n)}} = -\frac{1}{\ln 2} x_{u_l}^{(n)} B_{RB} \frac{1}{1 + \frac{S_{u_l,u_l}^{(n)} h_{u_l,u_l}^{(n)}}{x_{u_l}^{(n)} \omega_{u_l}^{(n)}}} \frac{h_{u_l,u_l}^{(n)}}{x_{u_l}^{(n)} \omega_{u_l}^{(n)}} = -\frac{x_{u_l}^{(n)} B_{RB} h_{u_l,u_l}^{(n)}}{\ln 2 \left(x_{u_l}^{(n)} \omega_{u_l}^{(n)} + S_{u_l,u_l}^{(n)} h_{u_l,u_l}^{(n)} \right)}$$
$$\tag{31}$$

$$\frac{\partial \Re}{\partial T_{u_l,l}^{(n)}} = -\frac{1}{2 \ln 2} \bar{x}_{u_l}^{(n)} B_{RB} \frac{1}{1 + \frac{T_{u_l,l}^{(n)} h_{u_l,l}^{(n)}}{\bar{x}_{u_l}^{(n)} \mu_{u_l}^{(n)}}} \frac{h_{u_l,l}^{(n)}}{\bar{x}_{u_l}^{(n)} \mu_{u_l}^{(n)}} = -\frac{\bar{x}_{u_l}^{(n)} B_{RB} h_{u_l,l}^{(n)}}{2 \ln 2 \left(\bar{x}_{u_l}^{(n)} \mu_{u_l}^{(n)} + T_{u_l,l}^{(n)} h_{u_l,l}^{(n)} \right)} \tag{32}$$

Continue to find the derivative about $S_{u_l,u_l}^{(n)}, T_{u_l,l}^{(n)}$ respectively to obtain the Hessian matrix H in the following formula

$$H = \begin{vmatrix} \dfrac{\partial^2 \Re\left(S^{(n)}_{u_l,u_l}, T^{(n)}_{u_l,l}\right)}{\partial S^{(n)}_{u_l,u_l}{}^2} & \dfrac{\partial^2 \Re\left(S^{(n)}_{u_l,u_l}, T^{(n)}_{u_l,l}\right)}{\partial S^{(n)}_{u_l,u_l} \partial T^{(n)}_{u_l,l}} \\ \dfrac{\partial^2 \Re\left(S^{(n)}_{u_l,u_l}, T^{(n)}_{u_l,l}\right)}{\partial T^{(n)}_{u_l,l} \partial S^{(n)}_{u_l,u_l}} & \dfrac{\partial^2 \Re\left(S^{(n)}_{u_l,u_l}, T^{(n)}_{u_l,l}\right)}{\partial T^{(n)}_{u_l,l}{}^2} \end{vmatrix}$$

$$= \begin{vmatrix} \dfrac{x^{(n)}_{u_l} B_{RB} h^{(n)}_{u_l,u_l}{}^2}{\ln 2 \left(x^{(n)}_{u_l} \omega^{(n)}_{u_l} + S^{(n)}_{u_l,u_l} h^{(n)}_{u_l,u_l}\right)^2} & 0 \\ 0 & \dfrac{\bar{x}^{(n)}_{u_l} B_{RB} h^{(n)}_{u_l,l}{}^2}{2\ln 2 \left(\bar{x}^{(n)}_{u_l} \mu^{(n)}_{u_l} + T^{(n)}_{u_l,l} h^{(n)}_{u_l,l}\right)^2} \end{vmatrix} \tag{33}$$

The matrix H is a second-order matrix with two eigenvalues, the two eigenvalues are

$$\tilde{\lambda}_1 = \frac{x^{(n)}_{u_l} B_{RB} h^{(n)2}_{u_l,u_l}}{\ln 2 \left(x^{(n)}_{u_l} \omega^{(n)}_{u_l} + S^{(n)}_{u_l,u_l} h^{(n)}_{u_l,u_l}\right)^2}, \quad \tilde{\lambda}_2 = \frac{\bar{x}^{(n)}_{u_l} B_{RB} h^{(n)2}_{u_l,l}}{2\ln 2 \left(\bar{x}^{(n)}_{u_l} \mu^{(n)}_{u_l} + T^{(n)}_{u_l,l} h^{(n)}_{u_l,l}\right)^2} \tag{34}$$

Because $\tilde{\lambda}_1 > 0$, $\tilde{\lambda}_2 > 0$, $\Re\left(S^{(n)}_{u_l,u_l}, T^{(n)}_{u_l,l}\right)$ is convex, the objective function (22) is concave. Therefore, the optimization problem is a convex problem, and there is an optimal solution. Therefore, the KKT conditions in convex optimization theory can be used to solve this problem.

Next, use the Lagrangian multiplier method to solve the problem. Let the Lagrangian multipliers of the constraints (23) to (29) in Eq. (22) be δ_n, ξ_{u_l}, ς_{u_l}, υ_l, ψ_n, ε_n, λ_{u_l}, $\rho^{(n)}_{u_l}$, $\kappa^{(n)}_{u_l}$, then the Lagrangian function is:

$$
\begin{aligned}
L = & -\sum_{l \in L} \sum_{u_l \in U_l} \sum_{n=1}^{N} \left[x^{(n)}_{u_l} B_{RB} \log_2 \left(1 + \frac{S^{(n)}_{u_l,u_l} h^{(n)}_{u_l,u_l}}{x^{(n)}_{u_l} \omega^{(n)}_{u_l}}\right) + \bar{x}^{(n)}_{u_l} \tfrac{1}{2} B_{RB} \log_2 \left(1 + \frac{T^{(n)}_{u_l,l} h^{(n)}_{u_l,l}}{\left(1 - x^{(n)}_{u_l}\right) \mu^{(n)}_{u_l}}\right) \right] \\
& + \sum_{n=1}^{N} \delta_n \left(\sum_{u_l \in U_l} x^{(n)}_{u_l} - 1\right) + \sum_{u_l \in D^P_l} \xi_{u_l} \left(\sum_{n=1}^{N} S^{(n)}_{u_l,u_l} - Q^{\max}_{u_l}\right) \\
& + \sum_{u_l \in M_l} \varsigma_{u_l} \left(\sum_{n=1}^{N} T^{(n)}_{u_l,l} - Q^{\max}_{u_l}\right) + \upsilon_l \left(\sum_{u_l \in M_l} \sum_{n=1}^{N} \frac{\gamma^{(n)}_{u_l,l,1}}{\gamma^{(n)}_{l,e} NB,2} T^{(n)}_{u_l,l} - Q^{\max}_l\right) \\
& + \sum_{n=1}^{N} \psi_n \left(\sum_{u_l \in D^P_l} S^{(n)}_{u_l,u_l} g^{(n)}_{u_l,u_l^*,1} - I^{(n)}_{th}\right) + \sum_{n=1}^{N} \varepsilon_n \left(\sum_{u_l \in M_l} T^{(n)}_{u_l,l} g^{(n)}_{u_l,l^*,1} - I^{(n)}_{th}\right) \\
& + \sum_{u_l \in U_l} \lambda_{u_l} \left[R_{QoS} - \sum_{n=1}^{N} \left(x^{(n)}_{u_l} B_{RB} \log_2 \left(1 + \frac{S^{(n)}_{u_l,u_l} h^{(n)}_{u_l,u_l}}{x^{(n)}_{u_l} \omega^{(n)}_{u_l}}\right) \right. \right. \\
& \left. \left. \qquad + \bar{x}^{(n)}_{u_l} \tfrac{1}{2} B_{RB} \log_2 \left(1 + \frac{T^{(n)}_{u_l,l} h^{(n)}_{u_l,l}}{\bar{x}^{(n)}_{u_l} \mu^{(n)}_{u_l}}\right) \right) \right] \\
& + \sum_{u_l \in D^P_l} \sum_{n=1}^{N} \rho^{(n)}_{u_l} \left(I^{(n)}_{u_l,u_l,1} + \sigma^2 - \omega^{(n)}_{u_l}\right) + \sum_{u_l \in M_l} \sum_{n=1}^{N} \kappa^{(n)}_{u_l} \left(I^{(n)}_{u_l,l} + \sigma^2 - \mu^{(n)}_{u_l}\right)
\end{aligned}
\tag{35}
$$

First, take the derivative of the allocation variable of the transmit power of the direct D2D users $S_{u_l,u_l}^{(n)}$

$$\frac{\partial L}{\partial S_{u_l,u_l}^{(n)}} = -\frac{1}{\ln 2} x_{u_l}^{(n)} B_{RB} \frac{1}{1 + \frac{S_{u_l,u_l}^{(n)} h_{u_l,u_l}^{(n)}}{x_{u_l}^{(n)} \omega_{u_l}^{(n)}}} \frac{h_{u_l,u_l}^{(n)}}{x_{u_l}^{(n)} \omega_{u_l}^{(n)}} + \xi_{u_l} + \psi_n g_{u_l,u_l^*,1}^{(n)}$$
$$- \lambda_{u_l} \frac{1}{\ln 2} x_{u_l}^{(n)} B_{RB} \frac{1}{1 + \frac{S_{u_l,u_l}^{(n)} h_{u_l,u_l}^{(n)}}{x_{u_l}^{(n)} \omega_{u_l}^{(n)}}} \frac{h_{u_l,u_l}^{(n)}}{x_{u_l}^{(n)} \omega_{u_l}^{(n)}}$$

(36)

According to the KKT conditions, let $\frac{\partial L}{\partial S_{u_l,u_l}^{(n)}} = 0$, we can obtain $S_{u_l,u_l}^{(n)} = \frac{(\lambda_{u_l}+1)x_{u_l}^{(n)} B_{RB}}{\ln 2 \left(\xi_{u_l} + \psi_n g_{u_l,u_l^*,1}^{(n)} \right)} - \frac{x_{u_l}^{(n)} \omega_{u_l}^{(n)}}{h_{u_l,u_l}^{(n)}}$. Assume that $\Delta_{u_l,u_l}^{(n)} = \frac{(\lambda_{u_l}+1)B_{RB}}{\ln 2 \left(\xi_{u_l} + \psi_n g_{u_l,u_l^*,1}^{(n)} \right)}$, the optimal value of the transmit power of the direct D2D user is expressed as

$$Q_{u_l,u_l}^{(n)*} = \frac{S_{u_l,u_l}^{(n)*}}{x_{u_l}^{(n)*}} = \left[\Delta_{u_l,u_l}^{(n)} - \frac{\omega_{u_l}^{(n)}}{h_{u_l,u_l}^{(n)}} \right]^*$$

(37)

$[\xi]^+$ means that the result takes a value not less than zero as the effective value, that is $[\xi]^+ = \max\{\xi, 0\}$. Next, take the derivative of the allocation variable of the cellular user transmit power $T_{u_l,l}^{(n)}$

$$\frac{\partial L}{\partial T_{u_l,l}^{(n)}} = -\frac{1}{2\ln 2} y_{u_l}^{(n)} B_{RB} \frac{1}{1 + \frac{T_{u_l,l}^{(n)} h_{u_l,l}^{(n)}}{\bar{x}_{u_l}^{(n)} \mu_{u_l}^{(n)}}} \frac{h_{u_l,l}^{(n)}}{\bar{x}_{u_l}^{(n)} \mu_{u_l}^{(n)}} + \varsigma_{u_l} + \upsilon_l \frac{\gamma_{u_l,l,1}^{(n)}}{\gamma_{l,eNB,2}^{(n)}} + \varepsilon_n g_{u_l,l^*,1}^{(n)}$$
$$- \frac{1}{2\ln 2} \lambda_{u_l} \bar{x}_{u_l}^{(n)} B_{RB} \frac{1}{1 + \frac{T_{u_l,l}^{(n)} h_{u_l,l}^{(n)}}{\bar{x}_{u_l}^{(n)} \mu_{u_l}^{(n)}}} \frac{h_{u_l,l}^{(n)}}{\bar{x}_{u_l}^{(n)} \mu_{u_l}^{(n)}}$$

(38)

In the same way, according to the KKT conditions in the convex optimization theory, let $\frac{\partial L}{\partial T_{u_l,l}^{(n)}} = 0$, we can obtain

$$T_{u_l,l}^{(n)} = \frac{(\lambda_{u_l} + 1) \bar{x}_{u_l}^{(n)} B_{RB}}{2\ln 2 \left(\varsigma_{u_l} + \upsilon_l \frac{\gamma_{u_l,l,1}^{(n)}}{\gamma_{l,eNB,2}^{(n)}} + \varepsilon_n g_{u_l,l^*,1}^{(n)} \right)} - \frac{\bar{x}_{u_l}^{(n)} \mu_{u_l}^{(n)}}{h_{u_l,l}^{(n)}}$$

(39)

Then the optimal transmit power of the cellular user is

$$Q_{u_l,l}^{(n)*} = \frac{T_{u_l,l}^{(n)*}}{\bar{x}_{u_l}^{(n)*}} = \left[\Delta_{u_l,l}^{(n)} - \frac{\mu_{u_l}^{(n)}}{h_{u_l,l}^{(n)}} \right]^*$$

(40)

$$\Delta_{u_l,l}^{(n)} = \frac{(\lambda_{u_l} + 1) B_{RB}}{2\ln 2 \left(\varsigma_{u_l} + \upsilon_l \frac{\gamma_{u_l,l,1}^{(n)}}{\gamma_{l,eNB,2}^{(n)}} + \varepsilon_n g_{u_l,l^*,1}^{(n)} \right)}$$

(41)

Substituting $\bar{x}_{u_l}^{(n)} = 1 - x_{u_l}^{(n)}$ into the Lagrangian function and deriving a derivative about $x_{u_l}^{(n)}$, we can obtain the formula (42). According to the KKT conditions, let $\frac{\partial L}{\partial x_{u_l}^{(n)}} = 0$, the expression related to the Lagrange multiplier δ_n is obtained as (43). In formula (43), there are $\theta_{u_l,u_l}^{(n)} = \frac{S_{u_l,u_l}^{(n)} h_{u_l,u_l}^{(n)}}{\ln 2\left(x_{u_l}^{(n)} \omega_{u_l}^{(n)} + S_{u_l,u_l}^{(n)} h_{u_l,u_l}^{(n)}\right)}$, $\theta_{u_l,l}^{(n)} = \frac{T_{u_l,l}^{(n)} h_{u_l,l}^{(n)}}{\ln 2\left(\left(1-x_{u_l}^{(n)}\right)\mu_{u_l}^{(n)} + T_{u_l,l}^{(n)} h_{u_l,l}^{(n)}\right)}$.

$$
\begin{aligned}
\frac{\partial L}{\partial x_{u_l}^{(n)}} =& -B_{RB}\log_2\left(1 + \frac{S_{u_l,u_l}^{(n)} h_{u_l,u_l}^{(n)}}{x_{u_l}^{(n)} \omega_{u_l}^{(n)}}\right) + \frac{1}{2}B_{RB}\log_2\left(1 + \frac{T_{u_l,l}^{(n)} h_{u_l,l}^{(n)}}{\left(1-x_{u_l}^{(n)}\right)\mu_{u_l}^{(n)}}\right) \\
& - \frac{1}{\ln 2}x_{u_l}^{(n)} B_{RB} \frac{1}{1+\frac{S_{u_l,u_l}^{(n)} h_{u_l,u_l}^{(n)}}{x_{u_l}^{(n)} \omega_{u_l}^{(n)}}} \frac{S_{u_l,u_l}^{(n)} h_{u_l,u_l}^{(n)}}{\omega_{u_l}^{(n)}}\left(-\frac{1}{\left(x_{u_l}^{(n)}\right)^2}\right) \\
& - \frac{1}{2\ln 2}\left(1 - x_{u_l}^{(n)}\right) B_{RB} \frac{1}{1+\frac{T_{u_l,l}^{(n)} h_{u_l,l}^{(n)}}{\left(1-x_{u_l}^{(n)}\right)\mu_{u_l}^{(n)}}} \frac{T_{u_l,l}^{(n)} h_{u_l,l}^{(n)}}{\mu_{u_l}^{(n)}}\left(-\frac{-1}{\left(1-x_{u_l}^{(n)}\right)^2}\right) \\
& + \delta_n + \lambda_{u_l}\left(-B_{RB}\log_2\left(1 + \frac{S_{u_l,u_l}^{(n)} h_{u_l,u_l}^{(n)}}{x_{u_l}^{(n)} \omega_{u_l}^{(n)}}\right) + \frac{1}{2}B_{RB}\log_2\left(1 + \frac{T_{u_l,l}^{(n)} h_{u_l,l}^{(n)}}{\left(1-x_{u_l}^{(n)}\right)\mu_{u_l}^{(n)}}\right)\right) \\
& - \frac{1}{\ln 2}\lambda_{u_l} x_{u_l}^{(n)} B_{RB} \frac{1}{1+\frac{S_{u_l,u_l}^{(n)} h_{u_l,u_l}^{(n)}}{x_{u_l}^{(n)} \omega_{u_l}^{(n)}}} \frac{S_{u_l,u_l}^{(n)} h_{u_l,u_l}^{(n)}}{\omega_{u_l}^{(n)}}\left(-\frac{1}{\left(x_{u_l}^{(n)}\right)^2}\right) \\
& - \frac{1}{2\ln 2}\lambda_{u_l}\left(1 - x_{u_l}^{(n)}\right) B_{RB} \frac{1}{1+\frac{T_{u_l,l}^{(n)} h_{u_l,l}^{(n)}}{\left(1-x_{u_1}^{(n)}\right)\mu_{u_l}^{(n)}}} \frac{T_{u_l,l}^{(n)} h_{u_l,l}^{(n)}}{\mu_{u_l}^{(n)}}\left(-\frac{-1}{\left(1-x_{u_l}^{(n)}\right)^2}\right)
\end{aligned}
\tag{42}
$$

$$
\begin{aligned}
\delta_n = (\lambda_{u_l} + 1) B_{RB}\left(\frac{1}{2}\theta_{u_l,l}^{(n)} - \theta_{u_l,u_l}^{(n)} + \log_2\left(1 + \frac{S_{u_l,u_l}^{(n)} h_{u_l,u_l}^{(n)}}{x_{u_l}^{(n)} \omega_{u_l}^{(n)}}\right)\right. \\
\left. - \frac{1}{2}\log_2\left(1 + \frac{T_{u_l,l}^{(n)} h_{u_l,l}^{(n)}}{\left(1 - x_{u_1}^{(n)}\right)\mu_{u_l}^{(n)}}\right)\right)
\end{aligned}
\tag{43}
$$

The actual δ_n is not calculated by Eq. (43), but updated by sub-gradient iteration method, which will be described in detail in the following content. In order to obtain the integer value of the resource block allocation factor $x_{u_l}^{(n)}$, a threshold variable needs to be set as

$$
\begin{aligned}
\chi_{u_l}^{(n)} = (\lambda_{u_l} + 1) B_{RB}\left(\frac{1}{2}\theta_{u_l,l}^{(n)} - \theta_{u_l,u_l}^{(n)} + \log_2\left(1 + \frac{S_{u_l,u_l}^{(n)} h_{u_l,u_l}^{(n)}}{x_{u_l}^{(n)} \omega_{u_l}^{(n)}}\right)\right. \\
\left. - \frac{1}{2}\log_2\left(1 + \frac{T_{u_l,l}^{(n)} h_{u_l,l}^{(n)}}{\left(1 - x_{u_l}^{(n)}\right)\mu_{u_l}^{(n)}}\right)\right)
\end{aligned}
\tag{44}
$$

The discriminant formula of resource block allocation factor $x_{u_l}^{(n)}$ is shown in the following formula

$$x_{u_l}^{(n)*} = \begin{cases} 1, \delta_n \leq \chi_{u_l}^{(n)} \\ 0, \delta_n > \chi_{u_l}^{(n)} \end{cases} \tag{45}$$

After obtaining the optimal solution of the user-to-relay communication transmission power $Q_{u_l,l}^{(n)*}$, $Q_{u_l,u_l}^{(n)*}$ and resource block allocation factor $x_{u_l}^{(n)*}$, the sub-gradient iteration method is used to update each Lagrangian multiplier, and the Lagrangian multiplier of the $(t+1)$th iteration is updated according to the following formula, $\Lambda_\alpha^{(t)}$ is the step length during the first iteration, $\Lambda_\alpha^{(t)} = a/\sqrt{t}$ and a is a constant.

$$\delta_n(t+1) = \left[\delta_n(t) + \Lambda_{\delta_n}^{(t)} \left(\sum_{u_l \in U_l} x_{u_l}^{(n)} - 1 \right) \right]^+ \tag{46}$$

$$\xi_{u_l}(t+1) = \left[\xi_{u_l}(t) + \Lambda_{\xi_{u_l}}^{(t)} \left(\sum_{n=1}^{N} S_{u_l,u_l}^{(n)} - Q_{u_l}^{\max} \right) \right]^+ \tag{47}$$

$$\varsigma_{u_l}(t+1) = \left[\varsigma_{u_l}(t) + \Lambda_{\varsigma_{u_l}}^{(t)} \left(\sum_{n=1}^{N} T_{u_l,l}^{(n)} - Q_{u_l}^{\max} \right) \right]^+ \tag{48}$$

$$v_l(t+1) = \left[v_l(t) + \Lambda_{v_l}^{(t)} \left(\sum_{u_l \in M_l} \sum_{n=1}^{N} \frac{\gamma_{u_l l,1}^{(n)}}{\gamma_{l,eNB,2}^{(n)}} T_{u_l,l}^{(n)} - Q_l^{\max} \right) \right]^+ \tag{49}$$

$$\psi_n(t+1) = \left[\psi_n(t) + \Lambda_{\psi_n}^{(t)} \left(\sum_{u_l \in D_l^p} S_{u_l,u_l}^{(n)} g_{u_l,u_l^*,1}^{(n)} - I_{th}^{(n)} \right) \right]^+ \tag{50}$$

$$\varepsilon_n(t+1) = \left[\varepsilon_n(t) + \Lambda_{\varepsilon_n}^{(t)} \left(\sum_{u_l \in M_l} T_{u_l,l}^{(n)} g_{u_l,l^*,1}^{(n)} - I_{th}^{(n)} \right) \right]^+ \tag{51}$$

$$\lambda_{u_l}(t+1) = \left[\lambda_{u_l}(t) + \Lambda_{\lambda_{u_l}}^{(t)} \left[R_{QoS} - \sum_{n=1}^{N} \left(x_{u_l}^{(n)} B_{RB} \log_2 \left(1 + \frac{S_{u_l,u_l}^{(n)} h_{u_l,u_l}^{(n)}}{x_{u_l}^{(n)} \omega_{u_l}^{(n)}} \right) \right. \right. \right.$$
$$\left. \left. \left. + \bar{x}_{u_l}^{(n)} \tfrac{1}{2} B_{RB} \log_2 \left(1 + \frac{T_{u_l,l}^{(n)} h_{u_l,l}^{(n)}}{\bar{x}_{u_l}^{(n)} \mu_{u_l}^{(n)}} \right) \right) \right] \right]^+ \tag{52}$$

$$\rho_{u_l}^{(n)}(t+1) = \left[\rho_{u_l}^{(n)}(t) + \Lambda_{\rho_{u_l}^{(n)}}^{(t)} \left(I_{u_l,u_l,1}^{(n)} + \sigma^2 - \omega_{u_l}^{(n)} \right) \right]^+ \tag{53}$$

$$\kappa_{u_l}^{(n)}(t+1) = \left[\kappa_{u_l}^{(n)}(t) + \Lambda_{\kappa_{u_l}^{(n)}}^{(t)} \left(I_{u_l,l}^{(n)} + \sigma^2 - \mu_{u_l}^{(n)} \right) \right]^+ \tag{54}$$

4   Performance Analysis

Since there are random variables in each channel coefficient and interference link, the information rate of each resource block is also random. In order to reduce the influence of randomness on the simulation results, we have carried out a large number of simulations to calculate the average rate. This will eliminate the randomness of channel coefficients and obtain the fairness index of information rate in each resource block. This paper adopts RajJain fairness index to judge the information rate in each resource block. The definition of RajJain index is:

$$F = \left(\sum_{n=1}^{N} R_n \right)^2 \bigg/ N \sum_{n=1}^{N} R_n^2,$$ where N denotes the number of total resource

blocks in system, R_n stands for the information rate in resource block n. The parameters of simulation are shown in Table 1.

Table 1. System parameters of simulation.

Parameter of system	Value
Bandwidth of system	2.5 MHz
Number of total resource block	13
Path loss among D2D users	$102.9 + 18.7log[d(km)]$
Path loss between users and relay	$103.8 + 20.9log[d(km)]$
Path loss between relay and base station	$100.7 + 23.5log[d(km)]$
Standard deviation of shadow fading between D2D users	3 dB
Standard deviation of shadow fading between user and relay	10 dB
Standard deviation of shadow fading between base station and relay	6 dB
Range of transmitting power of relay	20–30 dBm
Range of transmitting power of user	13–23 dBm
Maximum distance among D2D direct users	20 m
Radius of coverage of relay	200 m
Distance between base station and relay	125 m
Power spectrum density of noise	−174 dBm/Hz
Interfering threshold	−70 dBm

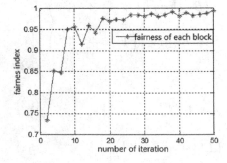

Fig. 2. Fairness index of each resource block.

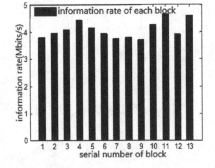

Fig. 3. Distribution of information rates in each resource block.

To check the correctness of theoretical analysis, we implement the following simulations. Assuming the number of resource blocks and total bandwidth of system are fixed. In our communication scenario, there are two relays, and the number of D2D pairs in each relay coverage area is the same as that of cellular users. For example, assuming there are four D2D pairs and four cellular users in relay 1 and relay 2 respectively. The simulation result in Fig. 2 shows that with the increase of number of iterations, the fairness index of information rate in each resource block is close to 1, which represents the user fairness becomes better gradually. These results show that averaging results of a lot of simulations indeed reduces the effect of random of channel. After 50 iterations, the information rate of each resource block is close to 4 Mbits/s as shown in Fig. 3.

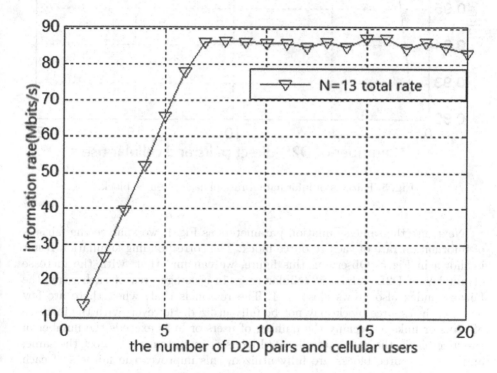

Fig. 4. Total information rate of system.

The simulation parameters of Fig. 4 is nearly 50 iterations and 13 resource blocks. Observing this figure, we can find that with the increase of number of D2D pairs and cellular users, the information rate of whole system first increases linearly, and then tends to a fixed value. Particularly, when the number of D2D pairs and cellular users are equal to 7 respectively, the peak information rate can be increased up to 85 Mbits/s.

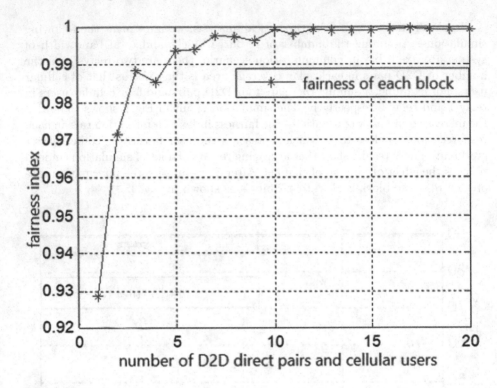

Fig. 5. Fairness of information rate of each resource block.

Next, use the same simulation parameters as Fig. 1, we analyze the fairness of information rate of each resource block. The corresponding simulation result is shown in Fig. 5. Observing this figure, we can find that, with the increase of number of D2D pairs and cellular users in coverage area of each relay, the fairness index also grows close to 1. The reason is that, when there are few users, each resource block may not be fully utilized. However, with the increase of users or links, especially the number of users or links exceeds the number of resource block, the resources allocated to users in system are almost the same, and total resource blocks are fully utilized, this improves the fairness of each resource block.

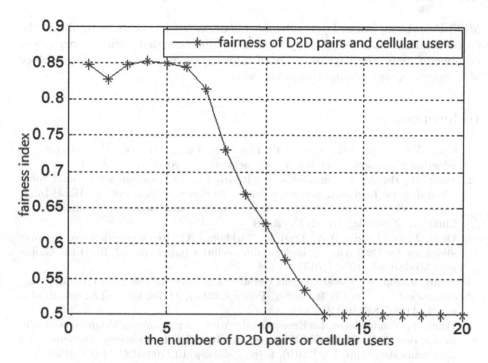

Fig. 6. The fairness of information rate of different users.

Use the same simulation parameters as Fig. 5, the fairness of information rate of different types of users are shown in Fig. 6. With the increase of number of D2D pairs and cellular users in covering area of each relay, the fairness of information rate of D2D pairs and cellular users decreases gradually. The reason is that, for each resource block, each slot can only be occupied by one user served by relays. When the number of users is larger than that of resource blocks, there is resource block competition between communication links. The above resource allocation scheme ensures that some of users have priority to use the current resource blocks and the other users have to wait for resource blocks. This leads to the decrease of fairness index of two kind of users in terms of information rate.

5   Conclusion

In this paper, we firstly set up a complex scenario, which includes base station of LTE-A, relays, and D2D pairs. Next, under the mode of direct D2D, we analyze the communication links of D2D pairs and cellular users, especially the interference of these links. Based on the above elements in scenario, we build the system model of information rate. Then we formulate this model into a

MINLP problem, utilize Lagrange multiplier and KKT conditions to obtain the optimal power allocation. The simulation results show that with the increase of number of users, the fairness index of information rate of each resource block also increases, and gradually approaches 1.

References

1. Cha, W.S., Song, J.K., Kim, S.T., Lee, T.J., Park, J.H., Oh, C.Y.: Method of selecting relay mode in mobile ad-hoc network. US 9060386 B2 (2015)
2. Yang, D., Bastos, J., Verikoukis, C., Rodriguez, J.: Location-aided round robin scheduling for fractional frequency reused LTE-A relay network. In: IEEE International Workshop on Computer Aided Modeling and Design of Communication Links and Networks, pp. 11–15 (2012)
3. Deng, J., Dowhuszko, A.A., Freij, R., Tirkkonen, O.: Relay selection and resource allocation for D2D-relaying under uplink cellular power control. In: IEEE Globecom Workshops. IEEE (2015)
4. Joung, J., Sun, S.: Power efficient resource allocation for downlink OFDMA relay cellular networks. IEEE Trans. Sig. Process. **60**(5), 2447–2459 (2012). https://doi.org/10.1109/TSP.2012.2187643
5. Wang, T., Vandendorpe, L.: Resource allocation for maximizing weighted sum minrate in downlink cellular OFDMA systems. In: IEEE International Conference on Communications, pp. 1–6 (2010). https://doi.org/10.1109/ICC.2010.5501904
6. Alam, M.S., Mark, J.W., Shen, X.S.: Relay selection and resource allocation for multi-user cooperative OFDMA networks. IEEE Trans. Wirel. Commun. **12**(5), 2193–2205 (2013). https://doi.org/10.1109/TWC.2013.032113.120652
7. Wen, S., Zhu, X., Lin, Z., Zhang, X., Yang, D.: Optimization of interference coordination schemes in device-to-device (D2D) communication. In: 7th International Conference on Communications and Networking in China, pp. 542–547 (2012). https://doi.org/10.1109/ChinaCom.2012.6417542
8. Yin, R., Zhong, C., Yu, G., Zhang, Z., Wong, K.K., Chen, X.: Joint spectrum and power allocation for D2D communications underlaying cellular networks. IEEE Trans. Veh. Technol. **65**(4), 2182–2195 (2016). https://doi.org/10.1109/TVT.2015.2424395
9. Ryu, H., Park, S.H.: Performance comparison of resource allocation schemes for D2D communications. In: 2014 IEEE Wireless Communications and Networking Conference Workshops (WCNCW), pp. 266–270 (2014). https://doi.org/10.1109/WCNCW.2014.6934897
10. Khosrowpour, M.: An overview of 3GPP long term evolution (LTE), 13–19 (2015)
11. Phunchongharn, P., Hossain, E., Kim, D.I.: Resource allocation for device-to-device communications underlaying LTE-advanced networks. IEEE Wirel. Commun. **20**(4), 91–100 (2013). https://doi.org/10.1109/MWC.2013.6590055
12. Periyalwar, S., Zhang, H., Senarath, N., Yu, D., Au, K.K., Mann, K.: System and method for peer-to-peer communication in cellular systems. US, US7548758 B2 (2018)
13. Park, K.J., Cho, H.G., Kwon, Y.H., Chung, J.H.: Method for transmitting an uplink signal and feedback information, and relay apparatus using the method. US, US20140286265 A1[P] (2016)

14. Yu, W., Lui, R.: Dual methods for nonconvex spectrum optimization of multicarrier systems. IEEE Trans. Commun. **54**(7), 1310–1322 (2006). https://doi.org/10.1109/TCOMM.2006.877962
15. Xu, Y., Yin, R., Chen, Q., Yu, G.: Joint licensed and unlicensed spectrum allocation for unlicensed LTE. In: 2015 IEEE 26th Annual International Symposium on Personal, Indoor, and Mobile Radio Communications (PIMRC), pp. 1912–1917 (2015). https://doi.org/10.1109/PIMRC.2015.7343611

Advanced Technology for 5G/6G (CROWNCOM 2021)

A Survey Channel Estimation for Intelligent Reflecting Surface (IRS)

Jiwayria M. S. D. Babiker and Xinlin Huang[⊠]

School of Electronics and Information Engineering, Tongji University,
Shanghai, China
{2090007, xlhuang}@tongji.edu.cn

Abstract. An intelligent reflecting surface (IRS), is a new era of wireless communication towards intelligent and reconfigurable wireless networks. IRS can enhance communication quality between the network terminals with a small cost, low complexity, and low energy consumption when the direct connection has been blocked. To obtain the IRS features, the acquisition of channel state information (CSI) is substantial but it's challenging in practice, due to the massive number of IRS elements without any capabilities of signal processing. To deal with this challenge in this survey, we first introduce an overview of channel estimation for IRS, then we address the main recent techniques proposed to estimate channels in IRS with various strategies in different applications. Furthermore, we summarize these recent works and list the main points that affect the estimation of the channel in IRS-aided communication system, and finally outline some future researches in IRS channel estimation and the conclusion of this survey.

Keywords: Intelligent reflecting surface (IRS) · Channel estimation · Pilot symbols

1 Introduction

IRS is a paradigm shift of wireless communications from traditional networks "just active components" to the hybrid networks "active and passive components". This hybrid network will be the backbone of the new technologies like beyond-5G, 6G, and so on.

In wireless communications, an IRS is used to assist the communication between the network terminals when the direct link is blocked [1]. IRS is an electromagnetic two-dimension (2-D) surface composed of a huge number of passive reflecting elements which are fabricated from meta-materials. It depends on altering the phase shift of the incident signals and then reflecting them to their intended destinations without transmitting or receiving signals, thus basically reducing power consumption, hardware cost, and complexity. There are many applications that used IRS- aided wireless communication systems such as physical layer security, a user at dead zone, a user at the cell edge, wireless information power transfer in internet-of-things (IoT) network, and massive device-to-device (D2D) communications [2]. Furthermore, there are many recent techniques that have the same behavior of reflecting the incident signals as the

© ICST Institute for Computer Sciences, Social Informatics and Telecommunications Engineering 2022
Published by Springer Nature Switzerland AG 2022. All Rights Reserved
H. Jin et al. (Eds.): CROWNCOM 2021/WiCON 2021, LNICST 427, pp. 169–180, 2022.
https://doi.org/10.1007/978-3-030-98002-3_12

IRS such as the metasurface or metamaterial reflectors [3, 4], the large intelligent reflecting surface [5–8], and the smart reflect-arrays [9, 10]. Despite the IRS's attractive advantages and applications, there are several challenges that clog using of the IRS in wireless communication systems, but, IRS reflection optimization, IRS deployment, and the IRS channel estimation are the main three challenges. In this survey, we treat the IRS channel estimation challenges.

To leverage the IRS techniques in wireless communications, channel estimation [7, 11–33], is essential because the IRS needs to acquire the CSI to set the reflection coefficients for its elements to reflect the incident signals. But it is the most critical challenge of the IRS due to the IRS's passive and massive elements. This means passive elements without any sensing capabilities to transmit or receive pilot symbols for channel estimation, the massive number of the IRS elements increase the number of paths to be estimated, and the CSI for the whole elements (i.e., full CSI) can't estimate during the limited channel estimation time.

Motivated by the above mentioned in this survey First, we review the main recent techniques used for IRS channel estimation and categorize them into three main methods, which are the cascaded channel estimation method when the IRS elements are fully passive elements, the partial channel estimation method when the IRS surface is equipped with some active elements beside the passive elements for channel estimation purposes, and the explicit channel estimation method when the IRS elements are equipped with some receive radio frequency (RF) chains to make the IRS has sensing capabilities to estimate the CSI. For each method, we explain how can estimate the CSI, show where the channel estimation has occurred (i.e., at the BS, the user, or the IRS), and review the recent related works. Furthermore, in the cascaded channel estimation, there are two manners, the reconstructing the full channel matrix manner and the beam training manner. For the first manner, we design a simple diagram to describe the main processes for IRS channel estimation and data transmission in a simple form. Second, to allow the IRS researchers and interested to clearly and directly acquire information, we summarize our review in a table by listing the current works in the IRS channel estimation ascending with their related methods, techniques, network scenarios, and the achieved outcomes. Lastly, we highlight some important future researches for the IRS channel estimation.

The rest of this paper is organized as follows. Section 2 presents the system model, the IRS channel estimation methods, and their related recent works. Section 3 summarizes the current works for the IRS channel estimation. Section 4 outlines several future works in the IRS channel estimation and Section 5 concludes the paper.

2   IRS Channel Estimation

In the IRS-aided communication systems, the estimate of CSI is quite significant but it is more challenging in practice due to the huge number of its passive elements. This section addresses the main types of IRS channel estimation, reviews, and summarizes the recent works which are carried out to estimate the CSI.

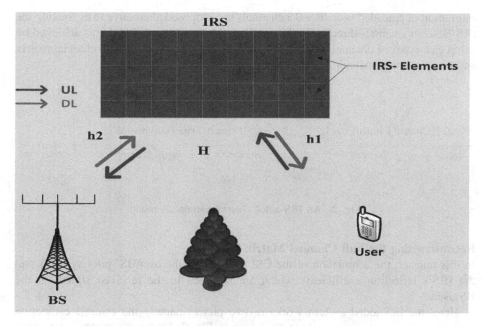

Fig. 1. An IRS-aided communication system

The IRS channel estimation methods are classified based on the type of the IRS elements which are passive, active elements, or elements equipped with some receive RF chains as shown in Fig. 1., into three categories: the cascaded, the partial, and the explicit channel estimation method, respectively.

System Model:
As shown in Fig. 1, the tree is blocking the direct channel between the user and the BS. Therefore, the user communicates with the BS through the IRS under the user-IRS channel (h_1) and IRS-user channel (h_2) which means the cascaded user-IRS-BS channel (H). The IRS consists of M passive reflecting elements each of which reflects the signals to their intended destinations. By considering the uplink (UL) transmission, the received signal Y(t) at the BS is:

$$Y(t) = H x(t)\Phi + n(t) \tag{1}$$

Where x(t) is the transmitted signal from the user, H is the cascaded user-IRS-BS channel reflection matrix, Φ is IRS reflection coefficients where $\Phi = \beta m$. Where are the reflection amplitude and the phase shift, respectively, and n(t) is the received noise.

In the following subsections, we present the IRS channel estimation methods one by one in more detail.

2.1 Cascaded Channel Estimation (Fully-passive IRS)

In the cascaded channel estimation, the IRS elements are totally fully passive without any active elements. So, in this case, due to the absence of sensing capabilities, the estimation of cascaded user-IRS-BS channels is a proposed alternative to estimating the IRS BS\user channels directly. in this method, the acquisition of CSI was achieved by using two types of channel estimation manners, reconstructing the full channel matrix and beam training manner.

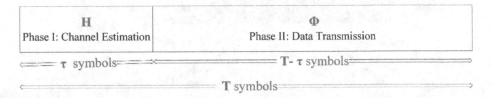

Fig. 2. An IRS-aided channel estimation mode

Reconstructing the Full Channel Matrix Manner

In this manner, the acquisition of the CSI depends on the user\BS' pilot symbols and the IRS's reflection coefficients which are included in the received signals at the BS\user.

Here, the IRS-aided system works in two phases namely the channel estimation phase and data transmission phase as shown in Fig. 2. Under the channel coherence time T symbols, in the channel estimation phase, the users (BS) send their UL (downlink (DL)) pilot symbols (τ symbols) to the IRS for channel estimation and the IRS reflects it to the BS (users). After the BS (users) estimates the channel reflection matrix (H), designs the passive beamforming (Φ), and feeds it (i.e., Φ) back to the IRS in the DL (UL). In the second phase, after adjusting the IRS, the users transmit their data over the residual of the channel coherence time T-τ symbols as shown in Fig. 3.

Related Works

Zheng *et al.* [11] considered an UL OFDM system, they groping the M IRS's passive reflecting elements with high channel correlation into K sub-surfaces to reduce the complexity of channel estimation and reflection design because the IRS's adjacent elements share a common reflection coefficient, this method was extended in [12]. Further, they proposed a full reflection of the IRS during both channel estimation and data transmission phases (i.e., the IRS elements are switched ON all the time).

You *et al.* [12] proposed a novel approach by exploiting the IRS elements grouping and partition, instead of the all-at-once approach which requires a number of pilot symbols depending on IRS elements which means the long length of pilot symbols, hence it increases the channel estimation time. The strategy followed in this work is as follows: the IRS elements are subdivided into K groups, each group partitioned into S sub-groups. First, estimate the CSI for effective channels in each group (per-group effective channel estimation) based on the designed basis training reflection matrix, after that collect the per-group effective channel estimation for each group. Next, resolve the subgroup aggregated channels, (Intra-group channel estimation) based on the designed subgroup training reflection matrix. At the last, from the estimated sub-group aggregated channels of all groups, optimize the passive beamforming vector for

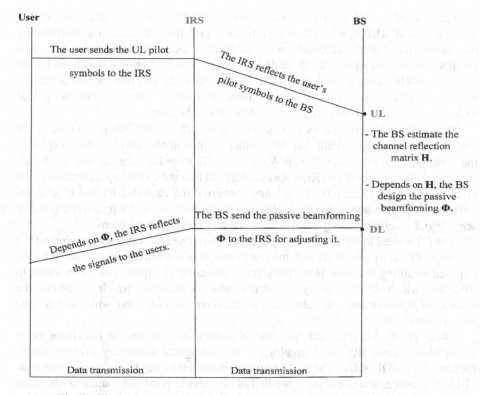

Fig. 3. The basic process to establish the IRS-aided downlink transmission

rate maximization. Here the required number of pilot symbols is reduced to the IRS groups instead of the number of the IRS elements as in the case of all-at-once channel estimation.

He *et al.* [13] introduced a framework for channel estimation with two stages algorithm, a sparse matrix factorization stage, and a matrix completion stage. They formulated the channel estimation problem for the reflected channels h_1 and h_2 from the received signal Y(t) as the matrix factorization problem and solved it by using the bilinear generalized approximate message passing (MiG-AMP) algorithm. Due to the diagonal ambiguity problem of a matrix factorization, they used the matrix completion stage with the Riemannian manifold gradient-based algorithm to solve this problem. Moreover, they provided the joint algorithm of the bilinear factorization (BF) and matrix completion (MC) channel estimation algorithms, which is denoted by (JBF-MC).

Mishra *et al.* [14] considered an ON-OFF state control strategy of IRS which is known as IRS binary reflection, under their proposed channel estimation protocol at each time slot only one IRS element is switched ON and the other elements are switched OFF so, their reflected channels h_1 and h_2 can be estimated one by one without any interference between reflected signals from other elements.

Jensen *et al.* [15] designed a channel estimation scheme to minimize Cramer- Rao lower bound (CRLB) under phase quantization and IRS attenuation constraints by proposing a novel method depends on the minimum variance unbiased estimator where all IRS elements are switched ON during the entire training period compared with the existing ON-OFF state control strategy. Moreover, they Showed that the IRS activation pattern impacts the performance of the channel estimation scheme, which is optimal under this scheme and suboptimal in the ON-OFF schemes.

Wang et al. [16] presented a channel estimation scheme for IRS in the case of the mm-Wave system. To formulation the channel estimation problem they first, exploited the inherent sparsity nature of mm-Wave channels to reduce the training overhead, then, used the Kronecker and Karti-Rao products to find the sparse representation of the cascaded h1 and h2 channels, lastly, they converted the cascaded h1 and h2 channel estimation problem into a sparse signal recovery problem. By applying the compressive sensing (CS) technique, they resolved the channel estimation problem.

The CS is used in signal processing systems to recover the signals by exploiting the property of sparsity of signals with the few numbers of measurements compared by the required sampling theorem. Here, the signal recovering is requiring two conditions to determine which signal recovery is probable, sparsity condition which is based on the sparsity of signal in some domains. And the incoherence condition, which is based on the isometric.

Zheng *et al.* [17] proposed two channel estimation schemes for broadband communication system IRS-aided employing the orthogonal frequency division multiplexing access (OFDMA). The first scheme is the simultaneous user channel estimation (SiUCE) scheme, which estimates the SCI of all users in parallel simultaneously at the BS. The second one is the sequential user channel estimation (SeUCE) scheme, which utilizes the fact that the IRS reflects the signals from all users to the BS via the same channel (IRS-BS channel). Specifically, first estimated the CSI for the arbitrarily selected user (it's called reference user), after that estimated the CSI for remaining users (it's called non-reference users) by normalized the CSI of reference user because the IRS reflected channels are the scale vectors of the reference user and to reduce the channel estimation time. For both schemes they derived minimum training time, the maximum number of supportable users, optimized the training design in terms of user pilot tone allocations and IRS reflection pattern to minimize the channel estimation error. Their results demonstrated that the SiUCE scheme has low complexity compared with the SeUCE scheme but the SiUCE scheme has able to support more users than the SeUCE scheme.

Wang *et al.* [18] proposed a novel pilot-based three-phase channel estimation framework for IRS-aided communication under sequential user channel estimation method by exploiting the correlation among the user-IRS-BS reflected channels of different users, which that each IRS element reflects the signals from all users to the BS via the same channel (as mentioned before). This framework is separated into three phases as follows, Phase I: They switched OFF the IRS and allow the BS to estimate the channel estimation by the traditional method. Phase II: They switched ON the IRS and allow for just one user to send its pilot symbols to the IRS, and IRS reflect it to the BS to estimate the channel estimation. Phase III: They allow for other users to send their pilot symbols to the IRS, and IRS reflects it to the BS to estimate the channel estimation.

Chen *et al.* [19] by utilizing the simultaneous user channel estimation method proposed a protocol for channel estimation in IRS-aided. Under this protocol, they formulated the channel estimation problem as a sparse channel matrix recovery problem using the CS technique to reduce the training overhead. In particular, they proposed a two-step procedure for multi-user channel estimation by exploiting the fact that, the sparse channel matrixes of the cascaded channels of all users have a common row-column block sparsity structure due to the common channel between BS and IRS. In the first step, project the signal into the common column subspace by considering common column-block sparsity to reduce complexity, quantization error, and noise. After that, in the second step, they apply all the projected signals and formulated a multi-user joint sparse matrix recovery problem by considering common row-block sparsity and they proposed an iterative approach to solving this non-convex problem efficiently.

You *et al.* [20] proposed two schemes for channel estimation problem in the case of using double-intelligent reflecting surfaces IRS-aided. The proposed double -IRSs are used to enhance the communication between the user and the BS when the reflected signals from a single IRS cannot pass all the barriers. In this work, they sub-divided the two IRSs elements into sub-surfaces as mentioned before in [11] and proposed two schemes to address the channel estimation problem under cascaded user-IRS1-IRS2-BS double-reflection channels (i.e., the user-IRS1 channel, the IRS1-IRS2 channel, and the IRS2-BS channel). The first scheme for any arbitrary inter-IRS (i.e., IRS1-IRS2) channel and the second scheme is customized under the assumption that the inter-IRS channel is line-of-sight (LOS) dominant. They showed that the second scheme has a smaller normalized mean square error (NMSE) with less channel time training compared with the first scheme.

Elbir *et al.* [21] proposed a framework for IRS channel estimation under mm-Wave massive MIMO systems. They proposed a double convolutional neural network (CNN) based on a deep learning network. The CNN is the joint use of convolutional layers (CL)s and fully connected layers (FCL)s and is fed by three channels data: real, imaginary, and the absolute value of each entry of the received pilot signals for channel estimation.

Elbir *et al.* [22] proposed a channel estimation framework for an IRS-aided massive MIMO system based on federated learning (FL). The proposed FL framework consists of three stages, namely training data collection, model training, and prediction stage. In the first stage, the users collect their training datasets from the received BS' pilot symbols for model training. In the model training stage, the users only transmit the gradients of the model parameters (i.e., model updates) to the BS rather than the whole datasets as in the centralized learning schemes so, the transmission overhead is reduced. After model training, in the prediction stage, users can estimate their channels by feeding the trained model with the received pilot symbols.

Beam Training Manner
In the beam training manner estimation, the passive IRS executes the set of operations that are known to the transceivers. Depending on these operations, the active terminals

on the network estimate the channel measurements and then send them to the IRS controller to design the beam patterns "beam directions" for data transmission.

Related Works

Ning *et al.* [23] considered beam training manner for IRS-aided channel estimation. They proposed a hierarchical codebook design for channel estimation and data transmission for a massive MIMO THz communication system. In this scheme, the IRS-aided system operates on two modes, return mode and direction mode. In the return mode: the cascaded transmitter (Tx)-IRS-receiver (Rx) channels are estimated by switching OFF the transmitter and receiver alternately. For the Tx-IRS channel estimation, switch OFF the Rx and allow the IRS to search the narrow beams which are knowns at all terminals on the network. After that, the IRS informed the Tx of the strongest return direction. Then, the Tx-IRS channel is estimated at the Tx. The IRS-Rx channel is estimated by switching OFF the Tx and following the same manner in the Tx-IRS channel estimation. In the direction mode, the Tx or Rx searches for the best direction depending on the estimated Tx-IRS-Rx channels and then sends it to the IRS controller for data transmission. Their work showed that accurate channel estimation can also be obtained by achieving beam training.

2.2   Partial Channel Estimation (Semi-passive IRS)

Here in the partial channel estimation, to facilitate the IRS channel estimation and beamforming reflection, the IRS surface is equipped with some active elements. Thus, the user\Bs sends the pilot symbols to IRS active elements for channel estimation, but in the reflection beamforming stage the active elements work as the residue of the passive elements that reflect the incident signals, and the machine learning techniques are used to learn the IRS how to interact with or reflect the incident signals.

Related Works

Taha *et al.* [24] proposed a novel solution for IRS channel estimation and reflection beamforming problems by using CS and deep learning approaches. In the CS approach after acquiring the channel knowledge at the active elements by using traditional method depending on the UL pilot signals, they developed the CS tools to recover all channels between the IRS and the transmitters/receivers from the channels at active elements (a.k.a sampled channels) without training overhead, and the IRS reflection beamforming vector was obtained by an offline search without beam training. In the deep learning approach, the IRS learns how to interact with the incident signals directly given the estimated sampled channel. This solution operates in two phases, the learning phase and predict phase. The deep learning model is trained through the learning phase while in the predict phase the system learns how to directly reflect the incident signals from the estimated sampled channels with the high data rates.

Their work was extended in [25] by proposing a novel framework by using the deep reinforcement learning (DRL) technique. The DRL is used to adjust the IRS reflection coefficients Φ without training overhead and to adjust the IRS reflection matrix for interacting with the incident signals because the DRL does not require an initial dataset collection phase. For the IRS interaction, the DRL-based IRS framework operates into two phases which are the agent interaction phase and agent learning phase. In the agent interaction phase, the IRS is interacting with the environment as follows: first, the IRS notices the present state (p) of the environment and take an action (c), based on the noticed state, the IRS then obtains a reward (w) for the action (c), lastly a new state notice (p') from the environment. In the agent learning phase, once the experience (p, c, w, p') is obtained, the DRL model is trained by the IRS by the present and past experience.

Liu *et al.* [26] proposed a deep denoising neural network-assisted compressive (CV-DnCNN) model for IRS channel estimation under millimeter-wave (mm-Wave) Massive MIMO system to reduce the training overhead. In this method, they activated some passive elements by equipping a few receive RF chains on it. First, they reconstructed the channel matrix H by using CS after that, they developed the angular-domain common sparsity of mm-Wave MIMO channels over different subcarriers to improve the accuracy, at last, they used their proposal CV-DnCNN for further enhancement. Their proposed model showed that the training overhead can be reduced by increasing IRS active elements and can use it at different signal-to-noise ratios (SNRs).

2.3 Explicit Channel Estimation (IRS Elements Equipped with Some Receive RF Chains)

In this method, the IRS elements are equipped with or connected to some receive RF chains to allow sensing capabilities for the explicit estimation. So, here the explicit channel from user\BS to IRS is estimated at the IRS based on the training signals.

Related Works

Alexandropoulos *et al.* [27] proposed a novel IRS hardware architecture by using a single active receive RF chain. In this architecture, the output of IRS is fed to the receive RF chain to estimate the channel at the IRS. Under the DL transmission, the BS sends its pilot symbols to the IRS to estimate the BS-IRS channel and the user sends its pilot symbols to the IRS to estimate the user-IRS channel. After the IRS was estimated the user-IRS-BS channel, it configured its phase shift and shared it with all of its elements for data transmission. Their simulation results demonstrated that using a single receive RF chain can achieve accurate channel estimation at the IRS.

Based on the above mentioned, the channel estimation in a cascaded manner occurs at the active terminals on the network (i.e., the BS or the user) and is achieved by the user\BS' pilot symbols or the beam training. In the channel estimation partial manner, it occurs at the IRS active elements based on the user\BS' pilot symbols. But in the explicit channel estimation manner, it occurs at the IRS depending on both user and BS' pilot symbols.

3 Summary

In this section, we summarize and classify the recent works of IRS channel estimation in a specific form as listed in Table 1. The summary includes five directions each of which has some classifications as follows: the IRS channel estimation method is based on cascaded, partial, or explicit channel estimation methods as we mentioned before in

Sect. 2, the IRS channel estimation problem formulation method which includes learning, mathematical and beam training method, the IRS reflection pattern depends on binary reflection or full reflection, the network context depends on the number of users (single-user or multi-user) and the type of the transmission (UL or DL transmission), and the evaluation of system performance which includes estimation error such as NMSE, mean-squared error (MSE), or least-squares (LS) and quantization error.

Table 1. Summary of the recent works of IRS channel estimation

Survey	Year	IRS channel estimation method			Problem formulation method			IRS reflection pattern		The Network context				System performance evaluation method			
		Cascaded channel estimation	Partial channel estimation	Explict channel estimation	Learning method	Mathimatical method	Beamtraining method	Binary reflection	Full reflection	Single-user	Multi-user	UL	DL	NMSE	LS	MSE	Quantization Erorr
Taha et al. [25]	2019			√	√				√	√		√					√
Mishra et al. [14]	2019	√				√		√		√		√				√	
Chen et al. [19]	2019	√				√		√			√	√	√	√	√		
He et al. [13]	2019	√				√		√		√		√		√			
Jensen et al. [15]	2019	√				√		√	√		√	√	√			√	
You et al. [12]	2020	√				√		√	√	√		√		√			
Zheng et al. [11]	2020	√				√		√	√	√		√		√			
Elbir et al. [21]	2020			√				√				√		√	√	√	
Liu et al. [26]	2020		√			√		√	√	√		√		√			
Wang et al. [16]	2020	√						√			√	√		√			
Elbir et al. [22]	2020			√				√			√	√	√	√			
Zheng et al. [17]	2020	√				√		√			√	√		√			
You et al. [20]	2020	√						√	√	√			√	√			
Taha et al. [24]	2020			√	√				√	√		√					√
Wang et al. [18]	2020	√				√		√		√		√	√	√			
Alexandropoulos et al. [27]	2020		√			√		√		√		√	√	√	√		
Ning et al. [23]	2020	√					√	√		√			√				√

4 Future Research

In the next few years, we expect that the IRS will change the face of wireless communications by combining active and passive terminals in one network. But until now, the acquiring of accurate CSI in practice still it is an open problem. So, the most important research direction is how to execute the existing IRS channel estimation proposals practically in the real world.

The second direction is in terms of estimating the channels related to all users in IRS-aided multi-user communication schemes, how to minimize the channel estimation time to maximize the data transmission time. The last direction is how to optimize the existing channel estimation scenarios in case of IRS elements grouping and partition to obtain high performance with low complexity, minimum channel estimation time, and minimum training overhead.

5 Conclusion

This survey presented an overview of channel estimation for IRS-aided communication systems, reviewed the recent related works, and highlighted the important future research directions for IRS channel estimation. We hope this survey becomes helpful in future research in this field and contributes to facilitating the IRS' challenges.

Acknowledgement. This work was supported in part by Shanghai Rising-Star Program under Grant 19QA1409100, in part by the National Natural Science Foundation of China under Grants 62071332, 61631017, and U1733114, and in part by the Fundamental Research Funds for the Central Universities. I would like to express my very great appreciation to Pr. Huang for his valuable and constructive suggestions during the planning and development of this research work. His willingness to give his time so generously has been very much appreciated.

References

1. Zhao, J.: A survey of intelligent reflecting surfaces (IRSs): Towards 6G wireless communication networks. https://arxiv.org/abs/1907.04789 (2019)
2. Wu, Q., Zhang, R.: Towards smart and reconfigurable environment: intelligent reflecting surface aided wireless network. IEEE Commun. Mag. **58**(1), 106–112 (2020). https://doi.org/10.1109/MCOM.001.1900107
3. Zhang, L., et al.: Space-time-coding digital metasurfaces. Nat. Commun. **9**(1), 4334 (2018)
4. Zhao, J., et al.: Programmable time-domain digital-coding metasurface for non-linear harmonic manipulation and new wireless communication systems. Natl. Sci. Rev. **6**(2), 231–238 (2018)
5. Hu, S., Rusek, F., Edfors, O.: Beyond massive MIMO: The potential of data transmission with large intelligent surfaces. IEEE Trans. Signal Process. **66**(10), 2746–2758 (2018)
6. Hu, S., Rusek, F., Edfors, O.: Beyond massive MIMO: The potential of positioning with large intelligent surfaces. IEEE Trans. Signal Process. **66**(7), 1761–1774 (2018)
7. Han, Y., Tang, W., Jin, S., Wen, C.-K., Ma, X.: Large intelligent surface-assisted wireless communication exploiting statistical CSI. IEEE Trans. Veh. Technol. **68**(8), 8238–8242 (2019). https://doi.org/10.1109/TVT.2019.2923997
8. Nadeem, Q.U.A., Kammoun, A., Chaaban, A., Debbah, M., Alouini, M.S.: Asymptotic analysis of large intelligent surface assisted MIMO communication. https://arxiv.org/abs/1903.08127 (2019)
9. Nie, S., Jornet, J.M., Akyildiz, I.F.: Intelligent environments based on ultra-massive MIMO platforms for wireless communication in millimeter wave and terahertz bands. In: IEEE International Conference on Acoustics, Speech and Signal Processing (ICASSP), pp. 7849–7853 (2019)
10. Tan, X., Sun, Z., Jornet, J.M., Pados, D.: Increasing indoor spectrumsharing capacity using smart reflect-array. In: IEEE International Conference on Communications (ICC), pp. 1–6 (2016)
11. Zheng, B., Zhang, R.: Intelligent reflecting surface-enhanced OFDM: Channel estimation and reflection optimization. IEEE Wireless Commun. Lett. **9**(4), 518–522 (2020)
12. You, C., Zheng, B., Zhang, R.: Intelligent reflecting surface with discrete phase shifts: Channel estimation and passive beamforming. In: Proceedings IEEE International Conference. Communications (ICC), Dublin, Ireland, June, pp. 1–6 (2020)
13. He, Z. Q., Yuan, X.: Cascaded channel estimation for large intelligent metasurface assisted massive MIMO. IEEE Wireless Commun. Lett. **9**(2), 210–214 (2020)
14. Mishra, D., Johansson, H.: Channel estimation and low-complexity beamforming design for passive intelligent surface assisted MISO wireless energy transfer. In: International Conference on Acoustics, Speech and Signal Processing (ICASSP), May 2019
15. Jensen, T.L., De Carvalho, E.: On optimal channel estimation scheme for intelligent reflecting surfaces based on a minimum variance unbiased estimator. https://arxiv.org/abs/1909.09440 (2019)

16. Wang, P., Fang, J., Duan, H., Li, H.: Compressed channel estimation for intelligent reflecting surface-assisted millimeter wave systems. IEEE Signal Process. Lett. **27**, 905–909 (2020). https://doi.org/10.1109/LSP.2020.2998357

17. Zheng, B., You, C., Zhang, R.: Intelligent reflecting surface assisted multi-user OFDMA: Channel estimation and training design. http://arxiv.org/abs/2003.00648

18. Wang, Z., Liu, L., Cui, S.: Channel estimation for intelligent reflecting surface assisted multiuser communications: Framework, algorithms, and analysis. IEEE Trans. Wireless Commun. (2020). https://doi.org/10.1109/TWC.2020.3004330

19. Chen, J., Liang, Y.C., Cheng, H.V., Yu, W.: Channel estimation for reconfigurable intelligent surface aided multi-user MIMO systems. https://arxiv.org/abs/1912.03619

20. You, C., Zheng, B., Zhang, R.: Wireless communication via double IRS: channel estimation and passive beamforming designs. IEEE Wireless Commun. Lett. **10**(2), 431–435 (2021). https://doi.org/10.1109/LWC.2020.3034388

21. Elbir, A.M., Papazafeiropoulos, A., Kourtessis, P., Chatzinotas, S.: Deep channel learning for large intelligent surfaces aided mm-wave massive MIMO systems. IEEE Wireless Commun. Lett. **9**(9), 1447–1451 (2020)

22. Elbir, A.M., Coleri, S.: Federated learning for channel estimation in conventional and IRS-assisted massive MIMO. https://arxiv.org/abs/2008.10846 (2020)

23. Ning, B., Chen, Z., Chen, W., Du, Y.: Channel estimation and transmission for intelligent reflecting Surface assisted THz communications. arXiv e-prints (2019)

24. Taha, A., Alrabeiah, M., Alkhateeb, A.: Enabling large intelligent surfaces with compressive sensing and deep learning. arXiv preprint https://arxiv.org/abs/1904.10136, Apr 2019

25. Taha, A., Zhang, Y., Mismar, F.B. and Alkhateeb, A.: Deep reinforcement learning for intelligent reflecting surfaces: towards standalone operation.https://arxiv.org/abs/2002.11101, May 2020

26. Liu, S., Gao, Z., Zhang, J., Renzo, M.D., Alouini, M.: Deep denoising neural network assisted compressive channel estimation for mmWave intelligent reflecting surfaces. IEEE Trans. Veh. Technol. **69**(8), 9223–9228 (2020)

27. Alexandropoulos, G.C., Vlachos, E.: A hardware architecture for reconfigurable intelligent surfaces with minimal active elements for explicit channel estimation. arXiv e-prints (2020)

28. Zhao, M.M., Wu, Q., Zhao, M.J., Zhang, R.: Two-timescale beamforming optimization for intelligent reflecting surface enhanced wireless network. In: 2020 IEEE 11th Sensor Array and Multichannel Signal Processing Workshop (SAM), pp. 1–5 (2020). https://doi.org/10.1109/SAM48682.2020.9104346

29. You, C., Zheng, B., Zhang, R.: Fast beam training for IRS-assisted multiuser communications. IEEE Wireless Commun. Lett. **9**(11), 1845–1849 (2020)

30. Wu, Q., Zhang, R.: Intelligent reflecting surface enhanced wireless network: joint active and passive beamforming design. IEEE Global Commun. Conf. (GLOBECOM) **2018**, 1–6 (2018). https://doi.org/10.1109/GLOCOM.2018.8647620

31. Lin, J., et al.: Channel estimation for wireless communication systems assisted by large intelligent surfaces. arXiv preprint https://arxiv.org/abs/1911.02158 (2019)

32. Wei, L., Huang, C., Alexandropoulos, G.C., Yuen, C.: Parallel factor decomposition channel estimation in RIS-assisted multi-user MISO communication. In: 2020 IEEE 11th Sensor Array and Multichannel Signal Processing Workshop (SAM), pp. 1–5 (2020). https://doi.org/10.1109/SAM48682.2020.9104305

33. Hu, R., Tong, J., Xi, J., Guo, Q., Yu, Y.: Matrix completion-based channel estimation for MmWave communication systems with array-inherent impairments. IEEE Access **6**, 62915–62931 (2018). https://doi.org/10.1109/ACCESS.2018.2877432

Artificial Intelligence (CROWNCOM 2021)

Minimum Class Variance Thresholding Based on Multi-objective Optimization

Liyong Qiao[✉], Huilong Jin, Chungang Liu, Jia Zhao, Wanming Liu, Ying Liu, and Zetong Lei

Hebei Normal University, Shijiazhuang, China
qiaoly@hebtu.edu.cn

Abstract. Variance-based thresholding is one of the most popular methods for image segmentation. The mechanism of variance-based thresholding methods is to minimize the class variance. A novel minimum class variance thresholding method based on multi-objective optimization has been presented, and the ideal threshold is achieved by minimizing the variance of each class and the sum of them, and this will lead to more satisfactory segmentation result. The presented method possesses the merits of restraining the class probability and the class variance effects, and it is more accurate. Firstly, the proposed method is compared quantitatively with other methods on lots of synthetic images with the convenience of obtaining the ideal thresholds precisely and the ground-truth images exactly. The presented method possess better performance at most magnitudes of the noise. At the same time, experiments over real infrared images and visual images also have illustrated the better performance of the presented method.

Keywords: Thresholding · Class variance · Multi-objective optimization

1 Introduction

In digital image processing, thresholding is one of the simple and effective methods for image segmentation. This method is based on the assumption that the intensity is similar within an object and different between different objects, and one appropriate threshold can be found to separate the object from the background [1–3]. And there have been many applications of thresholding for image segmentation, such as document image analysis, CT scan images, nondestructive testing, and so on. A large amount of thresholding methods have been developed due to their efficiency and simplicity, especially for two-class segmentation problems [1–3]. Among these methods, variance-based thresholding is a very popular technology for image segmentation [1–7]. The minimum within-class variance method proposed by Otsu is regarded as one of the classic methods [4]. Nonetheless, the Otsu method tends to shift the threshold towards the component with larger class probability or larger class variance. Hou et al. has explored the underlying mechanism responsible for Otsu method's bias, and proposed the MCVT method, which can overcome the Otsu method's disadvantages [5]. Li has proposed a new statistical thresholding method to avoid the negative influence caused by variance discrepancy between the object and the

H. Jin et al. (Eds.): CROWNCOM 2021/WiCON 2021, LNICST 427, pp. 183–191, 2022.
https://doi.org/10.1007/978-3-030-98002-3_13

background [6], but there is huge bias in the formula, and this method is called Li_1 for convenience in this paper. In addition, Li has proposed another statistical thresholding method for images in which the object and the background have similar statistical distribution [7], and this method is called Li_2 in this paper. Experiments on lots of corresponding images show that the two methods are not as effective as described, which has been analyzed in Sect. 2.

According to the theory of classifying and optimization, we have presented a novel minimum class variance thresholding based on multi-objective optimization (MCVT-MO). The presented method selects the threshold by a compromise solution. It can be applied to many classes of images effectively, such as infrared images, ordinary visual images, and even such images in which the object and background gray levels possess substantially overlapping distributions. Experiments in Sect. 3 show that the presented method possesses the MCVT method's advantages of overcoming the class probability and the class variance effects, but it is more accurate than the MCVT method.

This paper is organized as follows. In Sect. 2, the presented MCVT-MO method is formulated and a generalized MCVT method is defined. In Sect. 3, the performance of the presented method has been tested and compared with other methods on synthetic and real images. Finally, some concluding remarks are presented in Sect. 4.

2 Minimum Class Variance Thresholding Based on Multi-Objective Optimization

2.1 Theory of Multi-objective Optimization

A multi-objective optimization problem is formulated as follows [8]:

$$min(f(x) = (f_1(x), f_2(x), \cdots f_p(x))) \tag{1}$$

Over $x \in X$, X is the set of the non-inferior solutions of the vector optimization problem. This kind of problem is also called a vector optimization.

Generally, an optimal solution that minimizes all the objective functions simultaneous does not exist in multi-objective optimization problems, which are different from the programming problem with a single objective function. In this case, we can take the total balance of objectives into account to find a compromise solution. One of the most popular compromise solutions for the multi-objective optimization problems is the $l_p - norm$, which is defined as follows [8]

$$min\left\{ d_p\left(f(x), \widehat{f}\right) \triangleq \left\{ \sum_l^n W_j \left| f_j(x) - \widehat{f}_j \right|^p \right\}^{1/p} \right\} \tag{2}$$

Subject to $x \in X$.

Where $1 \leq p \leq \infty$, $\widehat{f}$ is the goal vector, W_j is the weight or priority given to the jth objective. $d(,)$ is the distance between $f(x)$ and $\widehat{f}$. If the goal $\widehat{f}_j$ is unattainable, the distance between $f_j(x)$ and $\widehat{f}_j$ can be considered to represent a measure of regret resulted from un-attainability of $f_j(x)$ to $\widehat{f}_j$. $min\left\{d_p\left(f(x),\widehat{f}\right)\right\}$ represents the minimum combined deviation from the goals $\widehat{f}_1,\widehat{f}_2,\cdots\widehat{f}_n$.

2.2   MCVT Based on Multi-objective Optimization (MCVT-MO)

As is known, the variance of a random variable X is a measure of dispersion or scatter from the mean in the possible values for X. Smaller variance corresponds to smaller dispersion from the center. The mechanism of variance-based thresholding methods is to minimize the class variance [5]. Therefore, the ideal threshold can be achieved by minimizing the variance of each class and the sum of them.

According the theories of variance and classifying, the goals to segment an image with two classes should be as follows

$$\sigma^2_{1min} = min\{\sigma^2_1(t), t = 0, 1, 2, \cdots L - 1\} \tag{3}$$

$$\sigma^2_{2min} = min\{\sigma^2_2(t), t = 0, 1, 2, \cdots L - 1\} \tag{4}$$

$$\sigma^2_{smin} = min\{\sigma^2_s(t), t = 0, 1, 2, \cdots L - 1\} \tag{5}$$

$$\text{with } \sigma^2_s = \sigma^2_1(t) + \sigma^2_2(t), t = 0, 1, 2, \cdots L - 1 \tag{6}$$

The above formulas (3–6) mean that when the object and background are well separated, the class variance $\sigma^2_1(t)$, $\sigma^2_2(t)$, and the sum of class variances $\sigma^2_s = \sigma^2_1(t) + \sigma^2_2(t)$ all should be minimized. However, they will not be minimized simultaneous with the same gray value t in most cases.

According to the theory of multi-objective optimization elaborated in Sect. 2.1, we adopt $l_2 - norm$ in this paper, and give three class variances $\sigma^2_1(t)$, $\sigma^2_2(t)$, $\sigma^2_s(t)$ the same weight or priority, $W_j = 1, j = 1, 2, 3$. Then, a compromise solution can be defined to have the minimum combined deviation of class variances from the desired goals $\sigma^2_{1min}, \sigma^2_{2min}$ and σ^2_{smin}.

$$J(t) = \left\{\left(\sigma^2_1(t)\right)^2 + \left(\sigma^2_2(t)\right)^2 + \left(\sigma^2_s(t) - \sigma^2_{smin}\right)^2\right\}^{\frac{1}{2}}, t = 0, 1, 2, \cdots, L - 1. \tag{7}$$

Then the optimal threshold t^* is determined as follows

$$t^* = Arg \min_{0 \le t \le L-1} J(t) \tag{8}$$

2.3   The Generalized MCVT Method

According to the theory of multi-objective optimization discussed in Sect. 2.1, if we adopt $l_1 - norm$, give the two class variances $\sigma^2_1(t)$ and $\sigma^2_2(t)$ the same weight or priority, $W_j = 1, j = 1, 2$, and do not consider the sum of class variances $\sigma_s^2 = \sigma_1^2(t) + \sigma_2^2(t)$, we can get another form of discriminating function $J(t)$. A compromise solution can be defined to have the minimum combined deviation from the desired goals σ_{1min}^2 and σ_{2min}^2.

$$J(t) = \sigma_1^2(t) + \sigma_2^2(t), t = 0, 1, 2, \cdots L - 1 \tag{9}$$

Then the optimal threshold t^* is determined as follows

$$t^* = Arg \min_{0 \le t \le L-1} J(t) \tag{10}$$

We can find that the MCVT method also can be obtained according to the theory of multi-objective optimization.

In addition, a generalized MCVT method can be defined as follows

$$J(t) = \left\{ \left(\sigma_1^2(t)\right)^p + \left(\sigma_2^2(t)\right)^p \right\}^{\frac{1}{p}}, 1 \le p \le \infty, t = 0, 1, 2, \cdots, L - 1 \tag{11}$$

the optimal threshold t^* is determined as follows

$$t^* = Arg \min_{0 \le t \le L-1} J(t) \tag{12}$$

According to aforesaid analysis, we can see that the MCVT method and MCVT-MO method are same in substance, and they just use different $l_p - norm$. Whereas the presented MCVT-MO method takes into account a more complete information including the distance between the sum of class variances $\sigma_s^2(t)$ and ideal σ_{smin}^2, and this will lead to more satisfactory segmentation result. The better performance of the MCVT-MO method has been proved in Sect. 3.

3 Contrastive Experiments and Analysis

A variety of synthetic of image and real images are chosen to test the five thresholding methods. To put into evidence the different performance features of these methods, we have used the following two performance criteria: misclassification error (ME) and segmentation error (SE). As paper [3], the two performance measures are adjusted so that their scores vary from 0 for a totally correct segmentation to 1 for a totally erroneous case. The arithmetic averaging of the normalized scores obtained from the two criteria is chosen as the indication of segmentation quality. Because the segmentation results of the algorithms are impacted seriously by the noisiness of the image, different performance of the algorithms are tested on the synthetic image added on Gaussian noise with different magnitudes.

3.1 Experiments on Synthetic Images

Firstly, the proposed MCVT-MO method is compared quantitatively with other methods on lots of synthetic images with the convenience of obtaining the ideal thresholds precisely and the ground-truth images exactly.

Figure 1(a) is a synthetic image with two intensities (the circle region is 50, the square region is 180), and Gaussian white noise is added to it, whose mean is 0 and variance is 0.015. Figure 1(b) is the histogram of the synthetic image, and the valley is at 104 marked as a dot in the figure. Figure 1(c) is the ground-truth image. Figure 1(d)–(h) are respectively the Otsu result, MCVT result, Li_1 result, Li_2 result, and MCVT-MO result.

From the thresholded images, one can see that the Otsu method almost perfectly segments the smaller circle component, but yields a noisier map in the largest square component. The Li_1 method, MCVT method and the proposed MCVT-MO method all lead to a cleaner segmentation map in the square component. The reason is that the Otsu method tends to shift the threshold towards the component with larger class probability or larger class variance [5], which is verified by the threshold 131 of the Otsu method. Nevertheless, the presented MCVT-MO method and the MCVT method can overcome the class probability and the class variance effects, and detect the valley more accurately than other methods as illustrated in Table 1. The threshold by the MCVT-MO method is exactly the valley, followed by the selected threshold 100 of the MCVT method. The difference between the threshold 131 determined by the Otsu method and the ideal threshold 104 is the biggest, which is followed by the Li_2 method and Li_1 method.

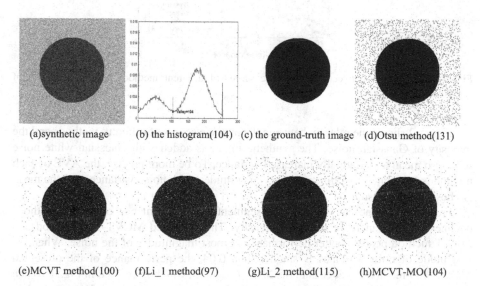

(a)synthetic image   (b) the histogram(104)   (c) the ground-truth image   (d)Otsu method(131)

(e)MCVT method(100)   (f)Li_1 method(97)   (g)Li_2 method(115)   (h)MCVT-MO(104)

Fig. 1. Experiment of different methods on the synthetic image (the number in the bracket denotes the valley of histogram or the threshold by the method)

Table 1. Experiment results of different thresholding methods on the synthetic image.

Method	Threshold	ME	SE	Average score (AVE)
Otsu	131	0.04404	0.13900	0.09152
MCVT	100	0.02010	0.04181	0.030955
Li_1	97	0.02235	0.05635	0.03935
Li_2	115	0.01953	0.02661	0.02307
MCVT-MO	104	0.01797	0.02334	0.020655

Table 1 lists the results in terms of threshold, ME, SE and the average scores (AVE), which are obtained by applying these thresholding methods to the synthetic noisy image shown in Fig. 1(a). From Table 1, one can see that the results of ME, SE and the AVE yielded by the proposed MCVT-MO method are the smallest among the five thresholding methods. Comprehensive speaking, the proposed MCVT-MO method should be considered the best among the five methods, followed by the MCVT method.

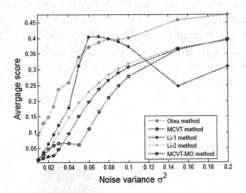

Fig. 2. The relation between the Average scores of different methods and the intensity of Gaussian noise.

Figure 2 shows the relation between the average scores of different methods and the intensity of Gaussian noise. The synthetic image is added with Gaussian white noise with zero mean and gradually increased variance. To be more precise, the AVE of each method is calculated five times at every magnitude of the noise variance, and the mean is chosen as the result.

From Fig. 2, one can see that the segmentation performance of all the methods declines with the increase of noise intensity. The presented MCVT-MO method and MCVT method possess better performance at most magnitudes of the noise. When the magnitude of noise variance is smaller than 0.04, the performance of the presented MCVT-MO method is better than the MCVT method, which is verified in Fig. 1. When the magnitude is bigger than 0.04, the result of comparison is reversed. However, when the magnitude is bigger than 0.1, the two methods' performance tends to be identical. The performance of the proposed MCVT-MO method, MCVT method and the Li_2 method varies gently, and the performance of the Otsu method and the Li_1 method varies sharply, especially the Li_1 method, which indicates that the stability of the method is poor.

3.2 Experiments on Infrared Images

The performance of the proposed MCVT-MO method has been tested and compared with other methods on lots of real infrared images. Owing to the intrinsic characteristics and abominable imaging environment, the infrared images are of poor contrast and faint edges, and the object and background gray levels possess substantially overlapping distributions, even resulting in a unimodal distribution, which can be seen in Fig. 3(a)–(b).

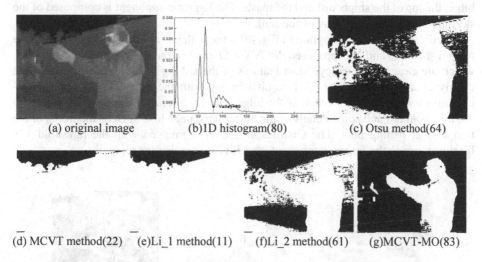

(a) original image   (b)1D histogram(80)   (c) Otsu method(64)

(d) MCVT method(22)   (e)Li_1 method(11)   (f)Li_2 method(61)   (g)MCVT-MO(83)

Fig. 3. Experiment of different methods on the real infrared images of irg04 group (the number in the bracket denotes the valley of histogram or the threshold by the method).

Figure 3(a) is infrared images selected from irg04 in Terravic Weapon IR Database of OTCBVS Benchmark Dataset Collection [9], which are video sequences showing muzzle blast and shell discharge. The size of the images is pixels.

From the histogram in Fig. 3(b), it can be seen that the image consists of three components. The darkest component mainly corresponds to the sky. The middle component is composed of the building and its shadow, the ground and trees. The brightest component is largely contributed by the shooter who is diffusing more heat. The valley between the middle and the brightest component is at 80. The threshold by the presented MCVT-MO method is 83, which is close to the valley. The shooter has been separated completely in the infrared image by the presented method. The threshold by the Otsu method is 64, which shifts towards the middle component with larger class probability. Portions of the building, the ground and the trees are misclassified as the object, and the segmented result is noisier by the Otsu method as illustrated in Fig. 3(c). The threshold by the Li_2 method is 61, and the result is worse. The thresholds by the MCVT method and Li_1 method are respectively 22 and 11. The building and its shadow, the ground and trees are all misclassified as the object, the shooter cannot be identified absolutely in Fig. 3(d)–(e).

3.3 Experiments on Other Images

The proposed MCVT-MO method has also been tested on lots of visible images, follows are two examples.

Figure 4(a) is a gray image chosen from the miscellaneous volume of USC-SIPI image database, which is maintained primarily to support research in image processing, image analysis, and machine vision [10]. The size of the image is pixels. The objects in Fig. 4(a) are three fishing boats. The darkest component mainly corresponds to the bilge, the top of the shipboard and the masts. The largest component is composed of the sky, the beach and most part of the hull.

As illustrated in the histogram in Fig. 4(b), the valley is at 80. The thresholds by the MCVT method and the proposed MCVT-MO method are respectively 75 and 85, which are close to the valley. Most features of the fishing boats can be discriminated clearly in their results. The Li_1 result is noisy with the threshold 96, which misclassifies some part of the beach as the bilge. The Li_2 result is under-segmented with the threshold 68, and some details of the object have been lost, such as the masts of the two smaller fishing boat. The Otsu result is over-segmented with the threshold 148 biasing towards the larger component, and it is very noisy perceptually.

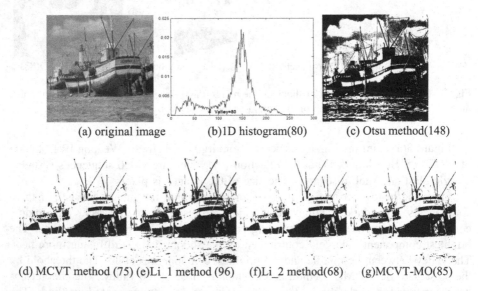

(a) original image   (b)1D histogram(80)   (c) Otsu method(148)

(d) MCVT method (75) (e)Li_1 method (96)   (f)Li_2 method(68)   (g)MCVT-MO(85)

Fig. 4. Experiment of different methods on the fishing boat image (the number in the bracket denotes the valley of histogram or the threshold by the method)

4 Conclusions

The mechanism of variance-based thresholding methods is to minimize the class variance. Therefore, the ideal threshold can be achieved by minimizing the variance of each class and the sum of them. According to the theory of multi-objective optimization, we have defined a compromise solution to have the minimum combined deviation from the desired goals.

In fact, the MCVT method can also be obtained through this theory as elaborated in Sect. 2.3. The presented MCVT-MO method possesses the MCVT method's merits of restraining the class probability and the class variance effects, and takes into account a more complete information including the distance between the sum of class variances and its ideal, which results in more reasonable thresholds. Experiments over synthetic images, real infrared images and visual images have illustrated that the performance of the presented method is better than the Otsu method, the MCVT method, Li_1 method, and Li_2 method.

Acknowledgements. This work was supported by Science Foundation of Hebei Normal University (Grant No. L2021B31). Our gratitude is extended to the anonymous reviewers for their valuable comments and professional contributions to their improvement of this paper.

References

1. Yang, P., Song, W., Zhao, X.: An improved Otsu threshold segmentation algorithm. Int. J. Comput. Sci. Eng. **22**, 146–153 (2020)
2. Messina, M., et al.: Modified Otsu's algorithm: a new computationally efficient ship detection algorithm for SAR images. Proc. IEEE **20**(2), 262–266 (2012)
3. Mehmet, S., Bülent, S.: Survey over image thresholding techniques and quantitative performance evaluation. J. Electron. Imaging **13**, 146–165 (2004)
4. Otsu, N.: A threshold selection method from gray-level histograms. IEEE Trans. Syst. Man Cybern. **1**, 62–66 (1979)
5. Hou, Z., Hu, Q., Nowinski, W.L.: On minimum variance thresholding. Pattern Recogn. Lett. **27**, 1732–1743 (2006)
6. Li, Z., Liu, C., Guanghai, L., Yong, C., Yang, X., Zhao, C.: A novel statistical image thresholding method. Int. J. Electron. Commun. **64**, 1137–1147 (2010)
7. Li, Z., Liu, C., Liu, G., Yang, X., Cheng, Y.: Statistical thresholding method for infrared images. Pattern Anal. Appl. **14**, 109–126 (2011)
8. Sawaragi, Y., Nakayama, H., Tanino, T.: Theory of Multi-objective Optimization, pp. 255–256. Academic Press Inc. (1985)
9. Otcbvs benchmark dataset collection: terravic weapon IR database. IEEE OTCBVS WS Series Bench. http://www.cse.ohio-state.edu/OTCBVS-BENCH/bench.html
10. The USC-SIPI image database, volume 3: miscellaneous. University Of Southern California. http://sipi.usc.edu/database/database.php?volume=misc

Pedestrian Detection Based on Deep Learning Under the Background of University Epidemic Prevention

Ruiyan Du, Jia Zhao[✉], Jiangfan Xie, and Tian Wen

Hebei Normal University, Shijiazhuang 050010, China
zhaojia2021@hebtu.edu.cn

Abstract. In the context of the current normalization of epidemic prevention, the nucleic acid detection process in colleges and universities is limited in human and material resources. Teachers and students who perform nucleic acid detection often cannot maintain a distance of more than one meter from others, and there is a pedestrian group behavior that has a large cross-infection safety hazard. This article uses Depthwise Separable Convolution to improve the YOLOv3 algorithm, and the improved network structure constructs a pedestrian detection, pedestrian tracking, pedestrian counting and pedestrian cluster system based on Deep Learning under the TensorFlow framework. The training parameters and training time of the improved network model are reduced to a certain extent, improved the operation efficiency of the network model. The advantage is that it realizes the function of monitoring centralized nucleic acid detection scenes in colleges and universities and assisting volunteers to maintain a reasonable order, which can effectively prevent cross-infection problems caused by cluster effects.

Keywords: YOLOv3 · TensorFlow · Pedestrian detection · Pedestrian tracking · Pedestrian counting

1 Introduction

1.1 The Development and Research Status of Pedestrian Detection Technology

The prevention and control of the epidemic situation in colleges and universities has long been a key link in the local prevention and control work. College students come from all over the country, and there is greater mobility within the school. In the process of regularly organizing and centralized nucleic acid testing for all relevant personnel, it was discovered that due to limited manpower and material resources, there are often group behaviors that pose safety hazards such as personnel gathering and trajectory overlap. Therefore, a pedestrian distance, trajectory, and number detection system based on deep learning has been constructed in colleges and universities. And a standardized nucleic acid detection execution mechanism is very necessary.

Pedestrian detection faces various challenges such as diverse human postures, complex detection scenarios, complex model building, and serious occlusion problems.

H. Jin et al. (Eds.): CROWNCOM 2021/WiCON 2021, LNICST 427, pp. 192–202, 2022.
https://doi.org/10.1007/978-3-030-98002-3_14

Therefore, there is a huge room for optimization and progress. Pedestrian detection essentially belongs to the category of target detection, and the effect of image feature extraction is the key factor affecting the detection quality. Pedestrian detection can be divided into the following two categories according to the extraction method of video features: one is traditional pedestrian detection algorithms that integrate machine learning, image processing and artificial design features, and the other is deep learning [1, 2] pedestrian detection method based on CNN feature extraction.

1.2   Traditional Pedestrian Detection Based on Machine Learning

In the 1990s, traditional pedestrian detection methods that integrated machine learning, image processing, and artificially designed features began to rise and gradually developed. Machine learning in the traditional mode uses the human body's own appearance characteristics for manual design to train classifiers. The target classification feature is obtained by pattern classification, and the extraction method of its main feature has gone through the following development process: In 1999, the SIFT scale invariant feature transformation can extract the scale information in the extreme points of the spatial scale [3]; in 2005, the edge orientation and intensity based on information research, a gradient histogram of all pixels in the grid was proposed [4, 5]; in 2008, a DPM variability component model using HOG features appeared, which can be independently modeled according to different parts of pedestrians. Generally speaking, the framework of traditional pedestrian detection can be divided into the following main modules, as shown in Fig. 1.

Fig. 1. The general sequence of the main modules in the traditional pedestrian detection

1.3   Pedestrian Detection Based on Deep Convolutional Neural Network

Traditional pedestrian detection based on artificial features and machine learning can achieve high accuracy under certain conditions. However, since Deep Learning has been applied to large-scale image classification, academia and industry have realized that the features learned by deep learning have excellent robustness. The CNN feature extraction technology can be traced back to the 1960s. Hubel and Wiesel [6] called the area sensed by neurons as the "receptive field" and discovered that the working mechanism of the nerve-center-brain is an iterative and abstract process. In 1980, Kunihiko Fukushima proposed a neurocognitive machine model that received two-dimensional analog signals to form a multilayer network with simple cognitive capabilities, that is, the earliest network form of CNN; Le Net-5 [7] came out in 1998, the training of the handwritten digit data set used back propagation to modify the network parameters. However, due to the hardware conditions of the computer at that time, the deep convolutional network entered the winter of research.

It was not until 2012 that Alex Net, an eight-layer neural network constructed with CNN technology and accelerated by GPU, was proposed for the first time, and more and more indepth neural networks came out in the upsurge. In the same year, R-CNN, a target detection algorithm appeared. The convolutional network in the algorithm is only used for feature extraction. The average accuracy of detection in standard databases is about 20% higher than that of traditional algorithms. Fast R-CNN was proposed in 2015, and the use of the SoftMax function greatly reduced the time consumed in the entire detection process.

Since the detection process is divided into candidate region generation and regression classification, the detection speed of the target detection algorithm based on region generation at that time was relatively slow. Later, the end-to-end skip region generation step YOLO [8] and SSD [9] algorithms appeared. Among them, the YOLO algorithm can achieve end-to-end target detection and divide the input image into S × S grids, and this grid will predict the bounding box and its confidence. If no object falls into the network cell, the confidence score should be zero.

In summary, in the current process of nucleic acid detection in colleges and universities due to limited human and material resources, there is a problem of pedestrian cluster behavior of the teachers and students who perform nucleic acid detection often cannot maintain a distance of more than 1 m from others. This article uses deep separable convolution to improve the YOLOv3 algorithm. Construct a pedestrian detection, pedestrian tracking, pedestrian counting and pedestrian cluster system based on Deep Learning under the TensorFlow framework to monitor centralized nucleic acid detection scenarios in colleges and universities to maintain a reasonable order, which can effectively prevent cross-infection problems.

2   Overview of Deep Neural Networks

As we all know, the ability of humans to think comes from the human brain, a complex network composed of billions of highly interconnected neurons. Therefore, the realization of brain-like intelligence [10] is inseparable from the study of the working mechanism of the brain. The computer can use "linear weighted sum" and "function mapping" to simulate the process of nerve cells receiving stimuli and outputting signals. Interpretation, labeling, and clustering of data features through the weight link and activation function algorithm of neural nodes between layers, class data features, the sequence data, the sequence data that we directly touch every day must be converted into numerical values before being sent to the neural network for deep learning before it can be operated on. A deep neural network consists of a network composed of multiple layers and several nodes that are connected and crossed to realize the specified algorithm. With the rapid development of computer hardware and performance, the three models of shallow fully connected network model, convolution network model and deep residual convolution network model can roughly represent the three change stages of neural network structure.

2.1 Shallow Fully Connected Network Model

The shallow fully connected neural network model has strong modeling capabilities for networks with few input features, and its structure is clear, which is easy to understand and operate. As shown in Fig. 2 below, the structure contains 10 input feature nodes. Calculation of the first layer (hidden layer): $z^{[1]} = W^{[1]} \cdot x + b^{[1]}$, $a^{[1]} = \sigma(z^{[1]})$ the calculation process of the second layer (output layer) network is similar to that of the first layer. There is a causal relationship between the network outputs y_1, y_2 and each input node.

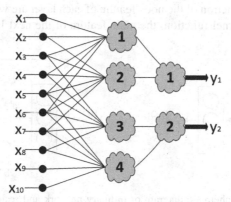

Fig. 2. Schematic diagram of shallow fully connected structure

Although the shallow neural network is relatively convenient to use, it is possible to build models for cases with more input features such as images, but the excessive number of weight matrices and offset vector parameters require higher computing capabilities for the computer, and the parameters to be trained too much, it is impossible to take into account the position information of the closer pixels between the pictures. In a network with a large number of layers, the loss function gradient transmission of this structure is more difficult, and the abstraction of the network expression will be affected, which limits the application scenario.

2.2 Convolutional Network Mechanism

With the introduction of deep learning and the improvement of hardware equipment, convolutional neural networks perform feature extraction and pattern recognition of image objects through an end-to-end learning method, and the local areas and functions of each layer of node features are weighted and activated by the convolution kernel function. After that, the node features of the next layer are obtained.

The convolution kernel of a convolutional neural network can share parameters. One of its advantages, which is different from ordinary neural networks, is its sparsity feature. This unique property can not only reduce the amount of model calculations, but also effectively limit its fitting ability; due to the maximum pooling operation of the feature map and its own computational characteristics, for the input features, the convolutional layer has the ability to move and not deform. The above features make the convolutional layer can still perform image feature extraction well under the premise of much fewer learning parameters work.

2.3 Deep Residual Network Model

Experiments have shown that after the number of layers of the neural network increases to a certain level, the convolution neural network carries out feature extraction and pattern recognition on the image object through an end-to-end learning method. After the local region and function of the node feature of each layer are weighted and activated by the convolution kernel function, the node feature of the next layer is obtained.

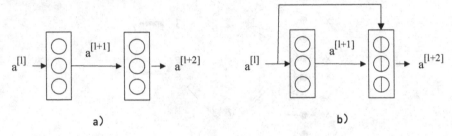

Fig. 3. Schematic diagram of ordinary network and residual unit

In Fig. 3, a) is a fragment of a plain network. The front and back layers of the Res Net network with the same feature map size. The necessary jump connections are added to each two layers to form a residual block. As shown in b), a shortcut is added. The network layer is between the l and l + 2 layers. This structure skips the feature matrix of the l + 1 layer and directly enters the l + 2 layer from the l layer for subsequent operations such as feature extraction. The residual network module learns $a^{[l+2]} = a^{[l]}$ is not difficult, so adding two jump layers to the neural network will not affect its performance.

3 Improved YOLOv3 Network Model

3.1 Brief Overview of YOLOv3 Algorithm

With the development of the concept of deep learning, the field of computer vision research and GPU computing performance continue to improve, allowing it to complete image analysis and processing tasks. Automatically marking the pedestrian bounding box position from the input video is the pedestrian target detection. This algorithm is the basis for intelligent analysis of pedestrian distance measurement, counting, and tracking in the nucleic acid detection video content of colleges and universities.

The YOLO algorithm proposed on the basis of deep learning in 2016 is an end-to-end learning method that inherits the algorithm idea of R-CNN, and performs classification and target regression in a convolutional network to greatly improve the detection speed and achieve for real-time target detection and multi-target detection tasks in the video field, the main idea of this algorithm is to divide the input image into $S \times S$ grid areas and detect the image whose center point falls into the grid. When YOLO is performing algorithm training, each cell with a target that is divided into $S \times S$ will select the prediction box with the largest IOU after the labeled data frame is compared to predict the target pedestrian object, making the other prediction bounding boxes of the grid indicates that the object is not included. However, the YOLO algorithm cannot achieve a very accurate prediction when the objects overlap. For example, when two objects fall into the same cell, only one object can be randomly selected for prediction.

3.2   Improved YOLOv3 Network Model

In the actual environment where the nucleic acid detection is concentrated in colleges and universities, it is found that YOLOv3 has high requirements for the GPU performance of the machine during training and prediction, and the actual detection effect is easily affected by external environments such as weather factors and scene layout. In order to further improve the universality of the algorithm, proposed to use depth separable convolution [11] to replace the convolution operation in the Res Net module, which greatly reduces the amount of model parameters.

Darknet-53 is a backbone network designed by YOLOv3 with 53 deeper neural network convolutional layers. It uses feature pyramid networks to design a multi-scale feature extraction structure. Its most notable feature is that it can perform target classification and location regression on three different scales. The network is composed of 3×3 and 1×1 convolutional layers, Res Net skip connection layer, upsampling layer for bilinear interpolation, feature fusion route layer and detection map output layer, etc. The three object detection processes are carried out by the 82nd, 94th, and 106th layers of the network. The input image sequence is divided into $S \times S$ grids, and a $52 \times 52 \times 255$ detection feature map is finally generated for classification and the location is back. On the basis of the backbone network Darknet-53, it is proposed to use deep separable convolution to replace the convolution operation in the Res Net module. Under the condition of reducing model training parameters, the function of improving the YOLOv3 algorithm to accelerate the network training speed is realized. The improved Darknet- 53 network structure is shown in Fig. 4.

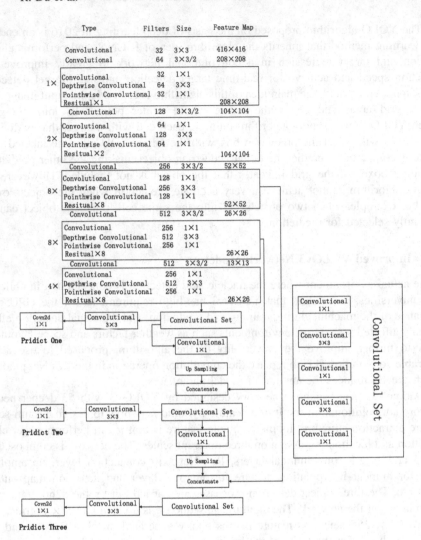

Fig. 4. Improved Darknet-53 network structure

Depthwise Separable Convolution extracts features by combining Depthwise (DW) and Pointwise (PW), reducing the amount of parameters and computing costs, and making the network more lightweight [12]. Channel-by-channel convolution performs independent convolution operations on each channel of the input layer, combined with point-by-point convolution, can further effectively use the feature information of different channels in the same spatial position, which is beneficial to the lightweight of the network. Improved YOLOv3 model the comparison before and after the feature extraction network is shown in Fig. 5.

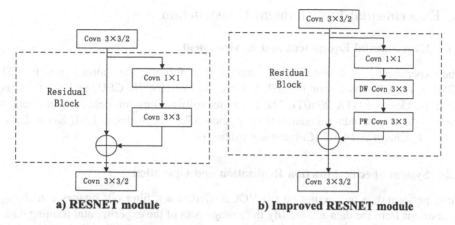

a) RESNET module　　　　　　**b) Improved RESNET module**

Fig. 5. Improved yolov3 model feature extraction network model structure

In order to realize the function of detecting the pedestrian detection, pedestrian tracking, pedestrian counting and pedestrian cluster system of collective nucleic acid detection in colleges and universities and maintain a reasonable order, a module for identifying and analyzing whether pedestrians have "cluster phenomenon" is added to the improved yolov3 network model. The specific output effect is shown in Fig. 6.

Fig. 6. Schematic diagram of "cluster phenomeno" output

This module mainly uses d(x, y): $=\sqrt{\sum_{i=1}^{n}(x_i - y_i)^2}$ to calculate the Euclidean distance between the person and the center point of the person, when the distance is less than twice its own width, it is judged as walking together, and the detection frames with cluster phenomenon are combined into a blue detection frame and output, marking group formation; people who are judged to be walking alone output a red detection frame, marking it as group destruction.

4   Experimental Environment Construction

4.1   Experimental Equipment and Environment

The experimental environment configuration is as follows: the motherboard is MSI B360M, the CPU processor is Intel(R) Core (TM)i9-10900K CPU, and the GPU is NVIDIA GeForce GTX 2080Ti. The computer software environment is: win10 operating system, anaconda-navigator1.9.12, python 3.7.6, TensorFlow 1.14, Keras 2.3.1, IDE is PyCharm 2019.3.2 (Community Edition).

4.2   System Specific Function Realization and Operation

First, perform data processing on the VOC2007 data set, filter out images containing pedestrians from the data set, modify the storage path of the experimental training data, run annotation.py to get 2007_train.txt and 2007_val.txt for training and verification, and then run check_data.py detects whether the data label is correct, and finally runs yolov_detector/trian.py to train the network to detect the location of pedestrians.

Train the deep residual network offline on the pedestrian re-recognition data set to train the DEEP SORT model, obtain pedestrian trajectories and count them through the Hungarian algorithm and Kalman filter, which are used to extract the features of the bounding box, and the appearance model is used to add rules for box matching. The appearance model adds rules for box matching, which can alleviate the occlusion problem and reduce the number of pedestrian ID switching.

Deep Sort uses a cascading matching algorithm. Each detector and each tracker that sets the time since update parameter can achieve one-to-one matching. The detection is constructed through the frame regression obtained by the bounding box learning, and the local maximum is filtered out by NMS. Finally, the probability of classifying the rectangular boxes that may be objects is screened out. After all the trackers of the previous frame are traversed and predicted, the results are stored and the effects of visualization, tracker update module, and feature set update module are achieved.

Pedestrian detection based on deep learning in the context of epidemic prevention and control in colleges and universities use PyQt to create a GUI application. Run main_ui.py under yolov3_ped_test. One-click to start the User Interface, click "Select Video" to retrieve the advance for the test video stored in the yolov3_ped_test folder, click "Start" to initialize the configuration of the running environment.

4.3   Experimental Results

After the configuration is complete, the detection system will start to detect, track, count and distinguish the cluster phenomenon of the input video. The total number of pedestrians displayed on the interface is the number of all pedestrians in the input video as shown in Fig. 7. The current number of pedestrians is the number of pedestrians in the video at this time. The number of pedestrians, each detected pedestrian will correspondingly output a detection frame and a corresponding color tracking line. The blue box indicates the cluster behavior of the detected object, that is, in the context of centralized nucleic acid detection in colleges and universities, there is a potential risk of

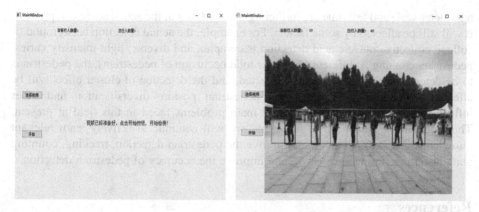

Fig. 7. User interface

cross infection in this cluster behavior. Relevant teachers and students should be notified to conduct nucleic acid detection at least at an interval of one meter or more according to the regulations.

The number of samples selected for one training of YOLOv3 is set to 16, and the Adam optimizer is selected. The initial learning rate is 1×10^{-3}. If the loss of the verification set does not drop for three consecutive times, the learning rate will be reduced to 0.1 times the original. Training for 100 epochs, after the training is completed, the pedestrian detection model training obtained by using tensorboard according to the training log is shown in Fig. 8. From the convergence curve, it can be considered that the network model training has reached the expected effect at this time.

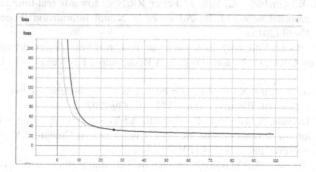

Fig. 8. Loss function curve

5 Conclusion

The pedestrian detection system based on deep learning in the context of epidemic prevention and control in colleges and universities implemented in this paper uses Depthwise Separable Convolution to improve yolov3 algorithm to effectively improve the accuracy and efficiency in a certain nucleic acid detection scene. Among them, the parameter scale and test time are further lightweight, but in the actual scene test process, it will still be affected by some factors. For example, the actual detection background of college collective nucleic acid detection is complex and diverse; light intensity varies; pedestrian clothing is different; partial or total occlusion of pedestrians; the pedestrians to be detected cannot be accurately selected, and the detection of cluster effect will be affected by small target passers-by; pedestrian posture diversification and other influencing factors, which are also the main problems faced in this field at present. Therefore, in the future study and work, we will continue to actively learn relevant knowledge and skills in the field, improve the pedestrian detection, tracking, counting and cluster discrimination system, and improve the accuracy of pedestrian detection.

References

1. Du, P., Chen, M., Su, T.: Deep Learning and Target Detection. Electronic Industry Press, Beijing, pp. 2–25 (2019)
2. Pooja, G., Varsha, S., Sunita, V.: People detection and counting using YOLOv3 and SSD models. Mater. Today. Proc. **44**, 2069–2079 (2021)
3. Li, L., Guo, B., Shao, K.: Geometrically robust image watermarking using scale-invariant feature transform and Zernike moments. Chin. Optics Lett. **06**, 332–335 (2007)
4. Zhu, Q., Yeh, M.C., Cheng, K.T.: Fast human detection using a cascade of histograms of oriented gradients. In: 2006 IEEE Computer Society Conference on Computer Vision and Pattern Recognition, pp. 1491–149. IEEE (2006)
5. Girshick, R.: Fast R-CNN. In: Proceedings of the IEEE International Conference on Computer Vision (ICCV), pp. 1440–1448 (2015)
6. Hubel, D.H., Wiesel, T.N.: Receptive fields, binocular interaction and functional architecture in the cat's visual cortex. J. Physiol. **160**(1), 106–154 (1962)
7. Ren, S., He, K., Girshick, R., Sun, J.: Faster R-CNN.: towards real-time object detection with region proposal networks. In: Advances in Neural Information Processing Systems (NIPS), pp. 91–99 (2015)
8. Redmon, J., et al.: You only look once: unified, real-time object detection. In: IEEE Conference on Computer Vision and Pattern Recognition, Las Vegas, NV, USA, pp. 779–788 (2016)
9. Cao, S., Zhao, D., Liud, X.: Real-time robust detector for underwater live crabs based on deep learning. Comput. Electron. Agric. **172**, 105339 (2020)
10. Redmon, J., Divvala, S., Girshick, R., Farhadi, A.: You only look once.: unified, real-time object detection. In: Proceedings of the IEEE Conference on Computer Vision and Pattern Recognition (CVPR), pp. 779–788 (2016)
11. Redmon, J., Farhadi, A.: YOLOv3: an incremental improvement. arXiv preprint: arXiv: 1804.02767 (2018)
12. Liu, W., et al.: SSD: single shot multibox detector. In: Leibe, B., Matas, J., Sebe, N., Welling, M. (eds.) ECCV 2016. LNCS, vol. 9905, pp. 21–37. Springer, Cham (2016). https://doi.org/10.1007/978-3-319-46448-0_2

Gesture Recognition Controls Image Style Transfer Based on Improved YOLOV5s Algorithm

Jiangfan Xie, Huilong Jin[✉], Tian Wen, and Ruiyan Du

Hebei Normal University, Shijiazhuang 050024, China
13131145063@163.com

Abstract. With the rapid development of artificial intelligence, human-computer interaction has drawn more researcher's attention. As one of the most important ways of human-computer interaction, Gesture recognition has been widely used in many fields. In this paper, an improved YOLOv5s gesture recognition algorithm is proposed, and the results of gesture recognition are used to carry out interactive experiments with the computer. Different gesture selects corresponding style, then the image style transfer network finishes the image style switch according to the image style. At the same time, PyQt5 is used to design an interactive interface to realize gesture recognition and image style conversion. Compared with YOLOv5s, the recall rate of gesture recognition by the improved algorithm is 94.77%, and the average accuracy is 96.46%, and the average accuracy of the improved YOLOv5s is 2.86% higher than YOLOv5s network, which is meeting the requirements of real-time and accuracy of image style transfer.

Keywords: Gesture recognition · YOLOv5 · Human computer interaction

1 Introduction

1.1 A Subsection Sample

In recent years, gesture recognition technology has been widely used and is a popular topic in computer vision field. Gesture recognition can be divided into contact type and non-contact type according to interaction mode.

Contact gesture recognition usually requires wearing a device with built-in sensors, and its recognition results have high accuracy and are not easily affected by external factors such as occlusion and illumination. Mina I. Sadek et al. divided Arabic Sign Language into multiple categories and used a few smart sensors to design gloves to judge gestures and obtain the meaning of Arabic sign language [1]. This method is simple in design and low in cost. Bin Fang et al. proposed a new type of data glove for capturing finger movements [2]. They carried out the finger motion capture experiment based on it, realizing the remote operation of manipulator through the acquired finger motion characteristics. This algorithm is easy to implement, and obtained more accurate and effective measurement results compared with existing methods. Yiyuan Zhang et al. reviewed the current research on using wearable sensors to identify the activities of the elderly in the bathroom, affirmed the important role of sensors in this research

H. Jin et al. (Eds.): CROWNCOM 2021/WiCON 2021, LNICST 427, pp. 203–212, 2022.
https://doi.org/10.1007/978-3-030-98002-3_15

[3], and advocated the combination with deep learning methods to achieve more accurate detection results.

Non-contact gesture recognition refers to gesture recognition method based on computer vision. This kind of method does not require the experimenter to wear any equipment, which has the characteristics of convenience, fast and easy to operate. Mohammed, A.A.Q et al. proposed an end-to-end method based on deep learning to detect and classify gestures [4]. In this method, the whole image is first extracted through the object detector for hand region, and then Convolutional Neural Networks (CNNs) carry out gesture recognition. The robustness and effectiveness of the proposed method are proved. Hua Li et al. proposed a gesture recognition system based on Leap Motion of the second generation [5], which could be used to recognize static gestures and dynamic gestures. The recognition rate of static gestures ranged from 94% to 100%, and that of dynamic gestures reached more than 90%. According to the experimental environment and the requirements of gesture recognition accuracy and speed, this paper chooses the non-contact gesture recognition method, and adopts YOLOv5s in the popular YOLO series algorithm to detect and classify gestures.

Style transfer is the transformation of general pictures into famous painting style, such as Van Gogh's Starry Night and Monet's Sunrise. Every painter has his own painting style. The purpose of style transfer is to transform the original picture into a specified painting style picture by computer, which can imitate the style. Meijun Sun et al. used MCCH feature selection model and Support Vector Machine (SVM) to describe Chinese painting styles and classify the works of different painters [6]. This paper chooses the algorithm proposed by Gatys et al. for image style transfer [7], which enables neural network model to learn different style images and generate corresponding style models. The model has a fast speed for new images, meeting the real-time requirements of this project.

2   Theoretical Foundation and Key Concepts

2.1   YOLOv5 Algorithms

Object detection algorithms based on deep learning can be roughly divided into two-stage algorithm and one-stage algorithm. In 2016, Redom et al. proposed one-stage object detector YOLO (You Only Look Once) [8] to solve the problem of inefficient two-stage object detection algorithm. In 2020, Jocher proposed YOLOv5, which has four network models: YOLOv5s, YOLOv5m, YOLOv5l and YOLOv5x. This paper selects the YOLOv5s model with the smallest network depth and the smallest feature map.

YOLOv5 has many advantages in hardware deployment, flexibility, and speed of the model. The overall structure is divided into four parts, including Input, Backbone, Neck, and Prediction. It includes two BottleneckCSP structures. The Cross-stage Partial structure (CSP) [9] is added into Residual Block [10], and BottleneckCSP1 contained Residual Block is mainly applied in Backbone. In the BottleneckCSP2 used in Neck part, the Residual Block is replaced with CBL structure, the structure of them is shown in Fig. 1.

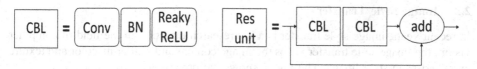

Fig. 1. The structure of CBL and Residual Block

The YOLOv5 network mainly uses the BottleneckCSP structure, as shown in Fig. 2. First, the classical residual structure Bottleneck operation is carried out, and the convolution results are added with the input through a 1×1 and 3×3 convolution operation. The other part is dimensionally reduced through 1×1 convolution, reducing the number of channels by half, and finally combining the two outputs. The number of Bottleneck structures in the LeneckCSP structure is the main point for residual learning and influences the improving of network performance.

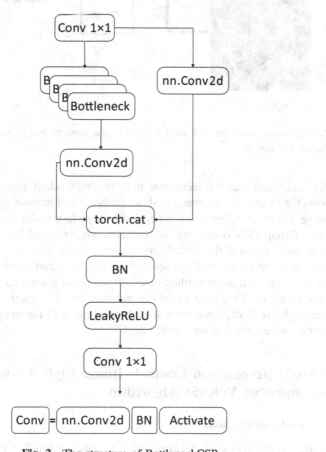

Fig. 2. The structure of BottleneckCSP

2.2   Image Style Transfer

In recent years, image style transfer is a hot research direction in the field of computer vision, the image style transfer keeps the image content and render its color and texture extracted from style image. The Fig. 3 shows the process.

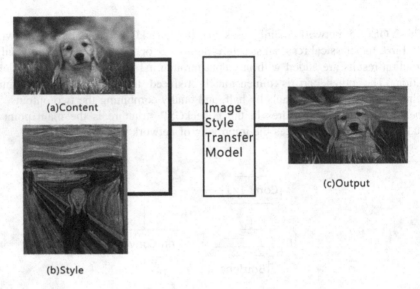

Fig. 3. The image style transfer model receives the content image and style image, then it generates a new image.

The traditional transfer technique uses the method of per-pixel compilation to transform the image, and its speed is slow, so the neural transfer style technique comes into being. Gatys et al. have developed a neural style transfer model based on Visual Geometry Group (VGG) network, which takes advantage of deep neural network and simultaneously extracts the underlying texture information and high-level semantic information of the image, and stylized images are generated by pixel iteration on noise images. Then the stylization method based on statistical parameters is used to match the style according to the global matching information. The method changes the pixel value through the Backpropagation at each pixel point of the image, which makes the composite image have a good visual effect.

3   Gesture Recognition Controls Image Style Transfer Based on Improved Yolov5s Algorithm

3.1   Project Introduction

PyQt5 used in this paper is a Qt application framework binding Python. Qt is a cross-platform framework for creating wonderful user interfaces and powerful native applications, and it is one of the best choices for human-computer interface development. Qt Designer allows us to design static interfaces that meet our needs. Using the Qt UI plug-in, we can convert interface files into a python callable format.

The interface is divided into two parts. The left part is gesture control area, which has two buttons called "start" and "end". The start and end button can open and close the camera, and control whether to display the shot picture. The right part is the image style transfer area, which has components to realize the selection and display of pictures in the local folder and the display of five style pictures controlled by five gestures. The project interface is shown in the figure below (Fig. 4).

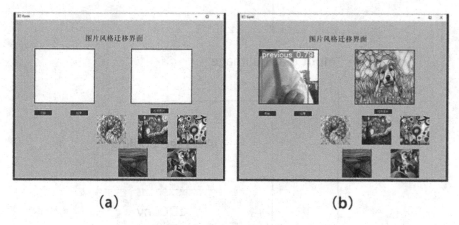

(a)   (b)

Fig. 4. Program interface

This project is based on YOLOv5s to achieve object detection of hand posture, and combines with the style transfer model, which can achieve real-time image style conversion. The two neural network models interact with each other through the interface designed by PyQt5. On the human-computer interaction interface, the human firstly shows gestures to the computer, which means giving instructions. The neural network model predicts gestures through each frame captured by the camera, and it obtains different instructions to complete the transformation of corresponding image styles. There are more and more applications in our daily life. For example, mobile phone camera can realize screen capture of mobile phone interface by recognizing hand gestures. In the field of smart home, it has been a trend to integrate multi-modal information such as visual information and sound information.

3.2 Improvements

The feature extraction network used by YOLOv5 algorithm is CSPDarknet. The network has a simple structure and low number of parameters.

With the rapid development of attention mechanisms, more and more studies have proved that channel attention mechanisms have great potential in improving the performance of CNNs. In order to balance the performance and complexity of the attention module, Qilong Wang et al. [11]. proposed the Effective Channel Attention (ECA) module. In order to further improve the efficiency and accuracy of gesture detection, we try to improve the feature extraction network structure of YOLOv5 and make it lightweight, and the attention mechanism is introduced to weigh the different channels of the feature map. The structure of the ECA is shown below (Fig. 5).

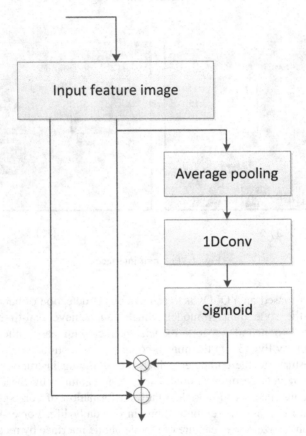

Fig. 5. The structure of ECA

As a result of the algorithm combined with the ECA layer design feature extraction network, the module has only a small increase in parameters, but has a significant performance gain. Adding the ECA structure into the Residual Block of the network can effectively fuse the information between different channels of the input feature graph, and improve the sensitivity of the algorithm to channel information. The structure of the algorithm in this paper is shown in the figure below (Fig. 6).

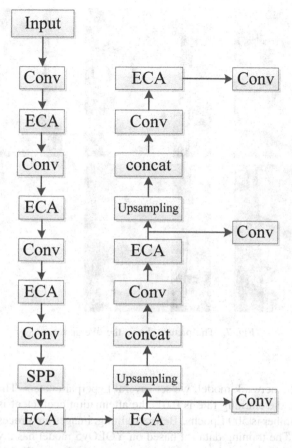

Fig. 6. The structure of the improved YOLOv5s

4 Experiments and Results

4.1 Dataset Description

The dataset used in this paper is a self-made dataset, including 1,597 training images and 400 test images. We use an application named LabelImg to label the dataset and label the minimum enclosing rectangle of the gesture in the image and save the annotations as XML. Then the training set and test set were randomly generated in the ratio of 4:1.

In order to enrich the data set and obtain better training results, the background is divided into two types when taking pictures, including pure color background and chaotic background. At the same time, the shooting distance is about 60 cm and the hand is in the center of the picture. Five gestures are selected as representatives, which represent the function of switching different styles in the picture style transfer.

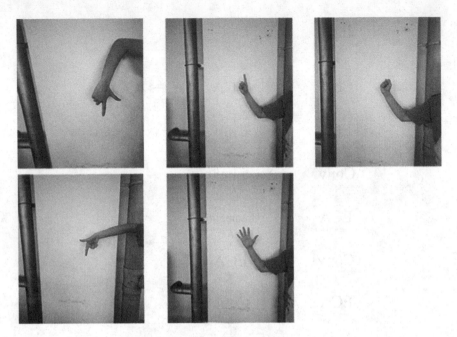

Fig. 7. The picture shows the five gestures.

4.2 Results

When training the network model, we set several hyperparameters. The iteration batch size is set as 16, the learning rate is 0.01, the attenuation coefficient is 0.005, and the total iteration number is 500 Epochs. Before training, images are processed to the same size 640 * 640. The training data set based on YOLOv5 model has a variety of image sizes, but due to the internal structure of the network, the image size is required to be a multiple of 32.

The experiment of this paper is carried out in windows10 system, equipped with Nvidia GeForce RTX 2080Ti graphics card, whose memory is 11 GB. We use Pytorch1.7 framework to set up the YOLOv5s model.

The gesture recognition accuracy based on the original algorithm has reached a high level. The recall rate of gesture recognition by the improved algorithm is 94.77%, and the average accuracy is 96.46%, which is 2.86% higher than the average accuracy of Yolov5s network. By comparing the mAP of the improved algorithm and the original algorithm in the training stage, we find that the convergence speed of the algorithm with ECA module is slightly faster than the original algorithm. The AP analysis of various gesture detection results shows that the improved algorithm has high detection accuracy for gesture.

Figure 7 shows gesture recognition using the improved YOLOv5s model. It can be seen from the figure if the color and shape of hands differ greatly from the background, the model will have a high accuracy in gesture prediction results. The recognition accuracy of the same gesture is slightly different under the background of pure color and cluttered background, the former is better than the latter (Fig. 8).

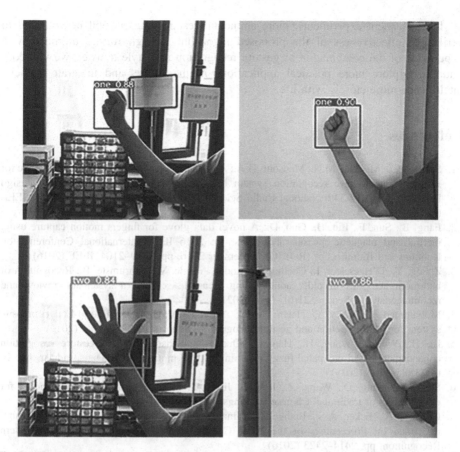

Fig. 8. The four images show the results of gesture recognition. The accuracy is more than 83%, regardless of whether the hand is on a solid or cluttered background.

5 Conclusion

This paper proposes an improved YOLOv5s gesture recognition network based on the existing YOLOv5 model and combined with practical applications, which can recognize hand posture more quickly and accurately. In this paper, the ECA module is added into the BottleNeckCSP, which improves the performance of the network architecture and the generalization capability of the model. Through the comparison experiment of different network models on self-made datasets, it shows that the MAP of the improved network has been improved to some extent, achieving the expected effect, laying a good foundation for the next image style transfer. Finally, in the static interface, the camera monitors gestures in real time to change the style of the imported image. The gesture recognition is accurate and fast, and the image style can be changed correctly, which proves the effectiveness of the algorithm.

In subsequent experiments, more abundant gesture datasets will be collected to verify the effectiveness of the proposed algorithm through further training. With experience of the combination of gesture recognition and style transfer, we will continue to explore more practical applications in the future, and integrate artificial intelligence more closely with life.

References

1. Sadek, M.I., Mikhael, M.N., Mansour, H.A.: A new approach for designing a smart glove for Arabic sign language recognition system based on the statistical analysis of the sign language. In: 2017 34th National Radio Science Conference (NRSC), pp. 380–388. IEEE (2017)
2. Fang, B., Sun, F., Liu, H., Guo, D.: A novel data glove for fingers motion capture using inertial and magnetic measurement units. In: 2016 IEEE International Conference on Robotics and Biomimetics (ROBIO), December 2016, pp. 2099–2104. IEEE (2016)
3. Zhang, Y., D'Haeseleer, I., Coelho, J., Vanden Abeele, V., Vanrumste, B.: Recognition of bathroom activities in older adults using wearable sensors: a systematic review and recommendations. Sensors 21(6), 2176 (2021)
4. Mohammed, A.A., Lv, Q., Islam, M.D.: A deep learning-based End-to-End composite system for hand detection and gesture recognition. Sensors 19(23), 52–82 (2019)
5. Li, H., Wu, L., Wang, H., Han, C., Quan, W., Zhao, J.: Hand gesture recognition enhancement based on spatial fuzzy matching in leap motion. IEEE Trans. Industr. Inf. 16(3), 1885–1894 (2019)
6. Sun, M., Zhang, D., Wang, Z., Ren, J., Jin, J.S.: Monte Carlo convex hull model for classification of traditional Chinese paintings. Neurocomputing 171, 788–797 (2016)
7. Gatys, L.A., Ecker, A.S., Bethge, M.: Image style transfer using convolutional neural networks. In: Proceedings of the IEEE Conference on Computer Vision and Pattern Recognition, pp. 2414–2423 (2016)
8. Redmon, J., Divvala, S., Girshick, R., Farhadi, A.: You only look once: unified, real-time object detection. In: Proceedings of the IEEE Conference on Computer Vision and Pattern Recognition, pp. 779–788 (2016)
9. Wang, C.Y., et al.: CSPNet: a new backbone that can enhance learning capability of CNN. In: Proceedings of the IEEE/CVF Conference on Computer Vision and Pattern Recognition Workshops, pp. 390–391 (2020)
10. He, K., Zhang, X., Ren, S., Sun, J.: Deep residual learning for image recognition. In: Proceedings of the IEEE Conference on Computer Vision and Pattern Recognition, pp. 770–778 (2016)
11. Wang, Q., Wu, B., Zhu, P., Li, P., Zuo, W., Hu, Q.: ECA-Net: Efficient Channel Attention for Deep Convolutional Neural Networks. arXiv preprint: arXiv:1910.03151 (2020)
12. Redmon, J., Farhadi, A.: Yolov3: an incremental improvement. arXiv preprint: arXiv:1804.02767 (2018)

Wireless Communication and Network Technology for Internet of Things (IoT) (CROWNCOM 2021)

Detection of Malicious Nodes Using Collaborative Neighbour Monitoring in DSA Networks

Augustine Takyi[1,2]($\boxtimes$), Natasha Zlobinsky[1], Odametey Akuye-Shika[2], David Johnson[1], and Melissa Densmore[1]

[1] Department of Computer Science, University of Cape Town, Rondebosch 7701, South Africa
{atakyi,mdensmore}@cs.uct.ac.za
[2] Department of Computer Science and Informatics, University of Energy and Natural Resources, Sunyani, Ghana

Abstract. This work addresses position falsification attacks of malicious nodes against spectrum users and devises a strategy to detect such nodes. We conducted over 6 months of measurements to confirm the practicability of using RSSI under varying weather conditions, which confirms that RSSI fluctuates along the mean. Also, the simulation results obtained show that collaborative neighbour monitoring in hybrid (centralized and distributed) networks work well in detecting position falsification attacks in dynamic spectrum access networks, provided that the distance between the actual malicious node position and the falsified position is at least 0.3 km.

Keywords: Spectrum sensing · Collaborative neighbour monitoring · Malicious node detection · DSA networks · Position falsification attack

1 Introduction

This paper advocates the idea of getting rid of malicious nodes that attempt to falsify their position to abuse the sharing principles of the dynamic spectrum access (DSA) networks, which may reduce throughput and increase latency. This subsequently affects the spectrum utilization. In view of this, the paper identifies some possible attack scenarios within a threat model and subsequently develops a detection algorithm to detect malicious nodes that may exploit the identified attack scenarios. Malicious nodes may falsify location information to mount attacks in the spectrum, causing harm to a primary transmitter or a neighbour secondary node. By falsifying its position the malicious node can easily adjust its parameters such as transmit power and antenna height to unduly cause unwarranted interference to prevent original nodes from transmitting. We study the above malicious node position falsification attacks in a network setup

© ICST Institute for Computer Sciences, Social Informatics and Telecommunications Engineering 2022
Published by Springer Nature Switzerland AG 2022. All Rights Reserved
H. Jin et al. (Eds.): CROWNCOM 2021/WiCON 2021, LNICST 427, pp. 215–230, 2022.
https://doi.org/10.1007/978-3-030-98002-3_16

of dynamic spectrum access-using network devices. Firstly, this is a challenging problem because of the coexistence of both the licensed and the unlicensed transmitters within the same space. Abusing spectrum etiquette of transmitting above approved power levels and antenna heights could have a serious effect on the genuine nodes. Secondly, the problem is challenging because of the shadowing and multipath fading effects in wireless transmissions. In mitigating shadowing and multipath fading effects we employ collaborative spectrum sensing, which improves the probability of detection in the highly shadowed environment [22].

The problem of position falsification in dynamic spectrum access networks has not yet been addressed in the literature. However, several works [1,6–8,12,21–23] have been proposed for detecting other forms of malicious attacks in DSA networks. Closest to our work is [22], which considers *malicious false reporting attacks* in a large cognitive radio network. Their study employed an approach of crowdsourcing of collaborative sensing to detect malicious users. However, the crowdsourcing of collaborative sensing approach cannot detect position falsification attacks, as the authors assume that there is no position falsification by the malicious node [22]. Hence, we develop an algorithm to resolve position falsification attacks, which is critical to consider is DSA-based networks.

In this work we develop an algorithm based on received signal strength indicator (RSSI) and fingerprinting of the node to detect any malicious node (a node that abuses the network rules) within the network. The algorithm is designed to operate in a back-haul of the network design architecture. The contribution of this paper is fourfold. First, we design a new system and threat model that fits in the DSA-based network. Second, we develop a threat model for the DSA-based network. Thirdly, we develop a detection strategy algorithm and also develop a naive detection algorithm based on common knowledge of statistics, using averages and dispersion of averages from similar data sets that operate at the layer one of the TCP/IP network layering architecture. The naive algorithm only depends on averages and standard deviation values. The results obtained from the naive algorithm as compared to the proposed algorithm are all false positives. We also show that computing weighted decision factors on the RSSI values of a neighbour node helps in making accurate decisions. The weighted decision factor introduces a new hypothesis: whether the node is malicious or not. Hence, the RSSI values obtained by using any of the free space models or the data propagation model or by measurement cannot be reliably depended on to make decisions in the proposed algorithm, unless the weighted decision factor of the RSSI values are obtained and computed and its hypothesis deduced to obtain the true status of the node as being malicious or not. Again, from the naive approach, averages and deviation values alone cannot be relied on to prove whether a node is malicious or not. Our algorithm depends solely on averages and dispersion of averages without the weighted decision factor to make decisions as to whether a node is malicious or not. Finally, we conduct simulations to investigate the effects of antenna height and distance on the propagation signal in the spectrum and also validate the proposed detection algorithm through simulation. Simulation results show that the algorithm is able to detect all falsified nodes with the minimum distance between the falsified position and the genuine position of at least 350 m.

2   System Model

In our model, we position fixed secondary (or unlicensed) nodes and malicious nodes, connected by a Central Decision Center (CDC), which is the decision-making platform implemented in the master node that controls the network, as also used by Basavaraj, Mancuso, and Probasco [5]. The CDC shall be the decision centre of the algorithm. The positions of the secondary nodes and the malicious users are independently distributed in an $(L \times L)\mathrm{km}^2$. We assume that all secondary and malicious nodes are embedded with spectrum analysers to capture the transmission signals from the neighbours within their transmission range. The obtained RSSI values and the node identification information are sent to the CDC. The ith device has position coordinates $P_i = (x_i, y_i)$ where, $i = 1, 2, 3, ..., n$. All our secondary user nodes are transceiver nodes. Each of the secondary users has a transmission range of R within the area. Each secondary node transmits at a power of P_s and the malicious nodes at a power of P_m. The secondary and malicious users are located at a minimum distance of L km from the primary user (licensed user within the spectrum), to prevent interference. Any RSS value received by the CDC below a threshold of λ is not used by the CDC in the estimation of channel statistic parameters. Secondary and malicious nodes are sensed using energy detection [17].

There are N secondary nodes and M malicious nodes in the system. Each secondary node communicates to the CDC over a secure end-to-end connection, such as a TLS tunnel, between each participating secondary node and the CDC [17]. Since we are interested in using our secondary nodes as back-haul nodes for our network, we assume that the secondary nodes are static and do not change position.

We again assume that malicious nodes may not have prior knowledge of all the nodes within its transmission range. This enables anonymous reporting about malicious nodes to the CDC to avoid compromising secondary nodes. Again, all nodes transmitting at an energy level greater than the approved energy level are considered to be malicious. We assume that all nodes can hear and decode any modulation scheme, which will prevent nodes from hiding behind modulation schemes to cheat on the network. Finally, we assume that each node on the network has an in-built system that is able to decode its neighbours' received signals to obtain their identities.

3   Threat Model

In our model, we assume that the links between the CDC and the secondary nodes are wireless and provide IP connectivity. We also assume that an attacker

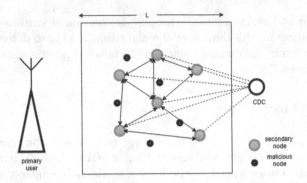

Fig. 1. Overall system model with six secondary nodes ($N = 6$) and five malicious nodes ($M = 5$).

has full access to the network medium between the CDC and secondary nodes and also between secondary neighbour nodes. We also assume that there is no mechanism to ensure confidentiality of the communication between the nodes. A malicious node on the network can cause an attack we refer to as a **position falsification attack (PFA)**. In a PFA the malicious node falsifies its location, resulting in physical and/or logical attacks. In a physical attack the PFA causes interference to neighbouring nodes on the network and in a logical attack the malicious user unduly takes channels that should be allocated to other nodes. An attacker exploiting PFA may pretend to be in the range of the network by adjusting its location information to conform to the propagation area of the network and request for a channel from the CDC just to deny genuine nodes from getting access to channels. Under such an attack the malicious node may increase its transmission power or antenna height above the agreed level in order to obtain a competitive advantage over the other secondary nodes. Any of the above can be exploited by the malicious node, thus negatively impacting on the performance of the network. Additionally, whenever any secondary node requests a channel from the CDC all the nodes within its transmission range hear the request. Again exploiting position falsification by a malicious node, the node can also create a Sybil attack [29] by creating several virtual nodes located in different locations as if those virtual nodes were part of the network.

All the attack scenarios considered in this threat model can highly affect the successful implementation of dynamic spectrum access based networks, especially opportunistic networks such as a TV White Space network deployment on a large scale. While the PFA as described in this work can occur in both fixed spectrum access (FSA) and dynamic spectrum access (DSA), it is a much more significant problem in DSA networks because of the scarcity of resources [14,15]. To detect these attacks, we propose to use collaborative neighbour monitoring.

4 Neighbour Monitoring in Cooperative Sensing

In neighbour monitoring, all nodes within transmission range of any transmitting secondary node in the network will hear it and measure its received signal strength (RSS). We do not rely on the individual nodes to report their RSSI values or distance from the CDC because malicious nodes can easily fake their RSSI values and their estimated range. Our proposed detection hypothesis is:

$$H_0 : \text{malicious node absent}$$
$$H_1 : \text{malicious node present}$$

We consider the main detection strategy proposed in the algorithm to detect malicious nodes if present.

4.1 Detection Strategy and Weighted Decision Factor at the CDC

In identifying a malicious node, we use a mean (average) received power indicator for all the individual neighbour nodes within the transmission range of the transmitter node. The CDC shall keep all the initially computed means of the received power values in dBm in its database and subsequently compare all the RSSI means calculated to check for deviations from the initially computed means. In the CDC, each node shall have separate means of the received power values measured for each neighbour node. Let the mean of the RSSI measurements from the ith neighbour of a given potential malicious node be represented by μ_i.

$$\mu_i = \frac{1}{S} \sum_{j=1}^{S} P_{ij} \quad \forall\, i,j \in \mathbb{N};\ i,j > 0 \tag{1}$$

where P_{ij} is the jth power sample obtained from the ith neighbour. Let σ_i represent the standard deviation of the power samples obtained from the ith neighbour node; that is

$$\sigma_i = \frac{1}{S} \sum_{j=1}^{S} (P_{ij} - \mu_i)^2 \quad \forall\, i,j \in \mathbb{N};\ i,j > 0 \tag{2}$$

The hypothesis decisions shall be the following:

$$\begin{cases} \text{if } |\mu_i - \mu_{ic}| \leqslant k\sigma_i \quad H_0 : \quad \text{no suspected malicious node} \\ \text{if } |\mu_i - \mu_{io}| > k\sigma_i \quad H_1 : \quad \text{suspected malicious node} \end{cases} \tag{3}$$

where μ_i is the initial mean of the received signal strength indicators and μ_c is the current mean of the received signal strength indicators and $k \in \mathbb{R}; k \leq 1$ is the threshold factor to account for interference and terrain conditions. To further compensate for the RSSI fluctuation we use weighted factors based on whether the node is potentially malicious and the initial advertised distance from the reporting neighbour node. In calculating the weighted factor, the estimated distance is compared with the advertised distance. We assume that any node whose estimated average received power is greater than or equal to twice the average advertised power of the node, is a potential malicious node as shown in Eq. (4). We therefore define the weighted factor in Eq. (5) based on the criteria defined in Eq.(4). If the null hypothesis is rejected by the Eq. (4), a weighted factor of 1 is assigned to the neighbour node; else the weight is assigned based on Eq. (5).

$$criteria = \begin{cases} -2\mu_i \leq \mu_i \leq 2\mu_i & \text{where either } H_0 \text{ or } H_1 \text{ is accepted} \\ \mu_{ic} > 2\mu_i & \text{where } H_0 \text{ is rejected} \end{cases} \quad (4)$$

where μ_i is the initial mean of RSSI and μ_{ic} is the current mean of the RSSI.

$$w_i = |\frac{\hat{d}_i}{D_i} - 1|, \ \forall i = 1, 2, 3, ..., N \quad (5)$$

where w_i is the estimated weight obtained from the estimated distance and the advertised distance, $\hat{d}$ is the estimated distance from the neighbour node, D is the initial advertised distance of the node and τ (which appears in Eq. (8)) is the tolerance factor to compensate for the variations in the RSSI values. The τ is set based on the initial advertised distance received at the CDC.

Therefore, for each node, the CDC computes the collaborative weight, W, on a node based on the neighbours within the sensed region using Eq. (6)

$$W = \frac{1}{N} \sum_{i=1}^{N} w_i \quad (6)$$

where N is the total number of the applicable neighbour nodes. We consider a weighted decision factor threshold at the CDC to be 10% of the total weights of the individual nodes calculated by the CDC of the individual nodes. Let I be the indicator variable for the weighted factor hypothesis.

$$I = \begin{cases} 0 & \text{where } H_0 \text{ is accepted} \\ 1 & \text{where } H_0 \text{ is rejected} \end{cases} \quad (7)$$

Therefore the hypothesis will be

$$\begin{cases} |\frac{\hat{d}}{D} - 1| \geq \tau & H_1 : \text{ malicious node present} \\ |\frac{\hat{d}}{D} - 1| < \tau & H_0 : \text{ malicious node absent} \end{cases} \quad (8)$$

This means that the collaborative weight W calculated by Eq. (6) is always less than 0.90 when H_0 is to be rejected. Based on this strategy we propose the detection algorithm that is as depicted in Algorithm 2.

4.2 Malicious Node Localization

The malicious node can then be localized using trilateration [35]. However, implementation of this component of the algorithm is out of the scope of this work. Let the location error be represented by lr and the location error threshold be represented as $lr_{threshold}$. Then the localization decision is given by the following:

$$\begin{cases} lr \leqslant lr_{threshold} : & \text{position not falsified} \\ lr > lr_{threshold} : & \text{position falsified} \end{cases} \tag{9}$$

5 Naive Detection Approach

We compare the naive detection algorithm with our cooperative weighted decision detection algorithm that goes further to compute weighted values and considers environmental factors of the terrain conditions. As shown in Tables 1 and 2 using our cooperative weighted decision detection algorithm shows more effective as compared to the naive approach. The naive algorithm is obtained from the idea of statistics which indicates that same datasets obtained should have the same deviation. According to common knowledge in statistics, when a node does not change its position, it shall produce similar signal strength at any time interval, which is expected to be the same dataset. However, according to this work, a node may falsify its position or change some of its parameters such as the power and antenna height to achieve its goal, by providing different datasets of RSSI values to cheat the system. So ideally, if a node in a DSA network does not change its position or parameters, then there will not be significant changes or deviations from the mean values obtained at any given data point such as n (for all n greater than zero and less than infinity).

5.1 Naive Detection Hypothesis

$$\text{naive hypothesis} = \begin{cases} H_0 : |\mu_i - \mu_c| > \sigma_i : & \text{the node is malicious} \\ H_1 : |\mu_i - \mu_c| \leq \sigma_i : & \text{the node is not malicious} \end{cases} \tag{10}$$

where μ_i is the initial mean of the initial dataset;
μ_c is current mean of the current dataset;
σ_i standard deviation of the initial dataset;
Each dataset is obtained from at least 20 simulation runs.

$$If \; lr \leqslant lr_{threshold} \; then, \; position \; not \; falsified$$
$$If \; lr > lr_{threshold} \; then, \; position \; falsified \tag{11}$$

5.2   Naive Detection Algorithm and Test Results

Table 1. Detection of malicious node M using naive algorithm by neighbour monitoring nodes

Node	μ_i	μ_c	μ_i-μ_c	σ_i	Hypothesis
A	−75.2889	inf		inf	accept H_0
B	−70.7047	−84.6650	−13.9603	7.2180	reject H_0
C	−52.7557	−73.3967	−20.6410	6.8531	reject H_0
D	−64.3251	−82.4262	−18.1011	7.1369	reject H_0

The simulation results as shown in the Tables 1 and 2 indicate that all the neighbouring nodes of node M shows that M is not a malicious node and accepted H_0 (null hypothesis), which confirms that node M as indicated in Fig. 2 is not a malicious node.

Algorithm 1. Naive Detection algorithm based averages

1: Set i, j := 0; Set $\{P_{ij}\}$:=∅;
2: Set N; Set S;
3:
  for (i, j) **do**
      Set d_{ij}:= 0;
  end for
4:
  for i; i ≤ N; i++ **do**
    for j; j ≤ S; j++ **do**
        Read received power values p_{ij}
        if $p_{ij} < \lambda$ **then**
          discard value
        end if
    end for
    Send P_i to fusion center
    Compute μ_i
    Compute σ_i
  end for
5: verify the detection using (3)
  if $|\mu_i - \mu_{ic}| \leqslant k\sigma_i$ **then**
      No suspicious malicious node
  else if $|\mu_i - \mu_{ic}| > k\sigma_i$ **then**
      Malicious node suspected
  end if
7: Compute the location errors using (11)
  if $lr \leqslant lr_{threshold}$ **then**
      malicious node position not falsified
  else if $lr > lr_{threshold}$ **then**
      malicious node position falsified
  end if

Algorithm 2. Cooperative Weighted Decision Detection Algorithm (CWDDA)

1: Set i, j := 0; Set $\{P_{ij}\}$:=$\emptyset$;
2: Set N; Set S;
3:
   for (i, j) **do**
      Set d_{ij}:= 0;
   end for
4:
   for i; i $\leq$ N; i++ **do**
      for j; j $\leq$ S; j++ **do**
         Read received power values p_{ij}
         if $p_{ij} < \lambda$ **then**
            discard value
         end if
      end for
      Send P_i to CDC
      Compute μ_i
      Compute σ_i
   end for
5: verify the detection using (3)
   if $|\mu_i - \mu_{ic}| \leqslant k\sigma_i$ **then**
      No suspicious malicious node
   else if $|\mu_i - \mu_{ic}| > k\sigma_i$ **then**
      Malicious node suspected
   end if
6: Compute weights according to (5)
   if $|\frac{\hat{d}_i}{D_i} - 1| \geq \tau$ **then**
      Malicious node present;
   else if $|\frac{\hat{d}_i}{D_i} - 1| < \tau$ **then**
      Malicious node absent;
   end if
7: Compute the location errors using (11)
   if $lr \leqslant lr_{threshold}$ **then**
      malicious node position not falsified
   else if $lr > lr_{threshold}$ **then**
      malicious node position falsified
   end if

Table 2. Detection of malicious node M using CWDDA by varying distances as indicated in Fig. 2

Node	μ_i	μ_c	μ_i-μ_c	σ_i	Hypothesis
A	0	−75.2889	0	6.9234	accept H_0
B	−84.6650	−70.7047	13.9603	6.7720	reject H_0
C	−73.3967	−52.7557	20.6410	6.1937	reject H_0
D	−82.4262	−64.3251	18.1011	6.5585	reject H_0

5.3   Comparison of Naive Algorithm to Cooperative Weighted Decision Detection Algorithm

In reference to Algorithm 1, the naive algorithm which is based on common statistical knowledge, i.e., it depends on the mean and standard deviation of similar datasets obtained from multiple simulation runs of RSSI values of neighbour nodes and determine how the current means deviate from the initial means obtained from similar datasets by comparing the means to its standard deviation and determine the hypothesis (the null (H_0) and alternative (H_1)). However, the cooperative weighted decision detection algorithm takes into consideration the expected differences in the RSSI values due to the environmental factors such as weather conditions and the intention of each node to cheat the system by introducing weighted factors and the threshold factors in the algorithm. The results of the two algorithms show that the naive approach in most times show that there is malicious node even when there is no malicious node and the vice versa. It can therefore be concluded that naive approach cannot be depended on in detecting malicious node, which may give false location information if computed. The cooperative weighted decision detection algorithm has three levels of hypothesis testing, whereas the naive approach has one hypothesis test, which is based on mean and standard deviation only. This indicates that the naive approach is not verified after the first hypothesis test, hence the result is not confirmed. Its output cannot be compared to the cooperative weighted decision detection algorithm, which verifies the first hypothesis twice before the algorithm completes.

6   Real World Measurements

As part of our work, we undertake real-world measurements on the University of Cape Town campus to verify the possibility of using received signal strength values to detect malicious nodes. In the measurement setup, we use two routers with 2.4 GHz WiFi, 5 GHz WiFi, and TVWS (television white space) network cards in each router as well as directional antennas for both the WiFi and the TVWS transmissions. We collected our data using a laptop on the 2.4 GHz WiFi band with the support of a measurement script we wrote. In the measurements, we considered the following variable parameters apply: channel number, channel width, transmission power and the distance between the two secondary nodes. The weather and terrain conditions were considered. The measurement results are shown in Table 3.

Table 3. Measurement of signal strength taken at a distance of about 200 m with one tree between the secondary nodes obstructing the signals

Ch no.	Ch width	TxPower	Min (RSSI)	Max (RSSI)	Mean (RSSI)	Std (RSSI)
1	20	20	−63	−54	−55.8	4.0249
1	20	15	−82	−58	−67	6.9585
1	10	20	−42	−28	−34.86	7.14
1	10	15	−28	−23	−25.83	1.309

Table 4. Experimental parameters

Parameter	Value
Secondary power	4 W to 10 W
Secondary height	10 m to 30 m
Frequency	470–694
Transmission range	1 km to 10 km
Antenna gains	5 dbi to 20 dbi

7 Experimental Set Up

We test this algorithm with by doing a simulation in Matlab. We adopt the Hata propagation model [4], which supports different terrain propagation. The values of the numerical parameters we consider for our simulation test are listed in Table 4. We consider Fig. 2 in the experimental setup when testing our detection algorithm above through simulation. In both Fig. 2 we positioned five nodes, of which node M was a malicious node that falsified its location. We run the simulation with different position coordinates and measure the effectiveness of our proposed algorithm.

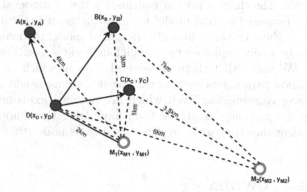

Fig. 2. Attacker may be positioned within the victim's network as M_1 but falsify its position as M_2 or the attacker may be positioned outside the victim's network as M_2 and falsify position as M_1 for verification by the CDC.

8 Results and Discussion

8.1 Simulation

In all the simulations, I fixed the k value at the threshold of 1. This is because I assumed there are no varying environmental effects that affected the propagation. The results obtained were much more interesting. In Table 3, I observed that when node A could not detect node M, it recorded the current mean as

Inf (infinity) and subsequently recorded node M as not malicious. Nodes B, C and D detected node M because the collaborative weights assigned to the three nodes were significant, node M was labelled by the CDC as a malicious node.

8.2   Models

This chapter designed a system model and a threat model which best fit in the scenario considered by this thesis. In the system model, the number of secondary and malicious nodes were independently distributed within a range in order not to create MAC layer issues. CDC was also considered as the part of the nodes that accepts and computes RSSI values and runs that detection algorithm. In the system model, it is assumed that all secondary and malicious nodes are embedded with spectrum analyzers to capture the transmission signals from the neighbour nodes and forward same to the CDC. In the system model, it is further assumed that the nodes are static and do not change positions. Again the model assumed that malicious nodes may not have prior knowledge of all the nodes within the transmission range. This enables anonymous reporting about malicious nodes to the CDC to avoid compromising secondary nodes. All nodes are embedded with equal moderation and de-moderation scheme which may prevent nodes from hiding behind different moderation scheme to cheat the system. The system model considered is a unique model applicable for DSA networks where channel availability is rare. The chapter further considers a threat model that assess the loopholes in the proposed system model for an attacker or malicious node may take advantage to cheat on the system. In the threat model the main attack that is considered to be easily exploited by a malicious node is Position Falsification Attack (PFA). We noted that there are several ways in which an attacker can pretend its position parameters such as varying it antenna height and changing its approve power transmission level, which are detailed explained in chapter 3 of the thesis. To prevent this attack from happening the chapter proceeded to develop an algorithm that seeks to detect malicious nodes that try to falsify their position.

8.3   Algorithm - CWDDA

The algorithm (CWDDA) is developed to check nodes either malicious or genuine secondary nodes that tries to alter its transmission power or antenna height to increase or decrease its transmission signal strength to cheat the system or faulty nodes that may transmit unevenly in the network. The algorithm computes averages of signal strength and employs other detection strategies such as weighted decision factor that computes weight on every RSSI value received by the CDC. In computing the weighted factor, every node have an advertised position so when RSSI value is received by the CDC, the CDC decoded to know the node that forwarded the RSSI value and by using an appropriate signal propagation model the distance is estimated from the RSSI value received. Reference Eq. (5) for computation of weighted decision factor. Our algorithm uses mean values but its different from naive approach that we considered above.

9   Naive Detection Approach

In order to better assess CWDDA, we have also simulated a naive detection approach for comparison.

The naive approach is based on common statistical knowledge, i.e., it depends on the mean and standard deviation of similar datasets obtained from multiple simulation runs of RSSI values of neighbour node and determines how the current means deviate from the initial mean obtained from similar dataset by comparing the means to its standard deviation and measure hypothesis (the null (H_0) and alternative(H_1)). However, the cooperative weighted decision detection algorithm takes into consideration the expected differences in the RSSI values due to the environmental factors such as weather conditions and the intention of each node to cheat the system. By introducing weighted decision and the threshold factors in the algorithm. The results of CWDDA compared to naive approach show that the naive approach in most times indicates that there is malicious node present (false positive) even when there is no malicious node and the vice versa. It can therefore be concluded that naive approach cannot be depended on in detecting malicious nodes, which may give false location information if computed. The cooperative weighted decision detection algorithm has three levels of hypothesis testing whereas the naive approach has one hypothesis test which is based on mean and standard deviation only which indicates that, the naive approach is not verified after the first hypothesis test hence the result is not confirmed. Its output cannot be compared to the cooperative weighted decision detection algorithm which verify the first hypothesis twice before the algorithm completes.

9.1   Limitation of the Algorithm

It is difficult to know the exact number of malicious nodes present at a time hence in distributing the number of secondary and malicious nodes it could be uniformly distributed. It is difficult to work on a simulation platform that do not support wireless sensing. According to the cooperative weighted decision detection algorithm in this chapter, each secondary node within the network area is expected to forward neighbour nodes RSSI to the CDC for computation of the threshold and decision of either malicious or not is determined by the CDC but not the individual nodes. The channel availability is scarce, therefore nodes within the network area cannot communicate at all times. The cooperative weighted decision detection algorithm is to detect the presence of malicious nodes in the DSA network; however, the algorithm is limited by the conditions under which it works. Conditions under which the algorithm works are

1. The presence of 3 nodes and above
2. When the environmental factors threshold is below 1.0
3. Availability of free white spaces

Conditions under which the algorithm may not work

1. When nodes are less than 3
2. When the environmental factors threshold is above 1.0
3. Unavailability of free white spaces

10   Conclusion

In conclusion, we have demonstrated that in spite of fluctuating RSSI values, it is still possible to use them to detect malicious nodes in our cooperative weighted decision detection algorithm. In our simulation, we observed that the algorithm was effective in detecting malicious nodes that falsified their positions. However, at the minimum distance of 300m the results received were mostly false positives. Also, we showed through simulation that between distances of 0.3–7 km, it is possible to reliably detect malicious nodes. The selection of k value greatly affects the performance of the algorithm, as large values resulted in false negatives. Nevertheless, more work needs to be done by optimizing the threshold and tolerance factors for highest accuracy. The simulation results demonstrated that, CWDDA works better than the Naive Detection Algorithm.

References

1. Matthee, K.W., et al.: Bringing Internet connectivity to rural Zambia using a collaborative approach. In: International Conference on Information and Communication Technologies and Development, 2007, ICTD 2007. IEEE (2007)
2. Chen, E.T.: The Internet of Things: opportunities, issues, and challenges. In: The Internet of Things in the Modern Business Environment, pp. 167–187. IGI Global, Hershey (2017)
3. Takyi, A., Densmore, M., Johnson, D.: Collaborative neighbour monitoring in TV white space network. In: Proceedings Southern Africa Telecommunication Networks and Applications Conference (SATNAC 2016), George, South Africa (2016)
4. Yuvraj, S.: Comparison of Okumura, Hata and COST-231 models on the basis of path loss and signal strength. Int. J. Comput. Appl. 59(11), 37–41 (2012)
5. Patil, B., Anthony M., Scott P.: Protocol to Access White-Space (PAWS) Databases: Use Cases and Requirements (2013)
6. Anand, S., Jin, Z., Subbalakshmi. K.P.: An analytical model for primary user emulation attacks in cognitive radio networks. In: 3rd IEEE Symposium on New Frontiers in Dynamic Spectrum Access Networks, 2008, DySPAN 2008. IEEE (2008)
7. Kamat, P., et al.: Enhancing source-location privacy in sensor network routing. In: Proceedings 25th IEEE International Conference on Distributed Computing Systems, 2005, ICDCS 2005. IEEE (2005)
8. Tapiador, J.E., Clark, J.A.: Masquerade mimicry attack detection: a randomised approach. Comput. Secur. 30(5), 297–310 (2011)
9. Richard Yu, F.: Defense against spectrum sensing data falsification attacks in mobile ad hoc networks with cognitive radios. In: MILCOM 2009 - 2009 IEEE Military Communications Conference, p. 2009. IEEE (2009)
10. van den Heuvel, M.P., et al.: High-cost, high-capacity backbone for global brain communication. Proc. Natl. Acad. Sci. 109(28), 11372–11377 (2012):

11. Subramanian, L., et al.: Rethinking wireless for the developing world. In: IRVINE IS BURNING, p. 43 (2006)
12. Jonathan, P., et al.: Successful deployment and key applications of Television White Space Networks (TVWS) Malawi (2014)
13. Albert, A.L., Moshe, T.M., David, L.J.: The television white space opportunity in Southern Africa: from field measurements to quantifying white spaces, In: White Space Communication, pp. 75–116. Springer, Cham (2015). https://doi.org/10.1007/978-3-319-08747-4
14. Kaligineedi, P., Majid, K., Vijay, K.B.: Secure cooperative sensing techniques for cognitive radio systems. In: IEEE International Conference on Communications, ICC 2008. IEEE (2008)
15. Zargar, S.T., et al.: Security in dynamic spectrum access systems: a survey. (2009)
16. Bhattacharjee, S., Shamik, S., Mainak, C.: Vulnerabilities in cognitive radio networks: a survey. Comput. Commun. 36(13), 1387–1398 (2013)
17. Fatemieh, O., Ranveer C., Carl , A.G.: Secure collaborative sensing for crowd sourcing spectrum data in white space networks. In: 2010 IEEE Symposium on New Frontiers in Dynamic Spectrum. IEEE (2010)
18. Zarrin, S., Teng J.L: Belief propagation on factor graphs for cooperative spectrum sensing in cognitive radio. In: 3rd IEEE Symposium on New Frontiers in Dynamic Spectrum Access Networks, 2008, DySPAN 2008. IEEE (2008)
19. Jayaprakasam, A., Vinod S.: Sequential detection based cooperative spectrum sensing algorithms in cognitive radio. In: 2009 First UK-India International Workshop on Cognitive Wireless Systems (UKIWCWS). IEEE (2009)
20. Zhang, W., Ranjan K.M., Khaled B.L.: Optimization of cooperative spectrum sensing with energy detection in cognitive radio networks. IEEE Trans. Wirel. Commun. 8(12), 5761–5766 (2009)
21. Saad, W., et al.: Coalitional games for distributed collaborative spectrum sensing in cognitive radio networks. In: IEEE INFOCOM 2009. IEEE (2009)
22. Visotsky, E., Kuffner, S., Peterson, R.: On collaborative detection of TV transmissions in support of dynamic spectrum sharing. In: 2005 First IEEE International Symposium on New Frontiers in Dynamic Spectrum Access Networks 2005, DySPAN 2005. IEEE (2005)
23. Meng, J.J., et al.: Collaborative spectrum sensing from sparse observations in cognitive radio networks. IEEE J. Select. Areas Commun. 29(2), 327–337 (2011)
24. Wang, W., et al.: Attack-proof collaborative spectrum sensing in cognitive radio networks. In: 43rd Annual Conference on Information Sciences and Systems 2009, CISS 2009. IEEE (2009)
25. Angelosante, D., Ezio, B., Marco, L.: Neighbor discovery in wireless networks: a multiuser-detection approach. Phy. Commun. 3(1), 28–36 (2010)
26. Pejovic, V., et al.: VillageLink: a channel allocation technique for wide-area white space networks. In: White Space Communication, pp. 249–280. Springer, Cham (2015). https://doi.org/10.1007/978-3-319-08747-4
27. Jin, Z., Anand, S., Subbalakshmi, K.P.: Mitigating primary user emulation attacks in dynamic spectrum access networks using hypothesis testing. ACM SIGMOBILE Mobile Comput. Commun. Rev. 13(2), 74–85 (2009)
28. Augustine, T., et al.: Performance analysis of a collaborative DSA-based network with malicious nodes (2017)
29. Bouassida, M.S., et al.: Sybil nodes detection based on received signal strength variations within VANET. IJ Netw. Secur. 9(1), 22–33 (2009)

30. Al-Khalid, O., Adams, A.E., Charalampos C.T.: Node discovery protocol and localization for distributed underwater acoustic networks. In: Advanced International Conference on Telecommunications, 2006/International Conference on Internet and Web Applications and Services, AICT-ICIW 2006. IEEE (2006)

31. Karthikeyan, V., Vinod, A., Jeyakumar, P.: An energy efficient neighbour node discovery method for wireless sensor networks. arXiv preprint arXiv:1402.3655 (2014)

32. Althunibat, S., et al.: On the trade-off between security and energy efficiency in cooperative spectrum sensing for cognitive radio. IEEE Commun. Lett. **17**(8), 1564–1567 (2013)

33. Alahmadi, A., et al.: Defense against primary user emulation attacks in cognitive radio networks using advanced encryption standard. IEEE Trans. Inf. Forensics Secur. **9**(5), 772–781 (2014)

34. Kaemarungsi, K., Prashant, K.: Properties of indoor received signal strength for WLAN location fingerprinting. In: The First Annual International Conference on Mobile and Ubiquitous Systems: Networking and Services, 2004, MOBIQUITOUS 2004. IEEE (2004)

35. Rida, M.E., et al.: Indoor location position based on bluetooth signal strength. In: 2015 2nd International Conference on Information Science and Control Engineering (ICISCE). IEEE (2015)

Research on Denoising Method in Pseudo-analog Video Transmission

Wanning He and Xin-Lin Huang(✉)

School of Electronics and Information Engineering, Tongji University,
Shanghai, China
xlhuang@tongji.edu.cn

Abstract. With the rapid development of mobile communication technology and the applications of 5G technology, video transmission, compared with file transmission, audio transmission and other media forms, has been more and more widely used. Today, the mobile video broadcasting needs to overcome some difficulties like the transmission noise. A knowledge-enhanced mobile video broadcasting (KMV-Cast) is a scheme utilizing joint source-channel coding and the correlated information in clouds, but in its calculation, there is still an item of noise that cannot be eliminated at the receiver side. In this paper, as same to KMV-Cast, the new scheme also exploits the hierarchical Bayesian model, the correlated information distillation in the clouds and Bayesian estimation algorithm to improve video quality. After the video reconstruction at the receiver, based on the items of the signal and the noise, selectively adds a Wiener filter to reduce the effect of noise. The simulation results show that the proposed KMV-Cast scheme with a proper Wiener filter at the receiver side is superior to that scheme without the Wiener filter and it achieves about 2 dB more of the peak signal-to-noise ratio (PSNR) gain at low-SNR channels (i.e., -10 dB) and about 1.5 dB more of PSNR gain at high-SNR channels (i.e., 10 dB).

Keywords: Wiener filter · Correlated information · Wireless video transmission

1 Introduction

With the prediction of Cisco Annual Internet Report 2020, over 70% of the global population will have mobile connectivity by 2023 and the total number of global mobile subscribers will grow from 5.1 billion (66% of population) in 2018 to 5.7 billion (71% of population) by 2023 [1]. The wireless communication technology, such as WiFi, LTE and so on, cannot meet the needs of the future with the increasing number of mobile users. So, reforming the traditional video transmission scheme is one of the current research hotspots of the mobile communication technology development.

As we all known, the traditional wireless video transmission adopts source-channel separation coding scheme and the coding between sources and channels limits the quality of transmission. When the channel quality is below a certain threshold, the quality of the received video declines linearly, which is called cliff effect. Cliff effect is

H. Jin et al. (Eds.): CROWNCOM 2021/WiCON 2021, LNICST 427, pp. 231–239, 2022.
https://doi.org/10.1007/978-3-030-98002-3_17

caused by the separation of source and channel coding and to solve this problem the new combined source-channel coding scheme was proposed [2]. It realized the joint control of source and channel coding and was applied into image transmission. Then, some joint source-channel coding schemes were proposed.

Among them, a conventional joint source-channel coding scheme proposed by Szymon Jakubczak and Dina Katabi, called Softcast [3], overcomes the cliff effect of a wireless video transmission well. The signal-to-noise ratio of the reconstructed image is linearly correlated with the channel quality. KMV-Cast is a brand-new video transmission framework and it is a joint source-channel coding scheme [4]. It can also overcome the cliff effect of a wireless video transmission like Softcast. Besides, it also makes a full use of correlated information to improve the quality and efficiency of reconstructed video and it utilizes the corresponding calculation to remove the mutual interference. But there is still a part of noise that cannot be eliminated through calculations and makes the image clearly segmented. In this paper, we mainly try to get rid of this part of noise and the Wiener filter is chosen to add into the KMV-Cast scheme.

During the transmission, we assume the noise in the channel is the additive white Gaussian noise, so the noise of the second item also follows the Gaussian distribution. It can be seen that the least mean square (LMS) principle is widely used in the noise elimination [5–9] and has a relatively good effect. For Wiener filter, the essence is to minimize the mean square value of the estimation error (defined as the difference between the expected response and the actual output of the filter), and the LMS algorithm is to minimize the mean-square error (MSE) performance function, define as $E\{e^2\}$ [6]. When using a Wiener filter, it needs prior knowledge of the power spectral density of the noise [8], which can be satisfied by its assuming noise Gaussian distribution. From above, adding a Wiener filter is a proper method to remove the second noise item of KMV-Cast scheme.

In this paper, firstly, we choose to add a Wiener filter to each block, to filter out certain noise and overall, there is an evident effect. But to some perfect blocks whose SNR is already higher, the effect is not ideal. This will be introduced in details later. Therefore, we decide to take block as a unit to selectively import the Wiener filter. The main functions are: 1) at the transmitter, correlated information extraction, evaluating and determining whether transmit and whether need to add the corresponding Wiener filter; 2) at the receiver, utilization of such information and Wiener filter for fast video recovery. We firstly search and extract correlated information in clouds based on certain criteria [10]. Secondly, based on KMV-Cast scheme [4], remove mutual interference and make full use of correlated information for image reconstruction. At last, selectively add Wiener filter to eliminate noise.

2 Related Work

2.1 Related KMV-Cast Transmission Scheme

From proposed KMV-Cast scheme, it can be seen that the reconstructed signal, at the receiver side, can be represent as [4]

$$\hat{\theta} = \left(\alpha^2\sigma_0^{-2}I + \Omega^{-1}\right)^{-1}\alpha\Phi^T\sigma_0^{-2}y = p\theta + \frac{\alpha\sigma_0^{-2}r\Phi^T v}{Cr+1} + \frac{\alpha\sigma_0^{-2}\vec{\theta}_i\vec{\theta}_i^T\Phi^T v}{(Cr+1)(Cr+C+1)}. \tag{1}$$

Here, each video frame is evenly divided into small pixel blocks (i.e., 8×8, $m = 64$), θ is the transmitted signal normalized vector ($m \times 1$), Φ is an $m \times m$ unitary matrix to reduce the peak-to-average power ratio, α is the power scaling factor, v is an independently and identically distributed Gaussian noise of a zero-mean and a known variance σ_0^2, $C = \alpha^2\sigma_0^{-2}$ is defined as the power scaling parameter, variance r is determined by maximum SNR, and p is donated as followings [4]:

$$p^2 = \left\{\left(\frac{Cr+1}{Cr}\right)^2\left[\frac{K^2}{[r(Cr+C+1)]^2} - \frac{2K^2}{[r(Cr+C+1)]} + 1\right]\right\}^{-1}. \tag{2}$$

where $K = \left(\vec{\theta}_i^T\theta\right)$ is the correlation coefficient of the pixel block. Since both the transmitter and the receiver know the information in clouds $\vec{\theta}_i$, we can remove the mutual interference item and get the final reconstructed signal expression [4]:

$$\hat{\theta} = p\theta + \frac{\alpha\sigma_0^{-2}r\Phi^T v}{Cr+1}. \tag{3}$$

The noise power in Eq. (3) can be represented as [4]

$$P_N = E\left\{tr\left\{\left(\frac{\alpha\sigma_0^{-2}r\Phi^T v}{Cr+1}\right)\left(\frac{\alpha\sigma_0^{-2}r\Phi^T v}{Cr+1}\right)^T\right\}\right\} = E\left\{tr\left\{\frac{\alpha^2\sigma_0^{-4}r^2\Phi^T vv^T\Phi}{(Cr+1)^2}\right\}\right\} = \frac{Cr^2m}{(Cr+1)^2}. \tag{4}$$

We donate two new variables for the easier calculation [4]

$$t = r(Cr+C+1) \tag{5}$$

$$A = \frac{\sqrt{C}(t+1)}{\sqrt{K^2 - 2K^2(t+1) + (t+1)^2}}. \tag{6}$$

The corresponding signal-to-noise ratio SNR_1 of the KMV-Cast model is [4]

$$SNR_1 = \frac{P_S}{P_N} = \frac{p^2}{P_N} = \frac{(Cr+1)^2p^2}{Cr^2m} \tag{7}$$

and take formular (2), (5) and (6) into the expression of SNR_1.

$$SNR_1 = \frac{A^2}{m}. \tag{8}$$

2.2 Wiener Filter Principle

The essence of Wiener filtering is to minimize the mean square value of the estimation error. The main process of the system can be represented as the following picture (Fig. 1):

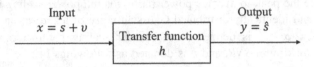

Fig. 1. The Wiener filter diagram.

where the signal and noise are both vectors. The transfer function is the matrix that we determine. The input of the filter is the origin signal and the noise of the transmission, and the optimal output of the filter is the origin signal without the noise. The estimation error is

$$e = |\hat{s} - s| = |x * h - s| \tag{9}$$

and the mean square value of the estimation error can be represented as:

$$E\{e^2\} = E\left\{(x * h - s)^2\right\}. \tag{10}$$

The goal is to get a proper transfer function h to minimalize the above formular (9), so we utilize its derivative with respect to h, like the following:

$$\frac{\partial E\{e^2\}}{\partial h} = 2E\{(x * h - s) * x\} \tag{11}$$

The point where its derivative is zero is the extreme point, so set the formular (11) equal to zero, and we can get:

$$HR_{xx} - R_{xs} = 0 \tag{12}$$

where H is the matrix of the optimal transfer function. R_{xx} is the autocorrelation matrix of the input signal and R_{xs} is the correlation matrix of the input signal and expected signal. The input signal consists of the origin signal and noise in the transmission, and the two parts are uncorrelated. As a result, we determine the transfer matrix as

$$H = R_{ss}(R_{ss} + R_{vv})^{-1}. \tag{13}$$

2.3   KMV-Cast + Wiener Filter

Add Wiener Filter at the Receive Side
Now we add a Wiener filter to reduce some noise in the second item of the formular (3). From formular (13), we can see that the transfer function of the Wiener filter only depends on the autocorrelation matrixes of the signal and noise, and the two auto-correlation matrixes can be calculated like the followings:

$$R_{ss} = E\{p^2\theta\theta^T\} = p^2 E\{\theta\theta^T\} = p^2\Omega = p^2 rI + p^2\vec{\theta}_i\vec{\theta}_i^T \tag{14}$$

$$R_{vv} = E\left\{\frac{\alpha^2\sigma_0^{-4}r^2(\Phi^T v)(\Phi^T v)^T}{(Cr+1)^2}\right\} = \frac{Cr}{(Cr+1)^2}I. \tag{15}$$

So the transfer function can be shown as

$$H = R_{ss}(R_{ss}+R_{vv})^{-1} = \frac{(Cr+1)^2 p^2}{(Cr+1)^2 p^2 + Cr}I + \frac{Cr(Cr+1)^2 p^2}{\left[(Cr+1)^2 p^2 + Cr\right]\left[(Cr+1)^2 p^2(r+1) + Cr^2\right]}\vec{\theta}_i\vec{\theta}_i^T. \tag{16}$$

The output signal through the Wiener filter can be written as

$$H\hat{\theta} = H\left(p\theta + \frac{\alpha\sigma_0^{-2}r\Phi^T v}{Cr+1}\right) = p\theta + H\frac{\alpha\sigma_0^{-2}r\Phi^T v}{Cr+1} - (I-H)p\theta. \tag{17}$$

As a result, the noise of the signal processed again is changed into

$$noise = H\frac{\alpha\sigma_0^{-2}r\Phi^T v}{Cr+1} - (I-H)p\theta. \tag{18}$$

As the same to the KMV-Cast, we can calculate the noise power through

$$P_N = E\{tr\{noise \times noise^T\}\} \tag{19}$$

After calculations, we can get the expression of SNR_2.

$$SNR_2 = \left\{\frac{1+r^2A^2 - 2rA}{(rA^2+1)^2} + \frac{[(-2r-1)A^4 - 2A^2]K^2 + [2r(r+1)A^5 - 2A]K + [2r(r+1)A^4 + (2r+1)A^2]}{(rA^2+1)^2[(r+1)A^2+1]^2}\right\}^{-1}. \tag{20}$$

From (5), we can calculate [4]:

$$r = \frac{-(C+1) - \sqrt{(C+1)^2 + 4Ct}}{2C}. \tag{21}$$

Determining Whether to Transmit and Whether to Add Wiener Filter

There are three ways to reconstruct the pixel blocks: (1) use the relevant information in the clouds and don't need to transmit or use Wiener filter. (2) use the KMV-Cast scheme without Wiener filter to some blocks with high power scaling parameters. (3) use the KMV-Cast scheme adding a proper Wiener filter.

If we use the relevant information and transmit the index of the similar pixel block $\vec{\theta}_i$, the SNR of reconstructed block is [4].

$$SNR_0 = \frac{1}{|\Delta|^2} = \frac{1}{2(1 - |K|)}. \tag{22}$$

Compared three formulars (8), (20) and (22), we can choose how to deal with the pixel block.

Power Scaling

In order to maximize the peak signal-to-noise ratio (PSNR) of the reconstructed video, we should minimize the total noise power of all transmitted pixel blocks with the given constrain of signal power P. Assume $l_{j(t)}$ is the noise power of the jth reconstructed block and it can be decided with the condition of maximum SNR.

The total noise power can be written as [4]

$$min\left\{\sum_{j=1}^{M} \frac{\lambda_j^2 l_{j(t)}}{C_j}\right\} \tag{23}$$

with the constraint condition [4]:

$$\sum_{j=1}^{M} C_j \leq P/\sigma_0^2 \tag{24}$$

where $\lambda_j^2 l_{j(t)}/C_j$ is the noise power of the jth reconstructed block. In order to minimalize the total noise of the reconstruct video, we need to allocate the power scaling parameter C_j by Lagrange multipliers, like the followings [4]:

$$C_j = \frac{\sqrt{\lambda_j^2 l_{j(t)}}}{\sum_{k=1}^{M} \sqrt{\lambda_k^2 l_{k(t)}}}, j = 1, 2, \ldots, M. \tag{25}$$

3   Experimental Results

In this section, we evaluate the performance of the proposed KMV-Cast + Wiener filter transmission scheme in terms of PSNR. We assume that the transmission channel is slow fading and its distortion can be cancelled by the equalizer. Besides, we compared the simulation results under additive white Gaussian noise channel. We mainly choose three typical transmission schemes to compare with the new proposed way, which are uncoded transmission, Softcast and KMV-Cast.

As same to KMV-Cast transmission framework, the transmitted video is segmented into frames and the correlated information can be known by both the transmitter and the receiver. From the standard video test sequence Foreman, we choose the 4th frame as the correlation information in clouds. As we can see from Fig. 2 and Fig. 3, we respectively choose 5th, and 215th frames as the transmitted signals which are highly correlated, and uncorrelated. On the whole, KMV-Cast with the Wiener filter is better than three other schemes. In details, from Fig. 2 with highly correlated information, compared with Softcast and KMV-Cast scheme, there are respectively more than 12.5 dB and 2.7 dB of PSNR gain for adding the Wiener filter at higher channel, but from Fig. 3 with no correlated information, are respectively 14 dB and 1 dB of PSNR gain. So it can be seen that the advantage increases with the increase of similarities between transmitted signal and correlated information in clouds.

Fig. 2. Reconstructed video quality comparisons with highly correlated information in clouds. Channel SNR: 10 dB. (a) Reconstruct #5 frame using uncoded video transmission (23.71 dB). (b) Reconstruct #5 frame using SoftCast (32.89 dB). (c) Reconstruct #5 frame using KMV-Cast (42.64 dB). (d) Reconstruct #5 frame using proposed KMV-Cast + Wiener filter (45.38 dB)

Fig. 3. Reconstructed video quality comparisons with no correlated information in clouds. Channel SNR: 10 dB. (a) Reconstruct #215 frame using uncoded video transmission (23.46 dB). (b) Reconstruct #215 frame using SoftCast (34.18 dB). (c) Reconstruct #215 frame using KMV-Cast (36.53 dB). (d) Reconstruct #215 frame using proposed KMV-Cast + Wiener filter (37.47 dB).

4 Conclusions

In this paper, the Wiener filter has been proposed to reduce the noise of the second item in KMV-Cast. The main difference with the related work is that we need to determine whether to add the Wiener filter to the transmitted pixel blocks based on corresponding expressions. This method has maximized the PSNR of reconstructed video and the simulation results have shown that selectively adding the Wiener filter performs better than the KMV-Cast scheme without a filter and others.

Acknowledgement. This work was supported in part by Shanghai Rising-Star Program under Grant 19QA1409100, in part by the National Natural Science Foundation of China under Grants 62071332, 61631017 and U1733114, and in part by the Fundamental Research Funds for the Central Universities.

References

1. Cisco: Cisco Annual Internet Report (2018–2023) White Paper (2020)
2. Modestino, J., Daut, D., Vickers, A.: Combined source-channel coding of images using the block cosine transform. IEEE Trans. Commun. **29**(9), 1261–1274 (1981)
3. Jakubczak, S., Katabi, D.: A cross-layer design for scalable mobile video. In: Proceedings of 17th Annual International Conference on MobiCom, Las Vegas, NV, USA, pp. 289–300 (2011)

4. Huang, X.-L., Jun, W., Fei, H.: Knowledge-enhanced mobile video broadcasting framework with cloud support. IEEE Trans. Circuits Syst. Video Technol. **27**(1), 6–18 (2017)
5. John, J.: Shynk: frequency-domain and multirate adaptive filtering. IEEE Signal Process. Mag. **9**(1), 14–37 (1992)
6. Ghogho, M., Ibnkahla, M., Bershad, N.J.: Analytic behavior of the LMS adaptive line enhancer for sinusoids corrupted by multiplicative and additive noise. IEEE Trans. Signal Process. **46**(9), 2386–2393 (1998)
7. Arazm, N., Sahab, A., Kazemi, M.F.: Noise reduction of SEM images using adaptive Wiener filter. In: IEEE International Conference on Cybernetics and Computational Intelligence (CyberneticsCom), Phuket, Thailand, pp. 50–55 (2017)
8. Kamiya, N., Sasaki, E.: Pilot-symbol-assisted phase noise compensation with forward-backward wiener smoothing filters. IEEE Trans. Signal Process. **65**(17), 4443–4453 (2017)
9. Petkova, L., Draganov, I.: Noise adaptive wiener filtering of images. In: 55th International Scientific Conference on Information, Communication and Energy Systems and Technologies (ICEST), Serbia, pp. 177–180 (2020)
10. Jun, W., Liu, D., Huang, X.-L., Luo, C., Cui, H., Feng, W.: DaC-RAN: a data-assisted cloud radio access network for visual communications. IEEE Wirel. Commun. **22**(3), 130–136 (2015)

Confidential Communications for Mobile UAV Relaying Network

Chenglan Ji, Zhenyu Na[✉], and Zilong Feng

School of Information Science and Technology, Dalian Maritime University,
Dalian, China
nazhenyu@dlmu.edu.cn

Abstract. In recent years, unmanned aerial vehicle (UAV) communication has not only attracted extensive discussion in academic circles, but also has been applied to practical scenarios. With the rapid development of UAV communication, its secrecy issues have gradually become prominent. In this paper, the physical layer security of mobile UAV relaying network is studied. We give a scheme of confidential communication to ensure the integrity and confidentiality of information. By optimizing the dynamic position of the UAV and transmit power, our goal is to maximize the minimum secrecy rate. Because the problem we put forward can not be solved directly by the solver, we divide the problem into two sub-problems to analyse. The simulation results show that our program improves the fairness of secrecy communication, and the physical layer security of the mobile UAV relaying network has been enhanced.

Keywords: UAV · Mobile relay · Secrecy · Convex optimization

1 Introduction

Unmanned aerial vehicle (UAV) has the characteristics of small size, low cost, convenient use, and so on. From the perspective of the global market, the industry demand and investment scale of UAV have grown steadily. In the future, UAV is likely to play a major role in express delivery industry, public safety, journalism, and other industries [1–4]. In recent years, the research and development of UAV at home and abroad has paid unprecedented attention, among which UAV communication is one of the key research. A detailed tutorial on the UAV communication networks are provided in [5]. Among them, the more comprehensive examples of UAV communication are introduced, such as aerial UAV base station, cellular-connected UAVs, flying ad hoc networks etc. On this basis, possible research directions and tools to solve such problems are given. With the deepening and comprehensive research of UAV communication, the secrecy of UAV communication has also received attention.

In [5], we can judge that the channel of the air-to-ground link is dominated by line-of-sight (LoS). Due to the broadcast nature of the wireless channel, while

© ICST Institute for Computer Sciences, Social Informatics and Telecommunications Engineering 2022
Published by Springer Nature Switzerland AG 2022. All Rights Reserved
H. Jin et al. (Eds.): CROWNCOM 2021/WiCON 2021, LNICST 427, pp. 240–250, 2022.
https://doi.org/10.1007/978-3-030-98002-3_18

the UAV communication system provides high-quality communication services to the destination, the possibility of eavesdroppers obtaining information is greatly increased. However, the complexity of traditional encryption and decryption algorithms is too high. Taking advantage of the randomness of the channel itself, physical layer security technology has become a key technology for UAV confidential communication, where some meaningful researches on this perspective can be found in, e.g., [6–10]. Among them, the survey articles [6–8] give several schemes for secure transmission of aerial UAV base station. Prior work [9] adopts the idea of multi-UAV relaying communication network to reduce the probability of eavesdropping and gives the expression under Rician fading channel. Gao et al. [10] maximizes the secrecy achievable rate of target user under the UAV relaying network.

To sum up, researchers have done a lot of work on how UAV acts as aerial base station to deal with malicious eavesdropping. Secure communication of mobile UAV relaying system is equally important. In [9,10], a secure relaying network for cooperative communication of multiple UAVs is given. However, in the above UAV relaying system, the UAV only communicates confidentially with one destination. Based on this, we propose mobile UAV relaying network in a multi-user scenario. Since the problem is not easy to solve directly, we separate it into two sub-problems and give the corresponding low-complexity algorithms. Finally, we give the simulation results to verify the effectiveness of the program.

2   System Model and Problem Formulation

2.1   System Model

This paper studies a mobile UAV relaying network, which is composed of a ground base station (S), a UAV relay (R), an eavesdropper (E), and a group of target users (D). Assuming that the base station, the eavesdropper, and the target users are located on a plane, which is denoted as the xoy plane. The coordinate system is established with the base station as the origin, then the eavesdropper's coordinate is $\mathbf{W}_e = [x_e, y_e]^{\mathrm{T}}$, and coordinate of the target user $k \in \mathcal{K} = \{1, ..., K\}$ is $\mathbf{W}_k = [x_k, y_k]^{\mathrm{T}}$. During the mission time T, the vertical coordinate of the dynamic UAV is fixed as H, and its horizontal coordinate is marked as $\mathbf{q}[t] = [x[t], y[t]]^{\mathrm{T}}, t \in T$. In order to solve the problem easily, we cut the task time T into N time slots, then the coordinate of UAV in the nth time slot is expressed as $[\mathbf{q}[n], H]^{\mathrm{T}}$, where $\mathbf{q}[n] = [x[n], y[n]]^{\mathrm{T}}, n \in \mathcal{N} = \{1, ..., N\}$. The position of the UAV in any time slot is limited by the maximum flight speed $V_{\max}$. The relationship between them is as follows

$$\|\mathbf{q}[n+1] - \mathbf{q}[n]\|^2 \le (V_{\max}\frac{T}{N})^2, n = 1, ..., N-1 \tag{1}$$

The trajectory of UAV in single route mode is constrained by the following

$$\mathbf{q}[1] = \mathbf{q}_{\mathrm{ini}} \tag{2a}$$

$$\mathbf{q}[N] = \mathbf{q}_{\mathrm{end}} \tag{2b}$$

Among them, $\mathbf{q}_{\text{ini}}, \mathbf{q}_{\text{end}}$ refer to the start point and end point of the UAV's trajectory.

On the basis of the LoS channel model, we can obtain the channel gains of link S-R, R-E, R-D, which are shown as follows

$$h_{\text{r}}[n] = \frac{\beta_0}{H^2 + \|\mathbf{q}[n]\|^2}, \forall n \tag{3a}$$

$$h_{\text{e}}[n] = \frac{\beta_0}{H^2 + \|\mathbf{q}[n] - \mathbf{W}_{\text{e}}\|^2}, \forall n \tag{3b}$$

$$h_k[n] = \frac{\beta_0}{H^2 + \|\mathbf{q}[n] - \mathbf{W}_k\|^2}, \forall n, k \tag{3c}$$

where β_0 refers to the channel power gain at the reference distance $d_0 = 1$m. The communication between the UAV and the target users adopts time division multiple access technology, which means that the UAV only secretly transmits information with a receiving terminal at any time slot. We introduce a significative symbol $\alpha_k[n]$ to record scheduling information, then $\alpha_k[n]$ should meet the following conditions

$$\alpha_k[n] \in \{0, 1\}, \forall k, n \tag{4a}$$

$$\sum_{k=1}^{K} \alpha_k[n] \leq 1, \forall n \tag{4b}$$

The transmit power of base station and UAV is given by $p_{\text{s}}[n], p_{\text{r}}[n], \forall n$ respectively. Its constraints may be expressed as

$$\sum_{n=1}^{N} p_{\text{s}}[n] \leq N P_{\text{s}}^{\text{ave}} \tag{5a}$$

$$\sum_{n=1}^{N} p_{\text{r}}[n] \leq N P_{\text{r}}^{\text{ave}} \tag{5b}$$

$$p_{\text{s}}[n] \geq 0, \forall n \tag{5c}$$

$$p_{\text{r}}[n] \geq 0, \forall n \tag{5d}$$

where, $P_{\text{s}}^{\text{ave}}, P_{\text{r}}^{\text{ave}}$ indicate average power of base station and UAV respectively. We introduce a new variable $\rho_0 = \frac{\beta_0}{\xi}$, where ξ represents the power of the noise. Then, the maximum achievable rate of the link S-R, R-D, R-E are respectively presented as

$$R_{\mathrm{r}}\left[n\right] = \log_2\left(1 + \frac{p_{\mathrm{s}}\left[n\right]\rho_0}{H^2 + x\left[n\right]^2 + y\left[n\right]^2}\right), \forall n \tag{6a}$$

$$R_k\left[n\right] = \log_2\left(1 + \frac{p_{\mathrm{r}}\left[n\right]\rho_0}{H^2 + \left(x\left[n\right] - x_k\right)^2 + \left(y\left[n\right] - y_k\right)^2}\right), \forall n, k \tag{6b}$$

$$R_{\mathrm{e}}\left[n\right] = \log_2\left(1 + \frac{p_{\mathrm{r}}\left[n\right]\rho_0}{H^2 + \left(x\left[n\right] - x_{\mathrm{e}}\right)^2 + \left(y\left[n\right] - y_{\mathrm{e}}\right)^2}\right), \forall n \tag{6c}$$

Therefore, our goal is specifically described as

$$R_{sk} = \frac{1}{N}\sum_{n=1}^{N}\alpha_k\left[n\right]\left[R_k\left[n\right] - R_{\mathrm{e}}\left[n\right]\right], \forall k \tag{7}$$

Because the UAV acts as a relay for confidential communication, we consider the following information causality constraints

$$\sum_{n=1}^{m}\alpha_k\left[n\right]R_k\left[n\right] \le \sum_{n=1}^{m}R_{\mathrm{r}}\left[n\right], \forall m, k \tag{8a}$$

$$\sum_{n=1}^{m}R_{\mathrm{e}}\left[n\right] \le \sum_{n=1}^{m}R_{\mathrm{r}}\left[n\right], \forall m \tag{8b}$$

2.2 Problem Formulation

Based on the above analysis, the single route optimization problem is formulated as follows

$$\max_{\alpha_k[n], p_{\mathrm{s}}[n], p_{\mathrm{r}}[n], x[n], y[n]} \varphi \tag{9a}$$

$$\mathrm{s.t.}\quad R_{sk} \ge \varphi \tag{9b}$$

$$\left(1\right),\left(2\right),\left(4\right),\left(5\right),\left(8\right). \tag{9c}$$

It can be observed that both the objective function and the causality constraints are non-convex. $\alpha_k\left[n\right]$ is an integer variable and involves multiple constraints. Therefore, this problem we proposed can not be solved directly with convex optimization tools.

3   Problem Formulation

Due to the complexity of the problem and the coupling of variables, we simplify it into two sub-problems: UAV-user association $\mathbf{A} = \{\alpha_k\left[n\right], \forall k, n\}$ optimization and transmit power and UAV trajectory $\mathbf{B} = \{p_{\mathrm{s}}\left[n\right], p_{\mathrm{r}}\left[n\right], x\left[n\right], y\left[n\right], \forall n\}$ optimization.

3.1 UAV-User Association Optimization

Since $\alpha_k[n]$ is an integer variable that is not easy to handle, we relax it into a continuous variable, so we can use $0 \leq \alpha_k[n] \leq 1, \forall k, n$ to replace the constraint (4a). Given the power and trajectory, the optimization problem of UAV-user association is expressed as follows

$$\max_{\alpha_k[n]} \quad \varphi \tag{10a}$$

$$\text{s.t.} \quad \frac{1}{N}\sum_{n=1}^{N} \alpha_k[n]\left[R_k[n] - R_e[n]\right] \geq \varphi, \forall k \tag{10b}$$

$$\sum_{n=1}^{m} \alpha_k[n] R_k[n] \leq \sum_{n=1}^{m} R_r[n], \forall m, k \tag{10c}$$

$$0 \leq \alpha_k[n] \leq 1, \forall k, n \tag{10d}$$

$$\sum_{k=1}^{K} \alpha_k[n] \leq 1, \forall n \tag{10e}$$

This problem contains linear objective function and constraints that can be easily solved using convex optimization tools.

3.2 Transmit Power and UAV Trajectory

Firstly, introduce two inequalities, whose process has been demonstrated in [11].

$$\ln(1 + \frac{1}{xy}) \geq \ln(1 + \frac{1}{x^r y^r}) + \frac{x^r y^r}{x^r y^r + 1}(2 - \frac{x}{x^r} - \frac{y}{y^r}) \tag{11}$$

$$\ln(1 + \frac{x}{y}) \leq \ln(1 + \frac{x^r}{y^r}) + (\frac{1}{1 + \frac{x^r}{y^r}})[\frac{1}{2y}(\frac{x^2}{x^r} + x^r) - \frac{x^r}{y^r}] \tag{12}$$

where $x > 0, y > 0, r > 0$.

Lemma 1. *The non-convex constraint* (9b) *is transformed into a convex constraint, as shown below*

$$\frac{1}{N}\sum_{n=1}^{N} \alpha_k[n]\left[R_k^{\text{lb}}[n] - R_e^{\text{up}}[n]\right] \geq \varphi, \forall k \tag{13}$$

where,

$$R_k^{\text{lb}}[n] = \log_2(e)\ln(1 + \frac{p_r^l[n]\rho_0}{d_k^l[n]}) + \frac{\log_2(e)p_r^l[n]\rho_0}{d_k^l[n] + p_r^l[n]\rho_0}(2 - \frac{p_r^l[n]}{p_r[n]} - \frac{d_k[n]}{d_k^l[n]}) \tag{14}$$

$$R_e^{\text{up}}[n] = \log_2(e)\ln(1 + \frac{p_r^l[n]\rho_0}{d_e^l[n]})$$

$$+ \frac{\log_2(e)d_e^l[n]}{d_e^l[n] + p_r^l[n]\rho_0}(\frac{1}{2d_e[n]}(\frac{p_r^2[n]\rho_0}{p_r^l[n]} + p_r^l[n]\rho_0) - \frac{p_r^l[n]\rho_0}{d_e^l[n]}) \tag{15}$$

where,

$$d_k[n] \geq (x_k - x[n])^2 + (y_k - y[n])^2 + H^2 \tag{16}$$

$$
\begin{aligned}
d_e[n] \leq &(x^l[n] - x_e)^2 + (y^l[n] - y_e)^2 + H^2 \\
&+ 2(x^l[n] - x_e)(x[n] - x^l[n]) + 2(y^l[n] - y_e)(y[n] - y^l[n])
\end{aligned}
\tag{17}
$$

Proof. Firstly, define a slack variable $d_k[n]$ to satisfy inequality (16), then $R_k[n] \geq \log_2(1 + \frac{p_r[n]\rho_0}{d_k[n]})$. According to inequality (11), we can get $R_k^{lb}[n]$, which is the lower bound of $R_k[n]$. Finally, establish the following inequality

$$d_e[n] \leq (x_e - x[n])^2 + (y_e - y[n])^2 + H^2 \tag{18}$$

which is a non-convex constraint of the UAV horizontal coordinate. The right side of the formula can be transformed into a convex constraint (17) by Taylor expansion.

According to the inequality (12) given above, the upper bound of the $R_e[n]$ is obtained, that is

$$R_e[n] \leq \log_2(1 + \frac{p_r[n]\rho_0}{d_e[n]}) \leq R_e^{up}[n]. \tag{19}$$

It can be seen that formulas (13)–(17) are convex constraints on optimization variables. Therefore, we can use them to approximate the non-convex constraint (9b).

Lemma 2. *Non-convex constraint (8a) can be transformed into convex constraint through successive convex approximation, namely*

$$\sum_{n=1}^{m} \alpha_k[n] R_k^{up}[n] \leq \sum_{n=1}^{m} R_r^{lb}[n], \forall m, k \tag{20}$$

where,

$$
\begin{aligned}
R_k^{up}[n] = &\log_2(e)\ln(1 + \frac{p_r^l[n]\rho_0}{d_{k1}^l[n]}) \\
&+ \frac{\log_2(e)d_{k1}^l[n]}{d_{k1}^l[n] + p_r^l[n]\rho_0}(\frac{1}{2d_{k1}[n]}(\frac{p_r^2[n]\rho_0}{p_r^l[n]} + p_r^l[n]\rho_0) - \frac{p_r^l[n]\rho_0}{d_{k1}^l[n]})
\end{aligned}
\tag{21}
$$

$$R_r^{lb}[n] = \log_2(e)\ln(1 + \frac{p_s^l[n]\rho_0}{d_s^l[n]}) + \frac{\log_2(e)p_s^l[n]\rho_0}{d_s^l[n] + p_s^l[n]\rho_0}(2 - \frac{p_s^l[n]}{p_s[n]} - \frac{d_s[n]}{d_s^l[n]}) \tag{22}$$

where,

$$
\begin{aligned}
d_{k1}[n] \leq &(x^l[n] - x_k)^2 + (y^l[n] - y_k)^2 + H^2 \\
&+ 2(x^l[n] - x_k)(x[n] - x^l[n]) + 2(y^l[n] - y_k)(y[n] - y^l[n])
\end{aligned}
\tag{23}
$$

$$d_s[n] \geq (x[n])^2 + (y[n])^2 + H^2 \tag{24}$$

The non-convex constraint (8b) *can be replaced with the following convex constraint*

$$\sum_{n=1}^{m} R_e^{\text{up}}[n] \leq \sum_{n=1}^{m} R_r^{\text{lb}}[n], \forall m \tag{25}$$

Proof. First, define an intermediate variable $d_{k1}[n]$ to satisfy the following inequality

$$d_{k1}[n] \leq (x_k - x[n])^2 + (y_k - y[n])^2 + H^2 \tag{26}$$

Then obtain the following continuous inequalities according to inequality (12)

$$R_k[n] \leq \log_2(1 + \frac{p_r[n]\rho_0}{d_{k1}[n]}) \leq R_k^{\text{up}}[n] \tag{27}$$

In addition, define a slack variable $d_s[n]$ to satisfy inequality (24), then $R_r[n] \geq \log_2(1 + \frac{p_s[n]\rho_0}{d_s[n]})$. According to inequality (11), we can get $R_r^{\text{lb}}[n]$, which is the lower bound of $R_r[n]$.

Formula (26) is non-convex, and the right part of it can be transformed into convex constraint (23) by Taylor expansion. Therefore, the non-convex constraint (8a) can be approximately replaced by (20)–(24). The derivation process of $R_e^{\text{up}}[n]$ in formula (25) has been proved in **Lemma** 1, and the derivation process of $R_r^{\text{lb}}[n]$ has also been proved. Therefore, the convex constraint (25) can approximately replace the non-convex constraint (8b).

Theorem 1. *Based on the* $p_s^l[n], p_r^l[n], x^l[n], y^l[n], d_k^l[n]$, *and* $d_{k1}^l[n]$ *obtained in the* r*th iteration, at the* $r + 1$*th iteration, the power and trajectory optimization problem is described as follows*

$$\max_{p_s[n],p_r[n],x[n],y[n],d_k[n],d_e[n],d_{k1}[n],d_s[n]} \varphi \tag{28a}$$

$$\text{s.t.} \quad (13) - (17), (20) - (25). \tag{28b}$$

4   Numerical Results

In this section, simulation results are presented to verify the UAV relaying scheme that improves physical layer security. First, we studied whether the UAV trajectory can be dynamically adjusted when the eavesdropper's position changes. Secondly, we investigated the average confidentiality rate of each target user before and after the variable optimization.

For the mobile UAV relaying network we proposed, the three-dimensional coordinate of the base station is fixed to $(0, 0, 0)^{\text{T}}$. UAV transmits information at a fixed height $H = 100$m. The eavesdropper is randomly distributed on the horizontal plane, and the target users are also randomly distributed on the horizontal plane, but there is a certain distance from the ground base station. Simulation parameters are set as follows: $K = 5, \beta_0 = -60$ dB, $\sigma^2 = -110$ dB, $V_{\text{max}} = 50$ m/s, $T = 60$ s, $N = 60, P_s^{\text{ave}} = 1$ W, $P_r^{\text{ave}} = 1$ W.

Figures 1 and 2 show the adaptive adjustment of the UAV's trajectory when the eavesdropper's position changes. For the location of the eavesdropper, we selected two representative cases, namely near to the base station and far away from the base station. It can be seen that in the two cases, the UAV can be far away from the eavesdropper and close to the each target user to transmit information. This shows that our algorithm is effective for any eavesdropping position. Figure 3 shows the transmit power of the UAV and base station during the mission time.

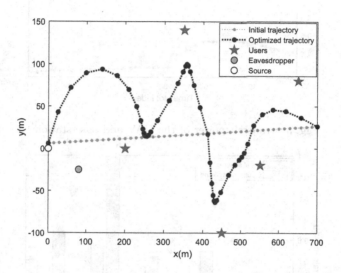

Fig. 1. UAV trajectory in the first position of the eavesdropper.

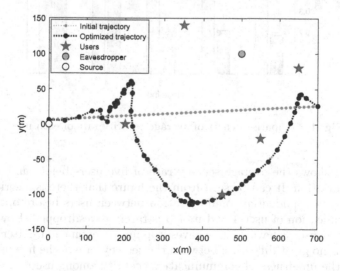

Fig. 2. UAV trajectory in the second position of the eavesdropper.

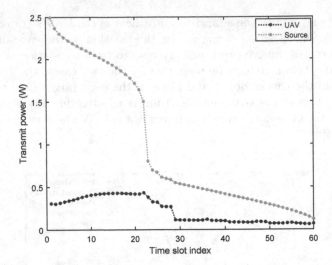

Fig. 3. Transmit power of the UAV and base station.

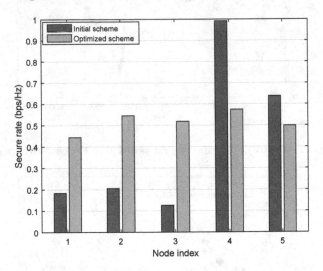

Fig. 4. Comparison chart of average security rate of each user.

Figure 4 shows the average secrecy rate of five users before and after algorithm optimization. It can be seen from the figure that there is a serious unfair phenomenon in confidential communication between users before optimization. The communication of user 4 and user 5 is rarely eavesdropped. However, user 1, user 2, and user 3 have serious eavesdropping phenomenon. After optimization, there is no great difference between the secrecy rate of the five users, which eliminates the unfairness of communication security among users.

5   Conclusion

This paper investigates the problem of confidential communication in mobile UAV relaying network from the perspective of physical layer security. Using time division multiple access technology, UAV can only communicate with one target user secretly in one time slot. By optimizing the three coupling variables of user scheduling, transmit power, and UAV trajectory, the minimum average secrecy rate among all users is maximized. The problem has been proved to be a nonconvex optimization. The original problem is simplified into two sub-problems, and the best results are obtained through standard convex optimization tools. The simulation results prove that the algorithm improves the secrecy of mobile UAV relaying network.

Acknowledgement. This work was supported in part by the National Natural Science Foundation of China under Grant 61971081, and in part by the General Project of Natural Science Foundation of Liaoning Province under Grant 2019-MS-026.

References

1. Vamvakas, P., Tsiropoulou, E.E., Papavassiliou, S.: On the prospect of UAV-assisted communications paradigm in public safety networks. In: IEEE INFOCOM 2019 - IEEE Conference on Computer Communications Workshops (INFOCOM WKSHPS), May 2019, pp. 762–767 (2019)
2. Feng, K., Li, W., Ge, S., Pan, F.: Packages delivery based on marker detection for UAVS. In: 2020 Chinese Control and Decision Conference (CCDC), August 2020, pp. 2094–2099 (2020)
3. Cavaliere, D., Saggese, A., Senatore, S., Vento, M., Loia, V.: Empowering UAV scene perception by semantic spatio-temporal features. In: 2018 IEEE International Conference on Environmental Engineering (EE), March 2018, pp. 1–6 (2018)
4. Wang, J., Liu, Y., Song, H.: Counter-unmanned aircraft system(s) (C-UAS): state of the art, challenges, and future trends. IEEE Aerospace Elcctr. Syst. Mag. **36**(3), 4–29 (2021)
5. Mozaffari, M., Saad, W., Bennis, M., Nam, Y.H., Debbah, M.: A tutorial on UAVS for wireless networks: applications, challenges, and open problems. IEEE Commun. Surv. Tutor. **21**(3), 2334–2360 (2019)
6. Wang, Q., Chen, Z., Cai, J., Tian, Z.: Establishing UAV-aided VBSs for secure multicasting. IEEE Wirel. Commun. Lett. **9**(7), 1009–1013 (2020)
7. Gao, Y., Tang, H., Li, B., Yuan, X.: Securing energy-constrained UAV communications against both internal and external eavesdropping. IEEE Commun. Lett. **25**(3), 749–753 (2021)
8. Hua, M., Wang, Y., Wu, Q., Dai, H., Huang, Y., Yang, L.: Energy-efficient cooperative secure transmission in multi-UAV-enabled wireless networks. IEEE Trans. Veh. Technol. **68**(8), 7761–7775 (2019)
9. Shen, T., Ochiai, H.: A UAV-aided selective relaying with cooperative jammers for secure wireless networks over Rician fading channels. In: 2019 IEEE 90th Vehicular Technology Conference (VTC2019-Fall), September 2020, pp. 1–5 (2019)

10. Gao, S., Ma, Y., Duo, B.: Safeguarding multi-UAVs relaying communications via joint trajectory design and power control. In: 2020 International Conference on Wireless Communications and Signal Processing (WCSP), October 2020, pp. 1182–1187 (2020)
11. Chi-Nguyen, D., Pathirana, P. N., Ding, M., Seneviratne, A.: Secrecy performance of the UAV enabled cognitive relay network. In: 2018 IEEE 3rd International Conference on Communication and Information Systems (ICCIS), December 2018, pp. 117–121 (2018)

Wireless Communications and Networking (WICON 2021)

Implementation and Performance Analysis of Smart Attendance Checking Using BLE-Based Communications

Lorenzo Gabriel Alcantara, Alphonso Miguel Taylor Balagtas, Trixia Britania, Sean Kristian Garibay, Joshua Wyndel Uyvico, and Nestor Michael Tiglao[✉]

Ubiquitous Computing Laboratory, Electrical and Electronics Engineering Institute, University of the Philippines, Velasquez Street, Diliman, 1101 Quezon City, Philippines
{lorenzo.alcantara,alphonso.balagtas,trixia.britania,
sean.kristian.garibay,joshua.uyvico,nestor}@eee.upd.edu.ph

Abstract. Current implementations of attendance checking in the University of the Philippines - Diliman (UPD) has been time consuming and easily cheated. The roll-call and pen-and-paper method cannot monitor student presence for the whole duration of the class session. Attendance checking systems using mobile technology and the Internet of Things attempt to mitigate these problems, but it also introduces new ones such as inclusivity, cost, and complex implementations. This study investigates the use of Bluetooth Low Energy (BLE) beacons, a mobile application, and a web server to create an attendance checking mechanism capable of eliminating queues and attendance cheating, monitoring student presence, and automating records. We created two procedures for sending information to our server, to determine the general advantages and disadvantages of each in terms of features, scalability, and cost-effectiveness. Procedure 1 mainly uses our Android application which was able to automate and record attendance checking in the background. Procedure 2 uses the ESP32 which was capable of scanning for information from these Android smartphones. Both of these Procedures send information to the web server to create reports based on available records. Overall, Procedure 1 served as the more scalable implementation due to its added features such as alarm systems, and ease of monitoring. However, Procedure 2 was simpler to set-up and more energy-efficient for smartphones since it relied on processing capabilities of the server.

Keywords: Smart attendance · Bluetooth low energy · Android · ESP32 · Cloud computing

1 Introduction

Recording student attendance is a common practice and is commonly mandatory in schools and universities. In a study conducted by Bekkering and Ward, there is a positive linkage between school attendance and academic performance [4].

© ICST Institute for Computer Sciences, Social Informatics and Telecommunications Engineering 2022
Published by Springer Nature Switzerland AG 2022. All Rights Reserved
H. Jin et al. (Eds.): CROWNCOM 2021/WiCON 2021, LNICST 427, pp. 253–268, 2022.
https://doi.org/10.1007/978-3-030-98002-3_19

The attendance rule in University of the Philippines - Diliman (UPD) stipulates that when the number of absences exceeds 20% of the total number of days for the semester, the student will be dropped from that class [10].

One method of attendance recording in the Electrical and Electronics Engineering Institute (EEEI) is by roll call. This is time consuming especially if the class lasts for only 1.5 h. Another method used is by passing an attendance sheet and encoding it in an electronic spreadsheet later on. As mentioned, the number of hours the student is present in class is important; however, both methods do not account for the students leaving the classroom earlier than scheduled.

In this study, a way to automate attendance recording was implemented. With the help of Bluetooth Low Energy (BLE) technology, two methods were implemented. A BLE beacon scans and advertises for the students' smartphones to record attendance. Depending on the Procedure, the attendance logs were sent to the server. Furthermore, the gathered information was stored in a database and was displayed both in the application and website. Smart attendance tracking also prevented students from cheating their attendance as it used their personal smartphones.

Paper Contributions: The major contributions of this paper are as follows: (1) testing the internal performance of an ESP32 as both scanner and beacon in a smart attendance checking system; (2) evaluation and comparison of the overall performance of the aforementioned Procedure 1 and Procedure 2; and (3) provides a basis for mitigating proxy attendance in hands-free attendance checking systems using ESP32 and BLE.

The rest of the paper is organized as follows. Section 2 provides a few related studies used as motivation and basis for our study. Section 3 describes the goals for our system in terms of the features it should provide. Section 4 discusses the methodology. Section 5 discusses our results and analysis. Finally, Sect. 6 presents our conclusion and recommendations for future work.

2   Related Work

Smartphone and Bluetooth Low Energy Implementations

Numerous studies have implemented different version of attendance systems through the use of BLE and smartphones. The main problems with the traditional attendance systems are cost, queues, and time. To address cost, several studies such as [3,8] used BLE beacons for a low-cost and inclusive system. While these systems are more convenient, their implementations are unable to prevent students from 'cheating' the system through proxy attendance. The works of [2,5,11] sought to prevent this through the use of the Bluetooth MAC address as unique identifiers per student. However, versions from Android 8 onward have made Bluetooth MAC address inaccessible. To solve this issue, AMAS, an attendance system made by Dankar et al. used the smartphone's IMEI address to verify the student instead of the MAC address [7]. Another issue is the possibility that students 'cheat' the system by recording attendance, then leaving the room after. To prevent this from happening, another study [5] implemented an algorithm where they timestamped information to be able to detect student presence all throughout a given class period. However, this needs a modified beacon which would require additional costs, and IMEI became inaccessible starting from Android 10. Zoric et al. [12] suggests having the application run in the background as it obtains beacon information. This allows the application to automatically check attendance wherever the user is for a hands-free experience.

Our study adopted some of the features from these studies. The timestamp mechanism, and the background scanning suggestion from [5,12] were adopted to give the system a hands-free experience. We also want to prevent cheating so we adopted a more controlled authentication mechanism similar to [7]. Additionally, an administrative login is needed to change accounts for easier monitoring of the 'one smartphone per student' rule.

Bluetooth Low Energy

Among several wireless technologies utilized in Internet of Things applications, BLE is new and gaining popularity. We looked at the real world performance of BLE communication.

For large communication networks, network collisions and traffic become a pertinent issue. Cho et al. [6] studied the BLE discovery process and calculated the influence of parameters such as discovery latency and energy performance. They showed that while discovery latency increases as the number of BLE devices which act as receivers increase, it is not affected by the number of transmitters sending advertisements since there are few collisions among advertisers.

Bawiec and Nikodem [9] studied the effect of collisions on the communication performance of BLE when under the presence of over 200 communicating devices. Here, they explored the features of BLE connectionless mode which allows for one-way communication from end-devices to a central device. The results of this study show that by performing multiple advertisement transmissions of the same information within a set data interval, over 200 devices can simultaneously transmit data successfully with a high reception rate.

In these studies, the parameters used to quantify their systems were defined based on their respective objectives. Thus, our study adopted a similar approach and defined a set of parameters based on the functionality of our system. Furthermore, our study adopted Bawiec and Nikodem's [9] approach of using BLE's connectionless mode since the payload between our devices was relatively small and our system had no need for a Bluetooth pairing process. To observe the effects of latency and collisions on our system, we tested it using different configurations to see what broadcaster-listener setup would perform better.

3   System Features

We aimed to create an automated attendance checking system that was able to do the following.

- Eliminated queues through automated attendance checking using smartphones
- Monitored student presence throughout the class session to prevent cheating in attendance records
- Automated attendance encoding for professors, and provide a summary of reports for both students and professors based on the attendance checked
- Sent data to a web server through the application and the Bluetooth beacon

To create such a system, the following were accomplished:

- A BLE beacon capable of sending a unique identifier represented by their room assignment to the students' smartphones. This communicated with the web server for transmission of student information.
- An application capable of receiving information from the BLE beacon. It checked attendance automatically without the need for user prompts. It verified validity of attendance with the server and showed attendance progress of students.
- A web server capable of receiving information from the BLE beacon, and application. This web server automatically updated attendance information in their respective class databases, and showed such records to both student and professors.

4   Methodology

This section describes the general Procedure of our implemented system. Our goal was to create a system that was capable of efficient data transmission through beacons and BLE and Wi-Fi enabled smartphones. To ensure that the students were indeed using their smartphone, they have to register in the centralized database. The database noted their basic information (name, course, year, schedule etc.). We limited the number of registered smartphones to one per student.

4.1   General System Architecture

Our study explored two procedures in data transmission to the server as seen in Fig. 1. Both architectures were implemented and tested in this study. They were evaluated based on specified performance metrics. Additionally, since we only conducted tests in a simulated classroom setting only, specified criterion were done along with the analysis of performance metrics to determine which was better for its intended use.

Figure 1a describes Procedure 1 where the system transmitted data to the server using smartphones. Students turned on the Bluetooth on their smartphone. Once they are in proximity of the beacon, an application scanned for the beacon's Universally Unique Identifier (UUID), major, and minor values. These were verified to match those values stored in the application. Also, to check for student presence throughout the class session, ping checks between

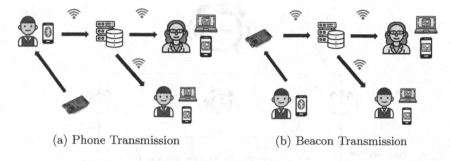

(a) Phone Transmission   (b) Beacon Transmission

Fig. 1. General system architecture

the smartphone and beacon were done to record time stamps [5] depending on the duration of the class. Once internet connection was available, it sends the information to the server. Finally, the professors and students were able to view their respective attendance records through the application or website.

Figure 1b shows Procedure 2. It worked similar to Procedure 1 except that the beacon transmits the data to the server and that internet connection must always be available to do so. Relevant information from the application is fed to the beacon, and the rest of the steps are followed.

4.2   Application

The software used for the development of this application were Android Studio as the Integrated Development Environment (IDE) and DB Browser for SQLite as the medium of access for the local database.

General Logic. On initial startup of the application after its download, the user is prompted to set the username and student number for that smartphone. To safeguard it from fraudulent intentions, an additional prompt for administrative credentials (e.g., admin username and password) is required before proceeding with this process. The application will then connect to the server and get information related to that student number (e.g., classes enlisted and their schedule). Once that information is available within the smartphone, a 3-stage alarm system shown in Fig. 2 takes care of the rest of the functionality of the application in the background.

First, a daily alarm is set every day at 12 AM then application will get the user's class list for that day. A new alarm will be generated for each of the classes for the day. These class alarms will be triggered at the start of their period and will then generate another set of 10 alarms spread evenly throughout the duration of that class as 'ping checks' to determine the presence of the user.

Bluetooth Communication. The application can act either as a listener for Procedure 1 or as a broadcaster for Procedure 2, both of which function for

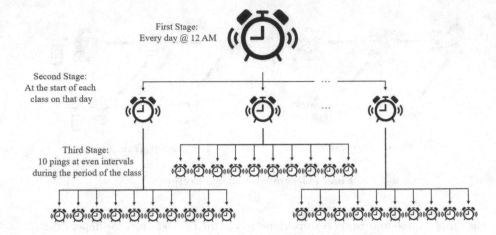

First Stage:
Every day @ 12 AM

Second Stage:
At the start of each
class on that day

Third Stage:
10 pings at even intervals
during the period of the class

Fig. 2. 3-stage alarm system

a small period at every 'ping check' alarm. As a listener for Procedure 1, the application will scan for Bluetooth advertisements, specifically those sent by ESP32s in their broadcaster mode. The scan will be filtered by the UUID, major, and minor values to determine the correct broadcaster which corresponds to the class at that moment. As a broadcaster for Procedure 2, the application will simply broadcast Bluetooth advertisements with information containing a UUID and the student number of that smartphone for the ESP32 in its listener mode to receive.

Interface. The main user interface (UI) of the application seen in Fig. 3 displays the basic functionalities the user would need, such as:

- A button to toggle the smartphone's Bluetooth on and off
- The status of the alarm system and a button to manually restart it
- A list of their classes for that day

On the top-right corner is a toolbar button which pops-up a list of a few more functionalities for the viewing of the user, such as:

- A list of all their classes
- A list of their recent attendance records
- A button to scan and list nearby Bluetooth devices

Communication with Server. The application communicates with the server through REST frameworks. All the necessary information was passed in JSON formats. The server used Django REST, while the application used Retrofit2 for their respective REST interfaces. Models were created for both the server and application for sending and receiving the datum in JSON. For the application,

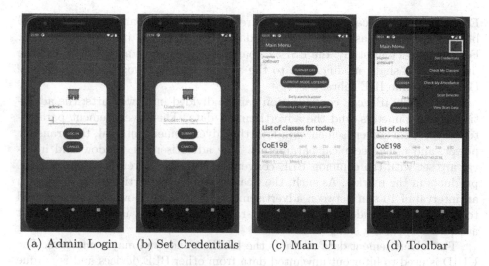

(a) Admin Login   (b) Set Credentials   (c) Main UI   (d) Toolbar

Fig. 3. User interface

these were used to get the list of JSON files in the different REST pages which were navigated using Retrofit's JSON API Interface. Majority of the communication happens whenever the user logs in, and updates the attendance. The server's attendance was updated by cross checking current server attendance with the local/application attendance list. This helps reduce redundancies when POST-ing by only sending the entries that are not yet uploaded.

4.3 ESP32

For the two Procedures defined in this study, an ESP32 is used as a broadcaster for Procedure 1 and as a listener for Procedure 2. The ESP32 also communicated with the web server in order to deliver the scanned data. The ESP32 programs were developed using C++ via the Arduino IDE. This study used the ESP32 boards package v1.0.4 by Esspressif Systems.

Fig. 4. An ESP32 used in this study

ESP32 as Broadcaster. In Procedure 1, the ESP32 board acted as a BLE beacon and broadcasts the necessary data to be received by the application. For this particular study, the ESP32 board is configured as an iBeacon and the program is a slight modification to the sample iBeacon program given by the ESP32 Arduino IDE Library.

The ESP32 iBeacon configuration can be divided into two parts: the advertisement parameters, and the advertisement data. The advertisement parameters involve the advertisement window, the advertisement interval, the transmit power, and other technical parameters. The advertisement window and interval are set with the common BLE convention used by currently available BLE products in the market. As such, the beacon is set to advertise for 100 ms with an interval of 10 s in between advertisements. The signal power was configured to transmit at the default high power rating such that it is able to transmit adequately within a small classroom.

The advertisement data contains the UUID, minor and major numbers. The UUID is used to filter out unwanted data from other BLE devices and is unique to all devices used in this study. It was also decided that the major and minor numbers in the beacon advertisement data would be used to identify each class's building and room number respectively. For the testing however, the study was not deployed in actual classrooms thus the major and minor number pair are used to represent classes instead. The following table shows a sample broadcast data that we used in our tests:

Table 1. ID assignments per class

Course	Room ID (Minor number)	Building ID (Major number)
CoE 198 MAB1	1	1
CoE 111	2	1
CoE 113	3	1
CoE 151	1	2
CoE 197D	2	2
EEE 100	3	2

When deployed, the ESP32 beacon is placed inside its corresponding classroom and continuously broadcasts its advertisement data to be received by participating smartphones. The low energy capability of the ESP32 allows it to enter deep sleep to conserve energy with a 10:0.1 sleep-to-broadcast ratio.

ESP32 as Listener. For Procedure 2, the ESP32 board acted as a BLE listener which listened to the periodic BLE broadcast of participating smartphones. The listener also connected to a Wi-Fi network to deliver the gathered data to the web server.

As a BLE listener, the scan window and interval must be configured to set the frequency at which the device listens for advertisements. Lower intervals and bigger scan times ensure faster detection, thus, it was set to listen for 100 ms with an interval of also 100 ms. For testing purposes, it was noted that a listening duration of 5 s is more than sufficient to detect at least 10 simulated BLE devices. The listener was also assigned integer values to act as the room and building ID. The same convention was used as in Table 1.

Every cycle of the listener must follow a specific sequence: get current time, listen for devices, then send data to server. This sequence occurs periodically as long as the device is turned on. Since the ESP32 does not have access to the current time locally, it must connect to the Network Time Protocol (NTP) server at the start of each sequence to get the actual current time. It will then switch to BLE to listen for any broadcasting smartphones. Each smartphone data is saved as a JSON object which is created as soon as that particular smartphone is scanned. The JSON object created for each smartphone contains the date and general time it was detected, the building and room ID of the listener device, and the Received Signal Strength Integer (RSSI). Each JSON object is compiled into a list which becomes the payload to be sent to the server. After the BLE scan, the device connects to the Wi-Fi and sends the JSON list via HTTP POST request. The following is a sample payload from the ESP32 listener to the web server:

```
[
{"dayStamp":"2021-05-31","timeStamp":"15:35:38","bid":1,"rid":1,"numID":201444444,"rssi":-64},
{"dayStamp":"2021-05-31","timeStamp":"15:35:38","bid":1,"rid":1,"numID":201355679,"rssi":-55},
{"dayStamp":"2021-05-31","timeStamp":"15:35:38","bid":1,"rid":1,"numID":202165432,"rssi":-64},
{"dayStamp":"2021-05-31","timeStamp":"15:35:38","bid":1,"rid":1,"numID":201222222,"rssi":-64},
{"dayStamp":"2021-05-31","timeStamp":"15:35:38","bid":1,"rid":1,"numID":201555555,"rssi":-70}
]
```

4.4   Web Server

The web server receives data coming from either the application or the ESP32 depending on the Procedure being used as specified in the General System Architecture.

Phone Side. For Procedure 1 implementation, the smartphone sends the relevant attendance information through the application to the web server. On the web server side, attendance data is simply received from the application and stored in the database. The changes made to the database are saved and are immediately available for download through the application to the relevant users. Note that the smartphone will only send a 'Present' attendance object if the smartphone satisfies the minimum number of pings. If a fewer number of pings is received, meaning the student did not stay within the classroom vicinity for the entire period, then the smartphone will send an 'Absent' attendance object to the web server.

ESP32 Side. For Procedure 2 implementation, ESP32 constantly sends data based on the smartphones it detects within its vicinity to the web server. Therefore, it can send multiple ESP32 data objects at once, depending on the number of smartphones detected. Once this data reaches the server, the server filters it out based on the room ID and building ID set by the given beacon's major and minor values respectively, as well as the data values that it receives which contains date, time, and student number. The server will only keep data that belongs to students registered in the system that have classes at the given date and time periods. The server needs to receive a certain number of ESP32 data objects (or pings) from the ESP32 to confirm that the student was there for the majority of the class. At the end of the day, additional scripts are run on the database to aggregate the received pings and update attendance accordingly.

Periodic Tasks. There are necessary periodic tasks that run daily in order to update the database. First, there is one script that will add 'Absent' attendances to the database based on the current attendance information. The script will check the current database to see if students that had classes that day do not yet have corresponding attendance data for each of the classes. This is necessary for Procedure 2 because it only records 'Present' attendances. For Procedure 1, it serves as a fail-safe if the application is unable to send the 'Absent' attendances for a given reason (e.g., smartphone runs out of battery during class period). Second, a pair of scripts that convert the ESP32 data objects (or pings) received from the ESP32 implementation and convert these pings into an actual attendance object at the end of the day. These scripts simply aggregate the number of pings that it received corresponding to each class per given user. Note that these scripts run at the end of the day in order to only update the database when all of the attendance-related information has already been received during the class hours.

5   Results and Analysis

This section tackles the internal performance of our system. Latency and Bluetooth advertisement reception were tested to quantify connectivity, and Bluetooth communication between the system components.

Procedure 1 Performance - System Connectivity. The application and beacon connection was tested by using the NRF Connect application by Nordic Semiconductors. The application was installed on a Samsung Galaxy A20s. The connection was measured by scanning the beacon multiple times while recording its RSSI value. The beacon was scanned at four distances with no physical obstruction in between. To provide a baseline, the ESP32 was configured to its default transmission power of 0 dBm at 1 m. Scanning was continuous until 500 entries were achieved. It is also important to note that alongside the ESP32, other wireless connections were present.

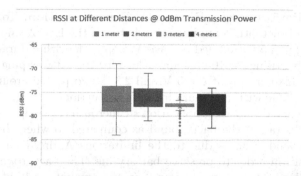

Fig. 5. RSSI at different distances @ 0 dBm transmission power

The compiled RSSI data is visualized in Fig. 5. Averaging the results of the 1 m, 2 m, 3 m, 4 m tests, the RSSI values are −76.257 dBm, −76.249 dBm, −78.0685 dBm, and −77.831 dBm, respectively. Here we see a slight decrease on the RSSI values as distance increases, which is expected. However, it is important to note that these values can differ depending on the voltage supplied to the ESP32. Although the attained RSSI values range in between the "Good" and "Low" range [1], it will not affect our system. In our case, the application does not need to connect to the beacon since they only scan for their information.

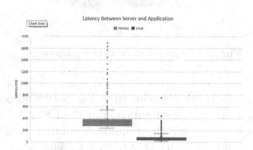

Fig. 6. Latency between the application and server

The application and server latency was measured through the application. A function was made to record the latency by subtracting the time before the HTTP request is sent, and time after the HTTP response is received. The data is visualized in Fig. 6. The deployment was done in Heroku and our local connection. The average latency is recorded at 394 ms for Heroku, and 80 ms for the local connection. If the outliers or spikes are removed, the average latency decreases to 337 ms and 65 ms respectively. Heroku gives higher latency than the local connection because Heroku is a free cloud service, and it is meant for early developments only. If lower latency is desired, the server must be ran either locally or in a better cloud service.

Procedure 1 Performance - Bluetooth Communication. To test the performance of the Bluetooth communication between the ESP32 and the application, the ESP32 was programmed to have a sleep cycle with a duration of 10.1 s where it was advertising for 100 ms and asleep for 10 s. It was plugged to a wall socket with an adapter outputting 5 V and 2.4 A and placed around 5 m away from the smartphone with minimal physical obstructions.

It should be noted that the application's Bluetooth scanning capabilities are weaker when it is ran in the background as compared to when the application is in the foreground. This is due to the limitations Android has imposed on background tasks in order to preserve battery life. The background work done by the application may take more time than the amount Android allocates for background tasks before killing them. Given this, a workaround was to disable the 'battery optimisation' feature for the application.

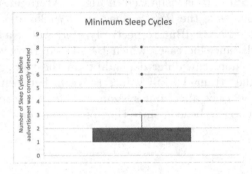

Fig. 7. Minimum sleep cycles parameter

For this test, the application's scan time was set to accommodate 12 sleep cycles of the 10.1 s sleep cycle configuration of the ESP32. Figure 7 shows 300 data points collected to analyze the minimum number of sleep cycles needed before the advertisement was correctly received. With a mean of 1.736 and a standard deviation of 1.2, it is sufficient to say that 3 sleep cycles worth of scan time is enough to account for most instances and correctly receive the advertisement within that time period. For one ping check, 30 s would be a reasonable time for the application to do some background work while keeping the smartphone's battery consumption to a minimum.

With the same setup, 200 data points were collected to analyze the ratio between the number of sleep cycles where the advertisement was correctly received over the 12 total sleep cycles. Figure 8 shows this data with a mean of 0.378 and a standard deviation of 0.154. While an average of 4 out of 12 sleep cycles where the advertisement is correctly received seems relatively low, what is important for our system is that it correctly receive the advertisement at some point and it does so during the first few sleep cycles as seen by the analysis on the minimum sleep cycles parameter.

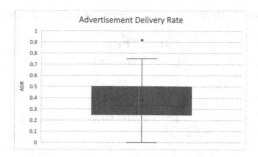

Fig. 8. Advertisement delivery rate parameter

Procedure 2 Performance - System Connectivity. The ESP32 to server latency was measured by recording the response time from sending packets to the local and Heroku servers. The packets, carrying the same payload, were sent to the server 500 times in order to collect the data points.

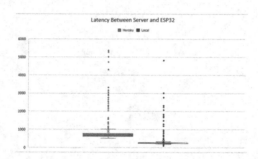

Fig. 9. Latency between ESP32 and the server

As shown in Fig. 9, the average response time of the Heroku server is 899.14 ms with a standard deviation of 748.036 ms while the average response time of the local server is 353.09 ms with a standard deviation of 391.79 ms. The higher latency of the Heroku server could be attributed to the fact that this transmission is done over the internet versus the transmission done over the local area network. A stress test was also conducted to determine the Packet Reception Rate (PRR) of the local server. Each test sent 1000 of the same packets consecutively to the server. The following table shows the PRR for each test:

With an average PRR of 99.25%, it is enough to correctly determine the presence of the students throughout each class.

Table 2. Packet Reception Rate for ESP32 to server

Test no.	PRR
1	99.30%
2	98.20%
3	100.00%
4	99.50%

Procedure 2 Performance - Bluetooth Communication. The Bluetooth communication test for Procedure 2 measures the speed and efficiency of the ESP32 listener when it comes to detecting smartphone broadcasters. For this test, we used a total of five smartphones each of different brands and models placed at various distances from the listener device. The listener scans in cycles of 100 ms with an interval of 100 ms. The smartphones advertise in bursts of one minute continuous broadcasts. The test recorded the multiple detection times for every smartphone regardless of distance from the listener. 500 data points were gathered.

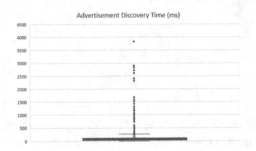

Fig. 10. Advertisement discovery time parameter

Figure 10 shows the advertisement discovery time for all smartphones during the multiple test runs. Most discovery times fall between the 20 ms to 300 ms range with the average scan time being 199.50 ms with a standard deviation of 2.24 ms. For this test, a scanning phase of 5 s was determined to be sufficient time to detect five smartphones within the area. Given the average scan time gathered from the data point, a regular classroom with about 30 students will need a scan duration of 6 s in order to detect the majority of smartphones while a larger classroom of 100 students will need a scan duration of 20 s assuming that every broadcasting smartphones is within range. We also measured the minimum scan cycles needed in order to detect any broadcaster given the 200 ms scan period defined earlier.

As shown in Figure 11, the vast majority of smartphones require only 1 scan cycle to be detected. Of the 572 data points for this test, 83.39% required only 1 scan cycle to be detected.

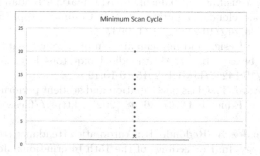

Fig. 11. Minimum scan cycle time parameter

6 Conclusion and Future Work

This study aimed to develop a smart attendance system using BLE using an Android application, an ESP32, and a web server. BLE served as an important mode of checking attendances through its advertising and scanning functionalities. Two Procedures were done to send the data to the server. The first Procedure uses the smartphone to scan beacons and update attendance. The second Procedure uses the ESP32 to do the same, except it scans for smartphones.

The application was able to successfully log attendance of the user. It was able to automatically start scanning for beacons depending on the class set in the user's schedule. The attendance log would then be stored within the application's local database after every class which would then be sent to the server to update the professors. It was also able to implement additional features such as schedule tracking, and class notifications. Lastly, the application was also able to broadcast itself to the ESP32 if the second Procedure is implemented.

The web server was able to successfully receive and process information from the smartphone in Procedure 1, and from the ESP32 in Procedure 2. Relevant attendance and class scheduling information are easily available for viewing through the web page as well. Certain user profiles (admin and teachers) were also able to access the database and make manual adjustments as needed.

Ultimately, Procedure 1 serves as the more scalable implementation between the two Procedures. It also has the added bonus of some helpful features such as an alarm system and the ability to easily check schedule information. On the other hand, Procedure 2 is simpler to set-up, and lessens the power consumption needed by the smartphones by taking advantage of the processing capabilities of the server. For future work, we recommend deploying the system in a real classroom setting. The UI can be also improved further.

References

1. RSSI level and a signal strength. https://www.netspotapp.com/what-is-rssi-level.html
2. Al-Shezawi, M., Yousif, J., Al-balushi, I.: Automatic attendance registration system based mobile cloud computing. Int. J. Comput. Appl. Sci. **2**(3), 116–122 (2017). https://doi.org/10.24842/1611/0037
3. Bae, M., Cho, D.: Design and implementation of automatic attendance check system using BLE beacon. Int. J. Multimedia Ubiquitous Eng. **10**, 177–186 (2015). https://doi.org/10.14257/IJMUE.2015.10.10.19
4. Bekkering, E., Ward, T.: Class participation and student performance: a tale of two courses. Inf. Syst. Educ. J. **18**(6), 86–98 (2020). https://files.eric.ed.gov/fulltext/EJ1258148.pdf
5. Boric, M., Fernandez, A., Redondo, R.: Automatic attendance control system based on BLE technology. In: Proceedings of the 15th International Joint Conference on e-Business and Telecommunications (ICETE), vol. 1, pp. 289–295 (2018). https://doi.org/10.5220/0006830202890295
6. Cho, K., Park, G., Cho, W., Seo, J., Han, K.: Performance analysis of device discovery of Bluetooth low energy (BLE) networks. Comput. Commun. **81**, 72–85 (2016)
7. Dankar, A., Kundapur, P.P.: Automated mobile attendance system (AMAS). In: 2019 International Conference on Advances in Computing, Communication and Control (ICAC3), pp. 1–6 (2019). https://doi.org/10.1109/ICAC347590.2019.9036787
8. Hidayat, M.A., Simalango, H.M.: Students attendance system and notification of college subject schedule based on classroom using iBeacon. In: 2018 3rd International Conference on Information Technology, Information System and Electrical Engineering (ICITISEE), pp. 253–258 (2018). https://doi.org/10.1109/ICITISEE.2018.8720948
9. Nikodem, M., Bawiec, M.: Experimental evaluation of advertisement-based Bluetooth low energy communication. Sensors **20**(1), 107 (2019). https://doi.org/10.3390/s20010107
10. University of the Philippines: Attendance (revised up code: Art. 346). https://our.upd.edu.ph/files/acadinfo/ATTENDANCE.pdf
11. Puckdeevongs, A., Tripathi, N.K., Witayangkurn, A., Saengudomlert, P.: Classroom attendance systems based on Bluetooth low energy indoor positioning technology for smart campus. Information **11**(6), 329 (2020). https://doi.org/10.3390/info11060329
12. Zorić, B., Dudjak, M., Bajer, D., Martinović, G.: Design and development of a smart attendance management system with Bluetooth low energy beacons. In: 2019 Zooming Innovation in Consumer Technologies Conference (ZINC), pp. 86–91 (2019). https://doi.org/10.1109/ZINC.2019.8769433

Intra-train Wagon Wireless Channel Connectivity Analysis of Ultra Dense Node Deployments

Imanol Picallo[1], Hicham Klaina[2], Peio López-Iturri[1],
Jose Javier Astrain[3], Mikel Celaya-Echarri[4], Leyre Azpilicueta[4],
Ana Alejos[2], Asier Perallos[5], Agusti Solanas[6],
and Francisco Falcone[1(✉)]

[1] Department of Electrical, Electronic and Communication Engineering,
UPNA, Pamplona, Spain
{imanol.picallo,peio.lopez,
francisco.falcone}@unavarra.es
[2] Signal Theory Department, University of Vigo, Vigo, Spain
analejos@uvigo.es
[3] School of Engineering and Sciences, Tecnologico de Monterrey,
Monterrey, Mexico
josej.astrain@unavarra.es
[4] Department of Statistics, Informatics and Mathematics, UPNA,
Pamplona, Spain
leyre.azpilicueta@tec.mx
[5] Engineering Faculty, University of Deusto, Bilbao, Spain
perallos@deusto.es
[6] Department of Computer Engineering and Mathematics,
Universitat Rovira i Virgili, Tarragona, Spain
agusti.solanas@urv.cat

Abstract. The advent of Internet of Things will provide massive connectivity and seamless interaction, mainly enabled by wireless communication systems. In this work, intra-wagon connectivity will be analyzed in terms of different system wireless system requirements. The specific application considers the use of standards such as 802.11 ah, Bluetooth Low Energy and Frequency Range 1 5G new radio spectrum, with the aid of in-house deterministic 3D Ray Launching algorithm, providing precise characterization of multiple parameters, such as interference distribution, received power levels and time domain characteristics.

Keywords: Intra-wagon communications · 802.11 ah · BLE · 5G NR · 3D Ray Launching

1 Introduction

The progressive adoption of Smart City and Smart Region paradigms is leading towards context aware environments, in which high levels of user interaction are one of the main characteristics. In this sense, wireless communication systems play a key role

H. Jin et al. (Eds.): CROWNCOM 2021/WiCON 2021, LNICST 427, pp. 269–279, 2022.
https://doi.org/10.1007/978-3-030-98002-3_20

in order to enable seamless interaction in multiple user/environment conditions. In this sense, given the advent of Internet of Things (IoT), highly variable and dynamic channel conditions can be established, in which scenarios of high complexity and large node densities are commonplace. In order to comply with quality of service and quality of experience requirements, interoperation between multiple wireless systems is envisaged, providing optimal coverage/capacity relations in the scenarios under test [1–5]. In this way, depending on node density, coverage area and transmission rate, different systems within the range of personal area communications, wireless sensor networks, wireless local area networks or public land mobile networks can be employed. In the case of IoT related applications, there are additional considerations to take into account, such as reduced form factor, low cost, high node density and limited energy availability. With this in mind, systems such as 802.11ah, Bluetooth Low Energy (BLE) or 5G New Radio operating in Frequency Range 1 (i.e., below 6 GHz) are some of the candidates under consideration in order to enable IoT oriented wireless connectivity.

In the context of train communications, the implementation of context aware user interactive environments is a goal related with the adoption of Intelligent Transportation System paradigms. By embedding dynamic communication systems within different elements of the train system infrastructure, different types of services can be provided, such as telecontrol and telemetry, passenger assistance, location/user-oriented marketing or multi-modal transportation handling, among others. Wireless systems play a key role in terms of providing interconnectivity within rail transportation systems [6, 7]. Among these, intra-wagon connectivity enables the development of different applications, given by different requirements by passengers as well as by train operators. These scenario pose specific challenges in terms of wireless system operation, owing to high transceiver density, the presence of users and interaction with human body in terms of blockage/dispersion and large scatterer density leading to strong multipath components, inherent to the underlying metallic structure within the wagon. Therefore, precise wireless channel characterization is compulsory in order to provide optimal device/network design in terms of coverage/capacity relations, particularly in the case of high node density conditions. In this sense, deterministic channel propagation methods can provide accurate results in order to extract information such as interference distribution or hot-spot identification, among others.

In this work, wireless channel characterization for intra-wagon train communications is performed, considering multiple wireless communication systems providing services for IoT enables applications, such as 802.11ah, BLE and 5G NR FR1 systems. Deterministic wireless channel estimation for the complete scenario volume, for frequency domain as well as time domain parameters is obtained, as a function of transceiver node location in the scenario under test.

2   Intra-wagon Wireless Channel Characterization

In order to perform the intra-wagon wireless channel characterization, an in-house implemented 3D Ray Launching code has been employed. the algorithm has been coded in Matlab and different modules have been added in order to reduce computational cost and increase simulation accuracy, including hybrid neural network interpolators, bi-dimensional electromagnetic diffusion equation or deep learning data base extraction based on collaborative filtering [8, 9]. A realistic simulation scenario has been implemented in order to consider all the effects of the surrounding environment, given by scatterer location (i.e., seats, intra-wagon cabinets and railings) and dispersive material properties. A schematic representation is depicted in Fig. 1.

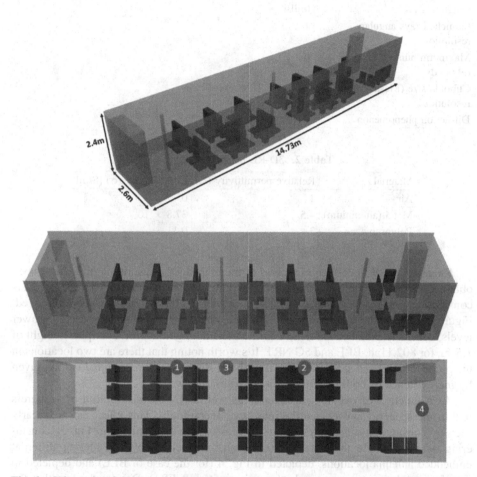

Fig. 1. Schematic of the intra-wagon scenario and the location of the embedded transceivers.

Simulation parameters have been set according to extensive convergence analysis, in order to optimize simulation time whilst maintaining high accuracy values (i.e., maximum number of reflections until extinction of launched ray, angle resolution in the polar plane, angular resolution in the azimuthal plane and cuboid mesh cell dimensions) [10]. The simulation parameters employed are detailed in Table 1 and the frequency dispersive material characteristics (which in this specific study remain practically constant for all the frequencies under analysis) are given in Table 2.

Table 1. 3D-RL simulation parameters.

Parameters	Values
Operation frequency	868 MHz (802.11ah-Europe), 2.4 GHz BLE, 3.5 GHz 5G NR FR1
Transmitted power	10 dBm
Antenna type	Monopole
Antenna gain	0 dBi
Launched rays angular resolution	1°
Maximum number of rebounds	6
Cuboids size (Mesh resolution)	10 cm × 10 cm × 10 cm
Difraction phenomenon	Activated

Table 2. 3D-RL material properties.

Material	Relative permittivity (ε_r)	Conductivity (σ) [S/m]
Air	1	0
Metal (aluminium)	4.5	37.8×10^6
Polypropylene	3	0.11

Received power levels as a function of the embedded transmitting node have been obtained for the complete volume of the train wagon, enabling coverage analysis considering potential location of receivers as well as the wireless system employed. Figure 2 depicts the estimation of bi-dimensional distributions of received power levels, considering embedded node 1 as the transmitting node, for a cut-plane height of 1.5 m, for 802.11ah, BLE and 5G NR1. It's worth noting that there are two locations in the plots (far left-hand side and upper right-hand side) there is deep signal fading, given by the existence of both metallic cabinets within the wagon.

As a function of operating frequency as well as by the distribution of scatterers within the scenario, power distributions vary accordingly. This effect can be clearly seen by considering different cut-plane heights, which are depicted in Fig. 3 (considering as an example the case of 802.11 ah), as well as by considering different embedded antenna locations, depicted in Fig. 4 (for the case of BLE) and depicted in Fig. 5 (considering as an example the case of 5G NR FR1). Despite the fact that the scenario under test has a limited volume size, the impact of interior furnishings (mainly seats, with a large density of highly reflective scatterers) can be clearly observed as potential location of receiver nodes is varied, as well as the vicinity of each one of the transmitting nodes considered.

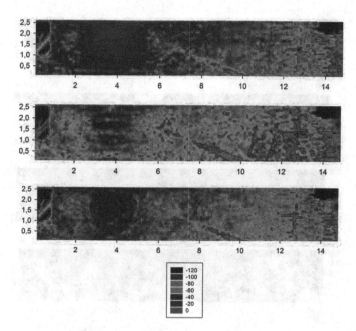

Fig. 2. Estimation of received power levels considering TX Antena 1 at a cut-plane height of 1.5 m, for 802.11 ah (top), BLE (middle) and 5G NR FR1 (bottom).

An example is given in the top 2 images in Fig. 4, which correspond to cut-plane height of 0.5 m and 1 m, respectively. Shadowing effects can be observed following a longitudinal distribution, approximately every 2 m. This is caused by the presence of the seats, with predominant non-line of sight links at those considered heights. Similar considerations can be seen for open space regions within the indoor train wagon cabin or the existence of elements such as cabinets, in which received power levels decrease considerably (specially in the case of considering metallic doors, which is the usual case within the indoor train environment). This effect can also be observed in Fig. 3 and Fig. 4, in the upper left hand of the received power level plots, corresponding to the presence of an operation cabinet within the train wagon, with losses in the excess of 20 dB owing to the presence of the metallic doors which enclose the cabinet volume.

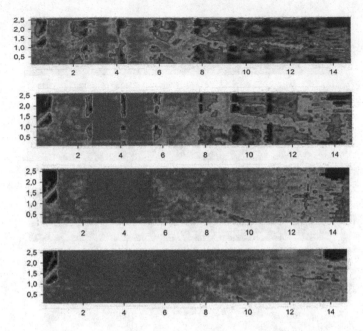

Fig. 3. Estimation of received power levels considering Antena -802.11ah and variations of cut plane height (from top to bottom) of 0.5 m, 1 m, 1.5 m and 2 m, respectively

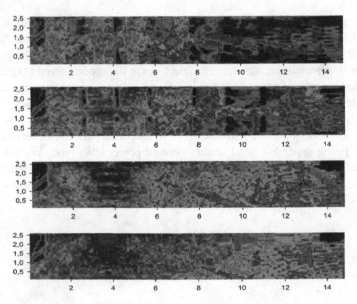

Fig. 4. Estimation of received power levels considering Antena 1-BLE and variations of cut plane height (from top to bottom) of 0.5 m, 1 m, 1.5 m and 2 m, respectively

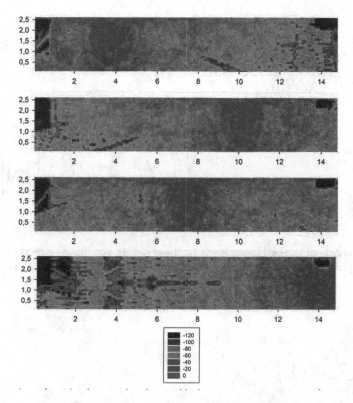

Fig. 5. Estimation of received power levels considering 5G NR FR1 at a cut plane height of 1.5 m for (top to bottom figures), node A1, A2, A3 and A4, respectively

Based on the estimation of received power levels, coverage/capacity relations can be obtained as a function of receiver sensitivity, which can be quantitatively evaluated by obtaining linear radial received power level distributions, such as the ones depicted in Fig. 6, for the case of 802.11 ah and in Fig. 7, for the case of BLE. The impact of height modification is clearly visible within this scenario, in which the location of seats leads mainly to non- line of sight conditions, as well as the impact of multipath propagation components, which build up with distance as interaction with scatterers increases. It is worth noting that estimations can be obtained within the complete intra-train wagon scenario, enabling to consider the location of transceivers at any given point within the wagon.

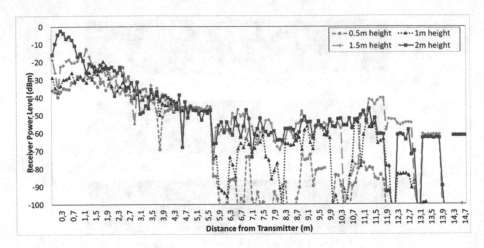

Fig. 6. Estimation of received power levels for linear radials, considering embedded transceiver A4 and cut plane heights of 0.5 m, 1 m, 1.5 m and 2 m, for the case of 802.11ah

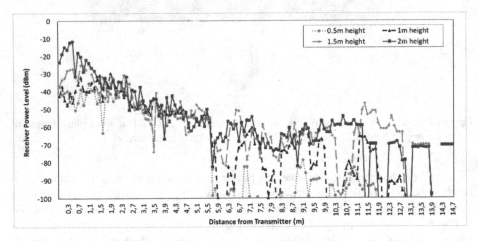

Fig. 7. Estimation of received power levels for linear radials, considering embedded transceiver A4 and cut plane heights of 0.5 m, 1 m, 1.5 m and 2 m, for the case of BLE

Multipath propagation characteristics can also be analyzed as a function of time domain parameters, such as power delay profiles or delay spread estimations, which can subsequently be employed to analyze elements such as coherence time or time of flight. Time domain characteristics can be extracted from the complete volume of the scenario under analysis. Examples of results for power delay profile estimations are depicted in Fig. 8 (for 802.11 ah) and Fig. 9 (for BLE), considering in both cases location of transceiver A1 and A4.

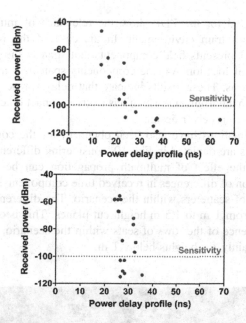

Fig. 8. Power delay profile estimations, considering 802.11 ah, for the case of location A1 (top figure) and A4 (bottom figure)

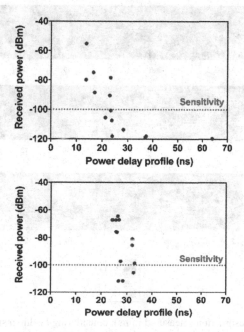

Fig. 9. Power delay profile estimations, considering BLE, for the case of location A1 (top figure) and A4 (bottom figure)

The results depicted for the PDP show the relevance of multipath propagation within the intra-wagon train environment. In the case of the results obtained for 802.11ah, location A1 presents field components that span in the 10 ns–70 ns range, whereas in the case of location A4, the components span in a much narrower time range, from 25 ns–35 ns. These results indicate that delay spread is strongly variable within the intra-wagon environment, which has a direct impact on channel equalization considerations within transceiver design.

Delay spread estimations have also been obtained, for the complete intra-wagon train scenario. Results are depicted in Fig. 10, considering different cut plane heights, for BLE, in which the effect of multipath propagation can be once again clearly observed, as a function of differences in received time components, owing to the effect of the large number of scatterers within the scenario. The differences are particularly visible when going from 1 m to 1.5 m height cut planes. This is once again given by the effect of the presence of the rows of seats within the scenario, which lead to non-line of sight links mainly for heights below 1 m.

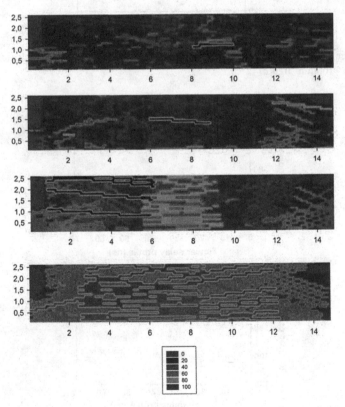

Fig. 10. Delay spread estimation (measured in ns), considering bi-dimensional cut planes at (top to bottom figure), for the case of node A3 BLE at cut plane heights of 0.5 m, 1 m, 1.5 m and 2 m

3 Conclusions

The integration of wireless communication systems in order to enable interactive passenger train applications plays a key role for the adoption of IoT within railway transportation systems. In this work, intra-wagon channel characterization for different systems (802.11 ah, BLE and 5G NR FR1) has been presented. With the aid of in-house deterministic ray launching code, the complete indoor intra-train wagon characteristics can be considered, such as furnishings (seats, handrails) or auxiliary elements (cabinets, doors). In this way estimations for the complete intra-wagon scenario have been obtained for frequency/power characteristics as well as for time domain characteristics, such as power delay profiles and delay spread distributions. The proposed methodology can be employed in order to perform coverage/capacity calculations which in turn aid in network/device design and planning process, enabling optimal network configuration. Future work involves the inclusion of human body models within the intra-wagon scenario, as well as the consideration of indoor/outdoor wireless link conditions.

References

1. Marcus, M.J.: Harmful interference and its role in spectrum policy. Proc. IEEE **102**(3), 265–269 (2014)
2. Ge, X., Huang, K., Wang, C.-X., Hong, X., Yang, X.: Capacity analysis of a multi-cell multi-antenna cooperative cellular network with co-channel interference. IEEE Trans. Wirel. Commun. **10**(10), 3298–3309 (2011)
3. Liu, F., Zhao, S.: Statistical resource allocation based on cognitive interference estimation in ultra-dense HetNets. IEEE Access **8**, 72548–72557 (2020)
4. Raza, A., Nawaz, S.J., Wyne, S., Ahmed, A., Awais Javed, M., Patwary, M.N.: Spatial modeling of interference in inter-vehicular communications for 3-D volumetric wireless networks. IEEE Access **8**, 108281–108299 (2020)
5. Karas, D.S., Boulogeorgos, A., Karagiannidis, G.K., Nallanathan, A.: Physical layer security in the presence of interference. IEEE Wirel. Commun. Lett. **6**(6), 802 (2017)
6. Tubaishat, M., Zhuang, P., Qi, Q., Shang, Y.: Wireless sensor networks in intelligent transportation systems. Wirel. Commun. Mobile Comput. **9**(3), 287–302 (2009)
7. Zhou, J., Chen, C.L.P., Chen, L., Zhao, W.: A user-customizable urban traffic information collection method based on wireless sensor networks. IEEE Trans. Intell. Transp. Syst. **14**(3), 1119–1128 (2013)
8. Azpilicueta, L., Falcone, F., Janaswamy, R.: Hybrid computational techniques for electromagnetic propagation analysis in complex indoor environments. IEEE Antennas Propag. Mag. **61**(6), 20–30 (2019)
9. Casino, F., Azpilicueta, L., López-Iturri, P., Aguirre, E., Falcone, F., Solanas, A.: Optimised wireless channel characterization in large complex environments by hybrid ray launching-collaborative filtering approach. IEEE Antennas Wirel. Propag. Lett. **16**, 780–783 (2017)
10. Azpilicueta, L., Rawat, M., Rawat, K., Ghannouchi, F., Falcone, F.: Convergence analysis in deterministic 3D ray launching radio channel estimation in complex environments. ACES J. **29**(4), 256–271 (2014)

Internet of Things and Smart Grids Security issues (WICON 2021)

Hardware-Accelerated Blockchain-Based Authentication for the Internet of Things

Joanne Marie V. Santos, Jeanne Eunice V. Pascua,
and Nestor Michael C. Tiglao(✉)

Ubiquitous Computing Laboratory Electrical and Electronics Engineering Institute,
University of the Philippines,
Velasquez Street, Diliman, 1101 Quezon City, Philippines
jvsantos@up.edu.ph, {jeanne.eunice.pascua,nestor.tiglao}@eee.upd.edu.ph

Abstract. Internet of Things (IoT) is steadily evolving which allows a new paradigm of smart sensors and lightweight devices interacting with one another without human intervention, also known as machine-to-machine (M2M) communication. This allows solution for various fields such as Smart Home Automation. In this scenario, the satisfaction of security and data privacy requirements play a fundamental role. Blockchain technology with the help of cryptography offers a solution by facilitating transactions and the coordination of devices without the need of a central authority. This study aims to improve the current smart home by developing and implementing a blockchain-based authentication system with the use of the Blockchain data structure, protocols and cryptographic algorithms such as Advanced Encryption Standard (AES), Secure Hash Algorithm (SHA-256), and Keyed-Hashing for Message Authentication (HMAC) on a microcontroller board equipped with hardware acceleration. Our performance analysis showed that hardware acceleration provided significant improvement in processing time with a speedup of 5.53 and 7.94 times for AES-128 and SHA-256, respectively, compared to a software implementation counterpart.

Keywords: IoT · Blockchain · Lightweight authentication · Hardware acceleration

1 Introduction

Internet of Things (IoT) has been gaining popularity over the past decade due to its contributions to automated services and the collection and processing of data [2]. Its capability for machine-to-machine and human-to-machine communication allows the emergence of smart homes, smart grids, and smart cities. These systems provide solutions to various global challenges such as the growing demand for energy services. A viable implementation is a power outlet monitoring system and automation, a *Smart Plug*, which raises the awareness of homeowners of their energy consumption. However, the integration of IoT in the

© ICST Institute for Computer Sciences, Social Informatics and Telecommunications Engineering 2022
Published by Springer Nature Switzerland AG 2022. All Rights Reserved
H. Jin et al. (Eds.): CROWNCOM 2021/WiCON 2021, LNICST 427, pp. 283–295, 2022.
https://doi.org/10.1007/978-3-030-98002-3_21

home presents challenges such as devices' security and data privacy. An overview of the current system framework of the smart plug is presented in Fig. 1. It is composed of four parts: the user interface, the main controller, the smart plug, and the server.

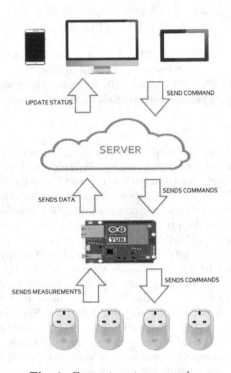

Fig. 1. Current system overview

Blockchain can be described as a distributed database with a data structure that consists of blocks which are linked back to a previously created block - its parent block. It creates a chain going back to the first block ever created, also called as the *genesis block*. This cascade effect of creating generations of blocks is the key feature of blockchain security because changing the whole blockchain means a recalculation of the subsequent blocks.

The security system, particularly the cryptographic algorithms can be implemented through the use of microcontrollers. Embedded systems, such as microcontrollers are preferred than general purpose CPU's due to space, power and cost saving reasons. Thus, a lightweight authentication system for the Smart Plug can be realized through microcontroller tools for developers. Additionally, various microcontrollers already support these cryptographic algorithms used by blockchain-based systems, as well as, non-blockchain-based implementations.

The implementation of such architecture is suitable for *machine-to-machine (M2M)* communication. M2M refers to communications between computers, embedded processors, and smart sensors with little or no human interaction [5]. As an example, wireless M2M communication lets machines communicate directly with one another (e.g. data transfer).

Commonly, an additional system with significant cost, area, and computation time is used to mitigate these issues. Thus, in this study, our goal is to design, develop, and implement an authentication system.

The specific objectives of this study are as follows:

- To implement cryptographic algorithms which provide data confidentiality from the smart plug's controller and server gateway
- To develop a hardware implementation of a blockchain-based authentication scheme for device integrity
- To compare various techniques and standards for lightweight devices in machine-to-machine (M2M) communications

Paper Contributions: The major contributions of this paper are as follows: (1) design and implementation of hardware-based blockchain authentication scheme; (2) comparison of various techniques for lightweight authentication algorithms for machine-to-machine communications; and (3) performance evaluation of the implemented schemes.

The rest of the paper is organized as follows. Section 2 provides the related work. Section 3 describes methodology of this study. Section 4 discusses the results and analysis. Section 5 provides our conclusion and recommendations for future work.

2   Related Work

In this section, we discuss lightweight cryptography and blockchain technologies. We highlight the need for efficient hardware implementation.

2.1   Lightweight Cryptography

A cryptographic system may aim to provide confidentiality, authentication, integrity, non-repufdiation, access control, etc. Basically, there are two classifications of cryptography - symmetric and asymmetric - based on how messages are encrypted and decrypted. Symmetric encryption uses a private key to encrypt and decrypt an encrypted message. On the other hand, asymmetric encryption uses the public key of the recipient to encrypt the message. To decrypt the message, the recipient will have to use his/her private key to decrypt.

Lightweight cryptography is studied for constrained devices for the IoT. Its properties have been discussed in ISO/IEC 29192. The properties are described based on their target platforms such that in hardware implementations, smaller chip size and lower energy consumption are desirable while in software implementations, smaller code and RAM size are preferable. Lightweight cryptography should also deliver adequate security. In symmetric cryptography, aside from

AES, block ciphers CLEFIA, PRESENT, and the hash function SHA-3 are considered. Meanwhile, there are no asymmetric cryptography primitives that meet enough lightweight properties or can execute at a reasonable time. However, Elliptic Curve Cryptography (ECC) is said to have a relatively small footprint than other asymmetric primitives [10].

2.2 Blockchain

A blockchain can be implemented in two ways: a (1) *public blockchain* and a (2) *private blockchain*. A public blockchain allows anyone to participate as long as the transactions are valid. On the other hand, in a private blockchain, reading data and sending transactions for validation may only be done by a predefined list of entities [8].

The original implementation of the blockchain comes from Bitcoin [16], which uses public key cryptography. Keys and bitcoin addresses and their transformation can be seen in Fig. 2a. Bitcoin uses a Merkle Tree or a Binary Hash Tree, which is a data structure used for summarizing and verifying the integrity of data [14]. This is based on the Merkle's signature scheme as seen in Fig. 2b.

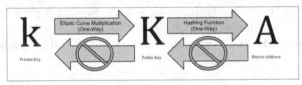

(a)   Private key, Public key and Bitcoin address (adopted from [3])

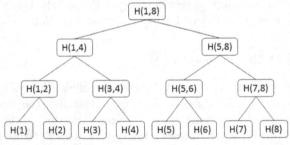

(b) A merkle hash tree from Niaz et al.'s work [17]

Fig. 2. Blockchain implementation of Bitcoin

Another work combines blockchain and cryptography which focuses on ensuring IoT device authentication to the gateway [7]. It uses hybrid cryptography - symmetric cryptography for the transmission of transaction and asymmetric cryptography for the transmission of the symmetric key. The IoT device generates a session key using Password-Based Key Derivation Function 2 (PBKDF2).

On the other hand, the encryption of the session key uses RSA. Meanwhile, blockchain transaction structure, as shown in Table 1, consists of the transaction ID, data length, data, signature of the sender and public key of the receiver [7].

Table 1. Transaction structure of blockchain for IoT from Gaurav et al. [7]

Field	Purpose
Transaction ID	Unique number of transaction
Data length	Number of bytes of data
Data	Actual message
Signature of sender	Identity of sender
Public key of sender	Used for encryption, decryption of data and data length

Due to the increasing number of M2M devices, hierarchical network architectures are proposed. Devices, or nodes, are usually embedded in smart devices which reply to requests or sends data packets to the gateway in a single hop or multi-hop patterns. The gateway, on the other hand, acts as an entrance to another network. Meanwhile, the software agents are the connections between the gateway and applications that report data to the user.

We see the emergence of more related on hardware acceleration using FPGA platform for cryptographic hash computations [4] and bitcoin mining for different cryptocurrencies [1,21]. Furthermore, more application-specific blockchain such as in P2P energy trading or transactive energy are being explored [13,20]. To address the scalability, latency, and energy requirement challenges of blockchain processing, work such as in [15] are focusing on integrating a more efficient hardware-based consensus algorithm.

3 Methodology

Advanced Encryption Standard (AES) is included in the ISO/IEC 18033-3 standard for encryption algorithms in the 128-bit block ciphers category. It is a symmetric block cipher that cuts a message into blocks, with a length of 128 bits, and encodes them individually using a pre-shared key which will be stored in the server and in the devices before system deployment [9]. The cryptographic algorithms such as AES-128 and the blockchain hashes will be implemented using the peripheral device which is the NXP Freedom Development Board (FRDM-K82F). This effectively decreases the amount of work to be done by the smart plug controller - Arduino 101. The communication between the smart plug and the peripheral device is done using Inter-Integrated Circuit (I2C).

The device to gateway communication will consist of nRF24L01+ wireless transceivers which is suitable for ultra low power wireless applications and operates in 2.4 GHz ISM band [18]. This uses SPI communication between the Arduino 101.

The *MultiCeiver* feature of the nRF24L01+ can also be utilized for a system with many devices. It can contain a set of six (6) parallel data pipes of star network topology. This provides unique addressability in the physical and link layer as seen in Fig. 3.

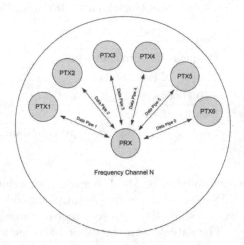

Fig. 3. Unique addressability in nRF24L01+ from [18]

Handling multiple devices can cause concern on packet collisions. Thus, the system utilizes Time Division Multiple Access (TDMA) where each device transmits data at a specific time intervals. The system architecture with the necessary communication between the devices, and the devices to gateway is shown in Fig. 4.

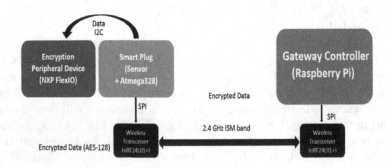

Fig. 4. Device to gateway diagram with wireless transceivers

3.1   Keyed-Hashing for Message Authentication (HMAC)

Message authentication codes (MACs) that are based on cryptographic hash functions are called Hash-based message authentication codes (HMACs).

HMACs combines public keys, private keys, and a hash for message authentication. An HMAC is computed by the following formula [12]:

$$HMAC(K, text) = H(K \oplus opad \,\|\, H((K \oplus ipad)\|(text)))$$

where,

K is the shared secret key

$text$ is the message input

$opad$ is 0x5C repeated B times ($B = 64 \equiv$ byte-length)

$ipad$ is 0x36 repeated B times

$\oplus$ is the bitwise exclusive-or operation

$\|$ is concatenation.

There is a well-known practice with MACs that truncates the output. It has an advantage of less information available to the attacker and a disadvantage of less bits to predict for the attacker. It is recommended, however, to limit the length of the truncated output to be not less than half the length of the hash output. For instance, HMAC-SHA-1-80 denotes HMAC computed using SHA-1 function with output truncated to 80 bits [12]. Additionally, *Authenticated Encryption (AE)* is necessary. For the study, *encrypt-then-authenticate* shown in Fig. 5 must be used since it is proven to be generically secure for implementing secure channels [11].

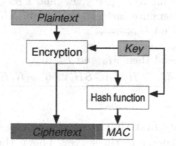

Fig. 5. Encrypt-then-authenticate mechanism [6]

3.2 Authentication of Genesis Block

To simultaneously provide authentication and encryption for new data to be linked in the blockchain, the authentication scheme is based on the (1) general protocol of symmetric message authentication using HMAC, (2) the blockchain and (3) AE's method of encrypt-then-authenticate. The algorithm to be used for the genesis block, the first block in the blockchain, which contains the data from the device to be verified by the server is shown in Algorithm 1.

The HMAC is truncated for the reason that the maximum payload length that the transceiver can operate only takes up to 32 bytes as shown in Fig. 6.

Algorithm 1. Genesis block symmetric message authentication and encryption

1: Devices A, B, C and D compute E_A, E_B, E_C and E_D.
2: Devices A, B, C and D compute their $M_n = HMAC\,SHA256_{128}(K, E_n)$.
3: Devices A, B, C and D send their M_n and E_n to S.
4: Server S checks whether $M_n \overset{?}{=} HMAC\,SHA256_{128}(K, E_n)$.

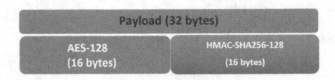

Fig. 6. Payload from devices to server S containing encrypted data and authentication code

3.3   Authentication of Subsequent Blocks

For a node to create a block in the blockchain, the incoming block header should contain the previous block hash. Thus, the algorithm to be used for the authentication of the subsequent blocks is shown in Algorithm 2.

Algorithm 2. Authentication and encryption of subsequent blocks

1: Devices A, B, C and D compute E_A, E_B, E_C and E_D.
2: Devices A, B, C and D compute their $M_n = HMAC\,SHA256_{128}(K, E_n)$.
3: Devices A, B, C and D send $H_{previous}$.
4: Server S checks $H_{previous}$.
5: Devices A, B, C and D send their M_n and E_n to S.
6: Server S checks whether $M_n \overset{?}{=} HMAC\,SHA256_{128}(K, E_n)$.

The server has to verify first that the incoming block's previous block hash field - $H_{previous}$ is a hash known to the server. This is the last block on the chain. The protocol can further be illustrated in Fig. 7.

3.4   Server

TCP/IP yields a better throughput and less packet loss compared to UDP when using the IEEE 802.11 standard. The current Application Program Interface (API) uses HTTP, which uses TCP/IP to communicate from the gateway to the web server which is built using Node.js. The HTTP Client will run in the gateway and send requests to the server in order to communicate with it and update the database for the data.

The *Requests* library for python was used in order to simplify the HTTP communication between the gateway and the remote server. It utilizes the urllib3 python library for automatic keep-alive and HTTP connection pooling [19].

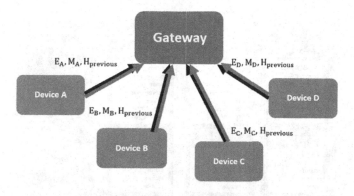

Fig. 7. Blockchain-based authentication protocol for devices' new data

3.5 Database

The web server is built using Node.js and MongoDB for the management of the database. We rearrange the database structure used in the current home automation system to fit the MongoDB data-as-documents architecture and add a new category to include the header of the previous block of transactions in order to create the blockchain. The new database structure can be seen in Fig. 8.

- **yun_devices** contains the list of devices connected to the main controller. Each device will be identified using a *node_ID*. It will also contain a table called the *block_headers*.
- **device_sched** contains the schedule of devices for actuation.
- **device_power** contains power consumption of each device connected to the smart plug. It will be sorted into *power_hour*, *power_day*, *power_week*, *power_month* and *power_year*.
- **device_status** contains the status of each smart plug (e.g. connected, identified, modified)
- **block_headers** contains the metadata of each blocks. This is separated from the node data for faster retrieval of the blocks for authentication.

4   Results and Analysis

Functionality Testing
To check the operation of AES-CBC-128 in Kinetis FRDM-K82F and Arduino 101, test vectors from NIST, specifically GFSbox, KeySbox, VarKey and VarTxt Known Answer Test Values were used.

SHA-256 is the hash function used in HMAC. To check its operation, the Secure Hash Algorithm Validation System (SHAVS) short messages tests for byte-oriented implementations were used. Aside from the NIST test vectors, RFC test vector was also used for the HMAC. Sample outputs of both the AES and HMAC which are displayed via PuTTY can be found in Fig. 9.

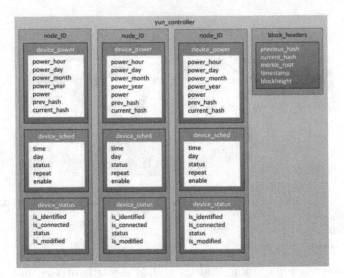

Fig. 8. Database structure

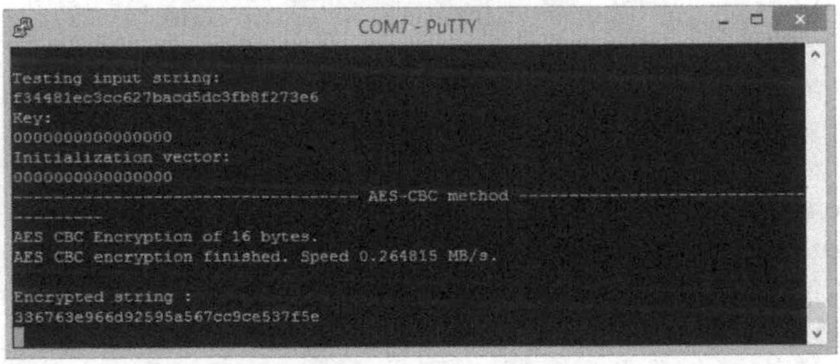

(a) Sample output for AES-CBC-128

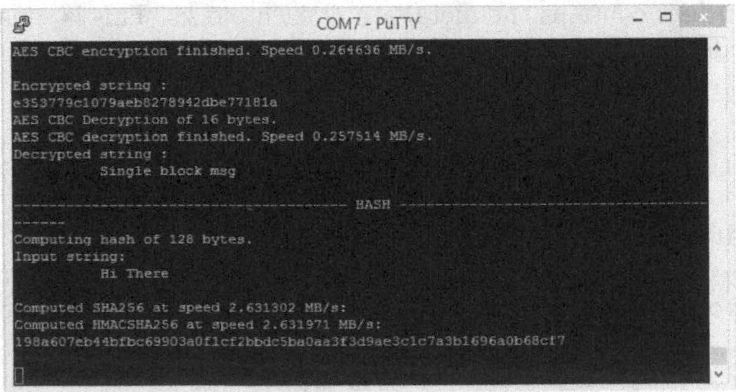

(b) Sample output for HMAC-SHA-256-128

Fig. 9. Sample outputs for test vectors on devices

Additionally, the encryption and decryption on the server was tested using the test vectors as seen in Fig. 10. Meanwhile, the test vectors for the HMAC validation was taken from RFC 4231. From the tests conducted, the integrity of implemented encryption, decryption and HMAC algorithms was proven.

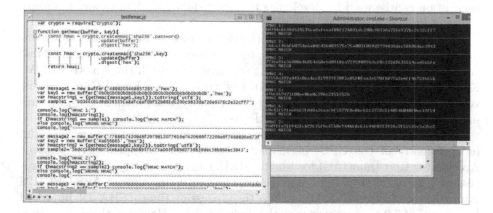

Fig. 10. Sample outputs for test vectors on server

Non-functionality Testing

The performances of the FRDM-K82F and Arduino 101 are compared by measuring the processing time of the algorithms. FRDM-K82F has ARM Cortex M4 with 150 MHz clock speed. It also has a Memory-Mapped Cryptographic Acceleration Unit (mmCAU). Meanwhile, the Arduino 101 has Intel Curie microprocessor with 32 MHz clock speed.

The algorithms for encryption (AES-CBC-128) and HMAC (SHA-256) are tested using 10 vectors from the functionality testing. The AES-CBC-128 ran at an average of 61 μs in Kinetis FRDM-K82F and 335 μs in Arduino 101. Meanwhile, SHA-256 ran at an average of 28 μs in Kinetis FRDM-K82F and 220 μs at Arduino 101.

Table 2. Average processing times (in μs) and speedup

Encryption algorithm	Kinetis FRDM-K82F	Arduino 101	Speedup factor
AES-128	60.665264	335.2	5.53
SHA-256	27.6773738	219.7	7.94

5   Conclusions and Future Work

The past implementation of the smart home automation system only had a login authentication which is a user authentication. An authentication system has been implemented for the machine-to-machine communication using blockchain and cryptographic algorithms such as AES-CBC-128 and HMAC-SHA-256-128 which made the system more secure.

The algorithms were implemented using familiar IoT devices e.g. Arduino, Raspberry Pi and Kinetis MCU. The proposed protocol for authentication and encryption can be used by developers to secure their IoT devices and to ensure the security and privacy of their users.

Several testing procedures were performed to test its functionality and non-functionality attributes. Functionality tests include the implementation of test vectors from NIST to check the output's accuracy for both the Kinetis FRDM-K82F and Arduino 101. There were 10 test vectors for AES-CBC and 10 test vectors for SHA-256. Meanwhile, non-functionality tests include the measurement of processing n time in the IoT devices.

It was found that using a hardware accelerator coprocessor which can run independently of the CPU, particularly the Memory-Mapped Cryptographic Accelerator Unit (mmCAU) for Kinetis MCU, can significantly increase the processing time of cryptographic algorithms. The processing time of AES-CBC-128 improved by a factor of 5.5. Meanwhile, the processing time of SHA-256 improved by a factor of 7.9 as compared with the Arduino alone. However, there are limitations in the communication between the Arduino 101 and the peripheral device (Kinetis FRDM-K82F) such as its accuracy and transmission duration.

It is also worth noting that there are differences in the implementation of the blockchain for this study as opposed to the original implementation of blockchain which is based on Bitcoin. The researchers have determined that implementing a private blockchain with symmetric cryptography is more suitable for the particular application of IoT security on account of the limitation of resources in IoT devices and their traditional threat model.

References

1. Abdulmonem, M.H., EssamEddeen, J., Zakhari, M.H., Hanafi, S., Mostafa, H.: Hardware acceleration of dash mining using dynamic partial reconfiguration on the ZYNQ board. In: 2020 32nd International Conference on Microelectronics (ICM), pp. 1–4 (2020). https://doi.org/10.1109/ICM50269.2020.9331815
2. Aggarwal, V.K., Sharma, N., Kaushik, I., Bhushan, B.H.: Integration of blockchain and IoT (B-IoT): architecture, solutions, and future research direction. IOP Conf. Ser. Mater. Sci. Eng. **1022**(1), 012103 (2021). https://doi.org/10.1088/1757-899X/1022/1/012103
3. Antonopoulos, A.M.: Mastering Bitcoin: Unlocking Digital Crypto-Currencies, 1st edn. O'Reilly Media Inc., Newton (2014)
4. Atiwa, S., Dawji, Y., Refaey, A., Magierowski, S.: Accelerated hardware implementation of blake2 cryptographic hash for blockchain. In: 2020 IEEE Canadian Conference on Electrical and Computer Engineering (CCECE), pp. 1–6 (2020). https://doi.org/10.1109/CCECE47787.2020.9255709
5. Chen, M., Wan, J., Li, F.: Machine-to-machine communications: architectures, standards and applications. KSII Trans. Internet Inf. Syst. **6**(2), 480–497 (2012). https://doi.org/10.3837/tiis.2012.02.002

6. Commons, W.: Authenticated encryption scheme (encrypt-then-mac), April 2015
7. Gaurav, K., Goyal, P., Agrawal, V., Rao, S.L.: IoT transaction security. In: 2015 5th International Conference on the Internet of Things. VMware Software India Pvt. Ltd. (2015)
8. Group, B.: Digital assets on public blockchains, March 2016
9. Kak, A.: Lecture notes on computer and network security (the advanced encryption standard). Lecture notes, April 2016. https://engineering.purdue.edu/kak/compsec/NewLectures/Lecture8.pdf
10. Katagi, M., Moriai, S.: Lightweight cryptography for the Internet of Things (2012)
11. Krawczyk, H.: The order of encryption and authentication for protecting communications (or: How secure is SSL?). In: Kilian, J. (ed.) CRYPTO 2001. LNCS, vol. 2139, pp. 310–331. Springer, Heidelberg (2001). https://doi.org/10.1007/3-540-44647-8_19
12. Krawczyk, H., Bellare, M., Canetti, R.: HMAC: Keyed-hashing for message authentication. RFC Informational 2104, February 1997. https://tools.ietf.org/html/rfc2104
13. Kwak, S., Lee, J.: Implementation of blockchain based P2P energy trading platform. In: 2021 International Conference on Information Networking (ICOIN), pp. 5–7 (2021). https://doi.org/10.1109/ICOIN50884.2021.9333876
14. Mahony, A.O., Popovici, E.: A systematic review of blockchain hardware acceleration architectures. In: 2019 30th Irish Signals and Systems Conference (ISSC), pp. 1–6 (2019). https://doi.org/10.1109/ISSC.2019.8904936
15. Mohanty, S.P., Yanambaka, V.P., Kougianos, E., Puthal, D.: PUFchain: a hardware-assisted blockchain for sustainable simultaneous device and data security in the internet of everything (IoE). IEEE Consum. Electron. Mag. 9(2), 8–16 (2020). https://doi.org/10.1109/MCE.2019.2953758
16. Nakamoto, S.: Bitcoin: A peer-to-peer electronic cash system (2009). http://www.bitcoin.org/bitcoin.pdf
17. Niaz, M.S., Saake, G.: Merkle hash tree based techniques for data integrity of outsourced data. In: GvD, pp. 66–71 (2015)
18. Nordic Semiconductor ASA: nRF24L01+ Single Chip 2.4 GHz Transceiver (2008), preliminary Product Specification v1.0
19. Reitz, K.: Requests: HTTP for Humans (2016). http://docs.python-requests.org/en/master/
20. Saha, S.S., Gorog, C., Moser, A., Scaglione, A., Johnson, N.G.: Integrating hardware security into a blockchain-based transactive energy platform (2020)
21. Zhong, G., Javaid, H., Saadat, H., Xu, L., Hu, C., Brebner, G.: FastProxy: hardware and software acceleration of stratum mining proxy. In: 2019 Crypto Valley Conference on Blockchain Technology (CVCBT), pp. 73–76 (2019). https://doi.org/10.1109/CVCBT.2019.00013

An Investigation of Vulnerabilities in Internet of Health Things

Saifur Rahman[1]([✉]), Tance Suleski[1], Mohiuddin Ahmed[1], and A. S. M. Kayes[2]

[1] School of Science, Edith Cowan University, Joondalup, WA 6027, Australia
{saifurb,tsuleski}@our.ecu.edu.au, mohiuddin.ahmed@ecu.edu.au
[2] Department of Computer Science and Information Technology,
La Trobe University, Melbourne, VIC 3086, Australia
a.Kayes@latrobe.edu.au

Abstract. Medical devices are the machines or instruments that play a vital role in diagnosis or treatment for patients in a healthcare ecosystem. As technologies advances so are these medical devices, and with time they are getting smarter and interconnected to themselves and other devices. These smarter devices attract attracts hackers to launch cyber-attack against these machines targeting vulnerabilities that exist within them. In this paper, we provide a brief description of medical devices in relation to different regulatory bodies, through which we try to understand the need to make the medical device safe for the users. We explore the vulnerabilities of medical devices and how they may be exploited to infiltrate the full healthcare system and other devices in the network. The paper covers three recent incidents of medical device vulnerabilities and explores the concept of blockchain that may be used to limit the vulnerabilities and their limitation. To ensure patient safety and privacy, it is essential that all relevant bodies including manufacturers, regulators, healthcare providers, etc. understand the risk and take proper steps to limit the threats.

Keywords: IoHT · Healthcare · Cybersecurity · Medical device · Vulnerability

1 Introduction

The devices intended to be used for medical purposes, to benefit patients by providing support to health care personnel for treatment, diagnosis so that patients can overcome sickness and disease can be termed as a Medical device. They are defined and regulated differently from one country or region to another country or region. This is due to different regulatory bodies in different countries and regions oversee their distribution. Medical devices have a risk classification level [25] associated with them, which allows regulatory bodies to scrutinize different medical devices differently and establish different levels of control. Regulatory bodies assess the medical device based on their safety towards maintaining

H. Jin et al. (Eds.): CROWNCOM 2021/WiCON 2021, LNICST 427, pp. 296–306, 2022.
https://doi.org/10.1007/978-3-030-98002-3_22

patient and facilitator safe. They also consider cyber threats [2] (See Fig. 1) in consideration when providing approval and follow different standards based on country, region, risk levels such as ISO 14971, ISO 13485, IEC 62304, AAMI/UL 2800, etc. [5].

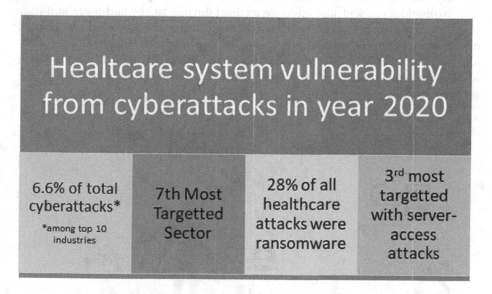

Fig. 1. Cyberattack on healthcare industry in year 2020.

As more and more devices are invented and developed, most of the devices are becoming smart medical devices generating and providing real-time data to health care professionals, for example, mySIgnals [7]. They are using state of the art software to improve the device performance and whose developments are regulated by regulating authority across the world. Smart devices are also generating in-depth diagnoses and report towards a better understanding of the cause of concern for patients. Patient's in interactions with smart medical devices are increasing day by day, similarly, the number of sensors, testing instruments, scanners, etc. evolving with the development of technological advances in minia-turization capacity of devices, computing power, and shifting towards wireless technology [6]. Due to the increasing usage of the Internet in the healthcare sector and state-of-the-art medical devices, cybercriminals are more than ever motivated to launch attacks on medical devices, and unfortunately in such a sce-nario, the result of the attack may even lead to loss of life. Compromised medi-cal devices can change the way how the device operates, generate false readings from sensors and result in life-threatening situations for patients [11,12,14,16]. Manufacturers are guided to consider potential cyber threats and encouraged to limit the risk for the lifecycle of the medical device [3]. The risk and vul-nerability of medical devices lie not only with connected devices but also with standalone devices. The weakness in technical and physical security controls of the device may be hardware or software-related. All these devices are at risk of being hacked (See Fig. 2) with unauthorized access and malware. Evolving nature of cyber threats should be addressed by the manufacturer of medical devices to address the security challenges of the present and potential future security threats [29,30] Systems, resources need to be managed in such a way that it provides efficient and effective medical devices to the end-users and constantly upgrading in such a way that it can combat threats with the help of device manufacturers, resulting in a quality and safe environment for patients and users of the medical devices. Organizations, especially health care providers at management level should have strategies to tackle the issue of medical device security issues.

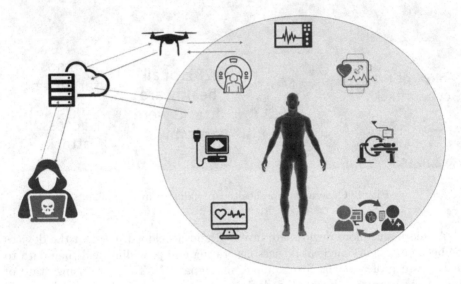

Fig. 2. Medical devices vulnerable to cyberattacks adapted from the Internet.

1.1 Paper Roadmap

The rest of the paper is organized as follows. Section 2 discusses the vulnerabilities found in digital healthcare and the critical analysis of medical device vulnerabilities. Section 3 highlights the recent incidents and motivations of cybercriminals. Section 4 discusses the solution trends for healthcare device cyber-attacks, notably the Blockchain. Section 5 concludes the paper followed by references.

2   Medical Device Vulnerability Analysis

As digitization and connectivity of medical devices are on the rise, these are devices are also vulnerable to following cyberattacks and bringing harm to patients Following Attacks are the ones most deadly to the healthcare ecosystem [5].

- Denial of service or therapy to patients.
- Directly alter the function of device and causing the patient harm.
- Loss of data and privacy of health data.
- Server Access attacks on healthcare device networks.
- Ransomware on medical devices.

All medical devices should pass through proper risk assessment and regulatory control before being deployed in the market. Following figure (See Fig. 3) shows some of the known cybersecurity vulnerabilities of medical device.

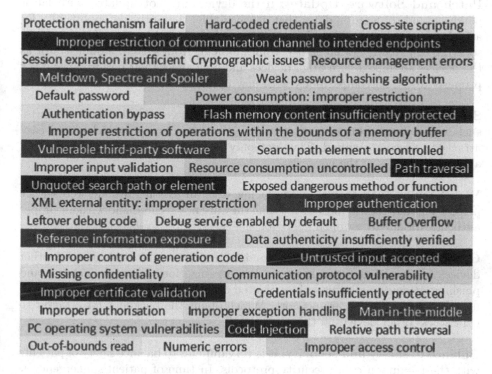

Fig. 3. Vulnerabilities of medical devices.

2.1 Vulnerability Exposure of Medical Devices

Medical devices falls victim to attacks due to vulnerabilities in them, which ranges from technical issues, management and human factors. These limitations contribute not only security threats to the medical devices itself but also on overall vulnerability of the health sector.

Information on Technical Specification: The technical information on working of the device through device manual, systems and their connectivity specification, and other vital data related to device is available not only from manufacturer also from certification body and patent databases. Which in turn provides opportunity for the attackers to reverse engineer [17] and find vulnerabilities of device for attack.

Legacy System and Software: When the device or the software becomes old, due to advancement in mode of cyberattack, it opens up security loop holes which were un-known before. This may also be due to unregulated system integration, misconfigured and incompatible system integration, mainly with third party software [18].

Patch and Software Updates: If the devices are not updated with latest patch [9] and software updates that are available, they provide opportunity for attackers to hack the system. Though it is recommended to upgrade as soon the software or patch is available, it becomes difficult from system administrator as the devices are linked with other devices and may affect their performance if not properly tested on compatibility with new updates.

Security Features: Some of the devices comes with very basic security features, such as continuous glucose level monitoring level machine [4], which can be easy attacked and compromised. Thus not only becomes vulnerable for themselves also other devices in the network.

Web Service Interface: For interfacing with an existing system web service [24] are popular choice, most of the time they are not secured and without proper authentication, leaving open doors for attackers.

Compromised Device: One compromised device may be used to attack other devices in the same network within the organization. Through malware and phishing schemes malicious scripts planted on devices to gain access to a particular device in a healthcare network. Which opens the backdoor for attacker to gain access other devices in the network [13].

Balance of safety and security: It is very difficult to balance safety of patients with the maximum cyber security protocols. In time of patient's emergency it may be difficult to follow all the practice and protocols for access control and encryption process in place, where time plays a vital role. This lapse opens up window of opportunity for attackers [19].

Limited Energy use: Many of the medical devices use very low or limited power and runs on battery [31]. Increased security protocols with many encryptions may actually reduce the battery life of the device [23], prompting the manufacturers not to use state of the art security features. As more communication, data transfer, system monitoring with use of micro controller is required more energy is consumed from batteries in the device. Limiting such activities may increase battery life but increases chance of security threats [19].

3   Motivation of Attacks and Recent Incidents

3.1   Attacker's Motivation

The motivation to exploit the medical devices and carry out an attack by attacker influenced by financial gain, state or national interest, sparking cyber terrorism, extract performance data of a device for corporate espionage, etc. [28]. Out of all the motivation factor money is the biggest motivator. The devices on hospitals and other medical facilities has lot of information, including sensitive personal information which attracts lot of attacker to extract the data and sell to potential buyers.

3.2   Recent Incidents

Sweyn Tooth Vulnerability [22] is a collection of 12 vulnerabilities and possible of more to be identified and released. It affects 7 different Bluetooth Low Energy (BLE) SoC manufacturers utilizing different models of software development kit (sdk). Medical devices from following BLE SoC manufacturer is said to be affected (See Fig. 4). The stated vulnerability allows an attacker to trigger deadlocks, buffer overflows, crashes or completely bypass the security from radio range, thus compromising the medical device.

GE Healthcare Clinical Information Central Stations and Telemetry Server [1] are exposed to vulnerabilities from using specific software version. These medical devices are used to monitor physiological parameters of patients (e.g. blood pressure, temperature, etc.). The vulnerability allows the attacker to take control of medical devices and silence the alarm, generate false alarm and interfere with patients monitors connected to these devices.

Urgent/11 is a collection of 11 identified vulnerabilities [8], in IPnet, a thirdparty software components, that supports network communication between computers. There are many medical devices may be affected by the use of software includes infusion pump, imaging system, anesthesia machines and more to be identified. The vulnerability allows attacker to take control of medical devices, change function, causes denial of service which may lead to information leaks or logical flaws and prevent device function.

4   Solution Trends for Healthcare Device Cyber Attacks Considering Blockchain and Constraints

Researchers are engaging in blockchain strategies to make healthcare ecosystem more secure. Medical devices are becoming more independent and dependent on more wireless connectivity, thus giving rise to decentralized healthcare institutions [21]. In blockchain transaction is done via public and private keys, where

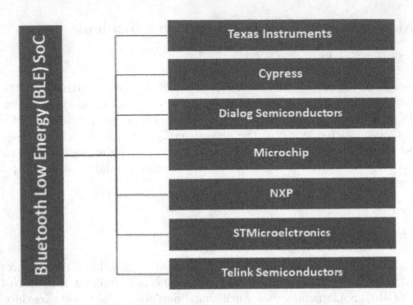

Fig. 4. Affected BLE SoC from manufacturer

private keys acts as security barrier for user authentication. Since the processing takes places at separate blocks it is independent of central server or database. Each node or decentralized block can perform the required task on its own [10].

4.1 Usage of Blockchains in Internet of Health Things (IoHT)

– Ethereum-Based Contributions: It proposes to implement smart contract for devices/user requests based on credentials on the domain. The authors [10] proposes proof medical stack (PoMS) to higher security against malicious attacks.
– Modified Consensus Protocol: The proposed system is consortium based blockchain architecture, where a patient agent (PA) software defines the blockchain functionalities [27]. The computing is done on Edge Computing network and data is stored in cloud based server in secure storage.
– Modified Cryptographic Technique: The proposal uses two software system integrated to original blockchain algorithm. For data encryption ARX algorithm and Diffie-Hellmman key exchange technique for transferring public keys [20]. The nodes must be certified before joining a blockchain and stores interconnected block with high data in cloud server with higher security. Cluster head is used to verify and store hash blocks in cloud servers and manages interactions between the clusters.
– Hyperledger-Based Contributions: The authors divides the blockchain in two segments, 1) Medical device blockchain to store data that were generated by medical device during treatment, 2) Consultation blockchain that store

patients records and data is maintained by health care provider [15]. Transactions are verified by smart contracts and execution is endorsed by Practical Byzantine Fault Tolerance algorithm.

- General Blockchain Concept Without Technical Specifications: The data is stored in shared between tamper-proof blocks between IoMT devices and healthcare providers. MedChain [26] proposes grouping the data generated by sensors in two groups 1) Blockchain network that store immutable data and 2) P2P network stores mutable data mainly focused on data query. MedChain uses BFT-SMaRt protocol.

4.2 Constraints to Use Blockchain on IoHT

Blockchain provides more security but it comes with constraints which makes it difficult to use in medical devices [21]. These are lsited below:

- Processing: The internal process of a block chain requires lots of resources for computation, thus also requires high energy. Which already a problem for medical device especially in context of energy use, more relevantly for wearable devices.
- Storage: The medical devices produces large amount of data with but not store them in different blocks and interacting through different nodes requires even larger space. This large space usually cannot be accommodated in IoHT devices.
- Real Time: In health care industry is very valuable to make decision, since blockchain involves connectivity between different blocks and nodes the computation time is increased, resulting loss of time for patient in care.
- Traffic Overhead: The inter-connectivity of the blockchains creates lots of traffic for data flow. This feature cannot be easily adopted by IoHT devices with limited bandwidth.

5 Conclusions

Medical devices are the keys to the well-being of human life. They must be protected from a cyber threat so that patients can take required health support from healthcare providers. The medical device regulatory bodies should come together with device manufacturers to formulate standards that are universally adopted and address the ever-changing technological environment. Concern bodies should work together and formulate the best solution via providing required funding so that researchers can develop an onvironment where human life will be safe from cyber threats. There exist limitations on technology and medical device computability which make them more vulnerable to security attacks, but the new process, innovations, algorithms are also being developed to address the issue. This paper briefly outlined vulnerabilities by keeping the focus on medical devices only, but there other areas of the healthcare system that is not discussed the paper also need attention. A further research scope on blockchain combined with edge computing may provide more secure and fast reliable solution to IoHT devices that is sought after.

References

1. Cybersecurity vulnerabilities in certain GE healthcare clinical information central stations and telemetry servers: Safety communication. https://www.fda.gov/medical-devices/safety-communications/cybersecurity-vulnerabilities-certain-ge-healthcare-clinical-information-central-stations-and. Accessed on 04 Oct 2021
2. Healthcare cyberattacks doubled in 2020, with 28% tied to ransomware. https://healthitsecurity.com/news/healthcare-cyberattacks-doubled-in-2020-with-28-tied-to-ransomware. Accessed on 04 Oct 2021
3. How fda medical device cybersecurity guidance affects providers. https://healthitsecurity.com/features/how-fda-medical-device-cybersecurity-guidance-affects-providers. Accessed on 04 Oct 2021
4. Making the case for medical device cybersecurity. https://www.darkreading.com/edge-articles/making-the-case-for-medical-device-cybersecurity. Accessed on 04 Oct 2021
5. Medical device cyber security guidance for industry. https://www.tga.gov.au/publication/medical-device-cyber-security-guidance-industry. Accessed on 04 Oct 2021
6. Medtech and the internet of medical things. https://www2.deloitte.com/global/en/pages/life-sciences-and-healthcare/articles/medtech-internet-of-medical-things.html. Accessed on 04 Oct 2021
7. Mysignals. http://www.my-signals.com/. Accessed on 04 Oct 2021
8. Urgent/11 cybersecurity vulnerabilities safety comm021cation. https://www.fda.gov/medical-devices/safety-communications/urgent11-cybersecurity-vulnerabilities-widely-used-third-party-software-component-may-introduce. Accessed on 04 Oct 2021
9. Va, ul collaboration advances case for medical device security standards. https://www.healthcareitnews.com/news/va-ul-collaboration-advances-case-medical-device-security-standards. Accessed on 04 Oct 2021
10. Agbo, C.C., Mahmoud, Q.H., Eklund, J.M.: Blockchain technology in healthcare: a systematic review. Healthcare **7**(2) (2019)
11. Ahmed, M.: False image injection prevention using iChain. Appl. Sci. **9**(20) (2019). https://doi.org/10.3390/app9204328
12. Ahmed, M., Barkat Ullah, A.S.S.M.: False data injection attacks in healthcare. In: Boo, Y.L., Stirling, D., Chi, L., Liu, L., Ong, K.L., Williams, G. (eds.) Data Mining, pp. 192–202. Springer, Singapore (2018). https://doi.org/10.1007/978-981-13-0292-3_12
13. Ahmed, M., Byreddy, S., Nutakki, A., Sikos, L.F., Haskell-Dowland, P.: ECU-IoHT: a dataset for analyzing cyberattacks in internet of health things. Ad Hoc Netw. **122**, 102621 (2021)
14. Ahmed, M., Pathan, A.S.K.: False data injection attack (FDIA): an overview and new metrics for fair evaluation of its countermeasure. Compl. Adap. Syst. Model. **8**, 1–14 (2020)
15. Attia, O., Khoufi, I., Laouiti, A., Adjih, C.: An IoT-blockchain architecture based on hyperledger framework for healthcare monitoring application. In: 2019 10th IFIP International Conference on New Technologies, Mobility and Security (NTMS), pp. 1–5 (2019)

16. Bostami, B., Ahmed, M., Choudhury, S.: False Data Injection Attacks in Internet of Things, pp. 47–58. Springer International Publishing, Cham (2019). https://doi.org/10.48550/arXiv.1910.01716
17. Burleson, W., Clark, S.S., Ransford, B., Fu, K.: Design challenges for secure implantable medical devices. In: DAC Design Automation Conference 2012, pp. 12–17 (2012). https://doi.org/10.1145/2228360.2228364
18. Chase, P., et al.: The evolving state of medical device cybersecurity. Biomed. Inst. Technol. **52** (2018). https://doi.org/10.2345/0899-8205-52.2.103
19. Clark, S.S., Fu, K.: Recent results in computer security for medical devices. In: Nikita, K.S., Lin, J.C., Fotiadis, D.I., Arredondo Waldmeyer, M.T. (eds.) Wireless Mobile Communication and Healthcare, pp. 111–118. Springer, Berlin, Heidelberg (2012). https://doi.org/10.1007/978-3-642-29734-2_16
20. Dwivedi, A.D., Srivastava, G., Dhar, S., Singh, R.: A decentralized privacy-preserving healthcare blockchain for IoT. Sensors **19**(2) (2019)
21. Ellouze, F., Fersi, G., Jmaiel, M.: Blockchain for internet of medical things: a technical review. In: Jmaiel, M., Mokhtari, M., Abdulrazak, B., Aloulou, H., Kallel, S. (eds.) The Impact of Digital Technologies on Public Health in Developed and Developing Countries, pp. 259–267. Springer International Publishing, Cham (2020). https://doi.org/10.1007/978-3-030-51517-1_22
22. Garbelini, M.E., Wang, C., Chattopadhyay, S., Sumei, S., Kurniawan, E.: Sweyntooth: unleashing mayhem over bluetooth low energy. In: 2020 USENIX Annual Technical Conference (USENIX ATC 2020), pp. 911–925. USENIX Association (2020). https://www.usenix.org/conference/atc20/presentation/garbelini
23. Kumar, S., Hu, Y., Andersen, M.P., Popa, R.A., Culler, D.E.: JEDI: Many-to-many end-to-end encryption and key delegation for IoT. In: 28th USENIX Security Symposium (USENIX Security 2019), pp. 1519–1536. USENIX Association, Santa Clara, CA (2019). https://www.usenix.org/conference/usenixsecurity19/presentation/kumar-sam
24. McCauley, V., Williams, P.: Trusted interoperability and the patient safety issues of parasitic health care software. In: 9th Australian Information Security Management Conference, AISM; Conference date: 05-12-2011 Through 07-12-2011, pp. 189–195 (2011)
25. Sametinger., J., Rozenblit., J.: Security scores for medical devices. In: Proceedings of the 9th International Joint Conference on Biomedical Engineering Systems and Technologies - SmartMedDev, (BIOSTEC 2016), pp. 533–541. INSTICC, SciTePress (2016). https://doi.org/10.5220/0005838805330541
26. Uddin, M.A., Stranieri, A., Gondal, I., Balasubramanian, V.: A patient agent to manage blockchains for remote patient monitoring. Stud. Health Technol. Inform. **254**, 105–115 (2018)
27. Uddin, M.A., Stranieri, A., Gondal, I., Balasubramanian, V.: Blockchain leveraged decentralized IoT ehealth framework. Internet of Things **9**, 100159 (2020)
28. Williams, P.A.H., Woodward, A.: Cybersecurity vulnerabilities in medical devices: a complex environment and multifaceted problem. Med. Dev. (Auckland, N.Z.) **8**, 305–316 (2015)
29. Xu, Y., Tran, D., Tian, Y., Alemzadeh, H.: Poster abstract: Analysis of cybersecurity vulnerabilities of interconnected medical devices. In: 2019 IEEE/ACM International Conference on Connected Health: Applications, Systems and Engineering Technologies (CHASE), pp. 23–24 (2019). https://doi.org/10.1109/CHASE48038.2019.00017

30. Yaqoob, T., Abbas, H., Atiquzzaman, M.: Security vulnerabilities, attacks, countermeasures, and regulations of networked medical devices-a review. IEEE Commun. Surv. Tutor. **21**(4), 3723–3768 (2019). https://doi.org/10.1109/COMST.2019.2914094
31. Yip, M.: Ultra-low-power circuits and systems for wearable and implantable medical devices. Ph.D. thesis, Massachusetts Institute of Technology, Cambridge, MA, USA (2013). http://hdl.handle.net/1721.1/84902

Faking Smart Industry:
A Honeypot-Driven Approach
for Exploring Cyber Security Threat
Landscape

S. M. Zia Ur Rashid[1], Ashfaqul Haq[2], Sayed Tanimun Hasan[2],
Md Hasan Furhad[3], Mohiuddin Ahmed[4], and Abu S. S. M. Barkat Ullah[5(✉)]

[1] Augmedix Inc., San Francisco, USA
[2] International Islamic University Chittagong, Chittagong, Bangladesh
tanimun@ieee.org
[3] Canberra Institute of Technology, Canberra, Australia
hasan.furhad@cit.edu.au
[4] Edith Cowan University, Joondalup, Australia
m.ahmed.au@ieee.org
[5] University of Canberra, Canberra, Australia
Abu.BarkatUllah@canberra.edu.au

Abstract. The digital evolution of Industry 4.0 enabled Operational
Technology (OT) infrastructures to operate and remotely maintain
cyber-physical systems bridging over IT infrastructures. It has also
expanded new attack surfaces and steadily increased the number of
malicious cyber incidents for the interconnected smart critical systems.
Within Industrial Control System (ICS), Programmable Logic Controller
(PLC) plays a crucial function to bridge between cyber and physical environments which made them the victim of sophisticated cyber-attacks
that are designed to interrupt and damage their operations. Honeypots have been used as a key tool for aggregating real threat data
e.g., malicious activities and payloads, to observe and determine different attack methods and strategies that can easily affect poorly secured
cyber-physical systems. In this research, we deployed T-pot honeypot
in Amazon Elastic Compute Cloud (AWS EC2) instance across six different regions to determine the current threat landscape as well as how
knowledgeable and ingenious threat actors could be in compromising
internet-facing Industrial Control System (ICS).

Keywords: ICS security · Cybersecurity · OT security · Honeypot ·
Cyber-physical security · Threat intelligence

1 Introduction

Industrial Control System (ICS) includes numerous types of control and management devices used by critical industries and smart factories, for instance,

© ICST Institute for Computer Sciences, Social Informatics and Telecommunications Engineering 2022
Published by Springer Nature Switzerland AG 2022. All Rights Reserved
H. Jin et al. (Eds.): CROWNCOM 2021/WiCON 2021, LNICST 427, pp. 307–324, 2022.
https://doi.org/10.1007/978-3-030-98002-3_23

Programmable Logic Controllers (PLC), Supervisory control and data acquisition (SCADA) etc. [1]. These are widely used to operate many critical infrastructures such as energy and smart grids, waste water treatment facilities, food and medicinal, oil and natural gas stations, transportation grids, and telecommunication which are essential to people's daily life. Disruption to these crucial public utilities may cause remarkable dam-ages and losses. The fourth industrial revolution (Industry 4.0) accelerated the integration of several industrial technologies in Information and Communication Technologies (ICT). The incidents of cyberattacks targeting ICS environments are steadily increasing due to the accessibility of interconnected modern ICS equipments and devices over the internet. Some noteworthy examples for rising the cyberattacks on ICS are inadequate security architecture and design, lack of baseline configuration and change management policy, inadequate security audits and standard monitoring procedures [2,3] etc.

In the last decade, cybercriminals had shown their notorious skills to undermine industrial core networks. In 2010, the infamous Stuxnet malware was used against Iran's nuclear installations which first showed that ICS networks are not secure [4]. Even in April 2021, we have seen another speculation of cyberattack at the Natanz uranium enrichment facility in Iran [5]. The network of a gas network operator in southern Germany and an energy network in Australia was injected by malformed commands caused disrupt controls in all flow operators in 2013 [6]. CrashOverride, which in 2015, triggered blackouts in Ukraine and left a large number of people with-out access to electricity for hours [7]. In 2017, Triton or Trisis malware was used to attack a Saudi petrochemical by the Xenotime hacking group, specifically targeting Triconex safety [8]. A recent report showed that critical industries across the world are being targeted by different notorious hacking groups [9]. Most attacks were carried out due to a lack of general protection in the communication protocols, applications, and operating systems used in ICS. While countless new threats are being generated on a daily basis, many of them depend on old security vulnerabilities to function. For too many malware looking to target the same few weaknesses over and over again, after they are found, one of the greatest risks an organization may face is failure to fix certain vulnerabilities. In addition, owing to severe real-time constraints and possibly fatal malfunction effects, these vital cyberphysical devices may sometimes not be upgraded or fixed, rendering it dangerous to conduct some kind of protection testing at all in live production systems. The necessity for security testing endures. To have an efficient threat defense system, we need to understand the current threat landscape and trending attack techniques.

This research contributes by illustrating large-scale threat analysis through deploying honeypots in various locations and it allows us to understand the vulnerabilities those are targeting Industrial Control System devices, collection of real intruders data including malware samples, exploits and post-exploitation activities for future analysis. The research conducted using a honeypot provides advantages over trying to spot intrusion in the real system. For example, a honeypot does not accept any legal traffic by design, so any logged behavior is likely to be a probe or intrusion attempt. This makes it simple and easier to track and classify a collection of IP addresses used to carry out a network sweep. In comparison, these tell-tale indicators of an intrusion are quickly overlooked in the background when we're gazing at the traffic on our core network.

2 Background and Related Work

Honeypot is a purposely vulnerable machine to look attractive to attackers or auto-mated scanners that can be probed, inspected and eventually exploited by adversaries [10], allows to collect and store information on any attempted exploits. Honey-pots are classified into a low-interaction honeypot and high inter-action honeypot. Low-interaction honeypots offer to learn quantitative informa-tion about adversaries intentions, tactics, techniques and procedures by emu-lating the operating system and different services over ports with limited inter-actions and minimal risk [11]. High-interaction honeypots are integrated with real-time operating system, applications and devices which are more complex to implement but attract sophisticated attackers to interact for a long time [11]. Researchers use both types of honeypots to conduct various kinds of threat landscape research. However, existing researches on ICS honeypots as exhibits in Table 1, were failed to simulate a wide range of services used by smart ICS and also incapable to aggregate vast amount of real data, in-depth threat analy-sis e.g., malware, exploit, post-exploitation activities. To overcome these short-comings, we utilizes an open-source honeypot called T-pot [12] developed by Deutsche Telekom (DTAG) that contains a couple of Intrusion Detection Sys-tem (IDS) sensors and can simulate a wide range of services and protocols. It is simple to set up and easy to investigate incidents using its user-friendly dash-board [13].

Honeypots is a useful technique to expose security vulnerabilities in major systems. It shows the high level of threat posed by attacks on different internet facing devices. It can also help to identify potential security gaps within the IT infrastructure which protection may need to be increased. There are some drawbacks of using a honeypot over attempting to detect interference into the actual system. For example, a honeypot does not accept any legal traffic by design, so any activity or event logged is likely to be a probe or intrusion attempt. That makes it much easier to spot payload patterns that are used to carry out a network sweep, such as common IP addresses (or IP addresses all coming from one country). For comparison, when you are looking at high volumes of legal traffic on your core network, those tell-tale signs of an intrusion are easy to miss in the chaos. The benefit of using honeypot encryption is that the only ones you see could be these malicious addresses, making it much easier to detect the threat. Since honeypots manage very small traffic, they are also light tools. They're not making major hardware demands; you can set up a honeypot with old machines that you don't need anymore.

Table 1. Summary of existing ICS honeypot related research.

Focus	Testbed	Protocols	Findings	Gaps
Honeynet [14]	Snort, Amazon EC2	Modbus, XMPP, DNP3, ICCP, TFTP, SNMP, IEC-104	Discovered SHODAN and non-SHODAN based peer interactions and correlation	Missing result on attackers techniques and payloads
CryPLH [15]	VMware	ISO-TSAP, SNMP HTTP, HTTPS	Effective simulation of Siemens PLC via Linux	Missing detail result and analysis on adversaries payloads, malware signature and post-exploitation activities
Conpot [16]	Splunk, Syslog	Modbus, HTTP, SNMP	Conpot sensor was used in pre-existing air gapped SCADA network	Lack of services simulation on more protocols
Custom Linux Based [17]	VMware	HTTP, HTTPS, SNMP, ISO-TSAP	Effective simulation using Siemens PLC with attacker's actions logging capability in high interaction environment	Testbed prepared with limited port services and in-depth result on attackers interactions are missing
Custom [18]	Snort	HTTP	BeEF tool was used to detect attacker locations accurately	Limited number of services were simulated over limited number of ports
Digital Bond Honeynet [19]	VMware, Snort	Modbus, SNMP, Telnet, FTP, HTTP, VxWorks Debugger	Limited interactions due to be deployed on university network	Limited interactions and attackers data for analysis

3   Methodology

3.1   Overview

In this research, our approach is to implement honeypots in AWS EC2 across multiple AWS regions to lure potential cyber criminals to make interaction with deployed honeypots and collect a huge amount of data for analysis as depicted in Fig. 1. Since low-interaction honeypots are easily identical, modification of default service banners and settings will be helpful to make them more real. The major goals are to monitor malicious intruders actions, analyze their origin and accrue different attack techniques, collecting malware samples and payloads. Furthermore, the obtained data could be shared to open-source community so that researchers and security engineers can utilize those data to extend their research as well as enrich intrusion detection systems.

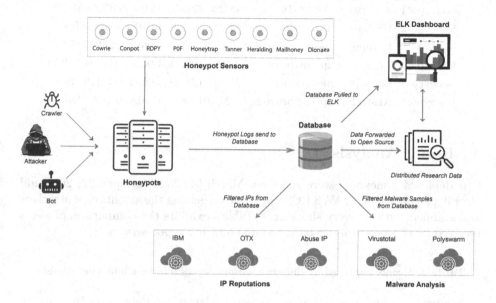

Fig. 1. Overview of experiment workflow.

3.2 T-Pot Installation

To handle a large number of attack processes and accumulate data from different places, Amazon Web Services Elastic Cloud Computing (AWS EC2) instances were chosen to install honeypot across six different regions. Following configuration was used for each instance:

```
Operating System: Debian (Stretch)
Ram: 32 GB, vCPUs: 8, Storage: 500 GB
Virtualization Type: HVM AMI
Instance Size: m5.xlarge
```

After configuring instances, Elastic IP or Public IP was allocated to each instance to avoid changing IP addresses after each reboot as well as make those instances publicly accessible through internet. SSH and Kibana dashboard were accessed over port 64295 and 64296, and security rules for both services were configured to restrict public access. Table 2 shows the information about deployed honeypots in six different regions using Amazon Elastic Compute Cloud (AWS EC2).

Table 2. Information about honeypot implementation in different AWS EC2.

Name	Region	Zone	Elastic IP	Instance ID
honeypot1	S. Africa	sa-east-1a	18.229.221.32	i-0fbe504f309251757
honeypot2	US East	us-east-2a	18.224.232.49	i-0106c86a7021f4ac
honeypot3	Europe	eu-north-1a	13.49.35.25	i-0fe18ac2494217ac5
honeypot4	Japan	ap-northeast-1a	52.194.106.24	i-00aba9778984dd671
honeypot5	Bahrain	me-south-1c	15.185.124.89	i-0be2b29a4a670f4e6
honeypot6	Australia	ap-southeast-2a	3.24.201.18	i-08be99ad2000ada56

4 Result Analysis

Our deployed honeypots were run from March 01, 2020 to April 22, 2020 and after deploying them on AWS EC2, they started getting the attention of attackers and scanners within a very short time. Table 3 exhibits the comparison of alerts received by different sensors based on different honeypot servers.

Table 3. Events captured by different sensors across different honeypot servers.

Sensors	Africa	USA	Europe	Japan	Bahrain	Australia
Dionaea	10711011	3218223	6361103	19281901	20771502	18222375
Cowrie	3273499	673290	3834526	1937548	2393980	1872987
Heralding	1072527	327941	2636491	1059014	395374	275885
Honeytrap	2122578	803156	1626080	933148	1120573	1018931
Rdpy	142722	12533	152024	619043	67578	28648
Adbhoney	7524	2811	13747	2190	135	944
Mailoney	4692	2455	12897	10636	6438	2601
Tanner	5170	1192	10533	7191	4083	2219
Conpot	1270	1086	872	800	876	1248
Total events	17340993	5042687	14648273	23851471	24760512	21425838

Dionaea: C and Python based low-interaction honeypot sensor which logging capabilities offer compatibility with log.json, hpfeeds, Fail2Ban and log.sqlite. The highest amount of log captured by this sensor is 18222375 in Australia region.

Cowrie: Cowrie is a medium SSH honeypot interaction that provides a Debian 5.0-based fake file system, enabling user to include and remove files as their wish. This program often stores in a safe and quarantined region all the downloaded and uploaded data, so if appropriate, we may conduct later re-view. This sensor recorded highest number of log which is 3273499 in Africa region and lowest amount of log in USA region.

Heralding: In Table 3 we got 1072527 logs from honeypot Africa on the honeypot service named Heralding. This honeypot sensor is nothing more but simply gathers credentials by emulating following protocols: ssh, ftp, telnet, http, https, imap, imaps, pop3, pop3s, smtp, vnc, socket5 and postgresql5. This sensor recorded 1072527 amount logs in Africa region which is the highest among other regions.

Honeytrap: Honeytrap is an extensible and open-source framework for honeypots to be run, tracked and maintained. In Africa region, there are 2122578 number of logs captured by this sensor.

Remote Desktop Protocol (RDPY): This python-based honeypot sensor was de-signed to function as vulnerable Microsoft RDP service (client and server side). In this service, the lowest and the highest number of logs are 12533 and 142722 respectively.

Mailhoney: Mailhoney is a Simple Mail Transfer Protocol (SMTP) Honeypot. There are various modules or types that provide custom modes.

Tanner: A remote data review and classification service to analyze and compose the response of HTTP queries, then served by Super Next Generation Advanced Reactive Honeypot (SNARE). When offering responses to SNARE, TANNER utilizes several program vulnerability style emulation approaches.

Conpot: Conpot is a low interactive honeypot engineered to be easy to install, change and extend. It encompasses with a set of standard industrial control protocols, capable of emulating complex infrastructures to persuade a competitor that he has just discovered a massive industrial complex.

Table 4 shows the connections received from different type of users and crawlers which are automatically categorized by honeypot sensor based on IP reputation.

Table 4. Interactions received from various sources.

Type	Africa	Australia	USA	Japan	Bahrain	Europe	Total
Known attacker	6026579	2564464	807187	689	2745911	4365988	16510818
Mass scanner	4909	28	1191	49	942	4140	11259
Bad reputation	1661122	14340	474263	10	3911	402237	2555883
Bot, crawler	32330	15	175	2	2957	1380	36859
Compromised	1054	–	9	–	11	95	1169

4.1 Attacks Origin Breakdown

In Table 5, we have presented the connections received by different ICS devices where IPMI device received the highest number of interactions and Siemens S7-200 PLC received the lowest number of interactions from attackers.

Intelligent Platform Management Interface (IPMI) is used to handle hardware over port 623 on a network. It is mainly used to track data such as temperatures or power status of devices in the network for industrial control systems. By booting, restarting, or switching them off, IPMI will monitor devices as well. Documentation of device action and data are also logged using IPMI. The number of IPMI connections received by geo-location are shown in Table 6.

Table 5. Interactions received by different ICS devices.

ICS devices	Africa	Australia	Bahrain	Europe	USA	Japan	Total
IPMI	441	364	269	232	362	318	1986
Guardian AST	379	382	201	227	317	220	1726
Siemens S7-200	246	228	129	116	85	125	929
Smart meter	204	274	277	297	322	137	1511

Table 6. IPMI connections received by geo-location.

Country	Africa	Australia	Bahrain	Europe	USA	Japan
United States	139	95	–	–	44	12
China	67	13	73	69	92	80
Brazil	95	135	–	40	1	152
UK	5	2	63	96	87	–
France	–	4	2	–	–	16
Hong Kong	94	75	26	4	–	–
Russia	41	–	86	23	125	58
Seychelles	–	40	19	–	13	–

Guardian AST is a gas tank monitoring system that was simulated through port 10001. Table 7 shows the interactions received by geo-location of Guardian AST. The most targeted gas tanks were the ones in the Australia (382), followed by the ones in Africa (379).

Table 7. Guardian AST interactions received by geo-location.

Country	Africa	Australia	Bahrain	Europe	USA	Japan
United States	286	103	12	23	–	–
China	–	32	–	13	–	43
UK	–	9	122	97	8	112
France	18	23	52	–	21	9
Seychelles	8	148	11	–	9	–
Russia	60	–	1	22	277	56
Hong Kong	–	–	–	57	2	–
Moldova	7	67	3	15	–	–

Conpot simulated Programable Logic Controller (PLC) through the S7 Communication protocol over tcp port 102. In Table 8 and 9 shows the interaction received by geo-location of Simens S7-200 and Smart Meter where S7-200 received the highest number of attacks in Africa based honeypot and Smart Meter received the highest number of interactions in USA based honeypot.

Table 8. Simens S7-200 interactions received by geo-location.

Country	Africa	Australia	Bahrain	Europe	USA	Japan
United States	60	–	11	–	–	11
China	85	–	–	23	43	24
United Kingdom	–	71	48	3	–	–
France	6	30	54	–	2	10
Seychelles	–	21	3	–	–	7
Russia	27	3	–	10	13	69
Hong Kong	54	15	8	51	–	3
Netherlands	14	9	–	9	27	1
Germany	–	79	5	20	–	–

Table 9. Originating countries for Smart Meter interactions.

Country	Africa	Australia	Bahrain	Europe	USA	Japan
United States	–	6	54	44	284	24
China	–	–	90	–	–	5
UK	195	177	77	83	2	32
France	6	–	35	4	–	50
Seychelles	2	78	–	140	36	26
Germany	1	13	21	26	–	–

4.2   Attacks Scenario

Different username and password combination were used by malicious attackers to carry out brute force authentication attack that was logged by honeypot sensors. These usernames and passwords were scanned against the largest dictionary wordlist rockyou.txt to find out the percentage of unique usernames and passwords received through all six honeypot servers as depicted in Fig. 2 and 3.

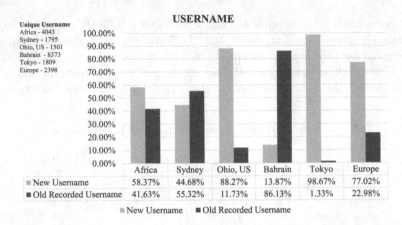

Fig. 2. Rate of unique and old usernames received.

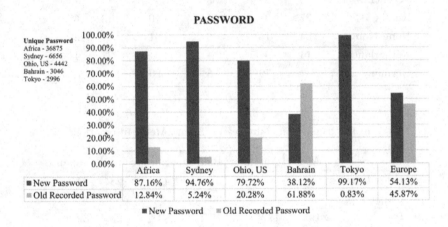

Fig. 3. Rate of unique and old password received.

Tokyo based honeypot recorded highest percentage of new username and password combination whether Bahrain based honeypot observed highest rate of previously used username and password combination. These commonly used weak username and password should be avoided for ICS devices and their corresponding services.

Table 10 illustrates the numbers of different types of authentication events captured across different region-based honeypots.

Table 10. Different types of authentication events recorded in all honeypots.

Event name	Africa	Europe	USA	Australia	Japan	Bahrain
Login attempt	20217	16771	16844	17380	7552	13659
Root failed authentication	319	388	397	366	208	483
Trying authentication password	1044	1003	439	408	438	879
Authenticated	2076	1747	1833	1826	793	1242
Remote error	19751	16200	15088	17158	6793	15232
Direct-TCP connection request	190	2912	44	36	76	14
Connection lost	25784	20668	18621	18262	15773	15663

Post-exploitation, as the term implies, literally involves the levels of action after the perpetrator has breached the mechanism of a target. The importance of the compromised device is calculated by the value of the real knowledge contained in it and how it may be exploited for harmful reasons by an intruder. Through this fact, the notion of post-exploitation has only emerged as to how you might utilize the data of the victim's corrupted device. In reality, this stage is about gathering confidential information, logging it, and getting an understanding of configuration configurations, network interfaces, and other channels of communication.

After honeypot systems were exploited, attackers executed different commands and conducted lateral movement, as seen in Table 11 and Table 12.

Table 11. Different types of post-exploitation activities.

Action type	Africa	Australia	USA	Japan	Bahrain	Europe
Pivot attacks	535	415	490	458	1010	646
CPU info	1671	1271	1507	1655	3493	2055
Crontab info	554	422	502	557	1162	681
Clean history	0	0	1	12	6	3
Operating system info	1129	1270	1009	1678	3467	2047
File execute	1130	850	1008	1127	2324	1364
Botnet	24	31	23	21	42	21
Change password	270	210	278	216	1717	434
Delete files	76	8	48	647	611	71
Shells	72	21	82	164	553	84

Table 12. Sample of commands executed after post-exploitation.

Command Type	Command input
Cleanup bash history	cat /dev/null >~/.bash_history && history -c && exit
	lscpu
CPU info	lscpu — grep Model
	cat /proc/cpuinfo — grep model — grep name — wc -l
	sudo lshw -short
System Info	hwinfo -short
	lsscsi
	rm -rf /var/tmp/.var03522123
Remove files	
	rm -rf /var/tmp/dota*
Lateral Movement	CMD: cd ~ && rm -rf .ssh && mkdir .ssh && echo "ssh-rsa AAAAB3NzaC1yc2EAAAABJQAAAQEArDp4cun2lhr4KUhBGE7VvAcwdli 2a8dbnrTOrbMz1+5O73fcBOx8NVbUTObUanUV9tJ2/9p7+vDOEpZ3Tz /+OkX34uAx1RV/75GVOmNx+9EuWOnvNoaJeOQXxziIg9eLBHpgLMuak b5+BgTFB+rKJAw9u9FSTDengvS8hX1kNFS4MjuxOhJOK8rvcEmPecjd ySYMb66nylAKGwCEE6WEQHmd1mUPgHwGQOhWCwsQk13yCGPK5w6hYp5 zYkFnvlC8hGmd4Ww+u97k6pfTGTUbJk14ujvcD9iUKQTTWYYjIIu5Pm Uux5bsZOR4WFwdIe6+i6rBLAsPKgAySVKPRK+oRw==mdrfckr">>.ss h/authorized_keys && chmod -R go= ~/.ssh && cd ~

Attackers used different types of known vulnerabilities to exploit our honeypot services. Figure 4 shows the number of various CVE used to exploit different services running within honeypots. CVE-2006-2369, CVE-2002-0013 and CVE-2002-2012 were mostly used to exploit our honeypot services. This indicates that known vulnerabilities and outdated services are lucrative endpoint for attackers to exploit and get into the internal networks.

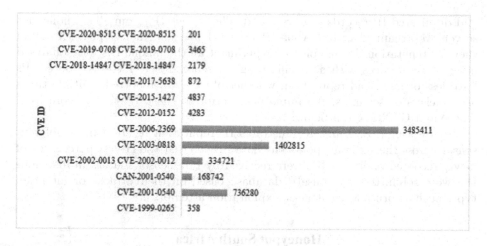

Fig. 4. CVE used to exploit honeypot services.

4.3 Malware Analysis

The malware samples received from all six honeypots were listed by unique hashes and uploaded to the VirusTotal website to find their categories. The VirusTotal scan provided results with 60% ransomware and 40% trojan. In Table 13, some sample malware hashes and corresponding malware type is provided.

Table 13. Types of malware with signature.

Malware types	Malware signature
Ransomware	414a3594e4a822cfb97a4326e185f620
Trojan	33d373e264dc7fdb0bcdbd8e075a6319
Trojan	759c8ee1f7042c118573a85407fec743
Trojan	414a3594e4a822cfb97a4326e185f620
Trojan	8c17c326a6be24f9fa845fea48106c3a
Ransomware	46e7d73f5bce2770af1e8626eb918af8
Trojan	6009b7eeced6e2ab0fb6df51887c2308
Trojan	ce223b231f2862124386c585e9b95ca1
Ransomware	ae12bb54af31227017feffd0598a6f5e
Ransomware	996c2b2ca30180129c69352a3a3515e4

4.4 IP Reputation

The reputation of the IP address is dependent on another IP address, such as whether it is registered with a data center, storage company, or a cellular or residential network. If their credibility is bad or if several IPs inside the subnet often participate in suspicious activity, certain services totally block whole neighborhoods of IP addresses. From the honeypot logs, all IPs were extracted and duplicated IP records were removed. The unique IPs from all six honeypot servers were scanned against AbuseIP, IBM X-Force and AlienVault OTX to find their IP reputation. In this part of experiment all the unique IPs were analysed using these services with a specific range of score. Newly recorded source IPs have less or mere bad reputation, whether old IPs are reported multiple times as attackers or scanners. A sample bash script to check IP threat score from AlienVault OTX is given below:

Figure 5, 6, 7, 8, 9 and 10 illustrates IP reputation received from different sensor across the six honeypots. The data reveals that the largest percentage of newly recorded malicious IPs were received by P0F sensor. Later, all malicious IPs were submitted to AbuseIP database based on their attacks or intention types such as brute force attacks, exploitation attempts etc.

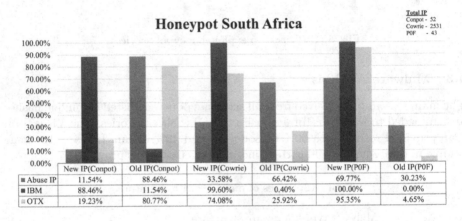

Fig. 5. Comparison of IP reputation (Africa Honeypot).

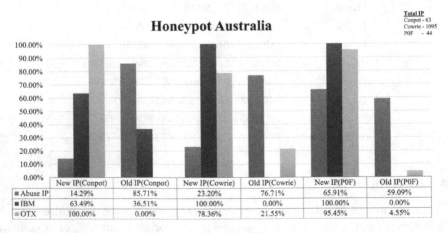

Fig. 6. Comparison of IP reputation (Australia Honeypot).

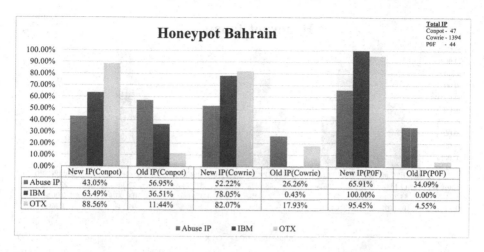

Fig. 7. Comparison of IP reputation (Bahrain Honeypot).

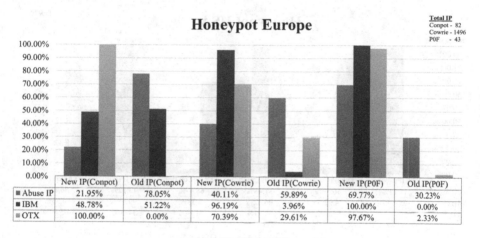

Fig. 8. Comparison of IP reputation (Europe Honeypot).

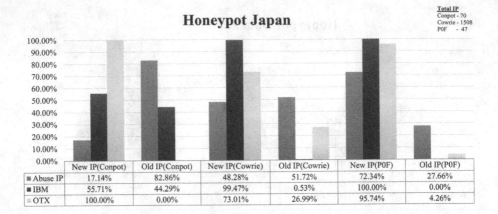

Fig. 9. Comparison of IP reputation (Japan Honeypot).

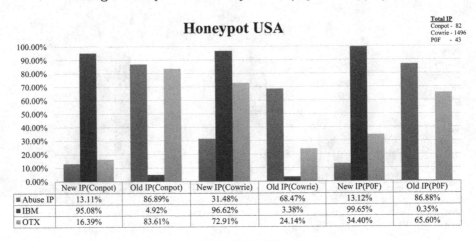

Fig. 10. Comparison of IP reputation (USA Honeypot).

5   Conclusion

Honeypot is an intentionally vulnerable computer system that plays a crucial role in moving away attacker's attention from the production systems. It enables us to better understand the attacker's motive, methods and strategies by collecting and logging attacker's information through mimicking the environment as a real system. Intruder's information received through honeypots could be used to develop machine learning-based intrusion detection. The more attackers lured to the honeypot systems, and the more real information could be obtained. As the research progressed, more and more curious peers are drawn to our system.

Threat actors also connected and exploited our honeypot systems, thinking of them as a real machine. The findings clearly indicate that current attacks in OT infrastructures follow similar attack trends for common IT environments. It is understood that each attacker follows his own "strategy" in order to be able to complete the attack. However, certain tasks of a general nature that they can carry out may be recognized as their goal. Specifically, the most common attack vectors against critical infrastructures include brute force authentication, remote code execution and buffer overflow attack on exposed devices through known vulnerabilities, malware attacks in the networks after post-exploitation. Our findings from this experiment should serve as cautionary examples for smart industries, particularly those that run internet-facing ICS, to ensure that adequate security measures are in place on their systems.

References

1. Stouffer, K., Pillitteri, V., Lightman, S., Abrams, M., Hahn, A.: NIST special publicayion 800–82, revision 2: Guide to Industrial Control Systems (ICS) Security (2014). https://doi.org/10.6028/NIST.SP.800-82r2
2. Weiss, J.: Protecting Industrial Control Systems from Electronic Threats. Momentum Press (2010). ISBN: 978-1-60650-197-9
3. Humayed, A., Lin, J., Li, F., Luo, B.: Cyber-physical systems security - a survey. IEEE Internet Things J. **4**(6), 1802–1831 (2017)
4. Hemsley, K.E., Fisher, E., et al.: History of industrial control system cyber incidents, Technical report, Idaho National Lab. (INL), Idaho Falls, ID (United States) (2018)
5. Corera, G.: Iran nuclear attack: mystery surrounds nuclear sabotage at natanz. In: BBC News (2021). https://www.bbc.com/news/world-middle-east-56722181.. Accessed 29 Sept 2021
6. Masood, R.: Assessment of Cyber Security Challenges in Nuclear Power Plants Security Incidents, Threats, and Initiatives. Cybersecurity and Privacy Research Institute the George Washington University (2016)
7. D. U. Case, Analysis of the cyber attack on the ukrainian power grid, Electricity Information Sharing and Analysis Center (E-ISAC), vol. 388 (2016)
8. Di Pinto, A., Dragoni, Y., Carcano, A.: Triton: the first ICS cyber attack on safety instrument systems. Proc. Black Hat USA **2018**, 1–26 (2018)
9. Slowik, J.: Evolution of ICS attacks and the prospects for future disruptive events, Threat Intelligence Centre Dragos Inc (2019)
10. Provos, N.: Honeyd-a virtual honeypot daemon. In: 10th DFN-CERT Workshop, vol. 2, p. 4. Hamburg, Germany (2003)
11. Mokube, I., Adams, M.: Honeypots: concepts, approaches, and challenges. In: Proceedings of the 45th Annual Southeast Regional Conference, pp. 321–326 (2007)
12. T-pot - The All In One Honeypot Platform. https://github.com/dtag-dev-sec/tpotce. Accessed 29 Sept 2021
13. Rashid, S.Z.U., Uddin, M.J., Islam, A.: Know your enemy: analysing cyber-threats against industrial control systems using honeypot. In: 2019 IEEE International Conference on Robotics, Automation, Artificial-intelligence and Internet-of-Things (RAAICON), pp. 151–154. IEEE (2020)

14. Serbanescu, A.V., Obermeier, S., Yu, D.-Y.: Ics threat analysis using a large-scale honeynet. In: 3rd International Symposium for ICS and SCADA Cyber Security Research 2015 (ICS-CSR 2015), vol. 3, pp. 20–30 (2015)
15. Buza, D.I., Juhász, F., Miru, G., Félegyházi, M., Holczer, T.: Cryplh: protecting smart energy systems from targeted attacks with a plc honeypot. In: International Workshop on Smart Grid Security, pp. 181–192. Springer, Cham (2014). https://doi.org/10.1007/978-3-319-10329-7_12
16. Scott, C., Carbone, R.: Designing and Implementing a Honeypot for a Scada Network, vol. 39. SANS Institute Reading Room (2014)
17. Buza,D., Juhasz, F., Miru, G.: Design and implementation of critical infrastructure protection system. In: Budapest University of Technology and Economics, Department of Networked Systems and Services, pp. 1–58 (2013)
18. Wilhoit, K.: The Scada that Didn't Cry Wolf. Trend Micro Inc., White Paper (2013)
19. Wade, S.M.: SCADA Honeynets: the attractiveness of honeypots as critical infrastructure security tools for the detection and analysis of advanced threats (2011)

Anonymous Key Agreement and Mutual Authentication Protocol for Smart Grids

Vincent Omollo Nyangaresi[1]([✉]), Zaid Ameen Abduljabbar[2,3],
Salah H. Abbdal Refish[4], Mustafa A. Al Sibahee[5,6],
Enas Wahab Abood[7], and Songfeng Lu[8,9]

[1] Faculty of Biological and Physical Sciences, Tom Mboya University College,
Homabay, Kenya
vnyangaresi@tmuc.ac.ke

[2] Department of Computer Science, College of Education for Pure Sciences,
University of Basrah, Basrah, Iraq
zaid.ameen@uobasrah.edu.iq

[3] Huazhong University of Science and Technology, Shenzhen Institute,
Shenzhen, China

[4] Computer Techniques Engineering Department, Faculty of Information
Technology, Imam Ja'afar Al-Sadiq University, Baghdad, Iraq
salah.hassan@sadiq.edu.iq

[5] College of Big Data and Internet, Shenzhen Technology University,
Shenzhen 518118, China
mustafa@sztu.edu.cn

[6] Computer Technology Engineering Department, Iraq University College,
Basrah, Iraq

[7] Department of Mathematics, College of Science, University of Basrah,
Basrah, Iraq
enas.abood@uobasrah.edu.iq

[8] Hubei Engineering Research Center on Big Data Security, School of Cyber
Science and Engineering, Huazhong University of Science and Technology,
Wuhan, China
lusongfeng@hust.edu.cn

[9] Shenzhen Institute of Huazhong University of Science and Technology,
Shenzhen, China

Abstract. The security and privacy protection of smart grid data exchanged over the open and public wireless communication channels is critical yet challenging in this environment. Conventionally, public key cryptography, group signatures, blind signatures, identity based schemes and elliptic curve cryptography could provide the much needed security and privacy. However, all these techniques either lack some smart grid security requirements or have intensive communication, storage and computation overheads. This obviously renders them inefficient for resource-constrained smart grid network devices. In this paper, an anonymous key agreement and authentication protocol to address some of these challenges is proposed. The simulation results showed that the proposed protocol is the most efficient in terms of bandwidth and computation requirements. It also required relatively less memory space during its entire execution than some of the related protocols. Further, it is demonstrated that it

© ICST Institute for Computer Sciences, Social Informatics and Telecommunications Engineering 2022
Published by Springer Nature Switzerland AG 2022. All Rights Reserved
H. Jin et al. (Eds.): CROWNCOM 2021/WiCON 2021, LNICST 427, pp. 325–340, 2022.
https://doi.org/10.1007/978-3-030-98002-3_24

offers both backward and forward key secrecy, anonymity, and is robust against impersonation, session hijacking, privileged insider, side-channels, packet replays, packet injection and privacy leaks attacks.

Keywords: Ephemerals · Mutual authentication · Nonce · Privacy leaks · Security · Session keys · Smart grids

1   Introduction

The inability of the conventional power grid to accurately control power transmission from power generators to users owing to operation center's lack of real time electricity consumption report [1] has led to the deployment of smart grids. The smart grids ride on internet of things (IoT) and offer intelligent generation, transmission and distribution of electricity. In so doing, smart grids enhance flexibility, efficiency, reliability and quality of energy delivered by power networks [2]. As a typical Indus-trial Internet of Things (IIoT) category, these grid systems offer dynamic electric power consumption adjustments based on users' needs. However, since the communication between utility service providers (USPs) and smart meters (SMs) is over the open public wireless networks, the transmitted data is vulnerable to numerous security and privacy attacks [3]. The connection of power grids to cyber networks offers advanced control and monitoring at the expense of cyber attacks [4]. Authors in [5] identify Home area networks (HANs) as the most susceptible smart grid components owing to lack of direct control by utilities. Consequently, device authentication needs to be deployed to enhance the security of these networks.

Authors in [6] point out that poor protection of the smart grid network may lead to intrusions that can bring down the entire network. Although security plays a crucial role here, the conventional security goals of integrity, confidentiality and authentication are not enough in this environment. For instance, privacy of the electricity consumption report needs to be assured [7]. Although security is meant to ensure that entities authenticate themselves before any data exchange [8], data leakages in smart grids has surged [9]. Since these real-time power consumption reports are associated with users' privacy such as economic status and lifestyle, robust protection is required. Authors in [10] have identified mutual authentication before the transmission of any sensitive data as being key for trusting identities within the smart grid. Through this authentication, the SMs and USPs verify each others' identity after which they negotiate a secret session key for data protection over insecure channels [10].

Unfortunately, authentication protocols based on the conventional public-key infrastructure (PKI) are computationally intensive and hence not ideal for resource con-strained smart grid systems and other IoT devices within this network [11]. Schemes based on certificate authority (CA) that issue certificates to devices exhibit high communication costs. Although the current identity based approaches eliminate cer-tificate management problems, the real identities of the communicating entities must be revealed during verification. Ring signatures and blind signatures can address the identity leakage problem [12] but these signatures render the tracing of smart grid malicious entities very cumbersome. In addition, they incur high computation and communication overheads [13]. Although group signature based authentication address this traceability problem, it has high computation and communication over-heads.

It is evident that despite the development of many authentication schemes for the smart grid environment, robust security and privacy protection still present some challenges [14]. As authors in [15] point out, although the current cryptographic protocols were designed to enable secure communication over the smart grid network, most of them do not offer flexible key management and anonymity. As such, the identified security, performance and privacy issues need to be addressed. The contributions of this paper are as follows:

I. We develop a protocol based on pseudo-identities for both smart meter and utility service provider so as to offer strong anonymity
II. The session keys are dynamically derived from random nonces for every authentication process to preserve backward and forward key secrecy
III. The stored user specific parameters are XOR-masked followed by one way hashing operations to thwart side-channel attacks.
IV. Using both Dolev–Yao and Canetti-Krawczyk models, we show that the proposed protocol offers protection from typical smart grid attacks such as message injection and replays.

The rest of this paper is organized as follows: Sect. 2 presents a discussion on related work while Sect. 3 elaborates on the deployed system model. On the other hand, Sect. 4 presents simulations results together with evaluations of the developed protocol. Finally, Sect. 5 concludes this paper and gives future direction in this research domain.

2 Related Work

Smart grid security and privacy has attracted much interest in both industry and academia, leading to the development of many schemes. For instance, authors in [16] develop a scheme for session negotiation but its bilinear pairing operations led to high computational costs. Elliptic curve cryptography (ECC) based identity-based key establishment protocol has been presented in [17] for smart grids but which resulted to high computation overheads at the SM side. In addition, the schemes in [16] and [17] fail to offer privacy protection during the key agreement and authentication process. Authors in [18] proposed a scheme which transmitted the SM real identity over the insecure channels and hence compromised SM anonymity. Therefore, the authors in [19] introduced an anonymous key agreement protocol, but which never offered mutual authentication since the SM does not validate the utility control. An efficient identity-based anonymous authentication scheme has been presented in [20], which fails to consider key management of communicating entities. On the other hand, a key management and authentication protocol in [21] does not provide device anonymity and revocation.

A protocol for conditional anonymity and dynamic participation using group and blind signatures was presented in [22] while authors in [23] have introduced a privacy preserving technique using group signatures. In addition, attribute certificates and ring signature based privacy protection approach has been presented in [24]. However, the schemes in [22–24] are computationally intensive due to the usage of group and rings signatures. On the other hand, a key distribution scheme has been presented in [25], but which is vulnerable to secret leakage attacks and does not offer session key security. ECC based key establishment protocol has been developed in [26] while authors in [27] have proposed a novel device authentication protocol. However, both schemes in [26] and [27]employ PKI which is computationally intensive for smart grid devices.

The protocol developed in [28] for smart grid key management is susceptible to man-in-the-middle (MitM) attacks while the scheme presented in [29] for secure key distribution is susceptible to impersonation attacks. Authors in [30] have presented a bilinear pairings based mutual authentication protocol in the smart grid environment but which is vulnerable to tracking and impersonation attacks. An authentication scheme based on bilinear maps was developed in [31] to address these issues, but it has high computational overheads. On their part, authors in [32] presented an ECC based scheme for SM anonymity, but which is still susceptible to ephemeral secret key leakages. A three-factor user authentication protocol has been presented in [33], which fails to offer flexible revocation of malicious SMs.

The anonymous authentication and key agreement approach in [34] employs time-stamps, which renders it vulnerable to de-synchronization attacks and the neighbor-hood area network gateway (NANG) need to store numerous symmetric keys for various HANs gateways. Authors in [35] present ECC based privacy protection pro-tocol, which experienced low computation costs while authors in [36] have developed ECC-based authentication protocol, which does not offer secure mutual authentication and is still vulnerable to impersonation and session key disclosure attacks. Moreover, the protocols in [25] and [30] fail to achieve smart grid security requirements while the techniques in [31–33] and [35] are computationally intensive due to elliptic curve point multiplication operations. Consequently, privacy protection under low computation operations during authentication process still remains challenging.

3 System Model

The current smart grid authentication and key agreement protocols have been observed to be susceptible to numerous security, performance and privacy challenges. Lack of anonymity and untraceability are some of the SM security requirements not considered in most of these protocols. In terms of performance, PKI based techniques have been observed to be computationally intensive. Although ECC based techniques offer anonymous authentication and key agreement at lower computation costs than PKI based approaches, most of these schemes incorporate bilinear pairing operations which are time-consuming. Consequently, the attainment of robust security and privacy in a smart grid environment at lower communication and computation costs still presents some challenges. As such, we propose a lightweight key agreement and authentication protocol based on only pseudo-identities, ephemerals, XOR and hashing operations. For these operations, the following definitions hold:

Definition 1: For a secure hash function $h(.)$: (a) given input message z of arbitrary length, the message digest of fixed length output h(z) can be generated (b) given $\mathcal{y}$, it is cumbersome to compute $z = h^{-1}(\mathcal{y})$ (c) given z, it is computationally infeasible to find $z' \neq z$ such that $h(z') = h(z)$.

Definition 2: In the Dolev–Yao model, adversary $\mathcal{O}$: (a) can be valid but malicious user (b) is able to control the open communication medium hence can modify, intercept, insert or erase transmitted messages (c) can obtain secrets stored in the smart device (SD) upon successful access of the SD through side-channel attacks (d) is a probabilistic polynomial time adversary and hence can guess low entropy passwords and other identity data within polynomial time (e) can physically capture and extract sensitive data stored in any smart meter within a smart grid since they are not tamper proof (f) cannot compromise the registration authority since it is fully trusted.

Definition 3: In the Canetti and Krawczyk's (CK) adversary model, adversary $\mathcal{O}$ has all Dolev–Yao model capabilities, and in addition is able to compromise ephemeral information such as session-specific states and keys.

Definition 4: Based on the one-time pad theorem, any value *XORed* with a random value yields a random output.

As illustrated in Fig. 1, the smart grid network model consists of three entities communicating over the insecure internet. The smart meter (SM) and the utility service provider (USP) communicate with each other via the Trusted Authority (TA), where the two first register before they are issued with security tokens to enable them mutually authenticate each other and establish a session key.

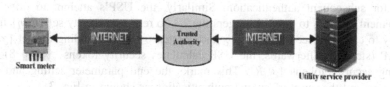

Fig. 1. Smart grid-utility service provider model

Since the exchanged power consumption reports are over the public internet, the security features pursued in this paper include anonymity, untraceability, mutual authentication, session key security, backward and forward secrecy and robustness against impersonation, side-channel, packet replay, session hijack, privileged insider, and packet injection attacks. Table 1 gives the notations used in this paper and their brief descriptions.

Table 1. Notations

Notation	Description
₫	USP center pseudo-identity
ƙ	SM pseudo-identity
η_i, $\bar{Q}_i$, Ϝ, Ċ	Nonces
Φ	TA's master key
ß, ɓ, Ƃ	SM authentication request messages
þ, ƚ, ɠ	USP authentication messages
Ⱬ	Session key
⊕	XOR operator
‖	Concatenation operator

The proposed protocol comprised of three major phases which included parameter setting, registration and mutual authentication.

Parameter Setting and Registration: During these phases, the TA registers both the SM and USP upon which unique pseudo-identities ƙ and ₫ are assigned to each of them (step 1). Afterwards, the TA buffers these parameters in the respective devices. As shown in Fig. 2, for the SM to receive power management services from the USP, the TA generates nonces η and $\bar{Q}$ for it (step 2) before computing security parameters R, ψ, Ƃ and H (step 3) for subsequent authentication. Then, the TA stores $\{\eta, R\}$ in its repository before transmitting $\{Ƃ, H, \bar{Q}\}$ to the SM (step 4). Upon receipt of these parameters, SM computes security parameter λ (step 5) and buffers the security set $\{Ƃ, H, \lambda\}$ for subsequent authentication. Similarly, the USP's attempt to offer power management services to the SM triggers the TA to retrieve security set $\{R, \eta\}$ from its memory to calculate security tokens z and ψ (step 6) before sending the set $\{\mathrm{z}, R\}$ to the USP (step 7). Afterwards, the USP calculates security tokens ç (step 8) before buffering security tokens $\{\mathrm{z}, R\}$. This marks the end parameter setting and device registration and the onset of mutual authentication as shown in Fig. 3.

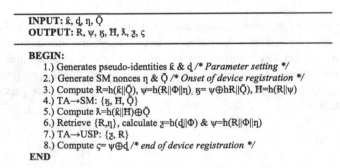

INPUT: ƙ, ₫, η, Q̄
OUTPUT: R, ψ, Ƃ, H, λ, Ⱬ, ç

BEGIN:
    1.) Generates pseudo-identities ƙ & ₫ /* *Parameter setting* */
    2.) Generate SM nonces η & Q̄ /* *Onset of device registration* */
    3.) Compute R=h(ƙ‖Q̄), ψ=h(R‖Φ‖η), Ƃ= ψ⊕hR‖Q̄), H=h(R‖ψ)
    4.) TA→SM: {Ƃ, H, Q̄}
    5.) Compute λ=h(ƙ‖H)⊕Q̄
    6.) Retrieve {R,η}, calculate Ⱬ=h(₫‖Φ) & ψ=h(R‖Φ‖η)
    7.) TA→USP: {Ⱬ, R}
    8.) Compute ç= ψ⊕₫ /* *end of device registration* */
END

Fig. 2. Parameter setting and device registration

SM-USP Mutual Authentication: The authentication session is initiated by having the SM compute security tokens $\bar{Q}$, R, ψ and H^* (step 1). Then security token H^* is validated against H such that if they are not similar, the authentication is aborted (step 2). However, if they are similar, then the SM proceeds to generate nonce $\digamma$ before deriving authentication messages $\{\beta, \eth, \boldsymbol{5}\}$ (step 3).

INPUT: $\digamma$, C, $\mathcal{k}$, $\mathfrak{d}$, λ, H, $\mathfrak{h}$, R, ς
OUTPUT: $\bar{Q}$, ψ, H^*, β, $\eth$, $\boldsymbol{5}$, β, $\mathfrak{l}$, Z, $\mathfrak{g}$, $\digamma^*$, R^*, $\boldsymbol{5}^*$, C^*, $\mathfrak{z}^*$, Z^*, $\mathfrak{g}^*$

BEGIN:
1. Compute $\bar{Q}=\lambda\oplus h(\mathcal{k}\|H)$, $R=h(\mathcal{k}\|\bar{Q})$, $\psi=\mathfrak{h}\oplus h(R\|\bar{Q})$, $H^*=h(R\|\psi)$
2.) **IF $H^*!=H$ THEN:**
    Abort authentication
3.) **ELSE:**
    Generate nonce $\digamma$ and compute $\beta=\psi\oplus\digamma$, $\eth=R\oplus h(\psi\|\digamma)$, $\boldsymbol{5}=h(R\|\psi\|\digamma)$
4.)   SM$\rightarrow$USP: $\{\beta, \eth, \boldsymbol{5}\}$
5.)   Retrieve $\{\varsigma, R\}$ and compute $\psi=\varsigma\oplus\mathfrak{d}$, $\digamma^*=\beta\oplus\psi$ & $R^*=\eth\oplus h(\psi\|\digamma)$
6.)   **IF $R^*!=R$ THEN:**
        Abort authentication
7.)   **ELSE:**
        Calculate $\boldsymbol{5}^*=h(R^*\|\psi\|\digamma^*)$
8.)   **IF $\boldsymbol{5}^*!=\boldsymbol{5}$ THEN:**
          Abort authentication
9.)   **ELSE:**
          Generate nonce C and calculate $\beta=C\oplus h(\psi\|C)$, $\mathfrak{l}=\mathfrak{z}\oplus C$, $Z=h(\digamma\|C)$,
          $\mathfrak{g}=h(R\|\psi\|\digamma\|C)$
10.)   USP$\rightarrow$ SM: $\{\beta, \mathfrak{l}, \mathfrak{g}\}$
11.)   Compute $C^*=\beta\oplus h(\psi\|C)$, $\mathfrak{z}^*=\mathfrak{l}\oplus C$, $Z^*=h(\digamma\|C)$, $\mathfrak{g}^*=h(R\|\psi\|\digamma\|C)$
12.)   **IF $\mathfrak{g}^*!=\mathfrak{g}$ THEN:**
        Abort authentication
13.)   **ELSE:**
        Trust SM and initiate packet exchange
14.   **ENDIF**
15.   **ENDIF**
16.   **ENDIF**
17. **ENDIF**
END

Fig. 3. SM-USP mutual authentication

This is followed by the transmission of authentication request message triplet $\{\beta, \eth, \boldsymbol{5}\}$ to the USP (step 4). Upon receipt of this triplet, the USP retrieves tokens $\{\varsigma, R\}$ from its buffer to re-compute ψ, $\digamma^*$, and R^* (step 5) before validating R^* against R. If these two security parameters are dissimilar, authentication is aborted (step 6), otherwise token $\boldsymbol{5}^*$ is re-computed (step 7) and validated against $\boldsymbol{5}$ such that is they are dissimilar, the authentication session is aborted (step 8).

However, if the two are similar, the USP proceeds with the generation of nonce C for the computation of security parameters triplet $\{\beta, \mathfrak{l}, \mathfrak{g}\}$ in step 9. In step 10, authentication messages triplet $\{\beta, \mathfrak{l}, \mathfrak{g}\}$ is transmitted to the SM. Upon receiving this triplet, the SM re-computes C^*, $\mathfrak{z}^*$, Z^* and $\mathfrak{g}^*$ (step 11) before validating $\mathfrak{g}^*$ against $\mathfrak{g}$ such that if they are dissimilar, authentication is aborted (step 12). However, if they are similar, the SM and USP can trust one another and commence packet exchanges. Figure 4 presents the message flow in the proposed protocol.

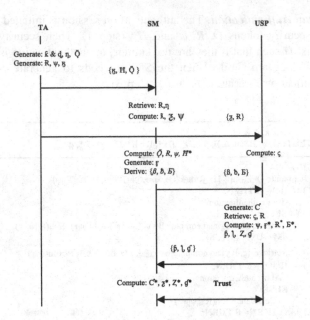

Fig. 4. Proposed message exchanges

As shown in Fig. 4, the TA controls the registration phase of both the SM and USP. After this registration, the SM and USP exchange a number of authentication messages. At the end of the successful mutual authentication process, some trust level is established between the SM and USP and hence they can commence payload exchanges.

4 Results and Discussion

The proposed protocol was simulated using NS2 2.35 network simulator running on Ubuntu 14.04 LTS platform. The simulation environment consisted of smart meters, the utility service provider and trusted authority. Table 2 presents the parameters that were deployed during the simulation process.

Table 2. Simulation parameters

Parameter	Description
Maximum number of SMs	50
Maximum SM transmission range	100 m
Number of USPs	1
Number of TAs	1
MAC protocol	IEEE 802.11
Platform	Ubuntu 14.04 LTS
Routing protocol	DSDV
Simulation duration	2000 s

As shown in Table 2, the maximum number of smart meter devices was 50 with each of them having a maximum transmission range of 100 m. On the other hand, there was only one utility service provider and one trusted authority. The media access control layer protocol was IEEE 802.11 while the routing protocol was Destination-Sequenced Distance Vector (DSDV). The simulations were executed for the duration of 2000 s.

In this section, performance of the proposed protocol is evaluated using communication overheads, computation overheads and space complexity. On the other hand, the security of the proposed protocol is evaluated using both Dolev–Yao (DY) and Canetti- Krawczyk (CK) models, which are widely utilized to prove the features of interactive cryptographic protocols. Section 4.1 describes the security analysis of the proposed protocol while Sect. 4.2 discusses the performance evaluation of this protocol.

4.1   Security Analysis

In both DY and CK models, network communications are assumed to occur over insecure channels and none of the communicating entity is trustable. Under adversarial properties in Definitions 2 and 3, the proposed protocol was evaluated against impersonation, side-channel, packet replays, packet injection and privacy leaks attacks as illustrated below. These attack models fairly represented all the assumptions of both DY and CK security evaluation models.

Impersonation Attacks: in this attack, it is assumed that an adversary is capable of physically capturing the smart meter and eavesdropping all the transmitted packets. For any successful impersonation, an attacker must generate valid authentication requests $\{\beta, \delta, \text{Б}\}$ and receive valid authentication responses $\{\rho, \ell, g\}$. However, the computation of these messages incorporates random nonces F and C, which are infeasible to guess correctly. Moreover, an attacker does not possess secret parameter ψ nor is the correct computation of session key Z possible due to the one way-hashing operation of the random nonces.

Side-Channel Attacks: suppose that an attacker has physical access to the smart meter and is able to extract a set of secrets $\{\text{Б}, \text{Ĥ}, \lambda\}$ stored in its memory. Due to the usage of XOR masking followed by one way hashing operation, user specific security parameters $\{\text{k}, \bar{Q}, \psi\}$ cannot be obtained from the memory extracted contents.

Packet Replay Attacks: in the proposed protocol, the freshness of transmitted messages is validated using $\{\text{Б}, \text{Б}^+, \text{y}, g^{\text{Ak}}\}$. Consequently, an attacker is unable to resend previously sent messages due to frequent updating of all sent messages for every authentication session.

Session Hijack Attacks: suppose that an adversary attempts to compute session key Z to facilitate this attack. Any such successful session computation requires correct calculation of a set of authentication messages $\{\beta, \delta, \text{Б}\}$. However, these authentication messages incorporate random nonce F and secret security parameter ψ which are unavailable to the attacker nor can they be computed accurately due to their stochastic nature. As such, this attack will fail.

Privileged Insider Attacks: in this attack, it is assumed that some entity at the USP is able to retrieve a set of parameters $\{R, \mathfrak{z}, \varsigma\}$ needed to authenticate the smart meter. However, since these parameters cannot yield specific smart meter pseudo-identity k and security parameter ψ, this attack fails. This is because the set $\{k, \psi\}$ can only be computed using correct nonce $\mathfrak{f}$ and q, which are unavailable to the privileges insider entity.

Packet Injection Attacks: the aim of this attack is to interrupt successful mutual authentication between the smart meter and the USP through the injection of bogus packets. However, upon receipt of authentication request message set $\{\beta, \, \mathcal{B}, \, \mathcal{B}\}$ from the smart meter, the USP validates message $\mathcal{B}^*$ using $\mathcal{B}$. In addition, the smart meter also validates the USP upon receipt of $\{\beta, \, \mathcal{l}, \, g\}$ using g^* and g. It is after the successful authentication that any messages can be exchanged between the SM and USP and hence this attack will fail.

Privacy Leaks Attacks: in the proposed protocol, the entire authentication process makes use of pseudo-identities for both the smart meter and USP which are further masked through XOR operations before being hashed. As such, it is infeasible for attackers to capture the real identities of the SM or USP.

The security features of proposed protocol are then compared with those of the schemes in [25, 30] and [36] as shown in Table 3.

Table 3. Security features comparisons

Security feature	[25]	[30]	[36]	Proposed
Impersonation	Yes	Yes	No	Yes
Packet replays	Yes	Yes	No	Yes
Privileged insider	No	Yes	Yes	Yes
MitM	Yes	Yes	Yes	Yes
Session hijacking	No	Yes	No	Yes
Privacy leaks	Yes	Yes	Yes	Yes
Forward key secrecy	Yes	Yes	Yes	Yes
DoS protection	No	No	Yes	Yes

Based on Table 3, it is evident that the proposed protocol offers all the security features followed by the protocol in [30] which lacked protection against DoS. On the other hand, the schemes in [25] and [36] lacked three security features each.

4.2 Performance Evaluation

The initial simulations that were executed encompassed the analysis of the end-to-end (E2E) latencies and throughput of the proposed protocol. Thereafter, the size of the exchanged messages, the time it took to compute the security tokens needed for session key agreement and mutual authentication, and the memory storage space required for the full execution of the proposed protocol are compared with other related schemes.

E2E: to analyze the E2E delay characteristics of the proposed protocol, the average time taken to route packets from the source to the destination was measured for different SMs densities as shown in Fig. 5 (a) below. It is evident that there is a general increase in E2E delays as the number of smart meters were increased from an initial value of 1 to a maximum value of 50. This is attributed to the surging number of messages exchanged among the TA, SM and USP for high SMs densities. As such, congestion crops in within the network which causes some processing delays at the endpoints.

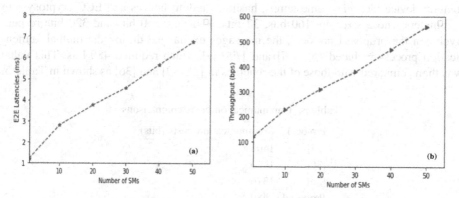

Fig. 5. (a) E2E variations (b) Throughput variations

Throughput: to determine the throughput of the proposed protocol, the number of bits conveyed within the network per unit time was measured. To accomplish this, the number of smart meters was increased from 1 to a maximum of 50 as the number of bits transferred was measured. The results obtained are shown in Fig. 5 (b), from which it can be seen that as the number of smart meters in the network increases, there is a corresponding increase in the network throughput. This is because the surge in the number of smart meters implies an increase in the number of exchanged packets within the network. As such, the network throughput for 50 smart meters was higher compared with the throughput for a single smart meter.

Computation Costs: based on values in [37], during mutual authentication, ECC point multiplication T_m, ECC point addition T_a, hashing T_h, bilinear operation T_b, exponentiation T_e, and symmetric encryption or decryption $T_{e/d}$ operations are normally executed, which take 2.226 ms, 0.0288 ms, 0.0023 ms, 5.811 ms, 3.85 ms, 0.0046 ms respectively. However, considering Fig. 2 and Fig. 3, the proposed protocol executed only 16 one way hashing operations and therefore its cumulative computation cost is 0.0368 ms as shown in Table 4.

Table 4. Computation costs comparisons

Protocol	Computation costs (ms)
[25]	30.4796
[30]	34.9273
[36]	8.9316
Proposed	0.0368

On the other hand, the schemes in [25, 30] and [36] take 30.4796 ms, 34.9273 ms and 8.9316 ms respectively. It is evident that our protocol had the least computation costs owing to its lightweight XOR and hashing operations. On the other hand, the scheme in [25] required $5T_m$, $2T_e$, $2T_b$, and $12T_h$ operations while the protocol in [30] needs $7T_m$, $2T_e$, $2T_b$, and $10T_h$ operations. On the other hand, the scheme in [36] requires only $4T_m$ and 12 T_h operations.

Communication Costs: many of the exchanged parameters during authentication include device identities, timestamps, hashes, random nonces and ECC cryptosystem parameters whose sizes are 160 bits, 32 bits, 160 bits, 160 bits and 320 bits respectively. In the proposed protocol, the messages exchanged during the mutual authentication process included $\{\beta, \, \delta, \, Б\}$ and $\{\beta, \, \lambda, \, g\}$ which required 480 bits. This value was then compared with those of the schemes in [25, 30] and [36] as shown in Table 5.

Table 5. Communication costs comparisons

Protocol	Communication costs (bits)
[25]	1408
[30]	1920
[36]	1376
Proposed	480

It is evident from Table 5 that the schemes in [25, 30] and [36] require 1408 bits, 1920 bits and 1376 bits respectively. These values were very high compared with the exchanged bits in the proposed protocol, as evidenced in Fig. 6.

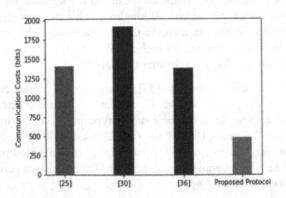

Fig. 6. Communication costs comparisons

In the proposed protocol, only two sets of messages were exchanged between the USP and SM during the authentication process. However, all these other schemes required three sets of messages to be exchanged. As such, our protocol is the most efficient in terms of bandwidth requirements.

Space complexity: a typical authentication protocol needs to store the public key cryptosystem parameters, random nonces, timestamps, hashes and device identity, which occupy 40 bytes, 20 bytes, 4 bytes, 20 bytes and 20 bytes respectively. In the proposed protocol, only message sets $\{\mathcal{B}, \mathcal{H}, \lambda\}$ and $\{R, \mathcal{z}, \psi\}$ required storage at the SM and USP respectively. Here, the storage requirements for $\mathcal{B} = \mathcal{H} = \lambda = 20$ byes hence the total space complexity for $\{\mathcal{B}, \mathcal{H}, \lambda\}$ is 60 bytes. Similarly, $R = \mathcal{z} = \psi = 20$ bytes and hence message $\{R, \mathcal{z}, \psi\}$ requires 60 bytes. Consequently, the cumulative storage requirement for the proposed protocol is 120 bytes as shown in Table 6.

Table 6. Space complexity comparisons

Protocol	Storage costs (bytes)		
	SM	USP	Cumulative
[25]	40	40	80
[30]	80	80	160
[36]	40	40	80
Proposed	60	60	120

On the other hand, the scheme in [25] required 40 bytes at the SM and 40 bytes at the USP, the scheme in [30] needed 80 bytes on the SM and 80 bytes on the USP while the protocol in [36] required 40 bytes on both the SM and USP. As such, the space complexities for protocols in [25, 30] and [36] are 80 bytes, 160 bytes and 80 bytes respectively, as shown in Fig. 7.

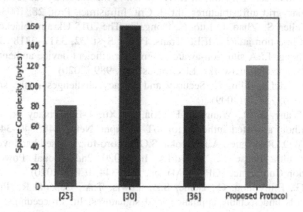

Fig. 7. Space complexity comparisons

Based on the graphs in Fig. 7, the proposed protocol had slightly higher space storage requirements than protocols in [25] and [36]. Although our scheme had higher space complexities than these schemes, it offers superior security features as shown in Table 3 above.

5   Conclusion and Future Work

Smart grid privacy and security has been noted to be challenging owing to the resource constrained nature of smart grid components. The bilinear pairing operations and elliptic curve point multiplication operations in ECC, certificate distribution and maintenance of revocation lists in PKI, signature signing and verification are all intensive in terms of the exchanged messages and the processing time involved. On the other hand, identity based schemes leads to the revelation of smart grid entities' real identities to the verifiers during authentication. Consequently, deploying conventional ECC, PKI, signature, and identity based schemes results in high communication and computation overheads or privacy leaks. The proposed protocol mutually authenticated the smart meters to the USP at lower communication and computation costs. It also required relatively low storage costs and was demonstrated to be robust against many of the conventional smart grid security and privacy attacks. Future work lies in the formal verification of the security features of this protocol and its evaluation using other metrics that were not within the scope of this paper.

References

1. Song, J., Liu, Y., Shao, J., Tang, C.: A dynamic membership data aggregation (DMDA) protocol for smart grid. IEEE Syst. J. **14**(1), 900–908 (2019)
2. Lyu, L., Nandakumar, K., Rubinstein, B.I.P., Jin, J., Bedo, J., Palaniswami, M.: PPFA: privacy preserving fog-enabled aggregation in smart grid. IEEE Trans. Ind. Inform. **14**(8), 3733–3744 (2018)
3. Shrestha, M., Johansen, C., Noll, J., Roverso, D.: A methodology for security classification applied to smart grid infrastructures. Int. J. Crit. Infrastruct. Prot. **28**, 100342 (2020)
4. Liang, G., Weller, S., Zhao, J., Luo, F., Dong, Z.: The 2015 Ukraine blackout: implications for false data injection attacks. IEEE Trans. Power Syst. **32**, 3317–3318 (2017)
5. Xiang, A., Zheng, J.: A situation-aware scheme for efficient device authentication in smart grid-enabled home area networks. Electronics **9**(6), 989 (2020)
6. McDaniel, P., McLaughlin, S.: Security and privacy challenges in the smart grid. IEEE Secur. Priv. **7**(3), 75–77 (2009)
7. Liu, Y.-N., Wang, Y.-P., Wang, X.-F., Xia, Z., Xu, J.-F.: Privacy preserving raw data collection without a trusted authority for IoT. Comput. Netw. **148**, 340–348 (2019)
8. Nyangaresi, V.O., Rodrigues, A.J., Abeka, S.O.: Neuro-fuzzy based handover authentication protocol for ultra dense 5G networks. In: 2020 2nd Global Power, Energy and Communication Conference (GPECOM), pp. 339–344. IEEE (2020)
9. Kalogridis, G., Efthymiou, C., Denic, S.Z., Lewis, T.A., Cepeda, R.: Privacy for smart meters: towards undetectable appliance load signatures. In: Proceedings of the 1st IEEE International Conference on Smart Grid Communincation, pp. 232–237 (2010)
10. Wu, L., Wang, J., Choo, K.R., He, D.: Secure key agreement and key protection for mobile device user authentication. IEEE Trans. Inform. Forensics Secur. **14**(2), 319–330 (2019)
11. Nyangaresi, V.O., Rodrigues, A.J., Taha, N.K.: Mutual authentication protocol for secure VANET data exchanges. In: Perakovic, D., Knapcikova, L. (eds.) FABULOUS 2021. LNICSSITE, vol. 382, pp. 58–76. Springer, Cham (2021). https://doi.org/10.1007/978-3-030-78459-1_5

12. Gong, Y., Cai, Y., Guo, Y., Fang, Y.: A privacy-preserving scheme for incentive-based demand response in the smart grid. IEEE Trans. Smart Grid 7(3), 1304–1313 (2016)
13. Guan, Z., et al.: Privacy-preserving and efficient aggregation based on blockchain for power grid communications in smart communities. IEEE Commun. Mag. 56(7), 82–88 (2018)
14. Nyangaresi, V.O., Rodrigues, A.J., Abeka, S.O.: Efficient group authentication protocol for secure 5G enabled vehicular communications. In: 2020 16th International Computer Engineering Conference (ICENCO), pp. 25–30. IEEE (2020)
15. Wang, J., Wu, L., Choo, K.K.R., He, D.: Blockchain-based anonymous authentication with key management for smart grid edge computing infrastructure. IEEE Trans. Ind. Inf. 16(3), 1984–1992 (2019)
16. Wan, Z., Wang, G., Yang, Y., Shi, S.: SKM: scalable key management for advanced metering infrastructure in smart grids. IEEE Trans. Ind. Electron. 61(12), 7055–7066 (2014)
17. Mohammadali, A., Haghighi, M., Tadayon, M., Nodooshan, A.: A novel identity-based key establishment method for advanced metering infrastructure in smart grid. IEEE Trans. Smart Grid 9(4), 2834–2842 (2018)
18. Mahmood, K., Chaudhry, S.A., Naqvi, H., Kumari, S., Li, X., Sangaiah, A.K.: An elliptic curve cryptography based lightweight authentication scheme for smart grid communication. Future Gener. Comput. Syst. 81, 557–565 (2018)
19. Mahmood, K., et al.: Pairing based anonymous and secure key agreement protocol for smart grid edge computing infrastructure. Future Gener. Comput. Syst. 88, 491–500 (2018)
20. Jia, X., He, D., Kumar, N., Choo, K.K.R.: A provably secure and efficient identity-based anonymous authentication scheme for mobile edge computing. IEEE Syst. J. 14(1), 560–657 (2019)
21. Kahvazadeh, S., Masip-Bruin, X., Diaz, R., Marín-Tordera, E., Jurnet, A., Garcia, J.: Towards an efficient key management and authentication strategy for combined fog-to-cloud continuum systems. In: 3rd Cloudification of the Internet of Things, CIoT 2018, Paris, France, pp. 1–7 (2018)
22. Zheng, H., Wu, Q., Qin, B., Zhong, L., He, S., Liu, J.: Linkable group signature for auditing anonymous communication. In: Susilo, W., Yang, G. (eds.) Information Security and Privacy, ACISP 2018. LNCS, vol. 10946, pp. 304–321. Springer, Cham (2018). https://doi.org/10.1007/978-3-319-93638-3_18
23. Ma, L., Liu, X., Pei, Q., Xiang, Y.: Privacy-preserving reputation management for edge computing enhanced mobile crowdsensing. IEEE Trans. Serv. Comput. 12(5), 786–799 (2018)
24. Zhao, J., Liu, J., Qin, Z., Ren, K.: Privacy protection scheme based on remote anonymous attestation for trusted smart meters. IEEE Trans. Smart Grid 9(4), 3313–3320 (2018)
25. Tsai, J.L., Lo, N.W.: Secure anonymous key distribution scheme for smart grid. IEEE Trans. Smart Grid 7(2), 906–914 (2016)
26. Li, Y.: Design of a key establishment protocol for smart home energy management system. In: Proceedings of the 2013 Fifth International Conference on Computational Intelligence, Communication Systems and Networks, Madrid, Spain, pp. 88–93 (2013)
27. Vaidya, B., Makrakis, D., Mouftah, H.T.: Device authentication mechanism for smart energy home area networks. In: Proceedings of the 2011 IEEE International Conference on Consumer Electronics (ICCE), Las Vegas, NV, USA, pp. 787–788 (2011)
28. Wu, D., Zhou, C.: Fault-tolerant and scalable key management for smart grid. IEEE Trans. Smart Grid 2(2), 375–381 (2011)
29. Xia, J., Wang, Y.: Secure key distribution for the smart grid. IEEE Trans. Smart Grid 3(3), 1437–1443 (2012)
30. Odelu, V., Das, A.K., Wazid, M., Conti, M.: Provably secure authenticated key agreement scheme for smart grid. IEEE Trans. Smart Grid 9(3), 1900–1910 (2018)

31. Chen, Y., Martínez, J., Castillejo, P., López, L.: An anonymous authentication and key establish scheme for smart grid: FAuth. Energies **10**(9), 1–23 (2017)
32. He, D., Wang, H., Khurram Khan, M., Wang, L.: Lightweight anonymous key distribution scheme for smart grid using elliptic curve cryptography. IET Commun. **10**(14), 1795–1802 (2016)
33. Wazid, M., Das, A.K., Kumar, N., Rodrigues, J.J.P.C.: Secure three-factor user authentication scheme for renewable-energy based smart grid environment. IEEE Trans. Ind. Inform. **13**(6), 3144–3153 (2017)
34. Kumar, P., Gurtov, A., Sain, M., Martin, A., Ha, P.: Lightweight authentication and key agreement for smart metering in smart energy networks. IEEE Trans. Smart Grid **10**, 1–11 (2018)
35. Abbasinezhad-Mood, D., Nikooghadam, M.: An anonymous ECC-based self certified key distribution scheme for the smart grid. IEEE Trans. Ind. Electron. **65**(10), 7996–8004 (2018)
36. Kumar, N., Aujla, G.S., Das, A.K., Conti, M.: ECCAuth: a secure authentication protocol for demand response management in a smart grid system. IEEE Trans. Ind. Inform. **15**(12), 6572–6582 (2019)
37. Kilinc, H.H., Yanik, T.: A survey of SIP authentication and key agreement schemes. IEEE Commun. Surv. Tutor. **16**(2), 1005–1023 (2014)

Vehicular ad Hoc Networks (VANET) (WICON 2021)

SAMA: Security-Aware Monitoring Approach for Location Abusing and UAV GPS-Spoofing Attacks on Internet of Vehicles

Messaoud Babaghayou[1] [iD], Nabila Labraoui[1] [iD], Ado Adamou Abba Ari[2,3] [iD],
Nasreddine Lagraa[4] [iD], Mohamed Amine Ferrag[5] [iD],
and Leandros Maglaras[1,2,3,4,5,6(✉)] [iD]

[1] STIC Lab, Abou Bakr Belkaid University of Tlemcen,
P.O. Box 230, 13000 Chetouane, Tlemcen, Algeria
`nabila.labraoui@univ-tlemcen.dz`
[2] LaRI Lab, University of Maroua, P.O. Box 814, Maroua, Cameroon
[3] LI-PaRAD Lab, Saint-Quentin-en-Yvelines University, 45 Avenue Etats-Unis,
78035 Versailles cedex, France
`n.lagraa@lagh-univ.dz`
[4] LIM Laboratory, UATL University,
P.O. Box G37, Route de Ghardaia (M'kam), 03000 Laghouat, Algeria
`ferrag.mohamedamine@univ-guelma.dz`
[5] School of C, University of Guelma,
B.P. 401, 24000 Guelma, Algeria
`leandros.maglaras@dmu.ac.uk`
[6] School of Computer Science and Informatics, De Montfort University,
Leicester LE1 9BH, UK

Abstract. The quick revolution on the wireless communication technologies had opened the gate towards promising implementations; Vehicular-Ad-hoc Networks (VANETs) and the safety-enhancing applications provided by the Internet of Vehicles (IoV) paradigm are one of them. By periodically broadcasting safety-beacons, vehicles can ensure a better safety-driving experience since beacons contain fine-grained location that is sent to the neighborhood. Nevertheless, some attacks basing on falsify or encrypt location-related data are threatening the road-safety considerably. In this paper, and by assuming a GPS-spoofing attack originated from Unmanned-Aircraft-Vehicles (UAV) system, we provide a Security-Aware Monitoring Approach (SAMA) that protects vehicles against such location abusing by allowing the Law-Side Authority (LSA) to monitor the potential malicious or tricked vehicles. SAMA is Implemented using the triangulation concept via Received-Signal-Strength-Indicator (RSSI) in conjunction with C++ map and multimap data-structures. The performances of SAMA are evaluated in terms of location-estimation precision and beacons collection per type.

Keywords: Location monitoring · Position detection · RSSI · Triangulation · Location privacy · Malicious attacks · UAV attacks · GPS-spoofing · Data falsification · IoV · VANETs

© ICST Institute for Computer Sciences, Social Informatics and Telecommunications Engineering 2022
Published by Springer Nature Switzerland AG 2022. All Rights Reserved
H. Jin et al. (Eds.): CROWNCOM 2021/WiCON 2021, LNICST 427, pp. 343–360, 2022.
https://doi.org/10.1007/978-3-030-98002-3_25

1   Introduction

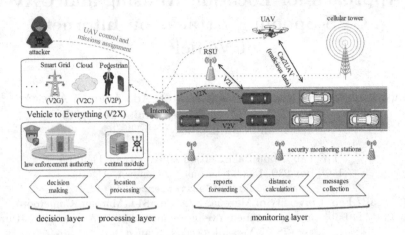

Fig. 1. System model, principle actors and security layers

Vehicular Ad-hoc Network (VANET) [1], the wireless network of cars had boosted the driving experience of road users enormously via communication types like Vehicle to Vehicle (V2V) and Vehicle to Infrastructure (V2I) [2], in addition to providing a bases for the Vehicle to Everything (V2X) [3] that serves as a core for the Internet of Vehicles (IoV) paradigm [4]. Moreover, location detection techniques such as Global Positioning System (GPS) [5], Road-side Unite (RSU)-aided and Location Based Service (LBS) [6] are getting much attention due to their high utility [7]. To avoid accidents and traffic jams, vehicles must broadcast safety-beacon messages [8] that contain the vehicle's status [9] including its location which, as a consequence, forms an environment instantiation. This beaconing is done in a range of 300 m and up to 10 beacons per second [10].

1.1   Problematic and Research Motivation

Since the world is diving more and more into the technology, many serious cyber attacks and exploits are emerging each time [11]. This beaconing had opened location-privacy issues which were an incentive for the research community to find mitigation to these limitations [12]; using pseudonyms and changing them over time was accepted as a fair solution [6] and much schemes had emerged [13]. In spite of being these schemes benign to the IoV users' location-privacy, they also open an attack vector to malicious vehicles as they can escape monitoring when modifying and/or encrypting such spatio-related beacons from the Law Enforcement Authority (LEA) [14] without a defending mechanism, in addition for giving the option to launch Sybil attacks [15]. Localization techniques are becoming a must in such a case. Generally speaking, much cryptography and trust-based mechanisms [16,17] were proposed and used to cope with the emerging security threats but they do not treat all kinds of security gaps. Another reason for the necessity of location techniques may be noticed when considering the critical vulnerability of the GPS technique [18]; we are talking about the GPS-spoofing attack [19]. The GPS-spoofing attack is defined as forging a falsified spatio-temporal data to the receiving devices using GPS-mimicker devices that aim at emitting a GPS signal but this later is falsified and coming from a malicious source and is hard to get verified [20,21]. With this said, we give a high importance to checking the transmitted location by vehicles to their vicinity where our assumed spoofer is considered to be a set of Unmanned-Aircraft-Vehicles (UAVs) [22] controlled by an attacker who aims at wreaking havoc on the system functioning. The exact scenario and used mechanisms are explained later on. Moreover, the used abbreviations in this paper are provided in Table 1.

1.2 Contributions and Paper Organization

The contributions of the paper are stated as follows:

- Introducing our system model that leverages the power and financial abilities of the Law-Side Authority to monitor and protect against the resulting vector attacks.
- Giving and shedding-light to a GPS-spoofing mechanism that exploits the possession of a UAV system to let vehicles send falsified locations.
- Recalling and formulating the used triangulation technique to detect a node (vehicle) by its Received Signal Strength Indicator (RSSI) and the nearby monitoring stations.
- Providing our proposed Security-Aware Monitoring Approach (SAMA) that estimates the location of potential malicious vehicles and explaining the used c++ map and multimap data-structures in addition to giving the pseudo-code of SAMA protocols and its results.

The remaining paper parts are presented as follows: Sect. 2, sheds light on legitimate privacy-schemes that encrypt beacon fields in conjunction with the GPS-spoofing attacks that let vehicles send falsified locations and discuss the localization-related state of the art. Next, the system model and coverage modes are described in Sect. 3. Then, the proposed SAMA approach is explained in details in Sect. 4. After that, Sect. 5 shows the location precision and collection per type results. Section 6 is consecrated for discussing the obtained results and potential future enhancements to the technique. Finally, Sect. 7 concludes this research.

2   Related Work

This section is three folds; (a) the used techniques to encrypt location data included in beacons, (b) the GPS spoofing problem that leads to sending a

Table 1. List of abbreviations

SAMA	Security-Aware Monitoring Approach
LSA	Law-Side Authority
RSSI	Received Signal Strength Indicator
RSU	Road-side Unite
LBS	Location Based Service
LEA	Law Enforcement Authority
CMIX	Cryptographic MIX-zones
REP	Random Encryption Periods
RADAR	An In-Building RF-based User Location and Tracking System
OBU	On-Board-Unit
ms_i	Monitoring station number i
CM	Central Module
mv_i	Monitored vehicle number i
PREXT	Privacy Extension for Veins

wrong geo-location data by vehicles and (c) the location detection techniques deployed for wireless networks:

(a) altering the safety-messages format (for good) was highly debated in the previous years. Freudiger et al. had proposed the Cryptographic MIX-zones (CMIX) scheme [23] that aims at encrypting beacon messages in some areas (mix-zones) to defend against unauthorized overhearing of these beacons, thus, having an opportunity to confuse the attacker when leaving the CMIX zones. Similarly, Wasef and Shen had presented the random encryption periods (REP) scheme [24] . REP lets vehicles encrypt their beacon messages in a group manner using a group key k_g. This is done after one of the group members (called coordinator) launches the random encryption process that is followed by a certificate updating to confuse the tracker. Ying et al. [25] had provided another mix-zone based scheme that uses the encryption but the mix-zones here are created on the fly (dynamically) according to the vehicle's predicted location and other parameters.

Despite being the location-privacy preserving schemes an addition to the privacy level, they also entail the use of such techniques for subversion purposes; i.e., encrypting the location for the bad. (b) Similarly, and indirectly, a vehicle may send wrong geo-location data due to a wrong GPS signal reception; we point out to the GPS-spoofing attack [26] that is by definition: leading the receiver GPS device to believe receiving a legit GPS signal while in fact it is falsified and forged from another malicious source. The powerfulness and usability of GPS-spoofing is shown to be a fact as stated in [27] where J. Noh et al. demonstrated the exploit of the Unmanned-Aircraft-Vehicles UAV safe-hijacking using the GPS spoofing technique for the good (defending against terrorist UAVs). Another work by Y. Guo et al. that investigated a covert spoofing algorithm [28] in the UAV context had shown the applicability of such spoofing techniques. This just proves the possibility of exploiting the GPS spoofing attacks on other fields; spoofing the location of vehicles. As a result, vehicles are expected to send falsified location data upon receiving forged GPS signals and from here the necessity of detecting such an odd behavior becomes a must.

With all of this said, finding mechanisms to deter such abusing becomes a must. (c) Location detection techniques are considered to be a plausible direction against such threats. In the context of location detection inside buildings, Bahl and Paramvir had suggested the use of a radio-frequency (RF) based system made for locating and tracking users inside buildings and was called An In-Building RF-based User Location and Tracking System (RADAR) [29]. RADAR gets benefit from the recorded and processed signal strength information received by multiple base stations situated at the area of interest. Their real world experiment showed that despite the signal's nature and the environment obstacles, they could achieve a precision ranging from 2 to 3 m which in fact can correctly pinpoint a room inside a building. In the same context, Youssef et al. [30] had investigated a WLAN location determination technique called (the Joint Clustering technique). They base on the signal strength probability distributions and the clustering of locations in their scheme. The scheme's best advantage is the complexity reducing as it uses cluster based techniques and can be applied indoor and outdoor environments. The scheme can be applied as a helping tool to other context-aware applications. In [31], Svečko et al. had evaluated a particle filter algorithm used for the distance estimation via multiple antennas that are attached to the receiver. They had conducted the study on a real world environment and their proposed particle filter achieved better results than other propagation models (e.g., the ground reflection propagation model) which permits it to be a reliable distance estimator.

Besides being the transmitted signal a mean to reduce the IoV users' location privacy, they also can defend against location abusing and data encryption used by attackers.

3   System Model

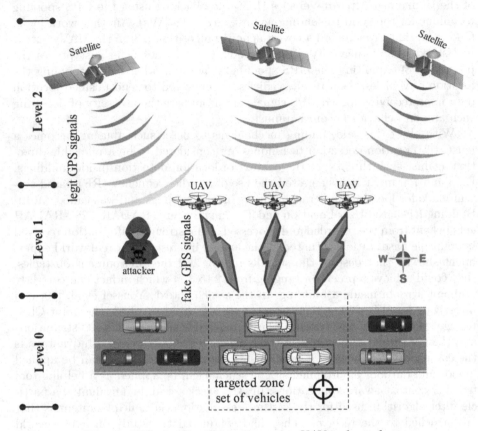

Fig. 2. GPS spoofing illustration using UAV technonology

In this section, we give our network and threat models. Then, we demonstrate our adversary's GPS spoofing technique that bases on UAVs. Additionally, we describing the security model and the used coverage modes.

3.1   Network Model

It consists of (a) the vehicles set S that is defined as $S = \{v_1, v_2, ...v_n\}$ where n represents the vehicles number and they communicate using the 802.11p standard (explained in [32]) via their On-Board-Units (OBUs) [33]. and (b) the infrastructure that allows the use of different provided services via Road-Side-Units (RSUs) [34], cellular towers and across the Internet to explore the V2X feature. This is illustrated in Fig. 1.

3.2   Threat Model

It refers to the malicious entity in the network. The main actor is (a) the attacker that possesses and controls (b) a set of vehicles S_a where $S_a \in S$. The attacker [35] is responsible for spreading malicious and suspicious messages that, for example, use unknown encryption algorithms and encrypting indispensable message fields. The trigger for spreading this kind of messages is supposed to be done via UAVs by giving UAV-missions [36] to deliver malicious orders. This is also illustrated in Fig. 1.

3.3   UAV GPS-Spoofing Attack

This kind of attacks is foreseeable with the advent of UAVs, their cheapness and their availability. Our scenario, which is illustrated in Fig. 2, consists of three levels:

- *Level 2 :* that is the origin of the legit GPS signal. Normally, vehicles take their locations by receiving the emitted GPS signal from the satellites to help determining their whereabouts.
- *Level 1:* that is the exploited point by the adversary who aims at emitting a stronger and faked GPS signal to mislead the vehicles on their location/whereabouts. The taken scenario considers two kind of attacks (a) zone targeting and (b) vehicles set targeting and in both of them, a set of UAVs are used to emit the falsified GPS signal.
- *Level 0:* that is the lower level where vehicles operate. When those vehicles are targeted, their sensing of the location are likely to be tricked especially that detecting a legit GPS signal from a fake one is still a big challenge to the research community; the GPS-spoofing attack [37].

By being the attacker able to forge falsified location and execute the GPS-spoofing attack, the targeted vehicles are expected to begin sending wrong geo-location data. Sending a wrong geo-location data may also be intentional in the case of attacker vehicles but considering the scenario of the GPS-spoofing attack, we do not want to instantly judge the behavior of the vehicle. Either way, comparing what is sent to where the vehicles is really at becomes mandatory to deal with such a possible attack scenario.

3.4   Types of Signal Receptions

When communicating, the sending vehicle emits a signal. Now when trying to receive that signal by a reception device, four main scenarios may occur: (a) an unsuccessful eavesdropping or reception with no collection at all, (b) single or mono-reception, (c) due-reception and a successful reception by getting the sent signal with at least three devices; that is the triangulation technique. Figure 3 shows the aforementioned scenarios.

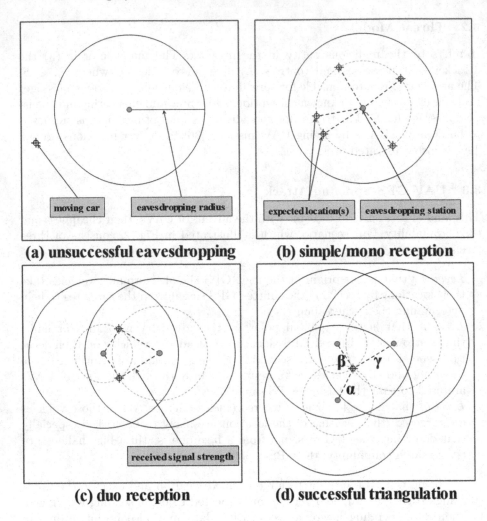

(a) unsuccessful eavesdropping   **(b) simple/mono reception**

(c) duo reception   **(d) successful triangulation**

Fig. 3. The different reception scenarios of an emitted signal by a moving car

3.5   Security Model and Coverage Modes

It is the law-side entity that aims at ensuring road-safety and data-security by only allowing legitimate vehicles to be present in the network. Thus, keeping an eye on the potential malicious and suspicious vehicles (also mislead vehicles; the GPS-spoofing attack victims) is its main task. For this purpose, the use of many security monitoring stations $ms(s)$ becomes a must. These $ms(s)$ are meant to collect the suspicious messages and reporting them to a security tracking module, also defined as Central Module (CM), and this later is responsible for performing the triangulation to pinpoint the monitored vehicle (mv_i)'s whereabouts. A LEA is connected to the system to make decisions (e.g., excluding an entity if proven to be guilty). The supposed available coverage modes are illustrated in Fig. 4. The densities are supposed to be applicable, we justify this by being the LEA a part of the government, hence, having both (a) the financial and (b) the reachability to deploy such a massive $ms(s)$ implanting would not be a problem (unlike for individual persons [38]).

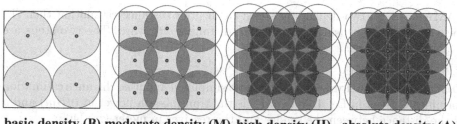

basic density (B) moderate density (M) high density (H)   absolute density (A)

Fig. 4. The assumed and used coverage modes

4   The Proposed Approach: SAMA

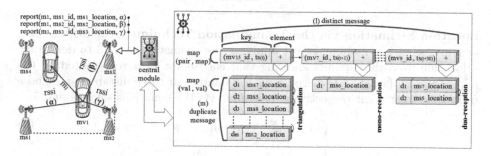

Fig. 5. SAMA implementation and functioning illustration

SAMA bases on the different received signal strengths from the proximal vehicles to the $ms(s)$. For the implementation, we use two c++ data-structures namely: map and multimap [39] and the detailed working is explained in the next point. Figure 5 shows the modus-operandi of SAMA.

4.1   Description and Motivation

The adversary is able to use UAVs either to give orders for data encryption; hiding his vehicle(s)' location or using his UAVs in order to execute the GPS-spoofing attack; misleading the targeted vehicles. Thus, location protection.

In light of this, finding a counter-mechanism is a fair motivation. Benefiting from the location detection techniques serves to protect, expose and thwart such malicious acts substantially.

4.2 The Techniques' Principles

SAMA bases on two depending steps: (a) a prior distance estimation then (b) location estimation using the calculate distances afterward. The two steps are explained as follows:

Distance Estimation. One of the most simplified and used distance estimation formulas is given in Eq. 1. Where Pt is the transmission power in (dBm) and d is the distance between the sender and the receiver in meter (m) [40]:

$$RSSI = Pt - 10n * log_{10}(d) \tag{1}$$

This allows to find and calculate the distance d as follows (Eq. 2):

$$d = 10^{\frac{Pt-RSSI}{10n}} \tag{2}$$

Location Estimation via the Triangulation Technique. The distance d is at hand, what is remaining is just applying the geometric method to determine a location from three points knowing that each point P_i is represented by the triple location (x_i, y_i, z_i) where $i \in \{1, 2, 3\}$ and their three distances a, b and c from the target point respectively. It is done via the equations set 3, 4 and 5:

$$\begin{cases} (x - x_1)^2 + (y - y_1)^2 = a^2 & (3) \\ (x - x_2)^2 + (y - y_2)^2 = b^2 & (4) \\ (x - x_3)^2 + (y - y_3)^2 = c^2 & (5) \end{cases}$$

By expanding and combining the equations (3 and 4) then (3 and 5), we get the equations set :

$$\begin{cases} 2(x_1 - x_2)x + 2(y_1 - y_2)y = -- a^2 + b^2 + x_1{}^2 + y_1{}^2 \\ \qquad\qquad -x_2{}^2 - y_2{}^2 & (6) \\ 2(x_1 - x_3)x + 2(y_1 - y_3)y = -- a^2 + b^2 + x_1{}^2 + y_1{}^2 \\ \qquad\qquad -x_3{}^2 - y_3{}^2 & (7) \end{cases}$$

We assume and define the following (the set 8):

$$\begin{cases} \alpha_1 = 2x_1 - 2x_2 \\ \alpha_2 = 2x_1 - 2x_3 \\ \beta_1 = 2y_1 - 2y_2 \\ \beta_2 = 2y_1 - 2y_3 \\ \gamma_1 = -a^2 + b^2 + x_1{}^2 + y_1 - x_2{}^2 - y_2 \\ \gamma_2 = -a^2 + c^2 + x_1{}^2 + y_1 - x_3{}^2 - y_3 \end{cases} \tag{8}$$

This results in a one more step to the final solution:

$$\begin{cases} \alpha_1 x + \beta_1 y = \gamma_1 \\ \alpha_2 x + \beta_2 y = \gamma_2 \end{cases} \tag{9} \tag{10}$$

Finally, the obtained location, in terms of x and y (assuming z is identical) coordinates, is gotten as follows:

$$\begin{cases} x = \dfrac{\alpha 2 \gamma 1 - \alpha 1 \gamma 2}{\alpha 2 \beta 1 - \alpha 1 \beta 2} \\ y = \dfrac{\beta 2 \gamma 1 - \beta 1 \gamma 2}{\beta 2 \alpha 1 - \beta 1 \alpha 2} \end{cases} \tag{11} \tag{12}$$

4.3 SAMA Implemented Protocols

In this part, the *on message reception by a monitoring station* and *on message reception by the central module* protocols are explained in details with additional pseudo-algorithms as follows:

On message reception by a monitoring station each ms_i is devoted to collect the nearby messages and supposed to be integrating a lightweight calculation module dedicated to find a distance d from a gotten RSSI value of the received message. A report is sent next to the central module. This is shown in kind of a pseudo-algorithm; Algorithm 1.

Algorithm 1. Message reception by a monitoring station ms_i

1: **procedure** RECEIVING_PACKET(MESSAGE* MSG)
2:    **if** ($Is\_Suspicious(msg)$) **then**
3:        $RSSI \leftarrow getReceivedPower(msg)$;
4:        $d \leftarrow calculateDistance(RSSI)$;
5:        send2Central(msg, ms_i.ID, ms_i.Location, d);

On message reception by the central module upon receiving a report from ms_i, CM proceeds to treating the obtained information like the distance between ms_i and the target vehicle in addition to the coordinates of ms_i which will be stored in the database of CM to be used next to calculate the vehicle's estimated location. The pseudo-code is given in Algorithm 2.

Algorithm 2. Message reception by central module from ms_i

1: **procedure** RECEIVING_REPORT(MESSAGE* MSG, INT ms_i.ID, COORD ms_i.LOCATION, DOUBLE D)

2:     **if** I had not received this msg before **then** create a new entry in the *Distinct_msg_Map* with the (**ms**ᵢ**.ID, ms**ᵢ**.timeStamp**) pair as a key and attach a multimap *duplicate_msg_Map* in the value field of *Distinct_msg_Map* and add (**d**) as a key and (**ms**ᵢ**.Location**) as a value.

3:     **else,** just add the received message to the multimap *duplicate_msg_Map* belonging to the entry of the received message **msg** by adding the distance (**d**) as a key and the location (**ms**ᵢ**.Location**) as a value.

4:     **end if**

---

5   Simulation Runs and Results

Table 2. Density details and achieved precision for Obstacle and Obstacles-Free scenarios

Density characteristics			Achieved Precision during triangulation (m)					
			With obstacles			Without obstacles		
Density mode	Overlapping (m)	Number of MSs	Average	Best	Worst	Average	Best	Worst
Absolute (A)	166	110	24.75	$5.9*10^{-5}$	87.55	$2.3*10^{-2}$	$3.7*10^{-7}$	52.26
High (H)	150	90	22.15	$1.1*10^{-5}$	83.59	$5.1*10^{-5}$	$5.5*10^{-7}$	$9.8*10^{-5}$
Moderate (M)	88	42	-	-	-	$7.1*10^{-6}$	$3.3*10^{-7}$	$1.5*10^{-5}$
Basic (B)	0	25	-	-	-	-	-	-

5.1   Simulation Setup

For the evaluation, the following tools are used: SUMO as the mobility simulator, Omnet++ as the network simulator and Veins [41] as the vehicular extension that acts as a bridge between SUMO and Omnet++. The used environment is an urban map consists of Munich city central taken by the Open-Street-Map tool. The exact model is found in [42]. As for the vehicles generation, we use the inter-arrival rate of 2.61 seconds per vehicle in a total simulation time of 300 s which leads to a generation of 115 vehicles. A variation of monitoring scenarios is also exploited and shown in Table 2. Additionally, we modified the PREXT [42] extension; that is a privacy extension, to integrate the central module and to add the triangulation technique to locate a specific node. For a holistic evaluation, we monitor every vehicle to measure the performances of SAMA under the toughest possible case with a frequency of one message per second. Thus, the case of only a set of targeted vehicles that are receiving the GPS-spoofing attack alone are not considered, but, all vehicles are considered.

5.2   Obstacles and Obstacles-Free Scenarios

In these two scenarios, we are interested on evaluating the effects of the *Simple Obstacle Shadowing* mode; that is an *Analogue Model* used to model the physical characteristics of the wireless medium. Thus, we consider the *Obstacles* scenario model when we are taking the obstacles' effect during the communication into account and when we are not, we consider that as an *Obstacles-Free* Scenario.

5.3   Simulation Results

For the Obstacles Scenario Figure 6 shows that the monitoring stations could only collect about half of the sent message in the network when applying the *basic* density and they were just mono-receptions. However, the collection was increased to 100% in the other densities and the *triangulations* achieved their pick (more than 18*k* message) when in the *absolute* density.

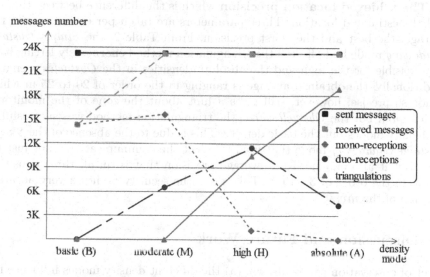

Fig. 6. The sent messages number and the different reception types in the Obstacles scenario

For the Obstacles-Free scenario as shown in Fig. 7, the almost same results happened, but, with a remarkable powerful messages collection than that of the previous scenario. The better collection of sent messages in the *basic* density is an example for that in addition to the approximate 100% of successful triangulations in the *absolute* density.

messages number

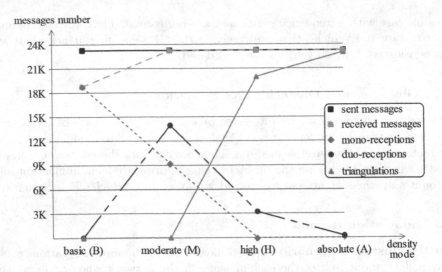

Fig. 7. The sent messages number and the different reception types in the Obstacles-Free scenario

The achieved location precision which is the difference between the real and the estimated location. Three parameters are taken per each scenario: the average, the best and the worst precision. From Table 2, the *Simple Obstacle Shadowing* mode had affected the triangulation method enormously letting it be only feasible for the high and the absolute densities in the *Obstacles* scenario. Additionally, the obtained average is ranging in the order of 20 to 25 m which is not so precise, however, still gives a hint about the zone of the monitored vehicle mv_i. For the *Obstacles-Free*, the triangulation method was successful in all density modes but the basic density. This is due to the absence of the *Simple Obstacle Shadowing* mode that used to affect the communications, not just for that, but it also enhanced the average precision that is, in all three densities, less than the order of $3 * 10^{-2}$. This, gives the security bodies a very accurate location of the mv_i.

6   Discussion and Future Work

A set of observation can be drawn: (a) the different density modes influence the amount of collected messages, the collection per type and the achieved precision. Also, (b) when considering the *Simple Obstacle Shadowing* mode, a lot of messages do not reach the monitoring stations appropriately leading to few receptions and less triangulations, hence, thwarting the location estimation. Additionally, (c) in the absolute density model, the dense overlapping stations, despite them giving higher number of triangulations, they unfortunately also degrade the achieved precisions. Finally, (d) when moving from the lowest (base) to the highest (absolute) density, the dominant type of collection will be that of the triangulations which is so natural as, theoretically, the intense implementation of monitoring stations leads to higher triangulation chances.

Even though being the *Simple Obstacle Shadowing* mode a real world effect that influences the precision of the monitoring stations considerably, it still gives some degree of precision which can be given as an entry to other location detection techniques. Moreover, the road map restriction can be used to infer the exact location of a monitored vehicle by excluding the non-common locations with the help of the different time instants and the moving context as shown in Fig. 8. This emphasizes a possible promising work direction with just mono-receptions instead of the reliance on triangulation for the location detection task.

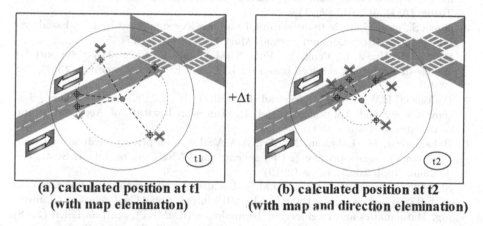

(a) calculated position at t1
(with map elemination)

(b) calculated position at t2
(with map and direction elemination)

Fig. 8. Exploiting the road restriction and time instances to eliminate false samples in just a mono-reception scenario

7   Conclusion

The location data hampering via encrypting and sealing the location fields in messages or launching GPS-spoofing attacks on a set of targeted vehicles can be seen as a serious security breach. In this work, we recalled the possibility of blurring the location by legitimate privacy schemes which highlight the negative effect if used maliciously in addition to the location misleading possibility resulted from the GPS-spoofing attacks. Fortunately, a set of location detection techniques does also exist; the set that uses the transmission signal as an indicator to the location. Among the applications, there is the triangulation method, explained and used on our proposed Security-Aware Monitoring Approach (SAMA). A malicious attacker that gives an order to his controlled vehicles and/or uses GPS-spoofing attacks via UAV-assisted missions in where, and for an extreme evaluation, we suppose that the orders are given to all present vehicles in the map which exposes the performances of SAMA under the worst possible situation. Two scenarios are considered: *Obstacles* and *Obstacles-Free* in addition to four density modes: basic, moderate, high and absolute. The obtained results are discussed in Sect. 6 where it showed the precision and the feasibility of SAMA, especially in the *Obstacles-Free* scenario.

References

1. Shilin, P., Kirichek, R., Paramonov, A., Koucheryavy, A.: Connectivity of VANET segments using UAVs. In: Internet of Things, Smart Spaces, and Next Generation Networks and Systems, pp. 492–500. Springer, Cham (2016), https://doi.org/10.1007/978-3-319-23126-6
2. Karagiannis, G., et al.: Vehicular networking: a survey and tutorial on requirements, architectures, challenges, standards and solutions. IEEE Commun. Surv. Tutor. **13**(4), 584–616 (2011)
3. Chen, S., et al.: Vehicle-to-everything (v2x) services supported by LTE-based systems and 5g. IEEE Commun. Stand. Mag. **1**(2), 70–76 (2017)
4. Sun, S.-H., Hu, J.-L., Peng, Y., Pan, X.-M., Zhao, L., Fang, J.-Y.: Support for vehicle-to-everything services based on LTE. IEEE Wirel. Commun. **23**(3), 4–8 (2016)
5. Parkinson, B.W., Enge, P., Axelrad, P., Spilker, Jr., J.J.: Global Positioning System: Theory and Applications, Vol. II. American Institute of Aeronautics and Astronautics, Reston (1996)
6. Babaghayou, M., Labraoui, N., Ari, A.A.A.: Location-privacy evaluation within the extreme points privacy (EPP) scheme for VANET users. Int. J. Strat. Inf. Technol. Appl. **10**(2), 44–58 (2019)
7. Saeed, N., Ahmad, W., Bhatti, D.M.S.: Localization of vehicular ad-hoc networks with RSS based distance estimation. In: 2018 International Conference on Computing, Mathematics and Engineering Technologies (iCoMET), pp. 1–6. IEEE (2018)
8. Kerrache, C.A., Calafate, C.T., Cano, J.-C., Lagraa, N., Manzoni, P.: Trust management for vehicular networks: an adversary-oriented overview. IEEE Access **4**, 9293–9307 (2016)
9. Al-Sultan, S., Al-Doori, M.M., Al-Bayatti, A.H., Zedan, H.: A comprehensive survey on vehicular ad hoc network. J. Netw. Comput. Appl. **37**, 380–392 (2014)
10. Babaghayou, M., Labraoui, N., Ari, A.A.A., Gueroui, A.M.: Transmission range changing effects on location privacy-preserving schemes in the internet of vehicles. Int. J. Strat. Inf. Technol. Appl. **10**(4), 33–54 (2019)
11. Ferrag, M.A., Babaghayou, M., Yazici, M.A.: Cyber security for fog-based smart grid SCADA systems: solutions and challenges. J. Inf. Secur. Appl. **52**,(2020)
12. Babaghayou, M., Labraoui, N., Ferrag, M.A., Maglaras, L.: Between location protection and overthrowing: a contrariness framework study for smart vehicles. In: 39th IEEE International Conference on Consumer Electronics (ICCE). IEEE (2020)
13. Babaghayou, M., Labraoui, N., Ari, A.A.A., Lagraa, N., Ferrag, M.A.: Pseudonym change-based privacy-preserving schemes in vehicular ad-hoc networks: a survey. J. Inf. Secur. Appl. **55** (2020)
14. Hasrouny, H., Samhat, A.E., Bassil, C., Laouiti, A.: VANET security challenges and solutions: a survey. Veh. Commun. **7**, 7–20 (2017)
15. Yao, Y., Xiao, B., Yang, G., Hu, Y., Wang, L., Zhou, X.: Power control identification: a novel Sybil attack detection scheme in VANETs using RSSI. IEEE J. Select. Areas Commun. **37**(11), 2588–2602 (2019)

16. Tchakounté, F., Calvin, K.A., Ari, A.A.A., Mbogne, D.J.F.: A smart contract logic to reduce hoax propagation across social media. J. King Saud. Univ. Comput. Inf. Sci. (2020)

17. Ferrag, M.A., Maglaras, L., Ahmim, A., Derdour, M., Janicke, H.: RDTIDS: rules and decision tree-based intrusion detection system for internet-of-things networks. Fut. Internet 12(3), 44 (2020)

18. Risbud, P., Gatsis, N., Taha, A.: Vulnerability analysis of smart grids to GPS spoofing. IEEE Trans. Smart Grid 10(4), 3535–3548 (2018)

19. Shepard, D.P., Humphreys, T.E., Fansler, A.A.: Evaluation of the vulnerability of phasor measurement units to GPS spoofing attacks. Int. J. Crit. Infrastruct. Prot. 5(3–4), 146–153 (2012)

20. Warner, J.S., Johnston, R.G.: GPS spoofing countermeasures. Homel. Secur. J. 25(2), 19–27 (2003)

21. Kosmanos, D., et al.: A novel intrusion detection system against spoofing attacks in connected electric vehicles. Array 5, 100013 (2020)

22. Shakhatreh, H., et al.: Unmanned aerial vehicles UAVs): a survey on civil applications and key research challenges. IEEE Access 7, 48 572–48 634 (2019)

23. Freudiger, J., Raya, M., Félegyházi, M., Papadimitratos, P., Hubaux, J.-P.: Mix-zones for location privacy in vehicular networks. In: ACM Workshop on Wireless Networking for Intelligent Transportation Systems (WiN-ITS), No. LCA-CONF-2007-016 (2007)

24. Wasef, A., Shen, X.S.: Rep: location privacy for VANETs using random encryption periods. Mobile Netw. Appl. 15(1), 172–185 (2010)

25. Ying, B., Makrakis, D., Mouftah, H.T.: Dynamic mix-zone for location privacy in vehicular networks. IEEE Commu. Lett. 17(8), 1524–1527 (2013)

26. Ahmad, M., Farid, M.A., Ahmed, S., Saeed, K., Asharf, M., Akhtar, U.: Impact and detection of GPS spoofing and countermeasures against spoofing. In: 2019 2nd International Conference on Computing, Mathematics and Engineering Technologies (iCoMET), pp. 1–8. IEEE (2019)

27. Noh, J., et al.: Tractor beam: safe-hijacking of consumer drones with adaptive GPS spoofing. ACM Trans. Privacy Secur. 22(2), 1–26 (2019)

28. Guo, Y., Wu, M., Tang, K., Tie, J., Li, X.: Covert spoofing algorithm of UAV based on GPS/INS-integrated navigation. IEEE Trans. Veh. Technol. 68(7), 6557–6564 (2019)

29. Bahl, p., Padmanabhan, V.N.: Radar: an in-building RF-based user location and tracking system. In: Proceedings IEEE INFOCOM 2000 Conference on Computer Communications, Nineteenth Annual Joint Conference of the IEEE Computer and Communications Societies (Cat. No. 00CH37064), vol. 2. pp. 775–784. IEEE (2000)

30. Youssef, M.A., Agrawala, A., Shankar, A.U.: WLAN location determination via clustering and probability distributions. In: Proceedings of the First IEEE International Conference on Pervasive Computing and Communications, 2003 (PerCom 2003), pp. 143–150. IEEE (2003)

31. Svečko, J., Malajner, M., Gleich, D.: Distance estimation using RSSI and particle filter. ISA Trans. 55, 275–285 (2015)

32. Jiang, D., Delgrossi, L.: IEEE 802.11 p: Towards an international standard for wireless access in vehicular environments. In: VTC Spring 2008-IEEE Vehicular Technology Conference, pp. 2036–2040. IEEE (2008)

33. Tengler, S., Auflick, J.: Vehicle on-board unit. US Patent 7,554,435, 30 June 2009

34. Park, S., Aslam, B., Turgut, D., Zou, C.C.: Defense against sybil attack in vehicular ad hoc network based on roadside unit support. In: MILCOM 2009-2009 IEEE Military Communications Conference, pp. 1–7. IEEE (2009)

35. Sumra, I.A., Ahmad, I., Hasbullah, H., et al.: Behavior of attacker and some new possible attacks in vehicular ad hoc network (VANET). In: Sumrain, I.A., et al. (eds.) 3rd International Congress on Ultra Modern Telecommunications and Control Systems and Workshops (ICUMT), pp. 1–8. IEEE (2011)
36. Wegener, S., et al.: UAV autonomous operations for airborne science missions. In: AIAA 3rd "Unmanned Unlimited" Technical Conference, Workshop and Exhibit, 2004, p. 6416 (2004)
37. Haq, S., Bashir, A., Sholla, S.: Cloud of things: architecture, research challenges, security threats, mechanisms and open challenges. Jordan. J. Comput. Inf. Technol. **06**(04), 415–433 (2020)
38. Babaghayou, A., Labraoui, N., Ari, A.A.A., Ferrag, M.A., Maglaras, L.: The impact of the adversary's eavesdropping stations on the location privacy level in internet of vehicles. In: 2020 5th South-East Europe Design Automation, Computer Engineering, Computer Networks and Social Media Conference (SEEDA-CECNSM), 2020, pp. 1–6 (2020)
39. <map>. http://www.cplusplus.com/reference/map. Accessed 01 Dec 2021
40. Du, J., Diouris, J.-F., Wang, Y.: A RSSI-based parameter tracking strategy for constrained position localization. EURASIP J. Adv. Signal Process. **2017**(1), 77 (2017)
41. Sommer, C., German, R., Dressler, F.: Bidirectionally coupled network and road traffic simulation for improved IVC analysis. IEEE Trans. Mobile Comput. **10**(1), 3–15 (2011)
42. Emara, K.: Poster: PREXT: privacy extension for veins VANET simulator. In: IEEE Vehicular Networking Conference (VNC). 2016, pp. 1–2. IEEE (2016)

Author Index

Printed in the United States
by Baker & Taylor Publisher Services